COAL, CAGES, CRISIS

Coal, Cages, Crisis

The Rise of the Prison Economy in Central Appalachia

Judah Schept

NEW YORK UNIVERSITY PRESS
New York

NEW YORK UNIVERSITY PRESS
New York
www.nyupress.org

© 2022 by New York University
All rights reserved

References to Internet websites (URLs) were accurate at the time of writing. Neither the author nor New York University Press is responsible for URLs that may have expired or changed since the manuscript was prepared.

Library of Congress Cataloging-in-Publication Data
Names: Schept, Judah Nathan, author.
Title: Coal, cages, crisis : the rise of the prison economy in Central Appalachia / Judah Schept.
Description: New York : New York University Press, [2022] | Includes bibliographical references and index.
Identifiers: LCCN 2021025170 | ISBN 9781479837151 (hardback ; alk. paper) | ISBN 9781479858972 (paperback ; alk. paper) | ISBN 9781479888924 (ebook) | ISBN 9781479866656 (ebook other)
Subjects: LCSH: Prison-industrial complex—Appalachian Region. | Prisons—Appalachian Region. | Coal mines and mining—Appalachian Region. | Appalachian Region—Economic conditions—21st century.
Classification: LCC HV9475.A55 S34 2022 | DDC 364.60975—dc23
LC record available at https://lccn.loc.gov/2021025170

New York University Press books are printed on acid-free paper, and their binding materials are chosen for strength and durability. We strive to use environmentally responsible suppliers and materials to the greatest extent possible in publishing our books.

Manufactured in the United States of America

10 9 8 7 6 5 4 3 2 1

Also available as an ebook

CONTENTS

Introduction: Capturing Appalachia   1

PART I. EXTRACTION AND DISPOSAL

1. "This Is a Place for Trash": Mountaintop Removal, Waste, and Prisons   37
2. Wars, Laws, Landscapes: Producing the Carceral Conjuncture   65

PART II. PROFIT AND ORDER

3. "What a Magnificent Field for Capitalists!": Convict Labor, Carceral Growth, and Craft Tourism   91
4. The Company Town: Remaking Social Order in the Coalfields   120

PART III. CARCERAL SOCIAL REPRODUCTION

5. Planning the Prison: Development, Revenue, and Ideology   155
6. "To Bring a Future and Hope to Our Children": Renovating Education, Identity, and Work   181
7. The Plot of Abolition: Solidarity Politics across Scale, Strategy, and Prison Walls, with Sylvia Ryerson   199

Conclusion: The Long, Violent History and the Struggle for the Future   227

Acknowledgments   235
Notes   241
Bibliography   275
Index   303
About the Author   321

Introduction

Capturing Appalachia

We stood on the side of a country road in the mountains of eastern Kentucky and opened the trunk of my car in order to begin unpacking Jill's camera equipment. Across the rural highway, nestled in an otherwise bucolic eastern Kentucky valley, was Little Sandy, the state's newest prison and, according to the Department of Corrections' own website, its most technologically sophisticated. As a researcher and a photographer studying the political economy and cultural geography of incarceration in the state, our intention was to get a sense of the place the prison takes in the landscape. As we began discussing what equipment to use, a white pickup truck with official tags pulled up behind us. A correctional officer stepped out of the truck and began walking toward us, all the while speaking into the walkie-talkie attached to his shoulder. Friendly but curt, he got right to the point: he would need to call the police and confiscate our equipment and photographs if we stayed any longer or took pictures of the facility. The police, he told us, could arrest us. "You see those signs?" he asked, pointing up and down the road to signs far in the distance on either side of us. "No photographs between those signs." He got back in his truck and started the engine. We could see him talking into his walkie-talkie. He shut off the engine and returned to our car before we could leave. "I'm going to need to see your IDs," he said, and promptly jotted down both of our driver's license information before ushering us on our way.

***

This encounter occurred in July 2012, during the very early stages of the research that informs this book. I had moved to Kentucky in 2011, only recently aware of the vast carceral geography that characterized the region. Even though I had been involved in various research and activist efforts opposing the carceral state for more than a decade, Central Appalachia's prison proliferation was new to me. Most attention to the rise of the prison has been directed to those places that have served as bellwethers for criminalization and incarceration policy and practice. And while Central Appalachia has received considerable attention in recent iterations of the drug war as well as for its perceived significant and even metonymic role in the 2016 presidential election, the region has been largely ignored in analyses of the carceral state until very recently.[1] But mass incarceration would not be possible, of course, without the prisons in which people are incarcerated. And Central Appalachia is home to many prisons.

Between 1980 and 2000, 350 new prisons were built in rural counties in the United States. Four particularly economically distressed regions together accounted for one-third of this new construction: the west Texas plains, the Mississippi Delta, south-central Georgia, and Central Appalachia.[2] The subregion of Appalachia that includes eastern Kentucky, southwestern West Virginia, western Virginia, and northeastern Tennessee is probably best known materially for coal production and symbolically by the myriad representations circulating in television, film, and books. But Central Appalachia is also home to fifteen prisons, twelve of which have been built in just the last three decades during the most accelerated period of mass incarceration. There are eight prisons alone in eastern Kentucky.

The prison where we had stopped to take a photograph that summer of 2012—Little Sandy Correctional Complex—is one of the newer prisons in the region. At this early stage of the research, I had a general interest in examining the region's prison growth, including its origins and economies. I also had a sense that there was an important visual story to document, as the prisons had risen in an area characterized by coal mining, and I wondered about their mingling in the physical and cultural landscape. My friend Jill Frank, an artist and professor of photography, was also interested, and we embarked on that first trip together with a general set of questions to guide us. Jill would accompany me on many more trips in the coming years of fieldwork, and her photographs are found throughout this book.

After being directed to leave by the correctional officer, Jill and I drove away, stopping thirty minutes down the road in the town of West

Figure 1.1a-c. West Liberty tornado damage. Photos by Jill Frank.

Liberty, Kentucky, the home of another prison—Eastern Kentucky Correctional Center—and the site of a severe tornado five months prior. We walked around the town, struck by the contrast between two prisons, undamaged in their fortress-like invincibility and humming in their daily operation, and a town whose main street was still devastated from tornado damage. The effect was a feeling of the prisons' permanence, a naturalization of their place in the landscape amidst the ruins of the town. It was precisely their construction in recent decades that had prompted my visit.

Fieldwork in the Interfaces

The correctional officer's role in this early encounter from my fieldwork demarcated a visual hierarchy: only authorized personnel could look with anything other than a fleeting gaze at Little Sandy. Between signs that extended the prisonscape a hundred yards in either direction beyond its walled perimeter, the only permitted look was the passing one obtained from a moving car. Those of us who might insist on a "right" to see prisons in a manner that is not officially permitted come up against the logic, language, and power of police in enforcing this ephemeral visuality: "Move on, there is nothing to see here."[3]

The denial of our attempt to photograph, our subsequent examination of West Liberty's destruction, and the initial consideration of the connections between these two experiences began to shift my analytical focus and methodological approach as I continued to examine the region's prison growth in the ensuing years. Rather than looking at or inside the prisons, it began to make sense to look to their *interfaces* with what surrounded them.

Thinking about the prison in this way requires a change in perspective, a different way of seeing. That change was not immediate for me; my own process has been iterative, shaped by the perspectives of those who have become interlocutors for this project, including research participants as well as the historians, geographers, theorists, artists, and others whose work has helped me recognize my own conceptual limitations as someone trained to study through a particular disciplinary lens that centers crime rates and punishment regimes.[4] Examining the prisons in relationship to the sites and struggles that border them in time and space in Central Appalachia—mountaintop removal sites and underground mines, coal waste storage ponds, company towns, trash incinerators, landfills, and struggles around land, labor, and democracy—requires an analysis that centers extraction, disposal, and order within a broader examination of racial capitalism and state power.

This book examines how the prison came to shape, and take shape in, Central Appalachia. It is based on eight years of periodic ethnographic and archival research, beginning soon after I arrived in Kentucky in the fall of 2011. During the course of those eight years, I would travel from my home in Lexington to eastern Kentucky communities like West Liberty, Wheelwright, Inez, Roxana, Whitesburg, and Hazard, to southwestern Virginia, and to eastern Tennessee, interviewing community residents, spending time in local and regional archives, reviewing official documents and local newspapers, and visiting the landscapes home to current, former, and future prisons in an attempt to better understand the extractive and carceral economies of the region. Following the leads of fieldwork—the shifting terrain of the landscape, analyses from coalfield residents, and emergent historical patterns—this book argues that the rise of cages in the coalfields reflects a new strategy for an old project: the state's ongoing need to manufacture and maintain capitalist social order and social relations.[5] The orbiting of both work and social reproduction around the coal company in the twentieth century—at times coerced or enforced by police power in the form of mine guards, state police, and sheriffs—is grinding to a halt, as coal employment and coal production continue to decline dramatically. Some Central Appalachian communities have turned toward prisons and jails to resolve and navigate the crises, positioning the carceral economy as a salve for structural unemployment, needed infrastructure upgrades and extensions, municipal revenue generation, and the ability to sustain education, health, and recreational opportunities. I refer to this process of community renovation through prison and jail growth as carceral social reproduction.

The methodological and analytical approach to studying the interfaces of the prisons—the relationships in which they are embedded—arose out of both formative moments of research in the region and a growing sense that the story of their emergence and prominence was bigger and more complex than a story of crime and punishment.

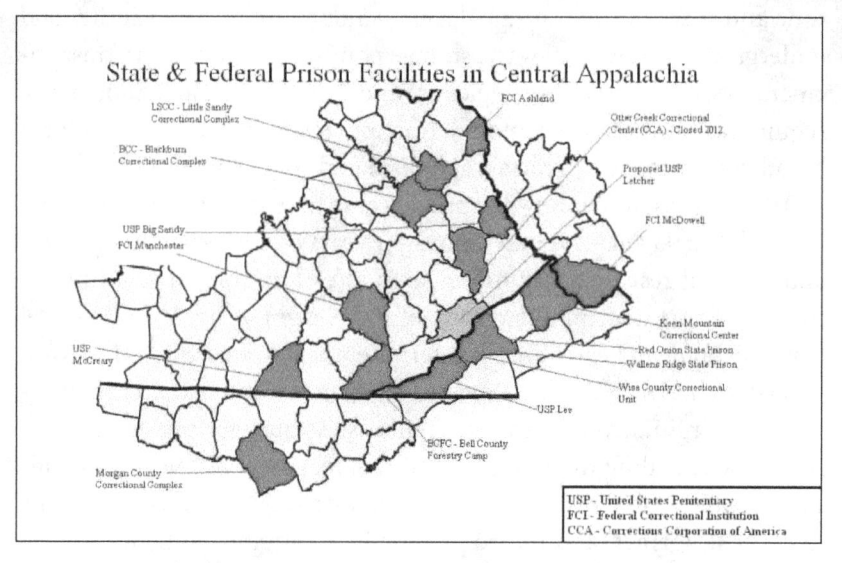

Figure I.2. Map of prisons in Central Appalachia by Elizabeth Sanders (Ryerson 2013).

Photography offered an additional methodological and analytical tool for wrestling with the "limits of representation" or the "edge of sight," those vantages that challenge existing frameworks.[6] Jill's photographs were generative for my own developing analysis, as her images often placed the prison in the broader landscape, which invariably included sites of extraction and disposal. Her photograph that serves as the cover of this book, for example, features an interface in eastern Kentucky between an old mining seam and the exterior fence of a prison, one of the many meeting points of the extraction and carceral geographies of the region. Another photograph found later in this book situates an east Tennessee prison in the mountains rising behind it, which are home to several mining entrances where prisoners were forced to mine coal for the state of Tennessee for seventy years.

The questions that motivated my interest in the research aligned with a particular photographic problem Jill was interested in exploring visually, namely, the optical-ideological work of the camera in framing and delimiting our vantages on and vocabularies for describing the depicted image. Our concerns sit within a prominent and provoking tradition of social theory and research on ideology, discourse, power, and photography. Photography can operate as "an index of an ideological theme," playing an *active* role in making the social world—confirming existing vantages, representations, and analyses.[7] Indeed, one only has to look at the long history of images and representations of Appalachia to glean how fraught the practice of photography can be in helping to calcify destructive depictions of people and places. As someone not from the region, I became acutely aware of the tensions between documentation—writing, photographing, publishing—and complicity in what Kate Fowler has called "the material and cultural extraction" of the region.[8] Researching and photographing prison growth in Central Appalachia required more than a reckoning with and accounting for my own positionality; it also required an examination of the long history of the region, within which representations of it figure heavily, including in its *ongoing* expropriation and exploitation. At the same time, by visually documenting the carceral geography of the region in a way that attempts to situate the prisons in a broader history of racial capitalism and state power, the photograph offers a way to move back and forth between the present moment and the historical contingencies on which it hinges.[9]

Historical inquiry offered another approach. While there is a common history to the rise of prisons and jails in Appalachia, there are veins of specific genealogies that branch off and structure the contours of particular places. In some communities, the specific history of coal camps looms large in understanding their trajectory toward becoming prison towns. In others, it is the War on Poverty, the history of strip-mine regulation, or the long and storied legacies of organizing and insurrection that help us to understand the fights over prisons today. Therefore, readers will find archival and other historical materials incorporated throughout the book in my attempt to tell the story of cages in the coalfields with attention to the context-specific ways in which broader historical moments have taken shape in different places. With that said, this book is not a conventional history of a region, even though it takes up historical questions in order to think through the violence of the present.

Understanding extensive prison and jail proliferation in Central Appalachia requires precise multiscalar work, examining specific configurations and contestations of local power as well as the broader politics and economy of the region, which itself is situated amidst flows of capital, political objectives, and ideological shifts that cross national and international borders. A quick gloss of one specific landscape in Letcher County, Kentucky, offers an instructive example. Letcher County was the location intended for the newest federal prison in the region and is the focus of the second half of this book, which examines in detail how local officials and residents attached to the promise of the prison everything from infrastructure upgrades to educational curriculum development to jobs. If it had been built, the prison would have sat near one of the few remaining operating coal mines in the county, currently owned by the Sapphire Coal Company. Sapphire was formed in 2004 out of the former assets of Golden Oak Mining and Cook & Sons Mining in Letcher County and employs about two hundred people across mines in eastern Kentucky. But Sapphire is one of six subsidiary companies in the region run by the United Coal Company (UCC), based in Tennessee. In 2009, Metinvest, a holding company, purchased UCC. Metinvest is the largest company in the System Capital Management Group, owned by Ukrainian businessman Rinat Akhmetov. Akhmetov's net worth is $6.5 billion, and numerous sources have alleged an earlier history in organized crime. Paul Manafort, the disgraced former campaign manager for then-candidate Donald Trump who was convicted in 2018 on a variety of state and federal charges ranging from tax and bank fraud to witness tampering and sentenced to prison, was a close friend and business partner of Akhmetov.

What does this brief examination of one small corner of the region's vast extractive and carceral geographies reveal? In the ability of coal companies to dissolve themselves and simply reincorporate as a distinctive LLC, one can see both the consolidation and the true international scope of the industry. Perhaps most importantly, that scope itself reveals central truths about Appalachia—that it is a region whose poverty is produced, again and again, by the theft of its natural resources by generations of capitalists operating in and outside of states: early settlers, speculators, industry titans, corporate executives, state officials, and global oligarchs. Today, while Letcher County's dwindling coal reserves funnel profits to one of the wealthiest men in the world, connected to transnational geopolitical currents, the county is in fiscal crisis, struggling to pay for basic infrastructure maintenance and upgrades, and county leaders have attached hopes for economic viability to the prospect of a federal prison. Moreover, the transnational scope of the coal industry, the global consequences of the climate change it hastens, and the reach of the prisons across geographies all caution against the understandable position that more than a century of destructive representations of Appalachia means that only those of the region should be able to speak about it. The reality, in the words of Harlan County activist Teri Blanton, is that "we all live downstream."[10]

The Making of Carceral Appalachia

One possible hazard of introducing rural Central Appalachia into the broader literature and conversation on the carceral state is being perceived as retreating from the centrality of race and racism, and pivoting to the kind of analysis that minimizes both.[11] Such a perception, while mistaken, would be understandable: Appalachia is often portrayed as an essentially white geography, a representation that makes three critical errors: (1) it ignores the historical processes that pushed out Native, immigrant, and Black people from the region; (2) it excises the contemporary presence of people of color, which is considerable in some parts of the region; and (3) it mistakes whiteness as nonracial. As an intervention into this series of mistakes, the approach I take in this book understands historical processes of racialization and racism as *constitutive* of capitalism. Whether one is discussing settler colonialism, industrialization, extraction, or incarceration, there is no moment of capitalism in the region that was not already racial. And, while incarceration indeed centers the way racial capitalism works against people of color generally and Black people specifically, racial capitalism is also operative when we are discussing white people, as well as those practices that might seem on their face to be nonracial. In Appalachia, whiteness is a complex construct, mobilized at times toward homogenization with a broader imagined white polity and (more often) at others employed to differentiate the region and its residents as deficient and even depraved. In this way, and as we will see, certain practices that may seem nonracial—struggles over wages, mineral rights, and land, even in communities that demographically are almost exclusively white—must be understood as part of racial capitalism's work to produce difference as it expropriates and exploits. A later section in this introduction will expand on racial capitalism further.

Prison growth in the region aligns in part with what we know from other scholars about rural areas across the United States increasingly suturing their economies to prisons, including in parts of Arkansas, Arizona, California, Colorado, Florida, New York, Indiana, Pennsylvania, Texas, and several other states in the West, including Oregon, Washington, Montana, and Idaho.[12] As these studies show for other areas of the country, in Central Appalachia the prison is used materially to respond to and putatively resolve various real and perceived crises at once, including manufactured crises like prison overcrowding and real crises arising out of the cycles of racial capitalism, including deindustrialization, structural joblessness, and revenue shortages. But Central Appalachia also requires context-specific consideration and historical examination. The region, after all, has been represented as synonymous with certain economic industries (coal), topographical features (mountains), and cultural tropes (white moral and financial poverty), which at times collapse into each other to form a composite representation of deficiency and dependency. These material features of the region, as well as their racialized and classed representations, are central to a deeper and historical reckoning with prison growth as they also bring into relief the limitations of a focus on crime and punishment.

Historians and other analysts of the region's political economy have alternately argued for Central Appalachia to be understood as an internal colony,[13] as an internal periphery of the world capitalist system,[14] and as a "national sacrifice zone."[15] The coal industry's success has depended in part on the insidious material and ideological practice of destroying land and lives while telling residents through targeted campaigns to be "friends of coal."[16] But even though coal came to characterize Appalachia, it is important to avoid the tendency to see the industry as a constitutive and even primordial part of the region. The story of both the dominance of the coal industry and the eventual rise of prisons in Central Appalachia must be understood within the broader historical developments of racial capitalism, which established the political-economic and spatial conditions of possibility for mineral rights to be sold to speculators and, eventually, for prisons to be imagined for and built on top of flattened mountains.

Scholars have offered important correctives to the notion that capitalist underdevelopment of Appalachia commenced with the coal industry.

Wilma Dunaway notes of early-eighteenth-century Appalachia, "Half a century before the decolonization of North America from the British Empire, southern planters and eastern capitalists expropriated vast territories of southern Appalachia from the Native American groups who lived and hunted there. . . . Once the frontiers had been depopulated of their indigenous inhabitants, speculator and settler capitalism expanded into the region."[17] Dwight Billings and Kathleen Blee note that these economic actors "engrossed more than four and a half million acres from Indian populations on the Appalachian frontier between 1763 and 1773," instigating the rapid transformation of "the land there from a common resource, as defined by indigenous peoples, to a privately possessed commodity."[18] It is important to pause and recognize the significance of this transition both for the sheer size of stolen land and for the historiography of Appalachia. First, consider the 4.5 million acres expropriated from First Nations in just a ten-year span in Appalachia compared to the 6.8 million acres, or 20 percent of the whole of England, enclosed and sanctioned by acts of Parliament between 1750 and 1820.[19] In other words, land expropriation in Appalachia was vast and rapid. Second, the history of enclosure in Appalachia challenges truncated narratives that periodize Appalachia and the coal industry together. The truth is that racial capitalism's brutal history in the region began not through nineteenth-century industrialization but rather with early-eighteenth-century settler-colonial expropriation and expansion. As Roxanne Dunbar-Ortiz puts it, "The Scots-Irish were the foot soldiers of British empire building, and they and their descendants formed the shock troops of the 'westward movement' in North America, the expansion of the US continental empire, and the colonization of its inhabitants. . . . They cleared forests, built log cabins, and killed Indians, forming a human wall of colonization for the new United States and, in wartime, employing their fighting skills effectively."[20]

Settler-colonial land expropriation from First Nations inaugurated capitalism's entry into the region, turning commons into property for white settlers, confirming in the process Patrick Wolfe's stunning observation that "the land that settlers seize is already value-added. There is no such thing as wilderness, only depopulation."[21] Ethnic cleansing and land seizure and transformation were the foundation for the eventual rise of the coal industry more than a century later. The emergence of the coal industry then ushered in a new round of enclosures as homesteaders lost their lands and became wage laborers in company towns, a process I explore in more detail in chapter 4. Importantly, these historical processes created the class structure of the region, as "land provided the economic basis for the structuring of a polarized Appalachian society in which the wealthy gentry amassed a majority of the acreage while more than half the settler households remained landless."[22] The transfers of land and the larger processes of enclosure and privatization have produced the striking spatial arrangement wherein "some of America's poorest people live on top of some of America's richest land."[23] Indeed, the extent of this spatial expression of the historical patterns of racial capitalism is perhaps indicated by both the need for and the findings of the major study *Who Owns Appalachia?*[24] Produced by a collective of community-based and university scholars across the region, the study, which was published in 1983, examined fifty-five thousand parcels in eighty counties, ultimately finding that major coal, oil, and gas companies owned 43 percent of the land in the region while largely avoiding paying the required property taxes.

This structure and its set of relations and tensions created and continues to remake Central Appalachia. In providing a foundation for how we have come to identify the area as a distinctive region, the historian Steven Stoll makes a profound point:

> The southern mountains are half a billion years old, but Appalachia did not exist before the industrial invasion of those uplands during the nineteenth century. It was created and constantly recreated by hunters and farmers of every ethnicity who employed the landscape for subsistence and exchange; by land-engrossing colonial elites; by corporate attorneys scheming to get hold of deeds; by investors wielding cadastral maps; by coal miners resisting company managers and starving on strike; by the social engineers of the New Deal; by the Appalachian Regional Commission; and by brokenhearted citizens watching beloved hollows buried by mountaintop removal mining.[25]

Appalachia as a region has no primordial existence outside of how it has been fabricated, both in the sense of being brought into material reality and in the sense of being a socio-spatial invention. To Stoll's list of individual and organizational bodies that have made and remade Appalachia, we must now also add prison boosters—the politicians, local elites, agency officials, and others who have helped to renovate land, labor, and identity through carceral development, including the fifteen regional prisons and a growing number of jails.[26] But as we will see, this process is neither inexorable nor indefinite. We must also add to Stoll's list those individuals and organizations that have offered a vision for the region that cuts against the grain of extraction and incarceration. In the very same county from which oligarch Rinat Akhmetov extracts wealth from one of the few remaining coal mines, and where the federal Bureau of Prisons worked with local elites to attempt to build the next prison in the region, a coalition formed to fight for a different future. Their historic defeat of United States Penitentiary (USP) Letcher, the focus of chapter 7, underscores that the remaking of Appalachia is the product of struggle.

Understanding Carceral Appalachia: Crisis, Order, Social Reproduction

Kentucky is one of more than two dozen states that have passed legislation that, on its face, aims to reduce the state prison population in what has come to be known as justice reinvestment.[27] Justice reinvestment was originally conceived of as a political mechanism whereby states could redirect funds from incarceration into the social and welfare services that had been abandoned under neoliberal restructuring.[28] In practice, however, the reforms to sentencing laws have often resulted in reorganizing, rather than reducing, state carceral capacities, a process some scholars have referred to as "transcarceration" or "carceral devolution."[29] Indeed, Kentucky's state prison population has *grown* since the 2011 passage of House Bill 463, the Public Safety and Offender Accountability Act, which had been intended to reduce state prison populations and the state prison budget. From 2000 until 2010, the state's incarcerated population had grown by 45 percent, compared to 13 percent for the US state prison system overall.[30] An 11 percent growth since the passage of HB 463 has continued a crisis of overcrowding. Kentucky has twenty-four thousand state prisoners but just under twelve thousand state prison beds and has turned toward county jails to house half the prisoners under the custody of the state Department of Corrections (DOC). County governments, particularly those in struggling rural areas, have been eager to oblige as the per-diem payments from the DOC (as well as from federal agencies like Immigration and Customs Enforcement and the US Marshalls) help to offset revenue shortages, which are particularly dramatic in eastern Kentucky because of the decline of coal.[31] The growth of incarceration even in moments characterized by legislative reform points to the recalcitrance of prisons and jails, produced in part by their importance to the everyday needs of the state at every scale.[32]

As this book details, then, rural counties have turned to incarceration to reap whatever benefits may be available due to the broad overreliance on imprisonment in the state and beyond. One way to think about this is as the state working across itself—across the scales of its expression—to try to solve crises it also helped to create. Local actors, working with federal representatives and state officials, worked hard to attract federal prisons and build local carceral capacity as mechanisms for both rural job creation and revenue generation in a context of economic crisis due to unemployment and revenue shortage. But local officials also misplaced the revenue surpluses they had during earlier times, sinking them into pet projects and into infrastructure designed explicitly to attract the prisons.

It is tempting to argue that the prison simply replaces the coal industry in Central Appalachia as a primary source of regional employment. At a glance, the employment numbers seem to support this argument. While coal jobs have declined rapidly, the number of prison jobs has risen steadily since the early 1990s, corresponding with the number of facilities built. As of this writing, in 2020, there are 3,760 existing coal jobs in Kentucky, by far the lowest total since the nineteenth century and down 38 percent from even 2019, when there were 6,073 employees in the coal industry in the state. In a telling comparison, there are now far more corrections jobs in the state—6,640—although that number does not include the medical, clerical, and mental health workers who also work inside of prisons.[33] In short, prison and jail jobs have overtaken coal jobs in Kentucky by *thousands* of positions. The federal prisons built since the late 1990s and early 2000s have no doubt inflated this number; as recently as 1997, there were 4,920 correctional officers in the state.[34] As one industry publication observed more than twenty years ago, in 1999, in a story headlined "Corrections Replace Coal in Eastern Kentucky," "In Kentucky's coal country, prisons have become the cornerstone of an economic renewal meant to offset the decline of coal mining."[35]

But thinking of the prison primarily as the replacement of one site of production for another is limiting. For one thing, the jobs that the prisons do provide do not even come close to matching the coal industry's historic employment levels in the state and region. At the height of coal employment (which is not the same thing as the height of coal production, as we will see) in 1949, the coal industry employed 75,707 people in Kentucky, or more than ten times the number of prison and jail workers in the state today. Moreover, the coal industry's dominance of the region's economy occurred for a century. And yet, there is no doubt that prisons remain a leading pursuit of politicians and community leaders looking for new and significant sources of employment. What does the prison do that requires an analysis beyond its attempt, however dubious, to replace coal as an engine of economic development?

Rather than as punishment or economic development, this book argues, prisons in the coalfields are best understood as central mechanisms for the ongoing need to manufacture capitalist social order amidst very real crises in the region. Crises, as Stuart Hall and his coauthors have defined them, occur when existing social formations cease to be able to reproduce themselves on the basis of current social and economic relations.[36] In the coalfields, the precipitous decline of coal employment and coal production has driven the region into severe crisis. The signing of the 1950 National Bituminous Coal Wage Agreement between the United Mine Workers of America and the largest coal operators avoided a strike and secured sought-after victories in the form of higher wages and benefits for miners. But the agreement also included a stipulation that the union would not oppose mechanization. In the ensuing decades, the industry mechanized rapidly, mining jobs began to fall rapidly, and millions of Appalachians would migrate out of the region.[37] Just during the period in which my research occurred, between 2011 and 2018, eastern Kentucky lost 73 percent of its already-dwindling coal jobs. Coal production's steep decline has hurt regional revenue streams because of the loss of receipts from the coal severance tax, a once-reliable source of millions of dollars for coalfield communities. Prisons have been deployed most explicitly to try to resolve issues of unemployment but also

Coal declines in eastern Kentucky

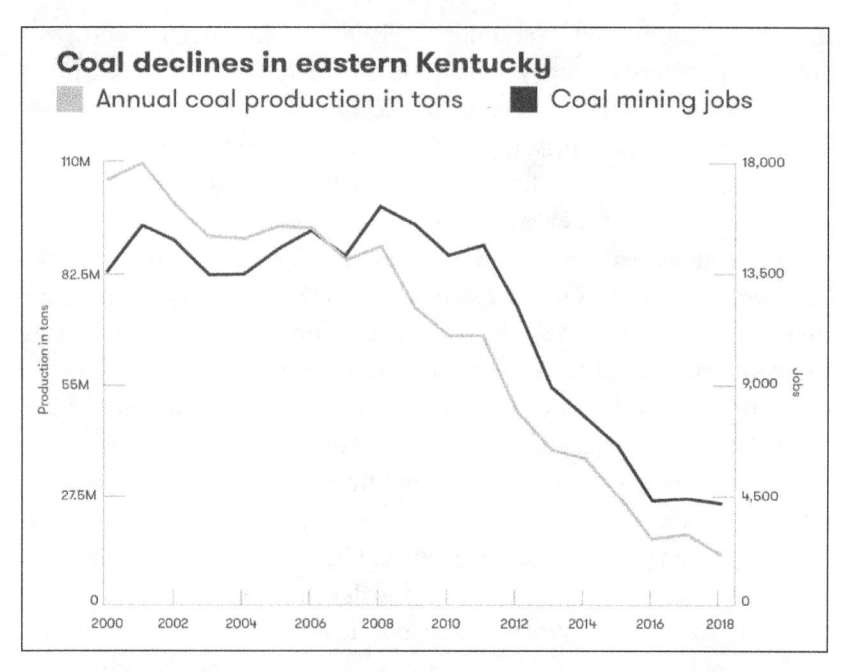

Figure 1.3. Coal declines in eastern Kentucky. Graph courtesy of Jacob Kang-Brown, Vera Institute of Justice.

have been the cornerstone of county applications for various infrastructure projects, where funding is contingent upon evidence of some kind of economic development project. As stated earlier, rural jails have recently proliferated in eastern Kentucky, holding significant numbers of state prisoners in exchange for per-diem payments in order to shore up revenue shortages.

Cages of all kinds, then, are utilized to address crises at the points of *both* production and reproduction, and offer important affective and symbolic recuperation to communities in crisis. As the historian Peter Linebaugh has noted, crime is "capital's most ancient tool in the creation and control of the working class."[38] There is an important legacy of this kind of analysis as it relates to the role of the prison in the management, control, and reproduction of the criminalized and racialized poor. The prison temporarily or permanently disappears people who are a part of the global working class and growing relative surplus population. In this regard, it also has a direct effect on the social reproductive capacities of the incarcerated as the prison has been shown to often guarantee the "jobless future."[39] But less attention has been paid to the ways in which the prison functions to manage the poor and working classes in the places where prisons reside. There, the prison both operates as a site of production or work in a postindustrial and postextractive economy and, at the same time, is positioned as critical to the social reproduction of and within those communities.

In these ways, the prison has transformed itself in the neoliberal era from a locally unwanted land use to a form of development perceived as offering stabilization and growth. In other words, the prison has moved from eliciting NIMBYism (or not in my backyard-ism) to generating YIMBYism (or yes in my backyard-ism), with communities courting prisons for years and competing for siting.[40] In multiple communities that this book examines, the prison has offered not only the prospect of employment opportunities but also the ability to envision a future for struggling rural hospitals, community centers, small businesses, and schools. Indeed, county education departments in communities home to or attempting to site prisons have reorganized school curricula and developed criminal justice degree programs around the promise or presence of the prison. This carceral social reproduction suggests a startling political and cultural transition and realignment as it points to the relationship between the political economy of the carceral state—i.e., the centrality of prisons and jails to the mundane operations of municipalities—and the force of its ideological work to inscribe subjectivities.[41] It is not just that the prison may provide some jobs, but rather that it threatens to deputize hundreds of people into one of the central institutional sites of racialized class war.[42] This is especially stark when understood in the historical context of the region, which has been home to militant struggles against capital and police. In the rise of the prison and jail, we might be viewing the collapse of the police powers at work in the twentieth-century coal camps and company towns into the new form of both work and social order. The modern-day correctional officer—and their communities in the region—may be best understood as not, in fact, the next iteration of the coal miner but rather as the fusion of miner and mine guard into a new subjectivity, activated by the carceral state and deployed as the most explicit manifestation of police power in the region.

Racial Capitalism, Waste, and the Political Economy of Representation

Many of the communities that this book examines are largely white. It is unfortunately common to misrecognize white people and white spaces as outside of, or incidental to, racialization. In fact, racialization was constitutive of the emergence of capitalism in Europe, "seeded in European social orders . . . creating racial hierarchies that formed early class structures" between and among people whom today we might identify as white.[43] The work of carceral social reproduction to renovate Central Appalachian communities through the rise of the prison is fundamentally racialized.

To begin, prisons are institutions that both are products and producers of racism. That is, they engage in what Barbara and Karen Fields call "racecraft," or the conjuring of race through the exercise of racism.[44] Many readers will be familiar with the statistics that demonstrate both the scope of the carceral state and the degree to which it polices and cages people of color. While these data can sometimes be mobilized narrowly to simply measure disparity, they nonetheless show the central role of the carceral state in "manufacturing racial meaning. . . . in materializ[ing] racism and therefore race."[45] As scholars of racial capitalism insist, race and racism are not always indexed to phenotype. Racism is best understood as "partitioning," "systems and processes that stigmatize and depreciate," and the structural "production and exploitation of group-differentiated vulnerability to premature death."[46] Racism, a constitutive feature of capitalism, separates, moving some toward undervalued lives and premature deaths in order to enhance the health, longevity, reproduction, property, profits, and other gains of others, in the process producing a racialized and unequal social order.

Appalachia offers edifying regional examples of racial capitalism's work. The violence of settler-colonial expansion into the region, the fueling of industrialization and war with Appalachia's coal, and the incarceration of thousands of people from outside of the area in the region's prisons all raise the centrality of Appalachia to the mundane and spectacular operations of racial capitalism and the state. In addition, Appalachia is often read as synonymous with whiteness, and in particular the so-called white working class. This construction floats outside of a more complex empirical reality and history. While the Central Appalachian communities home to the prisons that this book examines are mostly white, the broader Appalachian region is more demographically diverse. According to the historian Elizabeth Catte, there are more people in Appalachia who identify as African American than as Scots-Irish.[47] Data from the Appalachian Regional Commission further demonstrate the fallacy of the construct. People of color account for one in five Appalachian residents; in Southern Appalachia, one in three residents is a person of color.[48]

Moreover, the cultural imagination of Appalachia as white is part of a "double erasure" of people of color. Not only are they omitted from popular representations of the region but also the processes by which people of color have been expelled or pushed out from the coalfields are ignored, from formal processes of Native removal to the racialized impacts of mechanization, which hit Black coal miners first and hardest and led to mass migrations out of the mountains.[49] One of the consequences of these erasures is a failure to appreciate the true multiracial character of coalfield labor fights in the early twentieth century, a history that includes both the complexities of solidarity and its internationalism. This history includes, for example, Chicano miners in West Virginia coal camps in the 1930s engaging in "long political arguments between the Villistas, the Zapatistas, and the Carranzistas. The revolution was fought all over again."[50] It also includes Black leadership in rank-and-file organizations around the coalfields, including the significant role of Black men and women in the founding of the militant National Miners Union in 1928. Of course, the complex dynamics of racism are foundational to this history as well. As a Black miner in West Virginia put it to the investigative reporter Paul Nyden, multiracial solidarity in the mines was compromised when "we got outdoors . . . washed the coal dust from our faces . . . and white miners would become different. They remembered that they were white and we were black."[51] The erasures of this complex history, and the popular inscription of whiteness into Appalachia it has produced, prompted poet Frank X. Walker and many subsequent artists and writers to claim Affrilachia as geography and identity, subverting in the process both the standard spatialization of the region and its whiteness.[52]

In areas of Central Appalachia that are largely white, the rise of prisons in the region has returned large numbers of people of color to the mountains. Transported in and for captivity, they are formally counted as residents of the communities in which they are incarcerated and, at the same time, are denied any benefit that recognition may otherwise afford them, a denial that constitutes a third iteration of erasure.[53] Capitalism's inherent racial work is therefore apparent in communities that are home to prisons and that are overwhelmingly white. As Laura Pulido has argued, "It is essential to remember that racial processes also produce the environmental landscapes of white people as well."[54]

In this way, the structural economic crisis triggered by the precipitous decline of coal employment and production has deeply racialized and gendered affective and cultural contours. The extraction economy had bound a form of white hegemonic masculinity to coal mining.[55] The collapse of coal undoubtedly also elicited a crisis of "surplus masculinities."[56] The prison offers a path toward repairing and renovating the region's racialized and gendered social order through transforming once and would-be white (and largely male) miners into white (and largely male) prison guards.[57] In the work of criminalization and employment to bring two different, and differently racialized, groups of people together on opposite sides of the cage, we should understand the prison as enacting a key function of racial capitalism, what Jodi Melamed calls "densely connected social separateness."[58]

Finally, it is racial capitalism as both a historical force and an analytical framework that best explains the connections between the broader political-economic processes that have shaped the region—that is, its "capture" by settlers, industry, and incarceration—and representations of Appalachians—that is, their "capture" in narratives and images of material and moral poverty.

The construction of Appalachia and Appalachians in terms that distance and degrade has a long history. These representations have created a robust archive of tropes from which to draw, which continue to circulate within and across various media platforms and political discourses, and which are consequential for understanding the historical conditions that continue to produce Appalachia materially and ideologically.

Representing Race

Whether through explicitly invoking terms such as "hillbilly," "redneck," or "white trash," or relying on subtler tropes that similarly signify rural poverty, representations of Appalachia often racialize the region and people as essentially white (negating the systematic elimination of First Nations, the structural abandonment of one-time Black and immigrant residents, and the contemporary presence of residents of color) but as outside of hegemonic whiteness. Analysts of this dual racialization and its work to hierarchize and simultaneously include and exclude have argued that Appalachians are represented as "not quite white" or "unwhite."[59] These portrayals are deeply imbricated with the historical and ongoing expropriation of the region. As Steven Stoll has argued,

> No two dispossessions are the same. The white settler culture of the southern mountains did not share the same fate as the Cherokee, Choctaw, Chickasaw, Seminole and Creek. The compulsory removal of these five nations in 1838, known in Cherokee as the Trail of Tears, would seem to have no connection to the coming of corporations to West Virginia. Still, these events bear a resemblance. They rhyme. In both instances, a privileged commercial class depicted the members of a target group as a despised race before taking their land.[60]

The rhyming of different historical racialization projects is particularly notable for a couple of reasons. First, the language of racialism—the racist descriptions used to invent and identify races in order to justify imperialism, conquest, genocide, expropriation, and exploitation—is remarkably mobile, crossing continents, oceans, and epochs, and yet also contingent on and flexibly responding to context and struggle.[61] In that regard, what Stoll has observed in the rhyming of distinct racialized dispossessions in Appalachia is the historical syncopated rhythm of racism, recurring consistently and yet inflected differently in severity and context.[62]

Stoll's observations are important for a second reason. In the passage's focus on First Nations and white settlers, Stoll indirectly deepens our understanding of the function of racialization within broader objectives of dispossession and land expropriation. Even as we might understand

First Nations as primarily engaged in struggles over sovereignty, enduring and fighting against ongoing genocide and dispossession, rather than as an ethno-racial group subject to discrimination, it is clear that racism fuels the settler-colonial project.[63] In the case of white settlers and contemporary white residents of Appalachia, racialization operates to demarcate class positions among people who often serve as the basis against which the concept of race is formulated. What, then, does their racialization mean and what does it accomplish?

As mentioned above, race as a category and racism as a social practice are not necessarily indexed to phenotype, but rather are a technology (in the case of race) and a practice (in the case of racism) for the production of social difference.[64] Or, as Patrick Wolfe has argued, "What matters . . . is not phenotypical endowment . . . as if social processes come to operate on a naturally present set of bodily attributes that are already given prior to history. Rather, racial identities are constructed in and through the very process of their enactment."[65] What this confirms, then, is the centrality of racialization to capitalist processes even in places generally understood as racially homogenous and as foundationally about class, as if class and the political-economic processes that produce it operate outside of racial practices.[66]

The terms deployed to characterize Appalachia perform, foundationally, the production of social difference, distance, and deficiency.[67] "White trash" is perhaps the most germane to deconstruct because of what the term specifically instructs.[68] Reading the two words that comprise the term against one another, "white trash" expresses profound and even primordial contradictions, "between the sacred and the profane, purity and impurity, morality and immorality, cleanliness and dirt. . . . White trash names a people whose very existence seems to threaten the symbolic and social order."[69] At the same time, the term throws into explicit relief the tensions between race and class: white as an ethno-racial signifier and trash as indicating abject class status. But, terms like "white trash" and "hillbilly" did not originate in Appalachia and are not endemic to it. Anthony Harkins's cultural history of "hillbilly" notes that the term has applied less to a specific locale than to "anywhere on the rough edges of the landscape and economy."[70] Nancy Isenberg's masterful history of "white trash" notes the popular circulation of that term in the 1820s but also argues that the idea is much older, and was central to British plans for colonization. As she notes, the New World was understood as a "waste land" and the right place for dumping the idle poor, who were referred to as "waste people."[71] This original designation grounds its progeny, "white trash," even further in the political economy and symbolic representation of disposability. As Isenberg expands, waste people "have existed in the minds of rural or urban elites and the middle class as extrusions of the weedy, unproductive soil.... The worst ate clay and turned yellow, wallowed in mud and muck, and their necks became burned by the hot sun. Their poorly clothed, poorly fed children generated what others believed to be a permanent and defective breed. Sexual deviance? That comes from cramped quarters in obscure retreats, distant from civilization, where the moral vocabulary that dwells in town has been lost."[72] "Waste people" and its descendant terms collapse notions of class, breed, race, morality, diet, and landscape into one composite representation of distance, depravity, and deficiency. These constructs, and in particular their invocations of waste, dirt, and disorder, are inseparable from the racialized material and symbolic production of the nation and have been deployed in urban and rural contexts alike.[73]

Part of the work of racialization is to narrate and justify the violence of enclosure and ejection. In Appalachia, inventing a race of people and justifying the taking of their lands not only required "the force of law ... [but also] required a story."[74] A new literary genre known as "local color writing" and endemic to emergent nineteenth-century magazines like *Harper's New Monthly Magazine* communicated to urban elite audiences a kind of journalistic entertainment based on authors' travel accounts, and in which "a coherent place—Appalachia—and a unique people—the Appalachian 'mountaineers'—reached national consciousness." Between 1870 and 1890, "local colorists published over ninety travel sketches and 125 short stories about the region," including an early piece titled "A Strange Land and a Peculiar People."[75] One *Harper's* story from 1891 referred to older Middlesboro, Tennessee, "mountaineer" residents as "usually not attractive" but "rather yellow and cadaverous looking."[76] By the end of the nineteenth century the recurrence of tropes conflating the moral and economic poverty of the Appalachian resident with Appalachian topography was pervasive enough that there emerged "a generalization concerning the coherence of mountain culture and the homogeneity of mountain people ... which made possible the redefinition of Appalachia as a discrete region of the nation and the redefinition of the mountaineers as a distinct population, and thereby made possible the legitimation of Appalachian otherness."[77]

The idea gained traction, expanding through novels and scholarship, the latter of which ignored actual historical geographic evidence of migration patterns in order to argue for a culturally and even genetically deficient Appalachian resident.[78] This construct manifested through the trope of "two Kentuckies," which was first introduced by the poet James Lane Allen in 1886 and which identified a civilized bluegrass region and a primitive society in the mountains. Writing in the 1920s, author Horace Kephart noted that those who remained in the mountains "stood still or retrograded" and that the mountains "were cursed with a considerable incubus of naturally weak or depraved characters."[79] The notion of "mountain whites" emerged in 1933 with the release of *Hollow Folk* by the journalist Thomas Henry and the sociologist Mandel Sherman.[80] As the sociologist Rebecca Scott argues of this conflation between people and topography, "The mountainous landscape itself is implicated in the degeneration of the people who inhabit it. Appalachian stereotypes conflate land and people, with dark, trash filled hollows sheltering isolated, incestuous communities. These generic representations are instrumental in the cultural, social, economic and environmental marginalization of Appalachia."[81] These representations have been deployed with decent intentions in order to stir sympathy or outrage at persistent poverty, as when Michael Harrington, founding member of the Democratic Socialists of America, wrote of "the other America" and introduced the concept of the culture of poverty into wide circulation in the United States.[82] The problem, as Scott notes, is that this collection of images so saturates cultural accounts of Appalachia that it stands in for the place and people, and in the process naturalizes a kind of commonsense account of both endemic poverty and its biological or cultural causes.[83]

Contemporary expressions of this historic practice circulate widely, including from popular authors like Kevin Williamson and J. D. Vance, whose work in the pages of the *National Review* or, in the case of Vance, the *New York Times* best-seller *Hillbilly Elegy*, offer shoddy sociological observations and cartoonish character depictions grounded in racialized assertions of biological and cultural depravity.[84] In a series of essays, for example, Williamson refers to Appalachia as "the Big White Ghetto," a racial and spatial designation of poverty in and of itself, but which he animates with people who are unintelligible because of the mixture of "so much alcohol and Kentucky" in their voice and whose camouflage outfits suggesting outdoorsmanship are belied by "complexions [that] say 'Nintendo.'" The soundtrack for this sunken composite figure "isn't 'Shady Grove' but the 'thumpa thumpa thumpa' of Kanye West," and the setting is "the dank woolly wilds" of a real America.[85] Much of this depiction is consistent with and referential toward the historiography of the region. In this telling, substance abuse and a retrograde geography produce incoherence, an unhealthy lifestyle sallows and spoils residents' white skin, and the backwoods is both backdrop for and cause of their deficiencies. But Williamson updates the portrayal by further racializing the region. "Shady Grove," an Appalachian folk song from eastern Kentucky, operates in the article as a signifier for traditional and unsullied "white" music. The "'thumpa thumpa thumpa' of Kanye West" suggests a primitive and Black cultural encroachment and even displacement that further stain the whiteness of the region.

These depictions extend beyond these more notable authors and to journalistic accounts that fall into what the historian Elizabeth Catte calls "Trump country" pieces and that add a veneer of contemporary—if shallow—political analysis to an otherwise predictable adherence to this century-and-a-half-old script.[86] Crucially, the circulation of these accounts of Appalachia and Appalachians is rarely held to account for faulty methods and shallow analysis because they "reinforced the Atlantic elite's most versatile sociological category: race."[87] That is, this long history of representations reliant on enduring class signifiers of economic and moral poverty works to fabricate race—in this case, a degraded form of whiteness—in part by and through geography.[88] In this way, such representations help to construct and maintain a set of logics that racialize poverty "not as Black/white" but rather "in terms of genetic inferiority. [The poor] are deemed biologically incapable, disqualified from being Americans."[89]

The double racialization of Appalachia—as both white and not quite so—has produced complex and contradicting policies in the region, as powerful interests can organize and mobilize representations for particular political projects, with Appalachia serving "as a projection screen for both the liberal and conservative imagination."[90] In one early example, Central Appalachian coal had been so essential to the World War I effort that President Wilson had exempted miners from the draft. In literally fueling the war effort, the industry saw itself as a part of the larger national struggle, thanks also to political and media narratives that communicated that "mining coal was an expression of citizenship, an essential service to the nation."[91] Even as recuperated (white) American workers mining coal for their country, representations offered a callous instrumentalization of Appalachians. Just years later, however, during the height of the mine wars in West Virginia, national media relied on tropes that defined miners' essential differences from the rest of the nation, describing their militant organizing as a product of the region's "primitive culture" rather than as part of the larger class struggle.[92]

Figure 1.4. "Uncle Sam needs that extra shovelful."
F. Sindelar. United States, 1917. Brooklyn, NY: Latham Litho. & Ptg. Co. Photograph. https://www.loc.gov/ /

Figure 1.5. "Stand by the boys in the trenches. Mine more coal." Walter Whitehead. United States, 1918. Chicago: Edwards & Deutsch Litho. Co. Photograph. https://www.loc.gov.

Decades later, and as chapter 2 will detail, the bold economic vision of the War on Poverty was underwritten by particular representations of the people it would supposedly benefit. On the one hand, the Johnson administration sold the War on Poverty through sympathetic portrayals of Appalachian poverty to a "nation . . . [that] took obvious relish in the white skins and blue eyes of the region's children" and that was reticent about federal programs to help the Black underclass.[93] On the other hand, the phenotypic racialization of white poverty was limited by writers' decisions to credit genetic or cultural inferiority as the source of the region's ills. Some authors went so far as to endorse eugenics, an explicit embrace of the idea of an inferior form of whiteness. This "bourgeois imaginary" of Appalachia is constitutive of the ideological production of narratives of American exceptionalism.[94] In many cases, authors hitched their work—regardless of intentions—to an accelerating common sense about a region distinguished by remoteness and primitiveness that served to underwrite the continued exploitation of Appalachia by writing it out of the depiction.

Outline of This Book

Examining prison growth in Central Appalachia is fraught with analytical challenges. One of the central ones for me has been to evaluate the extent to which the region's particular histories of exploitation and expropriation structure the carceral present and future. One pitfall of hewing too closely to that story is to imply, as some authors do, that there is something peculiar about Appalachia, as if the region portends its own demise. Prison growth in Central Appalachia is at once a story about the region's central, if shifting, relationship to racial capitalism and state power through processes of extraction and disposal and, at the same time, a broader story about the dialectical relationships between urban and rural America. Recognizing the importance of Central Appalachia's extraction and prison economies as well as the relevance of regional history therein is different from arguing that Appalachia's long history of exploitation makes it exceptional, as some analysts who endorse the internal-colonialism model seem to indicate.[95] Rather, this book operates from a position that understands the analytical importance of *both* Appalachia's distinctive history, including its material and symbolic production, *and* its location as one regional geography among many hinterlands that can be characterized by exploitation, expropriation, survival, reproduction, and resistance.[96] The shared central characteristics of its story mean that there are lines of solidarity that can be, and in fact are, forged.[97]

Detailing this story as in part the transition from coal to cages, set within the possibilities delimited by racial capitalism as both economic system and ideology, is to explain, in the words of Ruth Wilson Gilmore, why "the outcomes are logically explicable but were by no means inevitable."[98] This is not only a story about the consequences of mass incarceration for rural communities, the failures of the War on Poverty, or evidence of the trend of rural prison proliferation. Rather, the rise and expansion of cages in the coalfields marks a transitional point in the history of racial capitalism, and is a clue—a major one—to the role of the state in needing to remake capitalist social order as the contradictions inherent to the political economy produce crises in need of resolution.

This book tells this story in three parts. Each part is organized around a different process that is central to understanding the carceral geographies of the region, and the chapters therein are built around the Central Appalachian communities that best illustrate the respective process. Part 1, "Extraction and Disposal," which includes chapters 1 and 2, examines the spatial and political relationships among coal, waste, and incarceration, focusing on sites of mountaintop removal that subsequently became the locations for prisons. Mountaintop removal (MTR) is the most extreme form of strip mining, using explosives to decapitate mountains in order to access the coal underneath. In its wake, MTR leaves hundreds of acres of flattened land, a spatial consequence that prison boosters readily mobilize to argue for prison siting. Both chapters are driven by the analyses of research participants, several of whom spoke of prison proliferation in ways that situated the prison as part of a regional historical geography of waste and enclosure. Chapter 1, "'This Is a Place for Trash': Mountaintop Removal, Waste, and Prisons," grounded in fieldwork in eastern Kentucky and southwestern Virginia, explores the contiguities among mining, waste management, and incarceration. In Martin County, Kentucky, residents took me on a tour of an illegal coal ash dumpsite and a new trash incinerator, both of which reside near United States Penitentiary Big Sandy, itself built on *both* an underground mine *and* a mountaintop removal site, and directly adjacent to various mining businesses, infrastructures, and waste sites. In southwestern Virginia, two "supermax" state prisons were built even as state incarceration rates had declined. A research participant there spoke of the long history of fighting coal companies, drug companies, and landfill companies, only to then fight the state in trying to stop prison construction. In Letcher County, Kentucky, at the site proposed for what would have been the newest prison in the region, residents offered competing visions of the space that both acquiesced to and resisted the prospect of carceral enclosure, acknowledging in the process the various uses of the land following MTR that would be foreclosed by the construction of the prison. The work of extraction and incarceration on the same land illustrates the dialectical relationship between waste and value. Within the vulgar calculus of capitalism, MTR transforms wasted land—a mountain—into a commodity: coal. But the extraction of coal produces another iteration of "waste": the denuded and flattened top of the MTR site. In the departure of the coal industry generally, and its abandonment of MTR sites specifically, the prison offers one mechanism to resolve this new round of waste, integrating the flattened planes into the region's carceral geography.

Neither the emergence of mountaintop removal nor the eventual prison proliferation it would partly enable were inevitable. Rather, both were produced by a confluence of historical processes operating through law, policy, political economy, and ideology. Chapter 2, "Wars, Laws, Landscapes: Producing the Carceral Conjuncture," examines the production of the historical moment in Central Appalachia in an attempt to better explain how places like those examined empirically in chapter 1 came to be home to sites of environmental and social violence, enacted through extraction and incarceration. Specifically, chapter 2 examines the War on Poverty, including its failures to implement structural changes and its tacit support for county elites at the expense of grassroots democracy; the convergence of the War on Poverty with the War on Crime, which seeded the rise of the carceral state and the eventual turn to prisons in rural communities; the role of regulatory law in enabling the coal industry to renovate it abilities to enclose land and maximize production, including the shift to mountaintop removal; and the power as well as incompleteness of both extractive and carceral ideologies.

Part 2, "Profit and Order," which includes chapters 3 and 4, looks to developments in the coalfields that query the relationship between profit and prisons. Upon close historical and ethnographic examination, the guiding logics and longer history of these formations broaden an analysis that might otherwise zero in on the profit motive. The reality is that the relationship between incarceration and profit changes over time, even when the formations in question are explicitly profit driven.

Chapter 3, "'What a Magnificent Field for Capitalists!': Convict Labor, Carceral Growth, and Craft Tourism," explores a new formation in the coalfields: the Brushy Mountain Development (BMD), a former prison in rural east Tennessee that has been developed into a site of eco- and prison-tourism. The chapter first discusses the rich history of the site, as the prison's construction in the 1890s—and the subsequent practice of forcing prisoners to mine coal for the state—was a direct response to militant labor uprisings against coal companies and their reliance on the convict lease system. The chapter then turns to the contemporary carceral formation, as the site's three owners have attempted to graft the current embrace of craft spirits and local food onto the unlikely host of the former prison as part of a plan for the economic "revitalization" of the county. In the process, the BMD produces a cultural afterlife of incarceration, mobilizing tropes of violence and depravity in order to sell the experience and a related set of products. This history of the one site indexes the changing role of carceral capacities under racial capitalism across different conjunctures and raises questions about what formations may follow the prison while continuing to extend its ideological work.

Chapter 4, "The Company Town: Remaking Social Order in the Coalfields," looks primarily at the small community of Wheelwright, Kentucky, a former coal company town. At present writing, Otter Creek Correctional Facility, a private prison in Wheelwright owned by Core Civic and decommissioned since 2012, is awaiting reopening (and renaming) as Southeastern Correctional Complex. Kentucky will lease the facility from the private prison company in order to house state prisoners and presumably to alleviate overcrowding at other prisons. While the presence of private prisons in the coalfields would seem to underscore the centrality of corporate profit to the region, this chapter's examination into both Wheelwright's history and its possible future suggests a more capacious understanding of racial capitalism's role in the community, forged in the twentieth century through police power and remade in the twenty-first through the prison. In examining the maneuvers to reopen the prison and describing the hopes of area residents for the prison to generate everything from job growth to infrastructure upgrades, this chapter examines the process of remaking social order in Wheelwright and introduces carceral social reproduction, the process around which part 3 is organized.

Part 3, "Carceral Social Reproduction," which includes chapters 5, 6, and 7, focuses in on one county in eastern Kentucky—Letcher

County—in order to examine the long contest over, and eventual defeat of, what would have been the newest prison in the coalfields, USP Letcher. Many of the justifications for construction hinged on the prison's putative ability to sustain the county amidst historic lows of coal employment and production levels. The chapters in part 3 further explore the dynamics of carceral social reproduction as well as the ways in which organizers, activists, and other area residents expressed and planned opposition to it.

USP Letcher would have resided on one of the former MTR sites examined in detail in chapter 1. The plan for the prison gained considerable momentum during the same period in which I was conducting the research for this book and thus offered "real-time" insight into the material and ideological struggles over both the prison and the future of the county it was purported to underwrite. Chapter 5, "Planning the Prison: Development, Revenue, and Ideology," examines in detail how local civic and political elites—what one participant has called the "Mountain Royalty"—attempted to position the county favorably to entice the prison. This occurred through shaping and policing local discourse as well as through mundane, although no less important, political and financial maneuvers designed to attract and retain the prison, in part to complete infrastructure projects and shore up revenue shortages. This chapter examines these granular efforts in order to better explain the importance of regional planning and development to the carceral state.

Chapter 6, "'To Bring a Future and Hope to Our Children': Renovating Education, Identity, and Work," extends these arguments further. With the decline of once-reliable revenue streams from coal production along with dwindling coal jobs, the county has turned to prisons as a way to imagine not only job growth but also the very possibility of a regional future, as evidenced by the outsized role of the prison in local residents' expressions of hope for schools, healthcare facilities, and community centers. The chapter examines what the prospect of a political and economic realignment around incarceration means for the county and considers the racialized and gendered contours of carceral social reproduction. While the focus in chapters 5 and 6 is fairly granular, examining the work of local public and quasi-public entities as well as public comments offered during the scoping and siting process for the prison, e analysis is (and must be) multiscalar, as USP Letcher was constantly positioned by supporters to resolve problems that cross county, regional, state, and national borders.

Chapter 7, "The Plot of Abolition: Solidarity Politics across Scale, Strategy, and Prison Walls," focuses on the coalition that formed to oppose USP Letcher and fight for a different future for the county. The coalition included local organizers, landowners, and concerned residents as well as national environmental activists and lawyers. Working on multiple fronts and through different strategies, the coalition delayed, disrupted, and eventually defeated the prison. Even as the proposal for USP Letcher moved beyond the environmental assessment stage required by federal environmental law and into the phase of construction, the work of the coalition had set the conditions of possibility for the project to falter. In a historic defeat, the Bureau of Prisons withdrew its Record of Decision on the prison, effectively foreclosing the possibility of construction. Coauthored with the scholar and activist Sylvia Ryerson, whose own work on Appalachian prison expansion is foundational, this chapter examines the creation and amplification of an *abolitionist geography*: a material and ideological terrain connected across time to earlier struggles in Appalachia and across space to other contemporary social movements, and mobilized to plot both a different story and a different vision for the region.

The conclusion, "The Long, Violent History and the Struggle for the Future," reflects on the book's arguments in the context of the 2020 crises of both pandemic and police. SARS-COV-2, better known as coronavirus, has overwhelmed the United States, with more than thirty-three million cases and six hundred thousand deaths as of this writing. Its spread has been particularly devastating in prisons and jails, where almost four hundred thousand people have contracted it. Meanwhile, the year has also seen trenchant organizing and a blazing insurrection against police violence. Crucially, a central tendency of the movement has been the call to defund and even disband the police, an expression and analysis made possible by decades of abolitionist intellectual production and political organizing. The conclusion, inspired partly by the song "Long Violent History" by eastern Kentucky musician Tyler Childers, considers these dual crises alongside the contested carceral geography of Central Appalachia. While the crises are exceptional in scale and scope, the violences of austerity (including disinvestment in public health), criminalization, and police are ordinary and central components of the banal configurations of state power that has invested so heavily in cops and cages quite literally at the expense of care. The struggle against USP Letcher, connected as it was across time and space to other movements, reminds us of Appalachia's place in both the long, violent history and its confrontation. For as this introduction has already begun to lay out, if prison growth is as much about land, labor, surpluses, revenue, order, and profit as it is about punishment, then abolition also "starts elsewhere, politically, culturally, aesthetically."[99]

PART I

Extraction and Disposal

1

"This Is a Place for Trash"

Mountaintop Removal, Waste, and Prisons

Industry and manufacturing require sinks—places where pollution can be deposited. Sinks typically are land, air, or water, but racially devalued bodies can also function as "sinks."
—Laura Pulido, "Geographies of Race and Ethnicity"

The hillbilly is . . . remote, ignorant, barefoot, lazy, and so has been a way of legitimating the dispossession of the mountains. It's a region full of people who are depraved, not part of the American dream, they don't really deserve the kinds of resources and wealth that lie beneath the land of Appalachia, particularly coal. It's only a region of trash, so why not trash it?
—Barbara Ellen Smith, in *Hillbilly*

On an overcast and drizzly day in May of 2014, I visited Letcher County, Kentucky, for the first time. Jill Frank, the photographer with whom I collaborated on this book, and I had traveled to the county to begin research into the plan to build the newest federal prison in the United States. United States Penitentiary (USP) Letcher would have been the fourth federal prison built in eastern Kentucky just since 1992 and the sixth federal prison in Central Appalachia. Our first interview appointment was with an older couple, Sharon and Rondell Meade, whose two-hundred-acre property in Roxana, Kentucky, was, at that time, the central acreage within one of the several sites under consideration by the Bureau of Prisons (BOP) to host the prison. Two years later, the BOP officially would select the Roxana site as the future home of USP Letcher and an adjacent minimum-security federal prison camp.

In the weeks leading up to our trip, I had spoken on the phone with Sharon and Rondell in order to introduce myself, request a visit to the site and an interview with them, and get directions to their house in Roxana, about seven miles outside of the county seat of Whitesburg. At that point in 2014, plans for the prison had been developing for close to ten years. In 2005, aides to US representative Harold "Hal" Rogers, who represents the fifth congressional district of Kentucky, which includes all of eastern Kentucky, first contacted members of the Letcher County Planning Commission to relay that their best chance at economic development was to pursue a federal prison. At that time, USP Big Sandy, two counties north in Martin County, had just been completed two years prior. On the recommendation of and ongoing communication from Rogers's office, the Letcher County Planning Commission, a private body of residents, most of whom occupied positions of political, civic, religious, and economic authority in the county, would spend the next decade pursuing the federal prison. With this in mind, and having heard that the family in Roxana was friendly with members of the commission, I was expecting to find two people enthusiastic about the prospect of the prison being built on their land.

We arrived at their house and Sharon met us out front. I could see a large garden stretching behind the house and toward the slope of the mountain behind it. Just after we exchanged pleasantries, Sharon gestured up the gravel road that led from their driveway where we had parked and up the mountain behind it, and said, completely unprompted, "Well, we're just dreadin' this prison." I was startled. Not only had I not inquired yet but also, I had assumed that they were courting the facility, or at least were aligned with what seemed to be the official line from the planning commission that the prison was key to local economic development. But Sharon was unequivocal and was also visibly upset. The BOP had shown up in 2006 and, rather than ask permission, had told them that the agency was going to explore their land. As the process narrowed the areas under consideration from six properties to two, the Meades' two hundred acres had jumped to the top of the list of contenders.

After we spoke with Sharon, and then her husband Rondell, who supported the prison, they opened up the chain that allowed access to the gravel road that led up the mountain behind their house in order for Jill and me to explore the site. It was a slow, steep, and winding drive up. But once we were at the top, it was startlingly beautiful. As I wrote in my field notes that day, "It is at once breathtakingly beautiful and deeply disturbing to stand at the top of this mountaintop removal site. You arrive at the top, which is obvious because you are almost level with lush peaks that surround you. But your immediate surroundings are remarkable for more than their beauty—you are at the top of a mountain and it is so flat. It looked like hundreds of acres of flat, open expanses with lots of grasses, shrubs, and surrounding trees." The writer Eric Reece, who spent a year observing the destruction of a single mountain in eastern Kentucky for his book *Lost Mountain*, noted of driving up on that five-hundred-acre mountaintop removal site, "And then there is nothing. Just acres of brown lespedeza. If I didn't know where I was, I might guess I was driving across a flat Kansas wheat field."[1] I would go back and visit the Roxana property another two times during my research, again with Jill and another time with the filmmaker and geographer Brett Story as part of her own research.[2] Each time I arrived on top of the site, I was struck by the juxtaposition of the flat expanse with the surrounding mountains.

Many mountaintop removal sites are barren and rocky expanses, the harsh terrain the casualty of explosive violence. Mountaintop removal (MTR), quite simply, involves the use of explosives to blow off the tops of mountains in order to access the coal seams underneath. Companies follow the decapitation by disposing of the rubble in surrounding streams and valleys. As Erik Reece has detailed, the semiology of a strip mine is instructive for understanding coal industry logic. As he writes of a mountaintop removal project in Breathitt County, Kentucky,

> One might begin, literally, at the top with the term *overburden*. What is burdened in this case is the coal seam down below; overburden is the oak-pine forest, the topsoil, and the two hundred feet of sandstone that stand between the coal operator and the coal seam. Of course, to whom this xeric forest is a burden depends largely on who profits from extracting this coal and who pays for living down below the mine site. When the overburden is dislodged, it becomes *spoil*. . . . Spoil that is dumped into the valleys below is no longer waste, but "fill." Streams are not buried; rather, valleys are filled.[3]

MTR has destroyed hundreds of peaks in Appalachia and buried thousands of miles of streams. The translation of forests to "burdens," former mountaintops to "spoil," and valleys and streams to sinks waiting for "fill" reveals industry logic to be underwritten by a crude calculus of value and waste. In their confinement of surplus populations and their attempt to transform surplus land into "production," prisons also express a relationship between waste and value. Based on field research in communities in Kentucky and Virginia where prisons have been built on or proposed for MTR sites, this chapter begins to explore and unpack this relationship in order to better explain the broader political and economic work of extraction and incarceration.

In its ruthless and destructive efficiency, mountaintop removal is, according to Bryan McNeil, the "logical product of neoliberalism."[4] Rebecca Scott expands on this, arguing that the practice should "be imagined as the realization in the landscape of the neoliberal translation of everything into market forms. It violently transforms the ground into a literal coalfield, where everything else—human communities, the forest, and other natural resources—have been erased."[5] Other writers and activists have helpfully situated the violence of MTR by comparing

Figure 1.1. Proposed mountaintop removal site for USP Letcher. Credit: Jill Frank.

the practice to other examples of explosive destruction. The environmental activist Bobby Kennedy Jr. put it in stark terms: "We are cutting down the Appalachian Mountains literally. They're blowing the tops off the mountains to get at the coal seams underneath. They detonate 2500 tons of explosives every day, an explosive power the size of a Hiroshima bomb once a week."[6] Eric Reece noted similarly that every day in Appalachia at the time he was writing in 2005, over four million pounds of industrial explosives, also known as ANFO (for ammonium nitrate and fuel oil), were used to detonate mountains. Timothy McVeigh used a more sophisticated variation of ANFO, ANNM (ammonium nitrate and nitromethane) in his attacks on the Murrah Federal Building in Oklahoma City. To put the quotidian violence of MTR in perspective, McVeigh's bomb, which registered as a 6.0 earthquake by seismologists, used about five thousand pounds of ANFM. In other words, on some days the equivalent of close to one thousand Oklahoma City bombs are detonated in Appalachia for the purposes of mountaintop removal.[7]

Such violence against the landscape has brought dramatic change to Appalachian communities in the form of decapitated peaks, denuded mountains, devastated streams, and depopulated communities. The areas of Kentucky's two largest cities, Louisville and Lexington, could fit on the combined square mileage of stripped mountains in eastern Kentucky.[8] MTR was essential in creating a new-to-the-region topographical feature—vast planes of flat land—onto which the idea of a prison could be projected. Were it not for the technological changes in the industry that shifted significant production from deep mining to strip mining, prison proliferation might have circumvented Central Appalachia.

"This Is Clearly a Place for Trash"
Martin County, Kentucky

United States Penitentiary Big Sandy sits off a rural highway in Martin County, Kentucky. In 2002, before construction was even completed, the prison suffered from controversy. Like many prisons in the region, Big Sandy's infrastructure is contiguous with the coal industry. The prison is built on top of a former underground mine shaft and sits on an MTR site as well. The Pocahontas holding company, which had acquired the land in 1992 and was responsible for the MTR process, had donated the property to the Bureau of Prisons once all of the coal had been extracted. The federal government then paid $40 million to remediate the site, the most ever for site preparation for a federal prison. But before construction was finished, the agency discovered that a guard tower was leaning and another building was sinking into an abandoned mineshaft below it. The federal government had to pay millions more dollars for additional site remediation, and USP Big Sandy became the most expensive federal prison ever built. Locals soon dubbed the prison "Sink Sink" and "Unleavenedworth," sardonic references to the infamous Sing Sing and Leavenworth prisons in New York and Kansas.[9]

Still, despite the problems, the prison opened in 2003. As the Martin County judge-executive said to a reporter at that time, "We're going to run out of coal in a few years, so this prison has tremendous potential and should have a tremendous impact on our local economy. My gracious, I can't over-emphasize how important it is to us." Gary Cox, the business manager for the Big Sandy airport, which services coal industry executives and sits on the same MTR site as the prison, noted the importance of MTR to the region's economic future to filmmaker Brett Story during an interview:

> We had no land for airports. Level land is at a premium here in eastern Kentucky. I always say, "The good lord didn't make level land here. The coal companies did." When you mine the coal, the easiest way to get to it is to blast the top of the mountain off, fill the valleys, expose the seam, and then you haul the coal outta here. And that left this enormous piece of level land when it was done. The area we were standing on right now once was two hundred feet higher than we are now. Everything on top of this particular mountain is built on a reclaimed surface mine. The airport, the industrial park, the federal prison was built on a reclaimed surface mine. With the coal industry gone I don't see eastern Kentucky getting better unless something else comes in here. The prison employs more than four hundred people.... It's recession proof. You close a factory down and you ship the jobs overseas. You can't do that to a federal prison.[10]

It is worth pausing for a moment to appreciate the magnitude of MTR and the coal industry in Cox's assessment. In his words, the coal companies improved upon the original flawed design of the region, flattening out topographical inconvenience in order to make way for industry. It is also important to point out the flaws in his understanding. Simply put, prisons are not recession proof. While it is a central argument of this book that prisons must be understood beyond the analytical confines of crime trends and punishment regimes, they are still indexed to both. When criminal justice patterns change, or when the cultural norms underwriting the credibility of imprisonment shift, institutions can and do close.[11]

Martin County's precarious economic situation has further deteriorated since the prison opened. Many of the prison's jobs have gone to people from outside of the county, either those who are long-time Federal Bureau of Prisons employees or those who have better credentials. Moreover, the total expenses for building the prison cost the public nearly $180 million, or more than $350,000 for each job the prison now provides.[12] In 2018, *U.S. News and World Report* ranked Martin County as "the worst-performing county with an above-average share of white residents" in the United States.[13] This is notable, of course, because USP Big Sandy, opened fifteen years earlier, was supposed to have provided needed economic development. But the county's ongoing economic decline, and its abject status as detailed in the report, is particularly stark for another reason: Martin County is the iconic site from which the War on Poverty was launched in 1964. Chapter 2 further explores the implications of this particular history.

Jill and I visited Martin County to talk about the prison with Mickey McCoy, a long-time anti–mountaintop removal activist and resident. McCoy and his wife, Nina, were both retired schoolteachers and lived in Inez, the county seat, twelve miles east of the prison and just miles from the border with West Virginia. McCoy invited us to meet him at his restaurant, a small lunch café located in the downstairs of a residential home in Inez. When we arrived, McCoy gave us a quick tour. Soups were on the stove in the back kitchen. The front room, with a couple of tables for diners, was decorated floor to ceiling with posters and photographs from the various causes and actions of which McCoy had been a part, as well as a number of paintings and photographs by Kentucky artists.

After the brief tour, McCoy turned to me and asked, "Now tell me again about your project?" I said something vague, along the lines of,

"Central Appalachia is home to a lot of prisons and I'm interested in asking 'why?'" Immediately, McCoy deadpanned back to me, "Well, did you hear we're getting nuclear waste next?" I was confused. He clarified, "Well, this is clearly a place for trash: prisons, coal slurry, coal ash dumps, and trash incinerators."

During our two-day visit, McCoy offered to take Jill and me on a driving tour of some of the sites he had alluded to in his comment. There are a number of points to be made here of both analytical and methodological significance. His comments about waste and his curated personal tour were his response to my inquiries about the prison. In order for us to better understand USP Big Sandy, he seemed to indicate, we needed to see and understand the incinerator, the illegal dumpsite, and the history of coal waste mismanagement. For him, regional prisons seemed to be linked to, or a part of, a broader waste geography, an analysis supported by national data mapping the proximity between prisons and contamination sites.[14] The immediacy and confidence of McCoy's assessment marked a pivotal moment in my emergent analysis.

McCoy made it clear that we needed to be vigilant during our visits to the sites. We left his shop and got in our car together to drive first to an illegal coal ash dumpsite. We pulled onto the main rural highway connecting Inez to Prestonsburg, the county seat of neighboring Floyd County. USP Big Sandy sits about halfway between the two communities. A few miles outside of Inez, McCoy had us slow the car down to let traffic pass on the left. He then looked in our rear-view mirror to make sure no cars were behind us. We slowed down more to make sure the cars ahead of us were far enough in front to not see us in their rear-view mirrors. Then, quickly, we pulled off to the right onto an unmarked and inconspicuous country road. The road immediately went steeply uphill, and turned from paved to gravel with large, water-filled holes. McCoy commented that there used to be both dogs and a guard stationed further up. Branches hung over, scraping the car as we drove. Finally, on the right the trees gave way to a large opening and we pulled the car over and parked. According to McCoy, a coal company had bought out whoever had owned the land and had simply been dumping coal ash and possibly other debris there, an action that violates federal law and has significant public health implications for nearby communities.[15] We got out and walked onto a flat part of land set between a hill and a steep decline, part

Figure 1.2. Cascading coal ash. Credit: Jill Frank.

of a cascading hillside sloping down to a stagnant and milky-looking iridescent pond at the bottom. But we were standing on what seemed like gravel, not ash. Mickey muttered to himself that they must have dumped gravel to cover it up. He kicked around at the ground. I didn't see much of a difference; it didn't appear as though he had unearthed the buried ash. We got back in the car, turned around, and headed back down the road to a flat expanse we had passed on the way up, one hill closer to the pond below. We parked and walked out again. Here, there was no mistaking that the gravel was just a thin coating over a much deeper, black substance. We were clearly walking on coal ash. At the edge where the flat platform precipitously cascaded down to the pond some forty feet below, it was easy to see that the gravel layer was just that—a thin crust to the dark and deep ash that literally made the mound we were standing on. I thought of the cross-sectional images of the earth where the crust looks like a coating to the thick mantle beneath.

That evening, over dinner in Prestonsburg, the McCoys also told us about their fight against the opening of a new trash incinerator in Martin County that promised to burn "cleanly." The incinerator sits several miles closer to the prison down the same road from the illegal coal ash dumpsite. If opened, the incinerator would burn 254 tons of garbage every day, only eight tons of which would come from the county. The remaining 246 tons would be brought in from other areas. The burning of that much trash would produce tens of thousands of pounds of hazardous materials, including mercury, cadmium, and arsenic. Mickey proposed another field trip the next day, this time to see the incinerator.

The following morning, we convened at a gas station outside of Prestonsburg in order to pile into the McCoys' car—a blue Prius, which was already conspicuous in that area—for an attempted surreptitious tour of the incinerator. We drove from the gas station, passing the entrance to the prison on our right, heading back toward Inez. Just a mile or so past the prison, Nina pulled off to the right onto a road that began ascending as it turned from paved to gravel. The McCoys insisted that it was a public road and we had every right to be there while also acknowledging the high-security atmosphere around the incinerator. Indeed, a few minutes later, we pulled up to its entrance, labeled "Recycling Solutions Technology," where there was a large gate across that made it difficult to enter even on foot. There was a prominent "No Trespassing" sign. We could see a guard booth, and Jill asked whether the McCoys thought she could take some photographs. Mickey replied, "Well, sure, though there's no way you'd be leaving here tomorrow," insinuating that photographing the site would surely get us arrested (a warning that reminded us of our interactions with the correctional officer years before in front of Little Sandy Correctional Complex). We backed their Prius away from the gate and kept driving around the tree-lined perimeter of the site, hoping for a view of the incinerator. We thought we saw one, and Nina drove past it, turning the car around to position us to leave before stopping so we could get out and see the view. Jill had just exited the car to take some photographs of the incinerator, camera up to her eye, when a white car came into view coming toward us. There was nothing

Figure 1.3. The incinerator. Credit: Jill Frank.

up on this small mountain road besides the incinerator and an old cemetery. Nina and Mickey beckoned us to get back in the car immediately. We hopped in and drove off, heading toward the white car, as that was back in the direction of the main road. As we approached, Mickey commented that this was surely "one of their goons." We passed the white car and the young man driving stared us down, his face plastered to the driver's side window, scanning our faces. We continued driving, pulling over after a few hundred feet so that Jill could quickly take the photograph that appears here, where the top of the incinerator is just barely visible through the dense trees. We obtained the image and then drove off. The white car followed us until we reached the paved part of the side road and then the rural highway. Jill and I watched from the back seat as the white car stayed on the gravel, its wheels just inches from the pavement, like a guard dog that had reached the end of its chain.

The image of the incinerator communicates a number of related messages, including of course documenting part of the "wastescape" of the region.[16] But the near imperceptibility of the image in the photograph, due both to the hidden nature of the incinerator and the literal policing of its visibility by the guards, suggests the limitations imposed on seeing certain images, including those that reveal capitalism's waste work.[17]

The more immediate landscape surrounding USP Big Sandy offers further evidence for considering the prison and/as waste. As mentioned earlier, USP Big Sandy sits on top of a former underground mine as well as on an MTR site. It shares the MTR site with a number of other notable neighbors. Adjacent to the prison is the Honey Branch Industrial Park, built just before the prison and partly justified in anticipation of the economic development USP Big Sandy was supposed to have generated. Across the road are operational mines, next to which sits a mining equipment company run by the Booth Energy Group. The group's CEO, James Booth, is referred to locally as "King James." He owns everything in town—banks, hotels, gas stations, a real estate company, a home insurance company, fast food stores, a cemetery, and more, effectively making him the boss of somewhere around fourteen hundred people in the county, or an astounding 41 percent of the workforce. He also owns a lot of the land, presides over the economic development board, is a former chairman of the state's Chamber of Commerce, and has been a trustee at the University of Kentucky. An investigation by the *Lexington Herald-Leader* in 2019 found that Booth also owed $2.9 million in back taxes to Martin County.[18]

Booth donated three acres on the other side of the equipment company, further up the road, to Haven of Rest Family Ministry, a faith-based organization providing overnight stays to people visiting their loved ones at USP Big Sandy. Haven of Rest offers low-cost and free accommodations to people traveling long distances to an area with very few options for places to stay overnight. But it also must be understood in the context of the investment of the state in prisons and its disinvestment from social welfare, including services to marginalized people like the families of the incarcerated. Faith-based initiatives and religious institutions have often filled in where the state has retreated.

Past Haven of Rest is the Big Sandy Airport, where Gary Cox works, and where Booth co-owns a plane with Don Blankenship. Blankenship, the disgraced former CEO of industry giant Massey Energy and former 2018 Republican candidate for United States Senate, spent a year in federal prison following a conviction for conspiring to violate mine safety standards in the 2010 explosion that killed twenty-nine miners at the

[Aerial photograph with labels: Inez, Davella, Office Park, Big Sandy Regional Airport, Three Coal Slurry Impoundment Ponds, USP Big Sandy, Active mines, Haven of Rest, Hoods Creek]

Figure 1.4. USP Big Sandy interfaces. Credit: Judah Schept.

Upper Big Branch mine in West Virginia. The airport serves predominantly coal industry executives. At the end of the road are three coal slurry impoundment ponds.

To summarize, a single road that snakes on top of former mountains links one of the newest prisons in the region to mining companies, active mines, mining infrastructure and logistics, and mining waste management. Viewed from these interfaces, we might consider that "Sink Sink" is more than just a play on the name of the infamous Sing Sing prison in New York. Following Laura Pulido's lead in the epigraph to this chapter, one can describe the prison—like the slurry ponds up the road from it, the incinerator across the valley, and the surrounding wastescape—as itself a "sink": a repository for racial capitalism's waste.

Southwestern Virginia

About two and a half hours south of Martin County is the small community of Pennington Gap, in Lee County, Virginia, just across the border from Harlan, Kentucky. The community sits proximate to three of the newer prisons in the region, including United States Penitentiary Lee just outside of town, as well as Red Onion and Wallens Ridge state prisons in neighboring Wise County. Red Onion is in Pound, in the northern part of Wise County and just thirty miles east of Roxana, the site intended for USP Letcher, and eighty miles south of USP Big Sandy in Martin County. Wallens Ridge is in Big Stone Gap, in the southern part of Wise County, and is fifty-five miles to the east and south of USP Letcher and a hundred miles south of USP Big Sandy. The two Virginia state prisons are identical in their design and intention as "supermax" facilities, and opened within a year of one another in 1998 and 1999, respectively. Red Onion was built on a former strip-mining site. But there had not been mountaintop removal mining in the Big Stone Gap area of the county. The former mountain on which Wallens Ridge now sits was subjected to mountaintop removal *precisely in order to build the prison.* As Joseph Hallinan writes of the process, "In 1995 the state of Virginia tore the top off Wallens Ridge. . . . The state cut down six thousand trees . . . then it dynamited the ridge, graded the rubble, and shortened the peak of Wallens Ridge by 323 feet."[19] Chuck Miller, a member of the Big Stone Gap Housing Authority, explained in an interview for the documentary film *Up the Ridge* that

> we weren't gonna have a prison here 'cause there was no money. It came to me, "Why don't we build it and rent it to the state?" It was kinda wild but oddly enough when we ran it by the state they thought it sounded pretty good. Within three weeks they had legislation on the floor of the House and it passed overwhelmingly giving us the authority to build this prison. . . . When the prison officials looked at it when we stood on top of the mountain they said, "You're kidding aren't you?" I said, "No, I'm not." As all of us who live in the coalfields know, we can flatten a mountain in no time. We know how to do that.[20]

Amelia Kirby grew up in Wise County and codirected *Up the Ridge*, which offers a critical and incisive examination of the opening of Wallens Ridge, its housing of prisoners from as far away as Connecticut, and the daily violence of imprisonment there. In an interview, Kirby spoke to me of her own jarring experience learning of the prison. She was back home during a visit from college and was driving in the county with her mother when they came upon the MTR site. She was startled and confused, because there had not been active strip mining in that part of the county. As Kirby noted, her mother had clarified, "No, it's for a prison." Kirby spoke of that moment as pivotal for her own political development, in part due to recognizing the transfer of technologies from coal mining to prison construction.

I had traveled to Pennington Gap to meet with Sister Beth Davies, a drug abuse counselor who had moved to the area in the early 1970s from Boston, after having grown up on Staten Island. As we sat down to chat, I mentioned to her that I had seen her in *Up the Ridge*; Davies had been a key interlocutor in the film. In what would become another decisive moment of the research for me, Davies responded directly by saying that the prisons had simply marked the newest fight in a decades-long struggle of which she had been a part. Soon after she had moved to the region, she explained, she got involved in challenges to strip mining in the 1970s. When waste disposal facilities tried to locate to Lee County, she fought them with the help of the stalwart social-movement organization the Highlander Research and Education Center, based in Tennessee. Of that campaign, she noted, "It was going to be some 'state of the art' trash facility. They're always 'state of the art,'" intimating the ways in which the language of technocratic improvement can act as political capital.

Indeed, in a manner that recalled Mickey McCoy's capacious answer to my question about USP Big Sandy, Davies began our conversation by first talking about Purdue Pharma, the disgraced manufacturers of Oxycontin, and the company's targeted marketing of the drug to Lee County in the late 1990s. Davies had witnessed firsthand the beginning of the opioid epidemic in the region, calling Oxycontin "a cancer that spread through the community." Purdue Pharma made national headlines in 2019 because of the volume of lawsuits against the company. Davies, along with a few other prescient local people, is recognized in at least some of this press as having sounded the alarm two decades earlier.[21] Of her many roles in the community, Davies's primary one had been at the Addiction Education Center, the clinic she helped to start in Pennington Gap. She remembered very painfully and viscerally in 1997 when her friend and local doctor, Art Van Zee, first investigated what appeared to be an overdose; the pills soon became ubiquitous.[22] She had since had many clients who saw her primarily for their Oxycontin addictions. Since the prisons had been built, Davies told me, she had seen a rising number of correctional officers as clients. Indeed, Wise County, home to Wallens Ridge and Red Onion, was the subject of national media coverage of the opioid epidemic in 2019 because of revelations from the federal Drug Enforcement Agency that pharmaceutical companies had shipped millions of pills to the small county.[23]

Purdue Pharma had marketed the drug as nonaddictive. Moreover, the company had targeted Lee County, the poorest county in the state of Virginia, because it had such a high percentage of coal miners and loggers, people with legitimate pain-management needs, as well as a substantial Medicaid population. Of this period in the 1990s Davies noted, "We had been taking the coal companies to court. Now I guess it was time to take the pharmaceutical companies!" When Purdue learned of their campaign to sue, the company reached out for a meeting. According to Davies, the company offered to fund local community development in an attempt to purchase acquiescence. Ultimately, decades later the company would admit in federal court to knowingly underplaying the risks of addiction. And while Purdue and its executives had paid out hundreds of millions of dollars in fines, Oxycontin sales alone had brought in $31 billion in revenue.[24] Finally, in September 2019, the company filed for bankruptcy because of the tens of billions of dollars it was liable to pay in lawsuits.

Davies also explained that the political fights in southwestern Virginia were connected to other struggles of which she had been a part, including racial justice organizing and education in New York City and Connecticut in the early 1970s. During that period, while working in schools in the Northeast, she implemented programs to involve students in social justice work, first in Latin America and then in Appalachia. Studying the production of poverty across global geographies clarified a particular question in the minds of her and her students: "Who owns the land?" She went on to tell me that this question formed the basis of her analysis of Appalachia. "This is a very rich area with very poor people," she told me, an observation echoed by some of the premier studies of the region.[25] As she told another interviewer, "These people are living on the richest land in the world, so why don't they have the best roads, the best health care, the best schools?"[26]

For Davies, opposition to the prisons was part of a broader economic and environmental struggle for what she called "Appalachian justice."

As another writer observed of Davies and a fellow Catholic sister with whom she worked, they helped to organize residents of southwest Virginia "around many issues which all have a common denominator: whether it is coal sludge, garbage, or using human beings as commodity, the Sisters will not allow central Appalachia to be America's dumping ground." As Davies explained, referencing industry boosters looking to locate waste management facilities and prisons in the area, "You hear jobs, jobs, jobs. What kind of image does that give our people? Is that all we are worth, to have outside trash dumped here?"[27]

Mitch's Birds

Even as prisons have risen on mountaintop removal sites in Central Appalachia, the future of these sites of extractive violence is not inevitable. MTR literally reshapes the physical and economic landscape of Appalachia, simultaneously destroying the region's most iconic signifiers and creating new spaces on which residents plan, contest, and enact possible futures. Back in Roxana, Sharon Meade was not the only one dreading the prison. Another resident whose property was included in the Bureau of Prison's original rendering of the site for construction, Mitch Whitaker, opposed USP Letcher and actively fought the BOP. Meade's reluctance and Whitaker's outright opposition were both fueled by the ways in which the land had been put to use since MTR. In fact, a closer look at the Roxana site, including both the Meades' property and Whitaker's, reveals considerable activity that centers and troubles the implicit categorization of the former MTR site as a wasted space. It is to this activity to which this chapter now turns.

The recent history of the land in Letcher County suggests a certain porosity among categories of private ownership, public use, and practices of "commoning." Even as MTR has dramatically altered the landscape, various forms of recreational, religious, cultural, and communal practices occur. At the very same time when politicians and county elites were planning USP Letcher, other local residents engaged with the space in significant ways. They hunted, foraged, rehabilitated injured birds, held family reunions, gathered for religious retreats, organized and held music festivals, and pursued hobbies like model airplane flying. Many of these activities were illegible within the discursive space created by the Bureau of Prisons, which focused exclusively on jobs and economic development, during the official scoping and siting process. These other activities, however, challenge the implicit notion of the MTR site as a wasted space as they reveal diverse practices both within and outside of capitalist modes of production and relation.

Rondell Meade recounted that the space had hosted a number of major events, drawing thousands of people, including "bluegrass shows, festivals, marriages, weddings, divorces, you name it, it's happened on top of that mountain. Family reunions and church reunions, stuff like that. The Shriners have had several shows on top of the mountain. . . . It's probably one of the biggest pieces of property we have in Letcher County for those kinds of events." The bluegrass concerts brought in people from "thirty-three to thirty-five different states" with fifteen to twenty musicians playing per show, including major recording artists like Bill Monroe and Ricky Skaggs. According to material from the Kings Creek Volunteer Fire Department, which is located near the property, the proceeds from the concerts held on the site helped to purchase new equipment and pay off the fire department's new building in addition to raising "hundreds of thousands of dollars for non-profits and merchants in Letcher County."[28] The Meades also noted the routine use of the site by other groups of people. Local residents forage for mushrooms and harvest ginseng. In line with the long history of ginseng harvesting in Appalachia by local people on private property, Rondell and Sharon did not have any official policy of charging people for their exercise of a kind of informal usufructuary right.[29] In fact, Sharon told me that the couple had provided several mushroom hunters with keys to the gate that otherwise bars vehicles from using the access road that leads up to the MTR site.

While visiting the site for the first time during my initial trip, I immediately noticed a sign in one area of the property, adjacent to a small open-air structure, which designated a long blacktop runway as the "Mountain Flyers Model Aircraft Field." Rondell confirmed that this was the home of a local club of recreational model airplane enthusiasts. They utilized the site because the flat and high expanse offered ideal topography in which to fly their airplanes. On the sign, underneath the larger writing designating the Mountain Flyers, was a quotation: "Any person that never flies in their lifetime is as a bird that is reared in captivity. To

Figure 1.5. Mountain Flyers. Credit: Jill Frank

Figure 1.6. Mountain Flyers' runway on proposed site for USP Letcher. Credit: Jill Frank.

live, grow old and die, never to have known it had wings with which to soar the sky!"

These existing uses of the site suggest that building USP Letcher would disrupt considerable and varied community activity. Moreover, the prison would necessarily enclose the space, with walls, fences, and cellblocks foreclosing the possibilities of local, recreational, semi-public, and semi-inclusive uses.[30]

The fight over Mitch Whitaker's adjacent parcel of land, which was included in the BOP's original rendering of seven hundred acres for USP Letcher, offered the most powerful material and symbolic challenge to the prison. Whitaker, who is in his sixties, is a fourth-generation Letcher County resident. He works for the University of Kentucky's agriculture extension office in Letcher County, where he rehabilitates injured raptors. Part of his job entails driving all over the region to rescue injured birds and bring them back to health. In addition, Whitaker is a certified master falconer for the state, teaching and certifying other falconers and hunting with his birds on his land. Mitch's birds, then, quite literally "soar the sky" just a few hundred yards away from the sign invoking flight and captivity. Mitch's steadfast opposition to the purchase and annexation of his land to the BOP ultimately forced the agency to redraw and shrink the prison's boundaries. The sign, situated in the heart of the acreage on which USP Letcher was proposed to sit, seems to speak directly to the tensions between commons and enclosure, freedom and incarceration. It marks one of the nodal points where the meeting of abolition and carceral geographies is visible.

Whitaker hunted with raptors for 120 straight days in the fall and winter of 2016–2017. He feeds the squirrels and rabbits that his birds capture to the injured raptors in his care for rehabilitation. He expressed his concern for his birds, as well as for other local environmental habitats, in a testimony to the BOP in response to its Environmental Impact Study report on the feasibility of the Roxana site. Whitaker noted,

> I release rehabilitated wild birds of prey back to nature on my property that is located next to the proposed site. I have rehabilitated and released numerous birds from this location in the past but am concerned about releases in the future. A prison with razor wires, fences, bright lights, and sirens would certainly defeat any efforts I have made or will in the future

Figure 1.7. Mitch's birds. Credit: Jill Frank.

Figure 1.8. Taking flight. Credit: Jill Frank.

> regarding their chance of surviving after rehab. This [prison] would also destroy all the efforts that have been done to return this strip-mining mountain top removal to a sustainable wildlife habitat it was intended to be reclaimed to. Since mining ceased on this location and the reclamation process began, wild life like deer, turkey and elk have begun to return and flourish.

Whitaker pointed out here that the prison not only would enclose land through wire and wall but also would threaten the air through which his birds travel freely. Bright lights, loud sirens, and gunshots from a firing range would threaten the habitats of his birds as well as several other species and a nearby stand of old-growth forest, as a group of biologists and other concerned scholars also argued.[31]

Whitaker elaborated on many of these same themes in our interview together. He spoke of being an environmentalist but also insisted that he is not against coal; he worked as a coal miner at one point. Rather, Whitaker clarified that he is against what the coal companies have done to the region. "You know those 'Friends of Coal' bumper stickers you see all around here?" he asked me, referencing coal industry propaganda that does, indeed, cover the bumpers of many cars in eastern Kentucky and beyond.[32] Whitaker continued, "I want to ask those folks [with the bumper stickers], 'why not "friends of water?"'" He proceeded to detail the long history of the coal industry's exploitation and expropriation of the region and its residents, connecting the potential loss of land to the prison to the changing relationship to water in his area. Many people in the more rural parts of the county had relied on well water, he explained, but coal mining, and MTR in particular, had so polluted the water table that residents were forced to switch to city water. Whitaker argued, "That water bill, that debt you owe every month to the county, should be billed to the coal companies. You had water for free—pulling the water from your own wells—but because the water became too polluted [residents] now have to pay for water." We had this conversation during the summer of 2017. One year later, and following the official Record of Decision that advanced USP Letcher beyond the environmental review process, the county announced that the imminence of the prison had enabled them to acquire $5.5 million in grant financing to extend water lines to the Roxana site and two hundred other area residents in the process. It was the prison, and not hundreds of county residents without municipal water access, that mobilized the political will and financing to extend water lines.

Whitaker understood coal extraction, water privatization, and prison building as forms of enclosure that destroyed the commons—land, water, air, forests, and mountains. Regarding the actual land on which the BOP had planned to build USP Letcher—his land and the hundreds of acres adjacent to it—Whitaker recalled to me that he had been at a local country store when some other area residents confronted him about his opposition to the prison. He said he actually felt scared about getting out of there safely. But, he argued, "I said to the fellers there" that "we've all hunted up there. During deer season we all hunt up there. You think when that prison's up there and they have a big old fence around it that we'll be able to go hunting?"

Whitaker's opposition to the building of USP Letcher derived in part from the history of his land, his family, and the relationship of both to outside interests. His grandfather, with the help of Whitaker's father and uncle, had fought off coal companies that had wanted to open mines on their property. Because of the broad form deed, the nefarious legal contract that was used by the coal industry in the late 1800s and early 1900s to sever land from mineral rights and that granted companies the right to mine coal on private property, Mitch Whitaker's grandfather did not own the mineral rights to their land. Nonetheless, the family fought off the coal company and forced them to circumvent his land. Whitaker understood the BOP, and the fight against them, in similar terms:

> I feel like back when those old folks sold their mineral rights to these coal companies, the coal company would send a land guy in, and say, "Hey we're gonna give you five thousand dollars for that old hill behind your house that you can't even till—we're not even gonna bother you, we're gonna get stuff out from under it—coal." Folks were desperate and needed money back then. They didn't see that they were selling theirselves off so *cheap*. . . . If they could have held out, or if they knew the *value* of it, they wouldn't have sold it for pennies. A lot of times they were told, "You can keep the land, we just want the coal." They were all sort of snookered. They were sort of lied to. Again—same thing is happening here. This was tried to slid right through before anybody could

do any research or see how these other prisons have done in the area, before you knew what the real consequence was. Boy it was a real *take advantage* type business move and I feel like this prison here is the same thing.[33]

Whitaker had a clear personal and political analysis of the connections between prison and coal in the region. Both were driven by imperatives and interests from outside of the region and were predicated on a presumption of local obedience and deference to elites—coal companies, the Bureau of Prisons, politicians, and local power structures. Whitaker's opposition is both reminiscent of and a product of the earlier rounds of enclosures in the region when homesteaders lost their lands and became wage laborers in company towns, a process I explore in more detail in chapter 4. One testimony from Letcher County suggests the brutality of this expropriation as it also points toward its relationship to today's struggles. Writing in 1909 of "Old Man Jackson on the border of Letcher County," whose farm and pasture allowed him to live with his sons and daughters in self-sufficiency, H. Paul Douglass captured the beginning of this round of enclosures:

> I thought of this spot . . . I would be safe for fifty years in telling the old story of the mountaineer. . . . Yet within three months I read [that] "The Blank and Blank Company of Indiana will spend a million dollars in Letcher County in the coming year. It will build thirty miles of railroad and open nineteen coke ovens." And why? Because the Lord sent a freshet which ran under Old Man Jackson's kitchen and laid bare a bed of coal. . . . Therefore, where never in all the world had the shadow of one human habitation fallen upon another, a narrow valley will be crammed with crowded miners' huts. [And] Old Man Jackson's sons, who have never been in bondage to any man, . . . will toil underground.[34]

The processes that expropriated "Old Man Jackson's" land, and that exploited his sons as new wage laborers, would shape the region for the next hundred years. Mountaintop removal would accelerate these expropriations, while moving many wage laborers from exploitation into new conditions of precarity as members of the relative surplus population. In the process, MTR's inherent violence against mountains, forests, streams, and their inhabitants would accelerate the destruction of the commons.[35] Today, "Old Man Jackson's" grandchildren and great-grandchildren, if they remain in the region, are likely facing the next iteration of this pattern of uneven development, as prison construction purports to rescue surplus populations and renovate wasted space, albeit through erecting explicit architectures of enclosure: walls, fences, and cages. These historical processes of dispossession—broad form deeds, mountaintop removal, prison construction—are precisely what Mitch Whitaker diagnosed, and what fueled his opposition.

In addition to his analysis of the history of enclosures in the county, Whitaker also offered an alternative vision for a future without the prison. He made the point that contrary to popular treatments of the region as remote and peripheral, the coal industry's history of extraction and distribution in national and international markets has produced the logistics and infrastructure that connect eastern Kentucky to the rest of the world. As he said to me, referencing the acreage intended for USP Letcher, "We could do anything up here! We have the trains. We could put anything on them to go anywhere in the country or shipped overseas. We have these social problems here, like cancer and addictions, so why don't we build things to address those two issues?" In an interview with Sylvia Ryerson, he spoke of approaching members of the Letcher County Planning Commission and asking,

> "How did you all come up with this [prison]?" I can think of a hundred different things we could do with that property. There's actually the last set of railroad tracks comes right to the foot of this hill. The last set of tracks in Letcher County is right at the bottom of that hill. We can make sunglasses, skateboards, whatever, and bring it out of there and put on a train and take it anywhere in the United States. We need to stop looking to the politicians to provide the solutions.[36]

In our interview, he listed all of the natural resources in the county, including lakes, mountains, a growing collection of craft small businesses, old-growth forests, and waterfalls, and commented that coordination and cooperation within and between counties in the region could make Appalachia a destination for tourism: "If Appalachia could organize and coordinate they could really create something."

Mitch Whitaker's analysis and opposition, as well as the existence of a variety of public and private uses of the Roxana site, warrant some consideration of the mingling of private-property defense and practices of commoning. The material and affective importance of private property exists largely as unquestionable common sense in the contemporary American political vocabulary. Accordingly, fighting MTR and prison construction does not necessarily occur on the linguistic and political terrain of defending the commons, but rather shifts over into the register of defending private property. On its face, this may seem so irreconcilable a difference as to undermine the relevance of the analytical point and compromise the political utility of the challenge. But looking to the ways in which residents in Letcher County actually discussed the land for which USP Letcher was proposed reveals that notions of property and the commons integrate in context-specific patterns of land use and meanings ascribed to it. Whitaker and others opposed to the prison staked their claims in *both* the language of property rights and the language of the commons. This has broad implications. First, it reveals the limitations of carceral ideology; residents offered counternarratives of place that directly challenged the narrative of rural economic development. Second, it suggests important strategic interventions in challenges to prison building. Indeed, as we will see in a later chapter, a coalition of attorneys, activists, and residents, including Mitch Whitaker, successfully defeated the prison, in part through strategies reliant on defending both the commons and private property.

Prisons, Extraction, Waste

In his book *Waste*, the scholar Brian Thill writes that "a responsible chronicle of the truly meaningful and consequential landscapes of waste would not consist of landfills and garbage cans but of things like oil sands, mines, and decapitated mountains—all of the extractive industrial processes that are ravaging the planet."[37] This is what the activism and analysis of Beth Davies, the McCoys, and Mitch Whitaker all seem to acknowledge. For them, the dumping and incineration of East Coast trash, the storage of coal slurry, the destruction of mountains, the construction of prisons, and even the marketing of highly addictive opioids to a region in pain all suggest that extraction and waste characterize the current relation between Appalachia and capitalist development.

Thinking about the predominance of waste urges a more acute understanding of the carceral state and its relationship to racial capitalism. How might we see the prison differently, as Mickey McCoy and Beth Davies seem to, if we consider it as part of a broader analysis of waste and disposal? Put slightly differently, if we list all of the ways we might think about waste as it relates to Appalachia both materially and symbolically—in terms of the imagined "waste people" and "white trash" who live there; the proliferation of landfills and incinerators; the prevalence of coal waste storage ponds and illegal coal ash dump sites; the hundreds of decapitated mountains; and, of course, prisons, understood here as a brutal kind of "humans-as-waste" disposal facility—how might that move us toward a new vocabulary of political analysis?[38]

The positions offered by Beth Davies and the McCoys in particular were striking to me at the time, as much for their analyses of prisons, extraction, and waste as for the confidence and immediacy with which they offered them. Importantly, some scholarship on mass incarceration has considered prisons in similar terms. Jonathan Simon has argued for understanding the contemporary form and function of incarceration as "waste management prisons."[39] Writing of the prison's contradictory existence and absence, in particular the ways its dominating presence works to disappear people, Angela Y. Davis has observed, "The prison has become a black hole into which the detritus of contemporary capitalism is deposited."[40] Cindi Katz has made a similar argument, connecting the school, the prison, and the military as sites for the management of disposable youth.[41] In examining the long history of incarceration in Los Angeles, Kelly Lytle Hernandez concludes that mass imprisonment—which she notes is a much older phenomenon than most scholars have realized—is *mass elimination*, a central logic and practice of settler societies and one for which the prison serves as a primary strategy.[42] Writing of waste more generally, Zygmunt Bauman observes the ideological work performed by its disposal in remote areas, noting that "we dispose of leftovers in the most radical and effective way: we make them invisible by not looking and unthinkable by not thinking."[43] Later in *Wasted Lives*, Bauman connects this explicitly to the work of prisons, noting the change in their mission from one of "recycling" during the heyday of rehabilitation to one of "waste management," in which the prisons perform a "final, definitive disposal" of waste that is "contaminating and disturbing to the proper order of things."[44]

But the work of "managing waste" and the rise of the prison itself demonstrate that "disposal" is as much about space as it is about time. In other words, the prison does not fully "get rid of" the people it incarcerates, even as it can enforce an enduring civil and social death and hasten actual death.[45] Moving people from, say, the street, an apartment, or a house into various stages of captivity and confinement—the back of a cop car, a jail or prison cell—is rarely the kind of final disappearance or elimination that "waste disposal" conjures.[46] Rather, most prisoners come home eventually. They, their loved ones, and allied social movements fight for recognition and for freedom.[47] They exist within, and also create, all kinds of representations, very much including resistant and insurgent ones from within the very carceral geographies that ensnare them.[48] This incompleteness of disposal points toward the prison's broader function vis-à-vis waste.

Mountaintop removal is deployed to transform nature perceived as wasted within the vulgar calculus of capitalism—a mountain—into value in the form of a commodity: coal. But this is not a closed circuit; destruction of the mountain and extraction of its minerals do not complete a transformation from waste to value. Rather, once the coal has been extracted, the decapitated mountain returns to a wasted space: an expanse of land whose potential for value is delimited within capitalist registers of meaning. The prison, and the people within it, are emplaced into the landscape as a fix, recuperating waste—land and people—and transforming it into value through attempting to resolve numerous crises: the containment of large segments of the racialized surplus population, revenue generation for host communities, profits for local elites, wage labor for some eligible workers, infrastructure extensions and upgrades for municipalities, and even support for community centers, schools, and healthcare sites.[49] Broadly, and as part 2 will examine specifically, the prison promises to renovate wasted space into opportunities for community-level social reproduction.

2

Wars, Laws, Landscapes

Producing the Carceral Conjuncture

The "dumping ground" and "place for waste" observed by coalfield analysts like Mickey McCoy and Beth Davies are the spatial and political contiguities among carceral, extractive, and waste economies. Mitch Whitaker offered similar observations, noting the destruction of the commons, while also expressing incredulity at the singular focus on building USP Letcher at the expense of the "hundred different things we could do with that property." But what is the broader and historical significance of this shared landscape? How did mountaintop removal, waste management, and prison building manifest on the same former mountains, and why in the historical moment in which they did?

The positions offered by McCoy and Davies in particular suggest that the proliferation of prisons cannot only be attributed to the punitive policies and culture of the era of mass incarceration. Instead, we must consider this moment as a carceral conjuncture, a historical period characterized by the rise and deployment of prisons and jails to resolve growing contradictions and their merging into crises.[1] In other words, we must situate the prisons within the ideological, legal, political, and economic forces that produced them. And while these forces were not unified or wholly coordinated, their alignment across several decades primed Central Appalachia for the crises for which prison growth—on former mining sites, and adjacent to waste management facilities—would serve as a putative solution. As the following sections make clear, these forces were never absolute or uncontested, but in fact were challenged and resisted on the ground. Martin County offers a particularly appropriate place from which to begin to examine them.

The War on Poverty

If you have heard previously of Inez, Kentucky, and Martin County, where the McCoys have made their home, it is likely for one of two reasons, one to be explored now and one, later in this chapter. First, and as chapter 1 briefly mentioned, it is the iconic site from which President Lyndon Johnson launched the War on Poverty in 1964. President John F. Kennedy had been developing a program for Appalachia with the region's governors called the "President's Appalachian Regional Commission," which would eventually lead to the birth of the eponymous agency. After Kennedy's assassination in November of 1963, Johnson resumed and expanded upon Kennedy's work, integrating Appalachia into a national vision to end poverty. Indeed, Adam Yarmolinsky, an advisor to both presidents, had responded to those inquiring about the framing of the War on Poverty around inner-city poverty with the corrective to "color it Appalachian if you are going to color it anything at all," a phrasing that signified white poverty in part by erasing Black Appalachians.[2] Fulfilling a promise Kennedy had made to travel to Central Appalachia to launch the regional commission, on April 24, 1964, Johnson flew to Huntington, West Virginia, as part of a "poverty trip" to inaugurate the War on Poverty. The president and his entourage then flew to eastern Kentucky by helicopter. Johnson would then meet unemployed sawmill worker Tom Fletcher on his porch five miles outside of Inez and hear about his efforts to raise eight children on an annual income of four hundred dollars. At that time, the average American family earned fifty-six hundred dollars a year, or fourteen times Fletcher's income. Later that day, from Paintsville in neighboring Johnson County, President Johnson promised tireless work to make sure that the people of the region would be a part of his vision for the Great Society.[3] While he would travel to Chicago and Pittsburgh on his poverty tour, according to the historian Elizabeth Catte, it was his stop in Martin County, and in particular the press images from his talk on the front porch with Fletcher, that "provided the public relations magic that transformed the war on poverty from a series of related legislation to an agenda with a deep moral purpose."[4]

The launch of the War on Poverty as an expression of a particular political formation arising out of Johnson's New Deal–style politics had an interdependent relationship with resurgent depictions of Appalachian desperation. Harry Caudill's articles and book, *Night Comes to the Cumberlands*, alongside Michael Harrington's *Other America: Poverty in the United States* and *New York Times* journalist Homer Bigart's now-famous article "Kentucky Miners: A Grim Winter," all caught the attention of Kennedy in the early 1960s and helped to focus his antipoverty efforts. These pieces shifted the attention of the country to the plight of the region and its residents. This translated into important policy changes, from mining regulations to decreases in poverty through various forms of investment in environmental conservation and justice efforts.[5] At the same time that this literature helped to mobilize the federal government, it also undoubtedly breathed new life into certain discourses about Appalachia and, in doing so, affirmed the paternalism at the root of Johnson's politics, impacted policies, and further instantiated narratives of difference and deficiency. Bigart, for example, who had traveled to Kentucky to meet Caudill and for whom Caudill served as a kind of poverty tour guide, observed of the region that "the tourist sees only the usual disorder of coal country. Creeks are littered with garbage, choked by boulders and silt dislodged by strip mine operations. Hillsides that should be a solid blaze of autumn color are slashed with ugly terraces where bulldozers and steam shovels have stripped away the forest to get at the coal beneath. . . . But to the sociologist, the erosion of the character of the people is more fearsome than the despoiling of the mountains."[6]

Appalachia has long been built in the national imagination using a scaffolding of ideas about cultural and even genetic difference and deficiency. Bigart's article is a particularly telling moment from the archive of representations of Appalachia. One sees the explicit conflation of trashed landscapes with trashed people, a sign of a primordially disordered coal country. This imaginary of the place and people requires excising the political and economic history of the region and country while finding firm footing in a kind of inherited inferiority. Both Bigart's article and Caudill's best-selling book broadcast Appalachian deficiency to a wide readership. In a passage that reveals the prescience of Caudill's ability to consolidate constructions of people and place, he wrote that the original settlers of Appalachian Kentucky—the ancestors of the people he saw as existing in an essentialized apartness—had been "social outcasts . . . as cynical, hardened, and bitter a lot as can be imagined outside prison walls."[7] While Caudill's work was central to the beginning efforts of the War on Poverty, he would later embrace radical eugenicist ideas for Appalachia, lamenting the growing presence of what he called "the trash element." Defending this particularly noxious idea in an unpublished and rejected letter to *Time* magazine in 1975, Caudill argued for the necessity of sterilization because, as he saw it, "the slobs continue to multiply."[8]

Inspired by Harry Caudill's *Night Comes to the Cumberlands*, President Johnson announced the federal government's series of programs to target poverty. There is no doubt that the Great Society policies unrolled during the War on Poverty and enacted through the newly formed Appalachian Regional Commission (ARC) transformed elements of life in Martin County and beyond. The ARC channeled more than $23 billion into Appalachia between 1965 and 2010, largely for infrastructure projects such as highway construction, water lines, and public buildings. In addition, hundreds of billions of dollars have come into the region through other programs established or institutionalized by the legislation that comprised the War on Poverty, including food stamps, Medicaid, Medicare, and expanded Social Security benefits, job training and placement programs, Head Start, and disability compensation. By most measures, efforts from the War on Poverty contributed to overall and significant reductions in poverty.

And yet, these successes were unevenly distributed around Appalachia. ARC data provide some clarity. While the efforts of the War on Poverty halved the number of Appalachians living in poverty, and lifted hundreds of counties out of their distressed status, there remains a concentration of both in Central Appalachia generally and eastern Kentucky specifically.[9] In Martin County, for example, the poverty rate remains exceptionally high when compared with the rest of the country: 37 percent generally and 56 percent for children, compared with national averages of 14 percent and 20 percent, respectively. Per capita income in the county is under fourteen thousand dollars. County residents are largely dependent on federal assistance. Since the 1996 changes to welfare passed by the Clinton administration, that assistance has often come through disability payments. Some authors, like J. D. Vance and Kevin Williamson, point to this as evidence of a problem of intergenerational dependency and a culture of poverty.[10] This lazy analysis ignores contradictory data as well as history. ARC research, for example, notes that while the federal government does pay out disability and retirement payments to Appalachians at a rate comparable to that of the rest of the country, the region receives 31 percent less in federal expenditures per capita than the national average.[11] Personalizing the problems of the region avoids grappling with the massive structural changes to the coal industry that have dramatically reduced employment and revenue, while increasing the environmental destruction that has impacted health and economy alike. Moreover, while the War on Poverty did channel monies through the ARC, those monies were dispersed across all states comprising Appalachia, and the implementation was left up to the discretion of state governors. People in Appalachia had been mobilizing for years through organizations like the Appalachian Committee for Full Employment (ACFE) in anticipation of the War on Poverty in order to prepare for receiving federal monies and to ensure they went to those most in need in the form of jobs. But rather than being channeled through the ACFE or other grassroots groups, the monies went "to the courthouse gangs, the people who had always run and controlled things here in eastern Kentucky."[12] As one observer of this process in Clay County, Kentucky, noted, regional political leaders "had no objections to giving more money or services to poor people" provided that those "resources were channeled through existing institutions and organizations controlled by the local power structure."[13] Furthermore, that money simply did not produce the kind of jobs program that would significantly reduce poverty in Central Appalachia. In 1965, more than fifteen thousand people in Kentucky and West Virginia vied for a mere 616 slots in the newly created Job Corps, one of the federal employment programs run by the Office of Economic Opportunity. Rooted in incomplete and individualized assessments of rural poverty, the signature piece of War on Poverty legislation, the Economic Opportunity Act, stopped short of enacting structural reforms.[14]

The War on Poverty created significant infrastructure capable of managing poverty and alleviating some of its manifestations. But it did not fund the kind of economic redistribution or jobs programs that would offer long-term solutions for urban and rural economies. Indeed, critics in Appalachia, like the ACFE, anticipated this even as the War on Poverty was rolling out. The organization released a response to the president's 1964 Appalachian Regional Commission Report, which had borne the title "A Region Apart." Challenging the narrative of a remote and retrograde geography, the ACFE argued instead, "We believe that it is a land that has been exploited and ravished, not for the benefit of the people who live here but for the benefit of the absentee owners who have been aided and abetted by the public officials of this state."[15] The response from the AFCE went further, noting at the very outset of the War on Poverty the program's inherent failure to apprehend the historical and structural production of Appalachian poverty as well as the tight relationship between capital and the state cemented through police power:

> The Commission has failed to recommend federal and state laws to remedy the conditions set forth—low income, inadequate education, deficits in living standards and protection of the people's rights, civil, political and economic[,] to unite for example in a strong trade union movement in order to better cope with the anti-labor concept of an industrial complex which has the assistance of the police powers of this state and nation to keep the unemployed in its grips and rule those people as industrial slaves.
>
> The commission honestly recognizes the fact that the wealth of this region is being drained away. It went down the streams with the great hardwood logs; it rode out on rails with the coal cars; it was mailed between distant cities as royalty checks from non-resident operators to holding companies who had bought rights to this land for sometimes a dollar or fifty cents an acre but most times for twenty-five cents. The failure of the commission to make recommendations to cure these atrocities of the free enterprise system is only an admission that the commission does not want to eliminate the discriminatory practices against the working people of this area.[16]

But the War on Poverty's failures to address the structural conditions of exploitation in Appalachia are not a singular explanation for the eventual turn to prisons as a solution to decades of economic crisis. At precisely this same historical juncture, the Johnson administration was pairing Great Society programs with legislation that would inaugurate the War on Crime, fertilizing the legal, political, and ideological seeds of what would eventually become the modern-day carceral state.

The War on Crime

In July of 1965, one year after signing the Civil Rights Act and one month before signing the Voting Rights Act and the legislation that would roll out programs like Job Corps in Appalachia and around the country, President Johnson stated, "I hope that 1965 will be regarded as the year when this country began in earnest a thorough, intelligent, and effective war against crime."[17] Just months before, in March, Johnson had presented the Law Enforcement Assistance Act to Congress. That August, and in response to the uprising in Watts, Johnson would equate so-called riots by Black people with the murderous violence of the Ku Klux Klan in a broader statement on the necessity of police.[18] He observed, "A rioter with a Molotov cocktail in his hands is not fighting for civil rights any more than a Klansmen with a sheet on his back and a mask on his face. They are both more or less what the law declares them: lawbreakers, destroyers of constitutional rights and liberties, and ultimately destroyers of a free America. They must be exposed and they must be dealt with."[19] Set within victories for civil rights and democracy, the response to the Watts rebellion nevertheless accelerated an emerging racialized common sense about the primary role of the police in resolving social and economic crises through securitizing urban spaces.[20] Three years later, in 1968, the Omnibus Crime Control and Safe Streets Act would pass, which created the Law Enforcement Assistance Administration (LEAA) to administer federal monies for the War on Crime. By the 1970s, the LEAA was the fastest-growing federal agency, with its budget growing from $10 million in 1965 to $850 million by 1973. As legal and political historians have demonstrated, the policies of the War on Poverty and the War on Crime converged in urban America, underwritten by a shared belief in the pathologies of Black poverty and a need to neutralize threats to racial capitalism posed by urban organizing and insurrection.[21] Indeed, law and policy braided the two wars together. The Johnson administration paired existing War on Poverty programs focused on education, housing, health, and welfare with police training and criminal justice research and practice aimed at crime control. In Johnson's view, "material aid to resist crime" was just as necessary as "federal assistance in the fields of housing, employment, mental health, education, transportation and welfare."[22] Crime control, in other words, was foundational to Johnson's vision for the War on Poverty: "The great society we are striving to build cannot become a reality unless we strike at the roots of crime."[23] In order to receive federal funding, employment, education, and service programs were required to partner with cops, courts, and corrections, a condition, writes historian Elizabeth Hinton, "that was perhaps more consequential in the long term than the modernization and militarization of American police forces."[24] Indeed, this convergence of law enforcement with Great Society social welfare provision created the vast infrastructure of social control that "metastasized into the modern carceral state."[25]

The state's reorganization since this period through police and carceral capacities has been well documented.[26] There are numerous entry points for describing and analyzing its contours—the millions of people incarcerated in prisons and jails, the greater number on probation and parole, the even higher number subjected to daily harassment, citation, or arrest by police, and the municipal, state, and federal budgets and policies that enable these practices. What rural prison proliferation offers generally, and in Central Appalachia specifically, is a sense of how the state's reorganization through carceral capacity fused with, and even displaced, elements of the War on Poverty. As later chapters will show, the emergence of what demographer Calvin Beale called "cellular rural development" promises to offer Appalachian communities what the War on Poverty failed to—a rural jobs program—while also at times serving as the keystone for those same communities' eligibility to receive grant monies from War on Poverty agencies like the Appalachian Regional Commission for basic infrastructure upgrades and maintenance.

The rise of Wallens Ridge and Red Onion state prisons on mountaintop removal sites in Wise County, Virginia, offers an illustrative example of how the war on crime and the failures of the War on Poverty converged to legitimate prison construction. As part of the wave of "get tough" legislation passing through state legislatures in the 1990s, Virginia passed Truth in Sentencing laws and abolished parole in 1994, while also funding new prison construction. At the same time, however, state crime rates were actually *falling* and state prisons were not full. Virginia began housing prisoners from other states at per-diem rates. At precisely this same time, in 1995, Wise County's biggest employer, the Westmoreland Coal Company, closed, laying off 750 miners and threatening financial crisis for the county. By the time the two Wise County supermax prisons were opened in 1998 and 1999, they lacked correctional justification and incarcerated people convicted of all kinds of offenses, serving short-term and long-term sentences. When Wallens Ridge opened, according to author Joseph Hallinan, the prison "was justified less by the crime it would prevent than by the jobs it would create."[27]

The Big Steal: The Role of the Law

The War on Crime, the rise of mass incarceration, and prison proliferation are of course important to this story. But understanding how the prison took shape in the Appalachian landscape also requires an examination of regulatory law, which has played a central role in empowering mountaintop removal and activating the eventual ideological work the practice was able to perform. The very federal law that was intended to *regulate* strip mining in fact *enabled* the rise and eventual predominance of mountaintop removal.

Legislative and technological changes in the mining industry in the 1970s would eventually create both the labor shortages and the surplus physical spaces that prisons would attempt to resolve. During this same period, Central Appalachia, and eastern Kentucky in particular, saw dramatic shifts in coal production from deep mining to strip mining. In 1960, 13 percent of coal in eastern Kentucky came from strip mining. Just fifteen years later, in 1975, strip mining accounted for 53 percent of the coal produced in the region. In some counties, including in Martin County, that percentage was over 70 percent, or some 6,126,461 tons of coal per year, more than twice the amount of coal mined in the county in deep mines.[28]

The shift to strip mining, and the environmental destruction and job losses the practice produced, led to more than a decade of political organizing and activism in Appalachia at the state levels to abolish or regulate the practice. This resulted in significant support from some politicians, but few meaningful policy changes because of the power wielded by the coal industry and some union leaders in state legislatures. In fact, regulatory laws in Kentucky and West Virginia were so compromised that strip mining actually *increased* following their passage.[29] Activists risked a lot during these years, often putting their bodies on the line in direct confrontation with coal operators to shut down strip mines.[30] Some groups, such as the Appalachian Committee to Save the Land and People, turned to the federal government to pursue a ban because state legislatures were so compromised. Six years after the 1972 Buffalo Creek disaster, in which a series of dams meant to contain coal waste broke due to heavy rains and killed more than a hundred Logan County West Virginians in the process, Congress passed the Surface Mining Control and Reclamation Act (SMCRA) in 1978. But like efforts at the state level, the SMCRA was the result of activist pursuits for abolition on the one hand and industry lobbying for little regulation on the other. The SMCRA produced some notable reforms to the practice of strip mining, but in the process opened a loophole that created the legal infrastructure for strip mining's most violent form, mountaintop removal, to take hold.[31]

The provision in the SMCRA that enabled MTR allowed for mining companies to avoid regulations requiring that stripping sites be restored to their "approximate original contour" if the stripped site could be put to "higher and better use." Coal companies recognized that MTR created flat planes in a region otherwise characterized by mountains and have had little trouble convincing policy makers and authorities of the potential for recruitment of businesses to the sites, which has exempted them from having to pay for remediation. By 2000, almost half of all the coal mined in Appalachia came from MTR sites.[32] A 2009 report commissioned by the Natural Resources Defense Council found that five hundred mountains had been blown up through MTR in Central Appalachia. Crucially, and contrary to the claims of the coal industry, the vast majority—89 percent—of these five hundred sites had seen no reclamation by other industries.[33] As Eric Reece notes, "Anyone who has ever looked down on the strip jobs from a plane knows that there is enough flat land in eastern Kentucky to plop down ten thousand Wal-Marts."[34]

Moreover, companies have figured out how to avoid the financial burden of adhering to the SMCRA's law regarding reclamation of the site. Coal operators have to put up bond money before they are granted a permit to mine. The intention of the bond is to act as insurance against the company abandoning the site once extraction is completed. The bond is released back to the company upon some amount of reclamation, such as reseeding the land. Companies have realized, however, that the cost of reclamation often exceeds the cost of the bond and have abandoned sites once extraction is completed, leaving in their wake a bare and destroyed mountain. Even when reclamation does occur, coal companies' choices of grass and rock to "reclaim" the site often fail to approach either the original contour or the previous biodiversity.[35]

The transnational scope of the industry militates against the law's effectiveness. Despite representations as a remote hinterland, Central Appalachia is in fact part of truly global flows: of capital, commodities, technologies, products, and people. Mountaintop removal might not have happened had the oil embargo of 1973 not driven up demand for coal. The SMCRA passed just years later, and subsequent adjustments made by the coal industry further reveal companies' shrewd ability to navigate statutory and case law to maximize profit amidst regulatory reforms. For example, coal companies' abilities to circumvent mandatory fines associated with violations at mines were enabled by a case in the US Court of Appeals for Washington, DC. In *National Mining Association vs. Department of the Interior*, the court found that permits could not be denied to companies for violations at mines they no longer controlled. In practice, this has translated into companies owned by larger conglomerates declaring bankruptcy and reincorporating as a new company in order to avoid having to pay for and engage in requirements like site remediation. Mitch Whitaker described this pattern in detail in Letcher County, noting that the newly reincorporated company will sometimes come right back into the same area to continue mining but freed now from legal and financial responsibility to pay a bond or clean a site by their establishment as a distinct LLC. As mentioned in this book's introduction, Sapphire Coal Company, which owns the mine in Roxana near Whitaker's land, was created out of the former assets of Golden Oak Mining and Cook & Sons Mining. Sapphire is a subsidiary of United Coal Company, itself owned by a holding company, which is part of the global portfolio of the System Capital Management Group, owned by Ukrainian oligarch Rinat Akhmetov.

By 2000, just two decades after the passage of SMCRA, almost half of all the coal mined in Central Appalachia came from MTR sites rather than deep mines.[36] In addition, the coal industry's substantial support for the candidacy of George W. Bush in the 2000 election translated, during his administration, into favorable reforms to regulatory legislation, enabled in part by appointments of industry lobbyists to cabinet and other regulatory positions. Specifically, Bush appointed Steven Griles to the position of interior department deputy secretary. Previously, Giles had been employed as a lobbyist for the mining industry and believed public lands were unconstitutional. In his position in the administration, he worked with representatives from the biggest coal companies in the country to strategically rewrite one word of the Clean Water Act so that the definition of the phrase "fill material" could be reinterpreted. After twenty-five years of the law prohibiting mining companies from dumping mine waste into streams, rivers, and other waterways, it became legal to do so.[37]

But the role of the law in enabling mountaintop removal did not begin with the passage of the SMCRA. In Kentucky, by the early nineteenth century, the state actively chose against legislating acreage to small homesteaders in favor of providing "land grants to 'monopolizing capitalists' for 'the purposes of speculation' and to promote industry."[38] Coal seams and other mineral deposits had been observed by the early settlers, and by the end of the Civil War, speculation and development accelerated. Various mechanisms enabled speculators representing northern capitalist interests to acquire both mineral rights and eventually land from local residents, a process one historian has called "the big steal."[39] Mineral rights were purchased cheaply from farmers who were poor and often illiterate. This was the beginning stage of the process that Mitch Whitaker identified as part of a generational struggle in his family to defend their land. Paperwork known in the region as the broad form deed "effectively transferred to the land agents all of the mineral wealth and the right to remove it by whatever means necessary, while leaving the farmer and his descendants with the semblance of land ownership," that is, until the industries penetrated the region through railroads and exercised their claims to both land and what lay beneath.[40] In this way, historian Ronald Eller continues, "Millions of acres of land and even greater quantities of timber and mineral rights, passed out of the hands of residents and into the control of absentee owners."[41]

Broad form deeds, which enabled the initial growth of the coal industry, would later serve as powerful mechanisms that empowered coal companies to revolutionize production, moving away from labor-dependent deep mining and toward the automated form of strip mining, which required far fewer miners and more advanced and heavy machinery. Owners of mineral rights exercised their access to properties without regard for the land use by the landowners. Courts sided with coal companies that the broad form deed allowed for their ability to access the minerals they owned "by any means convenient or necessary," including the destruction of the very land under which the minerals were located and on which the residents lived. As a result, "roads were cut across pastures, forests devastated, fields ruined and water supplies polluted to get at the coal."[42] Family farmers were left with little choice but to leave the farm to the mining companies and join the ranks of those roaming or leaving the region or now working in some capacity—as wage laborers—for the very companies to which they had lost their homes.

As a highly automated and destructive form of strip mining—"strip mining on steroids" is how Mickey McCoy described it to me—mountaintop removal's enhancement of production simultaneously has led to the precipitous loss of coal jobs. MTR's putative efficiency as a form of extraction is directly related to its seeming independence from actual workers; one operator on a mountaintop removal strip job can perform the same amount of work as twenty-two underground miners. Mechanization has enabled mining companies to reduce labor costs and lay off miners, while maintaining or expanding production.[43] As Eric Reece notes, "Forty years ago, Appalachia's poverty rate stood at 31 percent. Since then, nearly 2,300 miles of roads have been laid across the region and 800,000 or more families have indoor plumbing. And today, eastern Kentucky's poverty rate hovers around, well, 31 percent. Furthermore, one can look at a map of central Appalachia, and almost to the county—in Kentucky, Virginia, West Virginia, and Tennessee—the areas that the Appalachian Regional Commission deems 'distressed' are the ones that have seen the most strip mining."[44] Martin County is a testament to this observation. The site of the launch of the War on Poverty and thus an icon of the distress that federal efforts were supposed to ameliorate, the county remains one of the poorest in one of the poorest congressional districts of the United States. Twenty-seven percent of the county's mountainous surface lands have been strip-mined; the poverty rate is 37 percent. As chapter 1 mentioned, a 2018 *U.S. News and World and Report* analysis ranked the county as "the country's worst-performing county with an above-average share of white residents."[45]

A history of absentee land ownership is at least partly to blame. As the Appalachian Land Study of 1981 showed, by the late 1970s Harvard University owned 11,182 acres of oil and gas rights in Martin County. Indeed, Harvard owned the gas and oil rights under the property where USP Big Sandy was built and was leasing them to Columbia Gas at the time of the prison's construction.[46] Harvard had received the land from a wealthy northeastern family and paid just $2.82 in property taxes on those eleven thousand acres.[47] By the time of the SMCRA's passage, the Pocahontas-Kentucky Corporation had amassed 81,333 acres of mineral rights in Martin County alone. This was worth $7 million dollars. The company paid a total of seventy-six dollars in annual property taxes on that land, thus taking enormous profits out of the county while leaving environmental and economic devastation. Twenty-five years later, Pocahontas would donate acreage to the county in order for USP Big Sandy to be built. That donation of land, alongside efforts from local coal baron Jim Booth to leverage his mineral holdings to bring the prison, led a BOP official to comment on the "high level of cooperation" among local officials, the coal industry, and the BOP.[48]

Moreover, MTR is unquestionably destructive to environment and public health. Damage to ecosystems is devastating in part because Appalachian ecosystems are the most diverse on the continent. The mixed mesophytic forest is home to nearly eighty species of trees; it is North America's rain forest.[49] And yet MTR is responsible for the loss of one million acres of forest, the leveling of hundreds of miles of ridgeline, the burial of thousands of miles of streams, the destruction of entire ecosystems, and the decapitation of more than five hundred mountains.[50]

In addition to ecosystem destruction, MTR has alarming consequences for public health. This includes the resurgence of a particularly advanced form of black lung disease among Central Appalachian miners, continued contamination of water by heavy metals, and forms of cancerous growth, such as brain tumors, among populations concentrated near strip-mining operations.[51] In one small neighborhood in Prenter, West Virginia, which sits adjacent to one of the largest MTR jobs in the entire region, six neighbors, including children and young adults, have died of brain tumors. The national average for brain tumors is one in one hundred thousand people. The only common environmental variable these six people shared was the use of well water.[52]

The deadly environmental legacy of strip mining is at least partly responsible for the other reason why Inez and Martin County may be familiar to readers. In addition to its place in history as the site from which Lyndon Johnson launched the War on Poverty, the small community has a second and infamous designation: as the site of a massive coal slurry spill in the year 2000. Coal slurry, or sludge, is a highly toxic brew consisting of water mixed with a number of chemicals, including those used in the process of preparing coal as well as some that are naturally found within it, including arsenic, mercury, chromium, cadmium, and selenium. Slurry is often stored in impoundments, or "ponds," that reside all over the country but that are concentrated in Appalachia and often on top of former mountains. On October 11, 2000, the bottom of a coal slurry impoundment pond broke, sending the slurry into an underground and abandoned mineshaft below it. According to an inspector from the Mine Safety and Health Administration, the Martin County Coal Company (which had leased acreage from Pocahontas and is a subsidiary of industry giant Massey Energy) had submitted maps showing about a one-hundred-foot solid coal barrier between the abandoned underground mine workings and the impoundment. In reality, there was only as little as twelve feet of coal.[53]

The slurry flowed out of the old mine entrances and into two tributaries of the Tug Fork River, which runs the border of eastern Kentucky and West Virginia. In total, 306 million gallons of slurry spilled out of the impoundment and down hundreds of miles of tributaries and rivers, eventually seeping into the Big Sandy and Ohio rivers. The spill was thirty times larger than the Exxon Valdez spill in Prince William Sound in Alaska. In many of the smaller bodies of water, the highly toxic slurry killed all of the aquatic life. In total, the spill left twenty-seven thousand residents with contaminated water and killed 1.6 million fish. At the time, the EPA referred to it as "the worst environmental disaster ever in the southeast United States."[54]

Seventeen years later, as I began writing this chapter, Martin County residents were fighting a water crisis in their community so severe that schools had been shut down, residents could not drink or bathe, and the prison would only serve bottled water to prisoners. This crisis reflects the effects of the long history of mining, the wealth made off, but not retained within, the county, and the severe dilapidation of basic infrastructure. Estimates suggest 65 percent loss of water through the existing pipes. Mary Cromer, an attorney with the Appalachian Citizens Law Center, noted in a public forum that "no one drinks the water. No matter how poor. A family on a fixed income of eight hundred dollars a month will spend fifty dollars on bottled water plus fifty dollars for the newly increased water bill for water they can't drink."[55] As Gary Ball, the editor of the local newspaper the *Mountain Citizen* put it in 2018, "Inez is the very place where in 1964 LBJ declared a war on poverty. Well, we are fifty-four years later and we don't have clean water."[56] Against the odds, and in the long tradition of social movement work in the region, local residents formed groups such as the Martin County Water Warriors and Martin County Concerned Citizens in order to study the issue, pressure officials, and educate the larger public about the crisis.

The 2000 spill occurred three years before the opening of USP Big Sandy. While local officials and residents worked to clean up sludge, Massey Energy would go on to avoid significant liability and scrutiny. Later investigations and whistleblower testimony from the Mine Safety and Health Administration noted that not only had the company ignored numerous warning signs for years prior but also the initial MSHA investigations were severely hampered by political manipulations from Bush administration appointees trying to protect the company.[57] The crisis wrought by environmental disaster was not resolved with regulation, penalties for the company, a reckoning with absentee land ownership, or strip-mining abolition. Instead, hundreds of millions of dollars went to build the most expensive federal prison in the United States. The money to remedy the crisis wrought by decades of extractive violence against the people and land in Martin County, and to alleviate the water crisis of today, is there; it just resides in the wrong place, lining the pockets of coal executives and sunk into the infrastructures of enclosure and captivity. This is a story about water and the commons and the tireless work of many people to fight for what everyone should have. But this is also a story about the death-dealing decisions of capitalists and politicians. The histories and legacies of the wars on poverty and crime, as well as the changes to the coal industry, accumulated and converged in the building and operation of USP Big Sandy on an abandoned MTR site.

Ideology, Landscape, and the Prison Site/Sight

At the illegal coal ash dumpsite that we visited in Martin County and detailed in chapter 1, Mickey McCoy had pointed to an area on the lip of the slope where a pile of garbage sat on top of the coal ash. Someone had clearly come here to dump their personal trash. Mickey shook his head in disapproval, but also noted firmly that the coal company's trashing of the site preceded and invited its informal usage as a personal trash dump. That night, over dinner as the McCoys discussed the incinerator, Nina McCoy talked about her observations of the changing local attitudes toward the environment. When she first started teaching in Martin County in 1983, the coal companies posted signs even within the mines advocating recycling. Just a couple of decades later, in her classroom where she intentionally had recycling containers out, she faced hostile students who actively refused to recycle and intentionally littered. For Nina, this rapid change of attitude and behavior reflected the startling success of the coal industry's efforts to shape the ideological terrain of the region as a central front in the "war on coal" waged by environmentalists and politicians. The industry channels its propaganda through organizations and campaigns like "Friends of Coal" and the school-based CEDAR (Coal Education Development and Resource) program, which work to manufacture a sense of solidarity between the coal industry and many residents through everything from educational curricula to the holding of major community events to the sponsorship of college bowl games.[58] This saturation of daily life with coal industry talking points can manifest in a kind of individual-level habitus that responds to even largely symbolic gestures with open hostility.

But the attempt by the coal industry to "hegemonize common sense" is necessarily incomplete, as the contradictions of the political economy have become too acute. In turning to prisons and jails to manage the crises brought on by dry revenue streams and structural joblessness, alternative ideological efforts have necessarily emerged to try to naturalize carceral growth into the political common sense of coalfield communities. Indeed, chapter 5 looks specifically at the ideological efforts in Letcher County to do just that, as part of part 2's analysis of the struggle to build USP Letcher. As part of this chapter's examination of some of the forces that coalesced to produce the carceral conjuncture,

I conclude with a broader discussion of the ideological struggle in and for the landscape.

The testimonies from around Central Appalachia in chapter 1 reveal competing visions for the future of mountaintop removal sites and the region. I use that phrasing—"visions"—intentionally. Visiting the Roxana site, for example, centers the problem of sight to the political formations imagined for the space and the county. The land itself is both relatively empty—really, a vast plane in an otherwise mountainous terrain—and a space onto which ideas about work, waste, value, and futurity are projected and contested.

In my own experiences visiting these sites, the surrounding carceral geography of the region can shape one's imagination of and vocabulary for describing the future. There is some internal coherence to the Bureau of Prison's logic in choosing the Roxana site for USP Letcher, for example. It is accessible by a single, two-lane road, which means the Bureau of Prisons would need to do some infrastructural development but could control the access to and from the site. Moreover, there were substantial mining operations nearby, so the area is accustomed to some heavy traffic despite its remoteness. Indeed, on each of the three site visits I made to the property, I passed a number of coal trucks, most coming from or going to an open mining area just a mile north of the site and across the north fork of the Kentucky River. In addition, following the strip mining of the mountain and in anticipation of using the site for various events, utilities were connected to the top and a number of buildings were constructed. The BOP utilized the changing landscape, including the extension of utilities, as its own interlocutor, relying on it to assist in narrating and envisioning the prison.[59]

If one follows that narrative arc, there is a seemingly natural progression at work, from mountain to MTR site to the prison, with the facility supposedly resolving problems of both joblessness and surplus land, now unproductive and flattened—that is, wasted—following the extraction of coal. The poet James Lane Allen, who wrote of "two Kentuckies" in the late nineteenth century, foreshadowed the political, ideological, and morphological work of MTR. Writing of the necessity for capitalism to conquer nature in the region, he wrote, "A creek has to be straightened to improve drainage. . . . The mountain is in their way—that mighty wall of the Cumberland Mountains, which has been in the way of the whole United States for over a hundred years—they remove this mountain; that is, they dig through it a great union tunnel."[60] In this telling, mountains and mountaineers were barriers to America and Americanization in 1890, and tunneling, deep mining, and wage labor offered technological and political solutions. MTR's destruction of the mountains in the late twentieth and early twenty-first centuries is the ultimate realization of the vision expressed by Allen: the elimination of *the* spatial signifier of a different and deficient Appalachia as well as the creation of the spatial conditions necessary for property and industry.

The logics through which a practice as environmentally destructive as mountaintop removal is justified include implicit references to central pillars of American capitalism. MTR maintains credibility—even when used outside of its normative function in coal mining, as in the construction of Wallens Ridge—because it is foundationally rooted in capitalist logics and imperatives of development, improvement, and accumulation. As Rebecca Scott argues in her study of MTR in West Virginia, "In the eyes of industry supporters, the flat land created by MTR epitomizes the civilizational standard of property. Domesticated by corporate ownership, this flat land is an affirmation that nature is always already property waiting to be improved."[61] For Scott, the topographical change and its economic justifications also invoke an implicit disavowal of Appalachia. As she writes of some of her research participants, "Several coalfield residents exclaimed to me how beautiful the reclaimed flattops were. 'You'd think we were in Kansas,' said one. Another thought it looked like Wyoming. These emotional reactions suggest that if we are not in West Virginia perhaps we are just in America. According to these coalfield supporters, MTR, for all its destructiveness, offers a way to Americanize West Virginia."[62]

Scott's analysis of what follows MTR in West Virginia included business parks as well as examples of what she calls "spectacular accumulation," like golf courses. But in the final analysis, there may be no better example of a more quintessentially American "solution" than building a prison, an analytical shift that maps Scott's analysis of private property onto the political terrain of the (capitalist) state.

In Roxana, the surrounding carceral geography of Appalachia, including the numerous other prisons built on MTR sites, amplifies the resonance of this narrative and attempts to insulate it from alternative ones. The ongoing work of this transformation of mountains to property (whether state or private) through MTR can operate citationally, referencing and repeating what has occurred in the surrounding geography and reproducing itself as common sense.[63] The violence of private property, and even the inherent violence of the prison, can thus be seen "as impersonal, inevitable, and apolitical . . . part of the landscape and as such their violences can appear to be part of the order of things."[64] Indeed, as Scott's research participants intimated, MTR's transformations of the landscape—both the destruction of the mountains and the transferral of commons to property—can be understood as a kind of modernization or homogenization with the rest of the country. As Vinay Gidwani argues about the politics of waste, "The economic and moral collide as impropriety confronts propriety and its etymological sibling, property. Proper character or disposition, the original meaning of *propriété* . . . morphs after the seventeenth century to imply both property as 'material possession' and propriety as 'possession of or conformity to good manners.'"[65] The addition of the prison on MTR sites underlines the critical role of police power in the enactment of this etymological and material relationship.[66] The prison mimics the work of capital, converting wasted space into (state) property (itself a site of "waste management"), *while also* exerting the police power function of the state, disciplining wasted space into comportment with capitalist morality and economy.[67]

The view that the landscape portends its own enclosure by the carceral state is a product of the near-hegemonic narrative that extractive, waste, and carceral economies are the best that Appalachian residents can hope for and are, in fact, inevitable. The idea that the land itself is generative of the industries that exploit it and its residents evokes destructive mythologies of Appalachian residents as it also affirms and legitimates the region as a national sacrifice zone.[68]

The success of prison building in the region implicates the work of ideology and in particular its operation through the landscape to authorize the prison as a coherent choice for mountain communities in crisis. Geographers have made similar arguments about the connection among landscape, visibility, and the naturalization of power.[69] Don Mitchell has observed, for example, that "the look of the land plays a key role in determining the shape that a political economy takes."[70] W. J. T. Mitchell argues that "landscape ... has a double role with respect to ... ideology: it naturalizes a cultural and social construction, representing an artificial world as if it were simply given and inevitable, and it also makes that representation operational by interpellating its beholder in some more or less determinate relation to its givenness as sight and site."[71] In other words, the success of ideology can be perceived in the delimitation of discourses, classification schemes, and ways of seeing and understanding the potential of landscapes.[72] In political philosopher Mark Neocleous's pithy argument, "The fabrication of social order is simultaneously the fabrication of spatial order."[73]

Scott raises these issues specifically with respect to mountaintop removal in West Virginia. Writing of the pervasiveness of the practice, she argues that it becomes

> all but invisible to the casual observer ... [because] MTR is rapidly becoming part of the everyday landscape, making its drastic alterations of the landscape seem ordinary. Once a mountain disappears, how do we know it was ever really there? It becomes a ghost, nearly possible to ignore. The repetitive redoings of modernity, the planned obsolescence, the constant remaking of the dualism of future and past make it hard to see what was there only a few moments before. What we see appears natural. As if it had been there always.[74]

For Scott, removing mountains is so quotidian a process that the "drastic alteration of the landscape" appears natural, corroborating the success of landscape's ideological work across changes to its features or, in the language of W. J. T. Mitchell above, confirming its "givenness as both site and sight." The success of MTR despite its damaging environmental, economic, and health consequences is due, in part, to its occurrence out of sight, up on top of mountains, where access is limited or prohibited. Eric Reece writes that "unless you are flying over Perry County, Kentucky—half of whose mountains and forests have been literally blown away by explosives—you don't often see the damage."[75] Assisted by prison boosters' narration of the changing landscape, MTR's destruction and disappearance of the mountains can be seen as producing the very conditions of possibility for prisons, creating a growing carceral presence layered on top of the now-absent peak.

Indeed, one could argue that the prisons rely on a similar optical-ideological practice. They are difficult to actually view and yet easy to imagine on a putatively empty landscape. Moreover, the claims about their potential for reliable economic development are inherently tied to deeply calcified ideas about crime and punishment. Gary Cox, quoted in chapter 1, claimed that USP Big Sandy is "recession-proof"; Chuck Miller, in Big Stone Gap, made a similar argument in *Up the Ridge*: "Give me a prison. It's gonna be here tomorrow. . . . I think [criminals] are kinda like the poor, they'll always be with us, as the Bible says. There will always be criminals. 'Cause there's always somebody doing something wrong." In the course of its disposal function, the prison can affirm a particular worldview of the depravity or pathology of the people inside, in the process securing its own legitimacy.[76] In the coalfields specifically, the prison further naturalizes its own presence through continued expansion, and interpellates—indeed, deputizes—surrounding communities and individuals through relationships vis-à-vis work, taxes, infrastructure, revenue, and profit. Following Scott's line of argument, the proliferation of prisons can obscure the all-too-important questions of what was there before and what could have been there instead.

The carceral landscape, then, is not the passive backdrop on which political and cultural lives take place—just the land on which prisons are built—but rather plays an active part in setting the material and ideological conditions of possibility for those lives and institutions in the first place. But those conditions of possibility are not inevitable; they are not, in other words, the wholly instrumentalized domain of capital and the carceral state. The observations and efforts of residents like the McCoys, Beth Davies, Mitch Whitaker, Amelia Kirby, and many others in Letcher County complicate arguments about the optical-ideological success of extraction and incarceration. The long history of opposition to MTR in Appalachia, and the campaign against USP Letcher, suggest not only the incompleteness of the vision for an extractive and carceral economic geography but also an active and conscious struggle of sight (that is, ideology) and site (that is, the material).[77] Today's anti-prison activists extend the history and scope of a long tradition of people in Appalachia putting their bodies on the line to insist on a future for the land and people.[78] To analyses that hinge on the notion of invisibility and naturalization, we might ask, "For whom?"[79] Clearly, some residents actively see, and disrupt, the attempt to naturalize extraction and incarceration. As Mitch Whitaker remarked, in the midst of fighting for his land against the Bureau of Prisons, "We could do anything up here!"

Conclusion

This chapter has begun to consider the prison in Central Appalachia in a more capacious geography and in the longer history of social forces that have produced the region in our minds as well as in policy and practice. The War on Poverty improved regional infrastructure and ameliorated conditions in the broad Appalachian region, but failed to provide the structural material changes that could reverse the damages wrought by more than a hundred years of expropriation and exploitation in Central Appalachia specifically. At the same time, the War on Crime greatly enhanced the urban criminalization and securitization projects that accelerated the rise of the carceral state and that granted early credibility to prison building. The passage of the SMCRA enabled mountaintop removal to expand significantly. MTR's razing of both landscape and labor aligned with the turn to prison growth by both states and the federal government during the buildup of mass incarceration.

This same period included a parallel political and spatial shift. The systemic ordering of the urban through waste-removal practices eventually came to rely on rural America as a dumping ground.[80] While Appalachian coal fueled both world wars and the rapid industrialization of the cities, decades later those same cities would send their trash back to low-income rural areas in the region, which became "prime targets for commercial landfills, waste incinerators, and toxic storage facilities."[81] To be clear, *at the same time* that urban communities were sending their solid waste to new landfills and incinerators in Appalachia, they were also sending their populations "wasted" by capitalism to the same mountains for disposal in newly built prisons next door. This "spatial reorganization of waste," from urban to rural and including everything from Big Mac wrappers to human beings, affirms waste as a political category, applied in order to designate material that is out of, or actively threatening to, racial capitalist social order.[82]

Appalachia, which already exists in the "bourgeois imaginary" as a disordered and uncivilized space, is twice positioned as a disposable geography, a wasted place and a place for waste.[83] As Barbara Ellen Smith puts it in the documentary *Hillbilly*, representations of Appalachian people and place legitimate the dispossession of the mountains: "It's only a region of trash, so why not trash it?"[84] The prison and/as waste disposal must be understood in these varying contexts—in the long history of representations of Appalachia as a waste land for a waste people; in the broader "wastescape" of the region, where prisons sit adjacent to other sites of waste disposal; and in the function of the carceral facility in the neoliberal era to extract and house surplus populations. There is a related analytical point to be made here about the relationship between rural and urban. Rather than seeing them as static and opposed, or for that matter conceptualizing Appalachia as a colony wholly exploited by the urban metropole, it is most accurate to consider them dialectically, as a part of processes of movement of people, objects, and capital.[85] The prison, the landfill, the incinerator, and the mine, while sharing the Appalachian landscape as extraction and disposal sites, are also sets of relations that bring together rural and urban through patterns of consumption, extraction, criminalization, disposal, and logistics.[86]

PART II

Profit and Order

3

"What a Magnificent Field for Capitalists!"

Convict Labor, Carceral Growth, and Craft Tourism

What we need to make East Tennessee the most prosperous and desirable section of the South is capital. That would be a panacea for our financial ills and would disarm poverty of its terrors. It would put us on the high road to wealth. . . . We need hundreds of blazing furnaces distributed over this region, along the foothills of our mountains, lighting up their gorges and developing and utilizing the iron embedded in their bowels. . . . What a magnificent field for capitalists!
—C. W. Charlton, "Mineral Wealth of East Tennessee," 1889

Morgan County, Tennessee, and the small town of Petros sit about 150 miles to the south and west of Letcher County, Kentucky, and forty-five miles west and north of Knoxville. Once home to the notorious Brushy Mountain State Penitentiary, the former prison town is in the middle of an attempted cultural and economic "revitalization" thanks to the vision of three entrepreneurs from Chattanooga, who have developed the decommissioned prison into a tourist site called the Brushy Mountain Development (BMD). While primarily organized around tours of the prison grounds and cellblocks, the development also has grafted other ventures onto the prison site, including moonshine distilling and tasting, concert and wedding hosting, and various elements of eco-tourism. All of these additional enterprises are bound tightly to the material presence and symbolic reconstruction of the prison and its former captives and workers. The site, and its transformations across three different centuries, offers a sweeping view of the changing coal economy; the inaugural and shifting role of the prison in the American South; relationships between the prison and profit, revenue, and the state; and concerns in impoverished rural places about jobs and social reproduction.

Brushy Mountain State Penitentiary opened in Tennessee in 1896 as the state's second prison, and closed in 2009. During its lifespan, Brushy was known as a brutal and isolated prison, located within a particularly remote section of the Cumberland Mountains. The prison was called "The End of the Line" because of both its seclusion and its incarceration, for many decades, of exclusively maximum-security prisoners, many of whom were in prison for life sentences.

Ten years after it closed, in the spring of 2019, I visited the prison-turned-tourist site for the first time. I had been to the area before in order to conduct research in the archives held at the East Tennessee Historical Society, as well as to visit the mining entrances that are still visible just a couple of miles up the steep mountain behind the prison, where Brushy Mountain prisoners mined coal for more than sixty years. But in the spring of 2019, soon after the Brushy Mountain Development opened to the public, I finally visited and toured the old prison with Jill Frank, my friend and colleague whose photographs document this project.

I was interested in including the Brushy Mountain Development in this book for a few reasons. First, the site is dense with the violent history of coal mining, class war, and incarceration. Brushy Mountain's history as a state prison began with the enclosure of land and the opening of mines in which prisoners would be forced to work. But the state's decision to build the prison in the first place in the late nineteenth century was the result of a historic and militant challenge to the reigning carceral regime at the time, the convict lease system. Brushy Mountain is, perhaps, the site par excellence that illustrates the remarkable tenacity of states to refashion their carceral capacities in the face of, and as a response to, major shifts in political and economic formations brought about by crisis.

Second, tourism is often invoked as a possible and proven sector of economic development for Appalachian communities envisioning and strategizing about their futures. Indeed, a number of people opposed to USP Letcher discussed tourism as a viable alternative economic-development project. In other places in the coalfields where prisons have already been built, communities may one day need to transition away from incarceration if prison populations decline and facilities close, as they have elsewhere. The Brushy Mountain Development offers interesting and cautionary insight into that possible future as it actively narrates a particular story of the site to fit into and shape its present iteration.[1]

Relying on site visits, archival research, and ethnographic content analysis of marketing materials, this chapter examines the cultural and political work of the Brushy Mountain Development, as well as what the site may portend for the future of prison towns. In some ways, this chapter offers a cautionary examination of the prison's spectral presence long after the last prisoners have left. New iterations of capital investment have repurposed the remains of the infrastructure, in the process reactivating and recirculating the logics of the prison in ways that are both familiar and novel. The familiarity is a reliance on the racialized tropes of violence, depravity, and degradation that have long been deployed to represent prisoners, but that the BMD mobilizes and instrumentalizes in order to sell a commodity—in this case, an experience and a related set of products. But the violence on display on the tour and on sale in the gift shop also communicates something about the *present* social order. In its curated memorialization of carceral violence, Brushy should be understood as "not a neutral, apolitical location operating as a historical conservancy, but rather an inherently political space shaped by dominant narratives that reinforce a particular set of beliefs and values."[2] This chapter offers a close cultural examination of the BMD tourist experience, including observations conducted in person during my visits as well as a consideration of the BMD's own cultural production, including its media presence and marketing campaign. First, however, this chapter examines the history of the Brushy Mountain State Penitentiary, looking specifically at the five-year period before it was built, as a historic challenge to both capital and the racial state set into motion the events that would end one carceral regime and begin another.

Coal, Labor, and Racialized Class War

The year 1866 marked the beginning of the convict lease system in Tennessee, which commenced with convicts leased to a Nashville furniture firm. The company had built workshops on the grounds of the sole state prison in the state at that time. Just one year into the arrangement, however, prisoners burned the workshops in protest of the conditions, constituting perhaps the first documented uprising against the convict lease system.[3] Before the Civil War, Black people had comprised no more than 5 percent of the incarcerated population in Tennessee. By as early as 1866, they accounted for more than 50 percent of it.[4] The racialized system reinforced "the prevailing belief among both authorities and ordinary citizens . . . that prisoners should work to defray the expenses their keep had incurred. Hard labor on a grand scale could bring the state much needed budget relief. Tennessee was indeed ripe for a convict lease system. Some state legislators even believed that a convict lease system could bring profits for the state coffers."[5] In other words, a foundational and racialized calculus about profit and revenue—including for the state—underwrote the convict lease system.

During this period, Tennessee Coal, Iron, and Railroad Company (TCI) dominated coal production in the Appalachian region of Tennessee, and had an exclusive partnership with the state for leasing prisoners and then subleasing them to other companies. TCI relied heavily on convict labor both for mining coal and for rebuilding the railroad infrastructure that had been destroyed during the Civil War, an effort that would enable greater accumulation through expanding distribution networks. TCI executives admitted that relying on convict labor also served as a strategy for controlling the labor of free miners, with the former Confederate political leader and general counsel to the company, Arthur Colyar, noting, "For some years after we began the convict lease system we found that we were right in calculating that free laborers would be loath to enter upon strikes when they saw that the company was amply provided with convict labor."[6]

In 1891, a confluence of disciplinary measures by the coal companies in the region led to increased militancy among free miners, and brought the broader arrangement reliant on the convict lease system into crisis. First, free miners in the area of what was then called Coal Creek (which is now between the communities of Briceville and Rocky Top, and about twenty miles northeast of where Brushy Mountain Penitentiary would later be built in Petros) were paid entirely in company scrip and were barely surviving because of it. In addition, one of the companies in operation in the county, the Tennessee Coal Mining Company (TCMC), had demanded that the miners dismiss their union checkweigher as a testament to "an implicit confidence in the integrity of the company."[7]

This was a major point of contention as both state law and common sense provided for miners to choose a checkweighman so as to ensure both that a fair weight was taken at the tipple and that miners were correctly credited for the accurate tonnage. Finally, and relatedly, the company asked miners to sign what would come to be called "Yellowdog contracts," essentially relinquishing all of their rights, including their right to unionize.[8]

The miners refused to dismiss their checkweigher and to sign the contracts. The company retaliated by closing the Briceville mine in April 1891. On July 4 of that same year, the company announced the reopening of the mine, but with convict laborers subleased from the TCI company. Forty convicts arrived on July 5 and were put to work tearing down the housing of the free miners. In its place, the prisoners built a stockade, designed to house not only themselves but also the much larger group of convicts set to arrive in a few weeks to work in the mines.

In response to the company's actions, union miners began what would become a year-long campaign of militant labor organizing and insurrections that collectively came to be known as the Coal Creek War.[9] First, on July 14, just ten days after the reopening of the mines with convict laborers, hundreds of armed free miners stormed the Briceville stockade and freed the convicts, who were marched back to Coal Creek and put on a train for Knoxville. Then, on July 20, thousands of miners from Tennessee and southern Kentucky marched on the Tennessee Coal Mine, again freeing convicts and sending them on trains to Knoxville.[10]

Several months of legislative inaction and executive impotence followed. On the night of October 31, fifteen hundred miners marched back to the TCMC stockade and demanded the release of the convicts. Officials had to comply and released 163 prisoners. The miners then burned down the stockade. They would continue their insurrectionary campaign in the coming nights. They freed 120 convicts at the Knoxville Iron Mine, burning down a guardhouse and office later that same night. On November 2, they liberated two hundred convicts at the Cumberland Mine in Oliver Springs, just down the road from Petros.[11] As historian Perry Cotham pithily summarized this period and its militancy, "The Coal Creek rebellion . . . was nothing less than a working class uprising against upper class management and politicians."[12]

The uprising resulted in significant reductions in coal output for the state for the year as it revealed the complete dependency of TCI on captive labor. The company admitted the impact of the insurrections on profits in an internal report, noting, "We have sustained the most serious losses by reason of the 'Convict troubles'... which resulted in the actual destruction of much valuable property, the temporary stoppage of our works, the increased cost of the material produced by convict labor, and the general demoralization... of all of our labor."[13] In addition, Tennessee had begun paying militias to stay in the area in order to fight against the threat of continued insurrection by the unionized miners, an extra expense for the state at a time when its own revenue from the convict lease system was threatened. Tennessee opted to terminate its contract with TCI and, in the process, became the first southern state to end the practice of convict leasing. Outgoing governor James Buchanan, who had been in power during the uprisings, urged "that the [convict] lease system be abolished immediately, that the state erect a new penitentiary, and that coal fields be acquired by the state where the convicts might work."[14] Militant labor uprisings against capital and the racial state had forced the existing social formation into crisis. To resolve it, the state built Brushy Mountain State Penitentiary in 1896, a "spatial fix" to quell the unrest, recuperate profits, and restore order.[15]

From One Regime to Another: Brushy Mountain State Penitentiary

In the fall of 1893, Tennessee's new governor signed a penitentiary bill. Soon thereafter, the state purchased nine thousand acres in the coalfields of Morgan County, in the town of Petros, just ten miles west of Oliver Springs. The abolition of convict leasing threatened state revenues, and the construction of a large state prison posed considerable building and operations expense. The prison, therefore, was premised on the arrangement that prisoners would mine coal directly for the state of Tennessee. For seven decades beginning with the prison's opening in 1896, prisoners mined coal at mines opened and located in the mountains immediately around the prison.[16] Foundationally, then, Brushy Mountain was built in order to *maintain* the objectives of the convict lease system— profit, revenue generation, and racialized population management—but *reorganized* and *optimized* as a (capitalist) state project. The prison opened with 525 prisoners, of whom 441, or 84 percent, were Black. That percentage dipped slightly in the ensuing years, but never beneath 79 percent.[17] This was the only state-owned mining operation in southern Appalachia. Prisoners at Brushy Mountain mined 350,000 tons of coal per year for Tennessee.

Prisoner mining, and the administrative maneuvers to maximize its efficiency, were located within larger economic and geopolitical contexts. A report from the Tennessee Board of Control noted the total earnings of Brushy Mountain mines during the years 1915 and 1916, as well as some of the logic that guided the social-control efforts of the prison administration:

> Total gross earnings, coal ... $450,038.66
> Total gross earnings, coke ... $273,546.64
> Total gross earnings, miscellaneous ... $10,592.37
> Total: $734,177.67
> Less expenses 1917: $264,033.18
> Total net profits carried to surplus ... $470,144.49[18]

In 2019 dollars, the profits Brushy made that year for Tennessee amounted to $9,406,268.96. Moreover, the demand for coal was tied outwardly to World War I efforts and inwardly toward the assertion of penal discipline. The same report noted that

> the Board of Control has a feeling of just pride in the fact that the State's mines have been made to yield so large a quantity of coal and coke during the period when the people and their essential war industries were in such dire need of fuel.
>
> That the earnings have been large should be gratifying to the citizens and taxpayers of the State who otherwise would have been called upon to make up by bonds or taxes a larger deficit in the State's revenues. The Board is in no way responsible for, nor does it claim credit for, the high prices of coal and coke which come as a result of war conditions. It does claim credit for selling at the best market prices; for understanding conditions; for adopting wise business policies and for having given such supervision and direction of the operations as to materially contribute to

the gratifying results obtained. . . . The prisoners on several occasions were assembled together and told by members of the Board that they could help their country by putting forth their best efforts to furnish a maximum quantity of coal each day. They were told that the slacker in their ranks would receive scant recognition for either parole or pardon, and it may be said to the credit of the great majority of prisoners that they responded splendidly to such appeals.[19]

Tennessee officials instrumentalized a shallow wartime patriotism in order to coerce prisoners' hard work toward generating state profits. To that end, Brushy's prison cells were double-bunked during these decades,

Figure 3.1. An old guard tower outside of the entrance to a mine in the mountains surrounding Brushy Mountain State Penitentiary. Credit: Jill Frank.

Figure 3.2. An old mine entrance outside of Brushy Mountain State Penitentiary. Credit: Jill Frank.

but four prisoners shared the two-bed cell. Two prisoners from each cell worked twelve-hour shifts at the mines, so there were always two in and two out of each cell. This particular administrative strategy served the dual economic purpose of *saving* the state of Tennessee money (by essentially halving the amount of cell space it would otherwise have needed for the population of prisoners) and *making* the state money by having prisoners mine coal around the clock. The coal that prisoners mined in the hills behind the prison for decades was particularly high in methane, and many prisoners were killed in mineshaft explosions. Others who refused to work faced the wrath of a brutal regime of corporal punishment. Prisoners published a series of articles and letters documenting the brutality, which led to state officials condemning the prison as a fire hazard and a blight. Brushy Mountain was rebuilt in the mid-1930s, with sandstone harvested on site by prisoners themselves, and the new prison was built in the shape of a cross. But this architectural gesture to faith and redemption did little to affect quotidian violence. As a Knoxville media series observed of this period, "Even with these better facilities, Brushy Mountain was still a violent hell."[20] In the years following the rebuilding of the prison, prisoners organized and went on strike. In one instance, forty-eight prisoners remained in the mines after their shift and refused to come out. At other times, prisoners took guards hostage and stayed in the mines until their complaints were heard.

Finally, in 1966, due to both the continued hazards of the mines and the declining profits derived from them, the state ended the practice of mining at Brushy Mountain. The penitentiary had been built originally to consolidate several objectives—pacification, profit, revenue, and racial regime renovation—into one efficient project. As mining within Brushy Mountain's walls ended midcentury, just a year following President Johnson's pairing of Great Society programs with the War on Crime, the prison's relationship to profit specifically, and racial capitalism more generally, shifted. Like the prisons that would soon be built elsewhere in Appalachia and around the rural parts of the country, Brushy would now exist as a disposal site for the extraction of the growing relative surplus population, who were left out of the changing economy and whose activity—political organizing, enforced idleness, involvement in alternative work economies—was increasingly defined by the emergent new common sense of criminalization.

From Prison to Property: The Brushy Mountain Development and the Selling of Depravity

The final decades of Brushy Mountain's existence as a state prison were unremarkable. That is, Brushy Mountain in the era of mass incarceration was home to the violence, boredom, routines, and resistances that could be found in every prison around the country. Brushy was known during this era for hosting its share of notable prisoners, including James Earl Ray, the man convicted of assassinating Martin Luther King, Jr., and there were occasional escape attempts and brutal acts of violence among both prisoners and guards. It also, of course, was home to thousands of others who entered and exited its walls.

Brushy closed its doors in 2009. In 2012, the founder and president of a branding firm based in Chattanooga saw the prison while on a charity motorcycle ride. He and two business partners then pursued purchasing the site with the idea of developing it into a project rooted in both prison tourism and "world-class distilling." The plan was to use the prison as an anchor for other business ventures located on site that could draw from prison tourism.

The developers soon secured the assistance of several public and quasi-public agencies, which began channeling public monies to the project as well as funding local infrastructure updates and extensions in anticipation of it. First, the state sold the land to the county for a dollar; the county then leased the land to the three developers. A number of other bodies, including the Morgan County Economic Development Board, the East Tennessee Development District (ETDD), and the Appalachian Regional Commission, then worked to provide funding for infrastructure updates, including water line replacement and sanitary sewer line extensions, with the ETDD delivering additional hundreds of thousands of dollars in funding for other site improvements. The developers, now referring to themselves as the Brushy Mountain Group, turned their attention to convincing the dry county and its skeptical residents to allow them to distill and sell bottles of liquor on site. It did so, according to the branding website of one its founders, through a strategic campaign that promised to create a tourism site that honored the legacy of the prison, distilled and sold bottles of liquor without selling alcohol directly, and created jobs in the process. In the lead-up to a November 2013 special referendum on the issue, the Brushy Mountain Group circulated materials designed to get out the vote.

The vote to open the Brushy Mountain Development (BMD) passed, and the Brushy Mountain Group took ownership in late 2014. As mentioned earlier, I visited the area in 2017 in order to research Brushy's history in regional archives and to visit the old mining entrances, but the prison had yet to reopen to the public. Then, in the spring of 2019, Jill and I visited the BMD in order to examine its reincarnation as a tourist site. It might be tempting to understand the decommissioning of the prison, and the site's opening to the public, as a kind of democratization of the site, or at minimum a sign of its progressive evolution. But the experience of visiting the BMD and an examination of its own guiding logics and cultural materials cautions against this analysis. Rather, we might best understand the BMD as a new form of enclosure physically

> **BRUSHY MTN. = JOBS**
> THAT'S WHY I'M VOTING YES
> BrushyMtnGroup.com
>
> **I SUPPORT BRUSHY MTN.**
> **I SUPPORT JOBS**
> BrushyMtnGroup.com

Figure 3.3. Bumper stickers designed by the Brushy Mountain Group to get out the vote.

built on and inside of the old, dependent on a certain narration of the prison's history, and also indexed to contemporary discourses of capitalist ventures: "craft" alcohol, dark tourism, and eco- and local value-added products. A local television reporter covering the opening of the site in 2018 may have put it best: "Trying to profit on the prison brings Brushy's history full circle, because the whole reason Tennessee built this prison in the 1890s was to make money, a decision that only came after a bloody battle at the town of Coal Creek over the previous system of making money on convicts."[21] The Brushy Mountain Group had taken one form of enclosure par excellence, the prison, and turned it into another: private property.

Touring the Prison: Authenticity, Haunting, Memorialization

The Brushy Mountain Development sits in a small valley in the rugged Crab Orchard Mountains, a particularly remote range in the Cumberland Mountains, which comprise the southern Appalachians. Frozen Head Mountain, one of the taller peaks in the Crab Orchard range, sits directly adjacent to the prison, and its sheer palisade forms one of the prison's four outer walls, the only one of its kind in the United States. It is this severe and beautiful landscape that immediately surrounds the prison—indeed, dwarfs it—that I first noticed when driving to the prison from the east, having come through Oak Ridge and, before that, Knoxville.

As I approached the prison on that drive, a number of details emerged. First, a fence topped with barbed wire still demarcated the front perimeter of the entire property, stretching hundreds of feet between the façade of the mountain to the prison's southwest and left side and that of Frozen Head Mountain, to the right and northeast. The prison gate, made of the same fencing and barbed wire, stays open during the open hours. As one drives through it, a sign bearing the Brushy Mountain Development's logo and the phrase "Dangerous since 1896" immediately greets viewers. Once past the entrance, Jill and I drove past several buildings, one of which contains the new BMD distillery, and parked in a lot across from a refurbished building that now serves as the site's

Figure 3.4. Brushy Mountain. Credit: Jill Frank.

gift shop and restaurant, as well as the place where one purchases tickets for the prison tour. We noticed immediately a group of people, four men and one woman, standing and talking, all dressed in the uniform of correctional officers—closely cropped hair, black shirts tucked into grey pants, which were tucked into black boots, walkie talkies on hips. It was the spring of 2019, and the prison had been closed for ten years.

After we had been on the grounds for maybe a minute, and before we set foot inside any of the buildings, the Brushy Mountain Development already had succeeded in evoking an affective authenticity. The front gate, the sign, and the COs—the architectural, decorative, and personal curation of the initial moments of the experience—all communicated a certain credibility grounded in the shrinking of time and space between the site's former and current functions. With promises of a tour to be guided by both former COs and former Brushy Mountain prisoners and buildings that remained relatively untouched since closing in 2009, the experience seemed organized around claims to authenticity even though our visit occurred ten years after the last prisoner had been transferred.[22]

We walked past the group of officers and entered the building, buying tickets for the tour and planning to return later for an extended consideration of the gift shop. We then made the short walk from the first building up to the prison. Standing in front of the entrance was a woman who took our tickets and a man who introduced himself as Bill, a former captain at the prison. In contrast to the group in the parking lot, Bill was not dressed in any kind of formal correctional officer gear, but rather in shorts, a baseball cap, and one of the several Brushy-themed t-shirts that the former penitentiary sells. Interestingly, this former captain was wearing one that evoked the prisoner experience, a shirt that features hundreds of tally marks and the phrase "life to go," replicating the many such marks that document the slow passage of time and that are still visible in the cells inside the former prison.

Bill was one of several former correctional officers the BMD employed as a tour guide, even though the tour itself is self-guided. With us, at least, he acted as more of an escort from one area of the prison to another, but also periodically circled back to find us, offering commentary and fielding our questions. After we met him at the entrance, Bill led us through the open gates of the administrative wing, through a courtyard, past a block of cells, and into what is now the prison museum

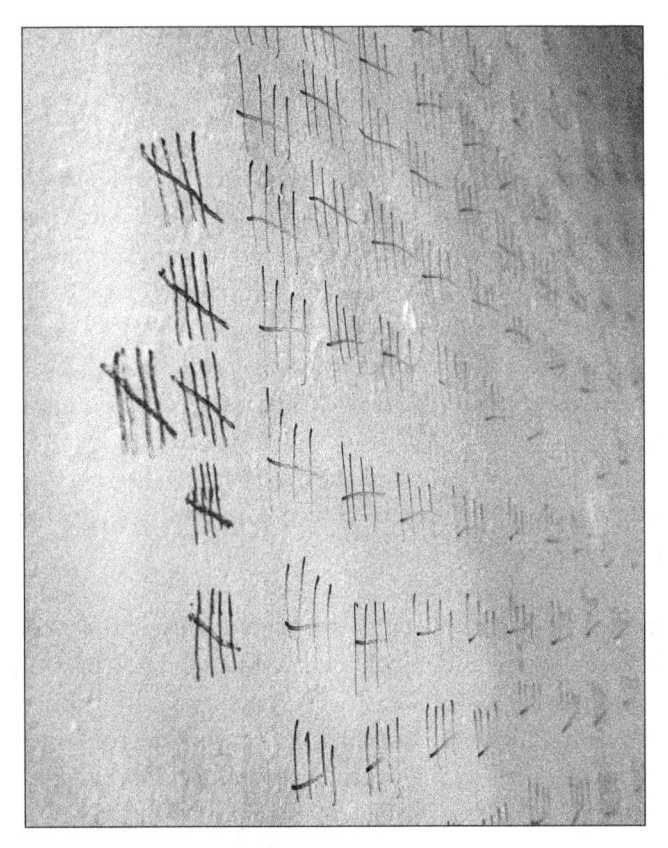

Figure 3.5. Time. Credit: Jill Frank.

in order to deliver us to the screening area where a seventeen-minute film would formally introduce us to the Brushy Mountain experience. The museum room had tables of weapons laid out for the public to view, exhibiting shanks, guns, and even nunchucks that were confiscated from prisoners, in addition to also displaying the infamous former whip used by guards at the whipping post until 1965. There were also tables full of photographs as well as old ledgers that showed the amount of coal former prisoners mined in various years for the state of Tennessee.

As Bill situated us in the viewing room, he offered brief tales of the prison's haunting, including the story of a group of "ghost hunters" who just the week prior had witnessed chairs moving and heard screams during their viewing of the film. Indeed, the Brushy Mountain Development relies heavily on the idea that the prison is haunted, charging groups of paranormal-curious tourists fifteen hundred dollars for a night at the prison to conduct their investigations. The BMD website offers,

> Evil men who did evil things were imprisoned here, with many locked away for the rest of their lives. And while the death penalty was never carried out at Brushy, more than a few died of natural causes or in the mines. Others met their end with the blade of a meat cleaver or a shiv, the final blow delivered by the violent hands of fellow inmate [sic].
>
> These are the souls that haunt this stone-cold fortress, whose spirits refuse to cross over. Who remain here because they have unfinished business.
>
> Visitors have been touched, shoved, scratched and even growled at. Nevertheless, they have a cautious fascination with this unexplained world of the undead.[23]

Later, on our self-guided tour and in a remote area on the second floor of one of the cellblocks, Bill snuck up behind us and yelled loudly, genuinely scaring both Jill and me. It was not clear whether Bill was just having fun or whether this "haunting" was part of the routine.

Given the scare tactic, the departing words before the film, and the considerable attention the BMD devotes to publicizing the paranormal tours, to say nothing of the money it makes from them, it is important to consider the role of these ghosts in the broader Brushy Mountain Development strategy. The ghosts also serve as a source of credibility for the narrative of violence on which the enterprise rests. Visitors to the BMD can experience a kind of spectral violence—touched, shoved, scratched by the ethereal presence of "evil men," but spared the gravest of consequences that befell their victims. The presence of the ghosts and their ability to reach out and touch us collapse time and allow, however fleetingly, for the visitor to Brushy Mountain to "experience" the prison in some role beyond that of spectator but short of captor or captive. At $480 for a four-hour tour for up to six people, and at $1,500 for an overnight stay for up to twelve people, the BMD instrumentalizes and capitalizes on ghosts as a strategy for additional revenue generation.[24]

Having introduced us to the prison's haunting, Bill left Jill and me in the viewing room to watch the seventeen-minute film. The video consisted almost exclusively of stories told by former guards and wardens about the violence of prisoners and the brotherhood formed by correctional officers. At no time in the video, nor on the tour more generally, was the violence that was described placed into any kind of explanatory context; there was no discussion, for example, of actual rates of violence, nor any comparison to other prisons in the state or elsewhere, nor any sense that the violence was anything other than natural and instinctive. To hear the former wardens and guards tell it on the video, prisoner violence was constant, brutal, and pathological, with the film's interlocutors reminiscing, "They knifed him in the jugular! Blood was spraying everywhere!"; "You couldn't believe the amount of blood"; "One of his arms was just hanging by a thread"; and "They cut him with a meat cleaver!" In short, much of the seventeen minutes consisted simply of descriptions of gratuitous and abject violence, from sources positioned as proximate and credible.[25] These same men also described the brotherhood formed among COs and the devastation they and the community felt upon the closing of the prison in 2009. One former CO noted, "The prison kept the community going," and another remarked that upon hearing that Brushy was being closed, "It was like being thrown out of your home." Another said, "I was disappointed to see it go. It's a part of the community."

At the end of the film, we left the screening room and walked out of the prison museum building past the former location of "the hole," a small hallway with five cells, each measuring a torturous four by eight by ten, with no windows or ventilation. A sign adjacent communicated that each "dreadfully dark dungeon" contained just one mattress and two buckets, one for water and the other to serve as a toilet. We then walked out of the building and around the grounds, taking note of the vast yard and surrounding wall, including the natural one formed on the prison's northern perimeter by Frozen Head Mountain. In the corner of the yard there was a newly raised stage that featured periodic performances. Advertisements on the website and grounds informed us of an upcoming show by country music star Dwight Yoakam. The stage is just a few hundred feet from the wall over which James Earl Ray escaped.

We then toured several cellblocks, where rows of cells seemed to be largely untouched since the prison closed. Interspersed on the grounds and through the hallways on the walls opposite the cells were

Figure 3.6. The stage. Credit: Jill Frank.

informational plaques that provided important details and perspective about the prison and its history. In one example, a sign titled "The Whipping Post" spoke of the four-foot leather strap used by guards to beat prisoners: "Prisoners were beaten until welts appeared, then again and again, until those blisters were broken. Screams were routinely heard by the townsfolk of nearby Petros. . . . Whippings were officially outlawed at Brushy in 1965, when the Warden declared the act to be inhumane." Another sign, one of several around the cellblocks and grounds titled "Did You Know?" and listing a variety of facts about the prison, noted the amount of money the state made and saved by using prisoners to mine coal as well as that the prison's overcrowding and conditions in the early decades drew comparisons to the Siberian gulags.

But these signs, while adding important details of the prison's various regimes over the years to the overall experience of the tour, did not otherwise deviate from the broader guiding logic of the experience. The Whipping Post sign, for example, noted of the practice of whipping that the "manner in which guards doled out discipline" was one of the more "notable and unfortunate facts of prison life." In the following paragraph, quoted above, the sign describes that discipline in detail but also in the passive voice. The violence is done to prisoners, but is both justified (as "discipline") and removed from its human source of distribution. Moreover, both signs noted above, as well as many others, spoke to issues of violence and misery that were in the *past* and were always attached to particularly egregious acts or conditions. In other words, violence was spectacular and exceptional as well as relegated to a bygone era. This stance avoids any reckoning with the inherent and quotidian violence of captivity. Moreover, the tour aligned with what scholars of prison tourism call the "memorialization" of punishment, or the process whereby narratives and artifacts encode the tourist experience with both a sense of authenticity and a particular positionality of witnessing something in the past, thus eliding engagement with the contemporary violent politics of imprisonment.[26]

In a radio interview conducted before the Brushy Mountain Development had opened, two members of the Brushy Mountain Group detailed an aspirational image of what a visit to the tourist site might entail:

> RADIO HOST: Pete, one of the things you mentioned to me kind of off the air is perhaps having folks who have worked there at the prison coming back and being part of this.
> PETE: Oh absolutely.... They've spent twenty, thirty years working at the prisons and they're still with us, they're still excited about the property and it's a part of their lives. That's the perfect tour guide to us. I mean, obviously we're going to do some automated type doors but we still want to have several of the ex-guards walking around and telling their stories. That is what makes the property...
> BRIAN: And they all have wonderful stories to tell.
> PETE: And can you just imagine what the museum's going to look like? We've got, we'll have access and we're working with the right folks to get the artifacts from years gone by, the shanks, but to have an ex-guard walking around and just...
> BRIAN: And just look at a photograph and say, "Hey, I knew that guy! He actually wasn't all that bad," or "he was horrible" or whatever. Only those people know those stories.[27]

In addition to Bill, the former CO, our tour relied on a second interlocutor: George, a former prisoner, whom the BMD also employs as a guide, perhaps to provide a sense of a balanced perspective and add additional legitimacy to the experience. We met George as we exited the prison museum after watching the film. He was sitting outside of an adjacent building, chatting with Bill and a woman who also works at the prison. They asked us about the video and remarked about the prison's bloody history. George said that during his time incarcerated at Brushy Mountain Penitentiary in the late 1980s, the guards were violent: "There were lots of beat downs." He noted that sometimes after a confrontation with a prisoner, a CO would "call in their buddies" and come back to exert a "group beat down." But, George then clarified, these beat downs were deserved. Bill, sitting near him, chimed in, "If you did your time and did what you were supposed to do, there was no problem." "That's right," Bill agreed, nodding. "But if you were an asshole, these guys would be assholes back and sometimes tenfold."

Branding Brushy

After the tour, Jill and I made our way back to the gift shop, where visitors can purchase shirts, drinkware, and keychains, and select from half a dozen flavors of "End of the Line" moonshine, including their unflavored variety, "Scared Straight." The Brushy Mountain Development brand strategy integrates and memorializes the story of violence and punishment into all of these products, with images of the prison and particular tropes that signify depravity featured on billboards, bumper stickers, shot glasses, shirts, and bottles of alcohol. In this way, visitors are invited to partake in Brushy Mountain's "past as lived and remembered experience" and to participate in "the spectacle of cruel cultural fantasy," taking home a "taste" of both the carceral history and a particular brand of Appalachia-ness.[28]

Originally, and influenced by data on growing economic sectors, the Brushy Mountain Group expressed a vision for the site that integrated prison tourism, craft liquor, and sustainability. Early images from their brand campaign bear this out. There is an implicit, primarily visual construction of Brushy Mountain as a potential "eco-tourist" destination. The initial website for the project was decorated with mock-up photos

Figure 3.7. Damnation. Credit: Jill Frank.

Figure 3.8. End of the Line Moonshine. Credit: Jill Frank.

Figure 3.9. Brushy Mountain billboard.

of farmer's market stalls full of produce, reconstructed aquatic environments, and picturesque views of nature trails, along with wide swaths of the proposed site designated for camping, walking trails, horse stables, and a large "working garden" and orchard. The prison looms in the background of these images, anchoring these speculative eco-futures to the site's carceral architecture.

One of the more interesting and central elements of the virtual experience of Brushy Mountain is the video that the BMD produced and that welcomed a visitor to the website. Over slow guitar picking and fiddle playing, with images alternating between landscape views of the prison sitting amidst fogged-in mountains and those of dilapidated prison infrastructure, a man with a southern Appalachian accent begins to narrate in what the BMD calls a "somber, emotional voiceover":

> When you made it to Brushy Mountain [Penitentiary] you'd hit the end of the line. You'd already spent too many nights in the drunk tank, worn out your welcome at the courthouse, and pulled your stints at the county jail. But when you stepped inside these walls, brother, let me tell you, you were down to your last one more. You think doing time's easy? Brushy

Mountain'll change your mind. You think you couldn't be broken? Brushy Mountain would break you. You think you could escape and make a run for it, go 'head! Brushy Mountain'll wait on you. He'll starve you, freeze you, maybe eat you. Mm-mm, brother, if you made it to Brushy Mountain you had exactly two choices: get right or give up. That's how it was here for more than a century. America saw ups and down and booms and depressions and victories and defeats but Brushy Mountain just saw time. Hard time for a real long time. Brushy Mountain was the damnation of many an evil man and it was the salvation of a humble few. This prison ate the sins of America so America could go on living. Out here in this beautiful, fearsome countryside was the anchor of this beautiful and fearsome country. So yeah, you can come and visit Brushy Mountain. You can pay for your tour, you can pay for your souvenirs, but above all you need to pay your respects, 'cause brother, we earned it.

The video's primary message, offered in colorful language, is of righteous punishment, enacted by the prison and offered in the service of—indeed, as a sacrifice for—the good of the country. In this telling, the land surrounding the prison is animate and deputized, assisting in the institution's functions of capture, captivity, and consumption: escapes are invited ("go 'head!") because the surrounding mountains will "starve you, freeze you, maybe eat you."[29] This consumption is taken a step further when the narrator notes the Christ-like sacrifice the prison made for the country, having "[eaten] the sins of America" so that "America could go on living." Indeed, the prison itself is built in the shape of a cross. But this framing of the prison's ingestion of the nation's sins performs important ideological work. It simultaneously positions the prison's political centrality to the success of "America" as the nation's waste disposal function as it also affirms the prison's spatial distance (as the "end of the line"). Indeed, the following sentence is even more explicit as "out here in the beautiful, fearsome countryside" was, in fact, "the anchor of this beautiful and fearsome country." Waste simultaneously marks the external limit of society and is also central to racial capitalist production and state formation.[30]

Set to a narration and soundtrack that evokes mountain men and mountain music, the video's construction of a carnivorous landscape

Figure 3.10. The Brushy Mountain landscape. Credit: Jill Frank.

ensnaring and consuming people unifies representations of Appalachians as "trapped by topography, stagnating in their remoteness and turning into the grotesque" with those of prisoners.[31] Even as the prison is visibly stark against the backdrop of the mountains behind and adjacent to it, the video and the prison's own architecture communicate a continuity between them. On the tour, Bill had boasted of the prison's *Guinness Book of World Records* feature: the natural wall created by Frozen Head Mountain that served as the fourth perimeter of the yard. The video invokes a similar carceral-natural geography forged through shared violence. The prison and mountains decide your fate, whether you are doing time, escaping, or mining coal.

The video also relies on a strong cultural narrative about the region, simultaneously representing its isolation from and essential role in the nation-state, reaffirming and legitimating its status as a "national sacrifice zone" and firmly situating itself within the larger discourse of Central Appalachia.[32] Of course, neither the video nor the website mention much about the Coal Creek War and convict leasing nor the present-day carceral state. This double silence conceals the literal battles between labor and capital fought where farm stands and distilleries would be built, memorializing the prison's violence as both a relic of, and a necessity for, the nation. In this way, the Brushy Mountain Development offers a spatial dimension to the memorialization endemic to prison tourist sites. The representations of an "imagined barbarous past and civilized present" map onto a particular geography, where the austere and vicious Appalachian Mountains are a condition of possibility for the civilized nation.[33]

The relationship among the prison, mountains, and cultural products featured on the website is very much "on brand." In fact, the brand management website for one of the developers of the Brushy Mountain Development notes the overall brand identity: "The shape of the core logo mark echoes badges worn by the prison's correctional staff, while the sharp contrasts on the prison itself indicate Brushy's impressive history and notorious reputation. In the background, the beautiful but daunting mountains of Morgan County, TN." That is, the core branding image is the prison guard's badge, which outlines and houses the prison and the mountains.

One of the developers who spoke with me expanded on the brand strategy of the BMD. He seemed at the outset of our interview to anticipate my questions, leading off our conversation by saying, "No offense, but academics tend to make things more complicated than need be as opposed to those of us who are involved in making money and creating jobs. It's not that complex." For him and his business partners, he explained, "We see the prison as the cornerstone of a brand. The history, story is there, no need to manufacture a story about a place. It's a great asset." His point here is crucial. The Brushy Mountain Development curates a certain history of depravity, spectacular and individualized violence, and remoteness in order to capitalize on its asset and build the brand. In the process, the BMD obfuscates a different history—one of crisis, class struggle, and racial state violence. The result is precisely the manufacturing of a story.

Violence, Memory, Profit: Brushy Mountain and Carceral Appalachia

C. W. Charlton's exclamation about the potential of east Tennessee in the epigraph to this chapter—"What a magnificent field for capitalists!"—was offered in 1889. It is not difficult to imagine that the three developers from Chattanooga behind the Brushy Mountain Development might have exclaimed similarly upon seeing the decommissioned prison.

In some respects, this chapter may seem incongruous with the rest of the book. After all, every other chapter examines communities that are home to prisons that were built or proposed for construction in recent decades. In contrast, Brushy Mountain State Penitentiary opened at the end of the nineteenth century and closed as a functioning prison in 2009. But the historical centrality of the site to labor, extraction, racialized captivity, and both corporate and state profit demands that we consider the Brushy Mountain Development as a part of Appalachia's carceral geography. This analytical decision aligns with calls from scholars to consider the carceral state's operations beyond its most obvious sites, including in places "where we might not be accustomed to look for it."[34]

Through curatorial choices about the prison tour, cultural production, and brand management, the BMD fastens the experience of the site to a narrative that centers the violence of the prison and the supposed pathologies of its captives. This representation results in minimal attention to the longer history of the site, an active omission that will affect how and in what analytical frameworks such a place is remembered. As the geographer Don Mitchell has argued, "Landscape is not just ideology, but *visual* ideology . . . a relation of power, an *ideological* rendering of spatial relations. Landscapes transform the facts of place in a *controlled* representation, an imposition of order in which one (or perhaps a few) dominant ways of seeing are substituted for all ways of seeing and experiencing."[35] To put it another way, Brushy Mountain's *cultural* representations of the penitentiary are foundationally about the very *political* practices of social order, memory, and place-making. Writing of the creation of museums and monuments, geographers Steven Hoelscher and Derek Alderman note that such sites demonstrate "the continually unfolding nature of memory; the importance of forgetting in every act of remembering; the pressures of the marketplace and commodification of the past; the unpredictability of group memory and its centrality in the maintenance and contestation of political identity . . . and the inextricable link between memory and place."[36] The sociocultural and spatial work of memory at a site like Brushy Mountain is especially fraught. The landscape is dense with meaning, its rugged terrain the site of iterations of carceral violence. The Brushy Mountain Development retains a defining power to shape the way the space is perceived and remembered. The company's vision for the tourist experience relies on claims of authenticity, tropes of interpersonal violence, and memorialized punishment. In imbuing that vision into a variety of mobile cultural products, and not just into an on-site tour, the political work of the BMD circulates beyond the boundaries of the prison.

In recirculating the carceral logics of Brushy Mountain State Penitentiary, the BMD also tampers with—and alters—the more complex cultural memories associated with the site. Perhaps, then, we might think beyond punishment and to another analytic that can better encapsulate the work of penal tourism sites. In the Brushy Mountain Development's reliance on interpersonal violence and depravity to narrate and sell the story of Brushy Mountain Penitentiary, it helps to circulate the *ideology of punishment*, or the notion that punishment is what motivated Brushy Mountain's life as a prison, rather than the longer history of racialized class war that set the condition for and activated the prison's initial construction and subsequent operation.[37]

This longer history reveals that the specific formations the site took in different moments reflected broader changes to both state and capital. These formations served different imperatives.[38] Convict leasing in the coal mines produced considerable profits for Tennessee Coal, Iron, and Railroad and other companies. The Coal Creek War uprising hastened a political and economic crisis, which Tennessee resolved by ending the convict lease system and building the prison, an endeavor designed both to reduce state expenditures around incarceration and to generate state profits, motivations that aligned the prison with guiding logics of prisoner labor at the time.[39] The last half of the prison's life, from the mid-1960s until 2009, saw the prison's relationship to racial capitalism shift again, as the mines closed and the prison was joined by a growing regional carceral geography tasked with managing the increasing numbers of people abandoned by capital and other segments of the state, their bodies the mechanisms through which a number of other political and economic objectives were satisfied: the justification of criminalization, the need for rural infrastructure development, and the payments of debt and paychecks.[40]

The reopening of the prison as the Brushy Mountain Development recenters profit to the site's function, largely through the curation and commodification of the experience and related products. In addition, the BMD's initial reliance on eco-tourism engaged in a symbolic reconstruction of the rural locality and surrounding community into a commodified ideal rurality that "transform[s] previously unproductive or noncapitalist forms of activity into sites of productive labor."[41] Two of the developers noted as much in a radio interview:

> We even wanted to look at helping people create some of their own sort of peripheral businesses where we say, "Hey, we've got this great website that's selling things to people in *Norway*, believe it or not." And we know that from research, we can do that. So why not sell preserves, or jam or honey . . . that's made by a local farmer or a local lady where someone says, "You know, this lady in my church makes the most unbelievable jellies or jams." So, we go to her and say, "Hey, what can you produce? If it's a small number that's fine. We'll put a label on it and we'll help you and all you have to do is make the jellies and jams. We'll handle the rest."[42]

Here the developers proposed to transform noncapitalist activities and social relations into forms of profit-driven activity, and to connect these newly commodified products to global markets. As geographers Smith and Phillips argue, "Rural places are 'theatres of consumption' . . . which may be crafted, marketed and sold to the new middle classes. . . . Socially constructed 'rural' spaces provide new leisure spaces, and positive (and exclusive) associations with nature and 'natural products.'"[43] Smith and Phillips term this type of middle-class consumption of rural nature and space "rural greentrification" as a means to emphasize the linkages between urban and rural gentrification processes.[44] Not wanting to leave ˌch to the imagination, the original website included mock-up ˌs of potential "natural products" such as "Momma's Morgan Co. ˌe Preserves," honey "direct from the bees at John Smith's Farm," and bottled "Brushy Mountain–Natural Spring Water." In the Brushy Mountain Development's vision, the rural county is indeed a "field for capitalists," with the prison both anchoring and driving the development of the county into a nodal point in capitalist exchange across a variety of scales.

Given that it is in one of the poorest counties in one of the poorest regions of the United States, it seems important to take Brushy Mountain's new life seriously as a possible economic stimulant for Morgan County. Moreover, while the cages and cellblocks remain and are mobilized to sell an experience and a set of products, they no longer hold humans; no one is talking about reopening Brushy as an actual prison. Ultimately, isn't Brushy Mountain's repurposing as a site of tourism preferable to its reopening as a site of imprisonment?

Yes and no. When Brushy Mountain Penitentiary closed in 2009, the state of Tennessee had just over twenty-seven thousand people in its custody in state prisons and county jails; as of 2018, that number had risen to over thirty thousand.[45] The prison's closure, in other words, should not be understood as signaling or enacting decarceration. Rather, the case of Brushy Mountain suggests that decommissioning a prison and transitioning it to a site of tourism can materially contribute to the *sustaining* of the carceral state while also providing it with new forms of ideological legitimacy. Given the long history of carceral regimes operating on the site, the state of Tennessee's ongoing investment in incarceration, and the broader surrounding landscape of prison and jail growth in the region, Brushy's contemporary operation as a tourist site locates it as part of, rather than distinguishes it from, the broader Appalachian carceral geography.

4

The Company Town

Remaking Social Order in the Coalfields

In 1946, folk singer Merle Travis released the song "Dark as a Dungeon," in which he analogized the danger of the coal mine to that of the prison cell. Johnny Cash popularized the song when he played it for prisoners at California's Folsom Prison in 1968, a performance that in itself further articulated the connection between coal and the cage. The song opens *Harlan County, U.S.A.*, the award-winning documentary examining the Brookside strike by miners in the southeastern Kentucky county. Travis, from a coal mining family in western Kentucky, also wrote the famous song "Sixteen Tons," which offers a severe critique of debt and wage labor: "You load sixteen tons and what do you get? Another day older and deeper in debt. . . . Saint Peter don't you call me 'cause I can't go, I owe my soul to the company store." In the case of "Dark as a Dungeon," Travis observed the spatial and photic homologies between the restrictions of the mine and the confinement of the cell:

> O midnight, or the morning, or the middle of the day
> It's the same to the miner who labors away
> Where the demons of death often come by surprise
> One fall of the slate and you're buried alive
> And it's dark as a dungeon and damp as the dew,
> Where danger is double and pleasures are few,
> Where the rain never falls and the sun never shines
> And it's dark as a dungeon way down in the mines.

Travis's turn of phrase in fact has substantial historical and contemporary weight. Fifty years before its release, the uprising by union miners against convict leasing effectively ended the practice in Tennessee; in the interim decades, other states would follow suit. While convicts across the South had been leased to industries ranging from turpentine to cotton to brick, and while all portended horrific conditions and brutal and premature death, those convicts who were leased to coal companies suffered the worst death rates of any industry that employed convict labor.[1]

As this book examines, the structural similarities between the mine and the cage have taken on an additional valence in the twenty-first century as prisons and jails proliferate in the coalfields of Central Appalachia. The prison in particular has come to occupy a central place in the discursive repertoire of political elites offering residents possibilities for employment and economic development in a post-coal economy. In some cases, the two industries are proudly articulated.

Inside the entrance to Otter Creek Correctional Facility, a private prison in Wheelwright, Kentucky, is a painting of the prison's logo. I have never seen it in person, having been denied entry to the prison when I attempted to visit. But the scholar and activist Sylvia Ryerson was able to snap a photo of it when granted permission to enter the facility to record a play being performed by women incarcerated at Otter Creek.[2] As she describes the image, "The iconic coalminer's helmet, pick and shovel [is placed] underneath the state of Kentucky, [which is] locked up from east to west [behind bars]. And so, Corrections Corporation of America defines the past, present and future of the state of Kentucky: prisons and coal."[3] The painting by Corrections Corporation of America, the private prison company now known as Core Civic, places coal and incarceration into the same economic, cultural, and physical landscape. While the incarceration of Kentucky was an aspirational goal for Core Civic, as it stood to profit directly, the painting should not be mistaken as just a piece of corporate propaganda (although it is also that). Rather, as Ryerson indicates, it expresses an accurate depiction of the political and economic geography of the state. Kentucky's rate of incarceration has far outpaced the national average since 2000, growing even since the state passed sentencing reform in 2011. At the current rate, every single resident of the state will be behind bars in 113 years.[4] In addition, as Ryerson notes in her analysis, Core Civic's rendering of this "imprisonment" of Kentucky above the mining equipment indicates a displacement, an observation that the cage is replacing the mine. As previous chapters

Figure 4.1. Prisons and coal. Credit: Sylvia Ryerson.

have discussed, and as is also true in Wheelwright, in many places in the coalfields, prisons are built literally on top of or adjacent to former mining sites.

Founded in 1916 by the Elkhorn Coal Company and named after its president, Jere Wheelwright, Wheelwright was one of hundreds of "company towns" established in the coalfields during the late nineteenth and early twentieth centuries. These communities were bought and sold between companies, and residents were entirely reliant on the presiding company for wages (often paid in company "scrip"), housing, work, food, school, and more.[5] With the construction and operation of a private prison in the former company town, and given the message of displacement expressed by Otter Creek's image, it would be easy to overdetermine corporate power and profit imperatives in any analysis. Of course, corporate power and profit *are central* to the story of the coalfields, including Wheelwright, and the eventual rise of the prisons there. At the same time, and even in regards to a private prison like Otter Creek, this is also a story about the *state's* use of prisons to respond to crises in urban and rural communities arising from deindustrialization, structural joblessness, the decline of the social wage, and municipal revenue loss. In other words, this is a story about the changing capacities of the state at various scales of its expression as it works to manage capitalist crises that it also helped to create.

Otter Creek is located about one mile north of the center of town. There is just one road in and out of Wheelwright, Highway 306, and the prison lies up a steep road that heads east off 306 and onto the small mountain that forms one perimeter of the "holler," or valley, in which the town sits. The prison has been closed since 2012, after then-governor Steve Beshear reluctantly ended the state's contract with Core Civic following both a sex scandal involving guards and prisoners and legislative changes intended to reduce state prison populations and therefore the need for additional prison beds.

Like other prisons that this book examines, the specific and surrounding landscape can serve as an index for a broader study of Wheelwright's and Otter Creek's story. US Corrections Corporation, a Louisville-based private prison company, built the facility in early 1992. Before that, the

Figure 4.2. Prison views. Credit: Jill Frank.

Figure 4.3. Otter Creek Correctional Facility. Credit: Jill Frank.

site served as a local garbage dump. Before that, it was the entrance to a mining site; on one of my visits to the town, two of Wheelwright's residents, both former coal miners and prison guards, proudly showed me where the coal seam is still visible across from the prison's outer gate. Old mining maps, created by a company that bought Wheelwright in the late 1960s called Mountain Investment, show many of the coal seams in and around the town, and in particular around the area that would eventually house Otter Creek.

But before Mountain Investment, and before the companies that owned Wheelwright prior to them, the mountain on which the prison sits was simply part of the larger chain that lies in between the left and right forks of the Otter Creek waterway and that forms the eastern perimeter of the valley in which Wheelwright resides. This morphology of the landscape—from mountain to mine, from mine to garbage dump, from garbage dump to prison, and from operational to decommissioned prison—illustrates the centrality of processes of extraction and disposal to patterns of capitalist uneven development. In particular, Wheelwright exemplifies what the geographer Neil Smith called the "seesaw movement of capital."[6] The departures and arrivals of capital have structured Wheelwright's constant state of both dependency on outside investment and proneness to taking whatever form in which it returns.

Wheelwright offers an opportunity to consider and pursue several concepts as through lines linking its early-twentieth-century founding as a company town with its twenty-first-century operations orbiting around the private prison. While corporate profit offers an obvious organizing concept, this chapter argues for a more complex reading of the prison's role in the history of the town. Figure 4.4, which depicts the interface between Otter Creek and the former mine, is the material and metaphorical space to which we must look in order to better understand the prison's rise, stability, and possible futures. Absent attention to and interrogation of that interface, our history of the prison in Central Appalachia would begin with its proliferation during the era of mass

Figure 4.4. The interface. Credit: Jill Frank.

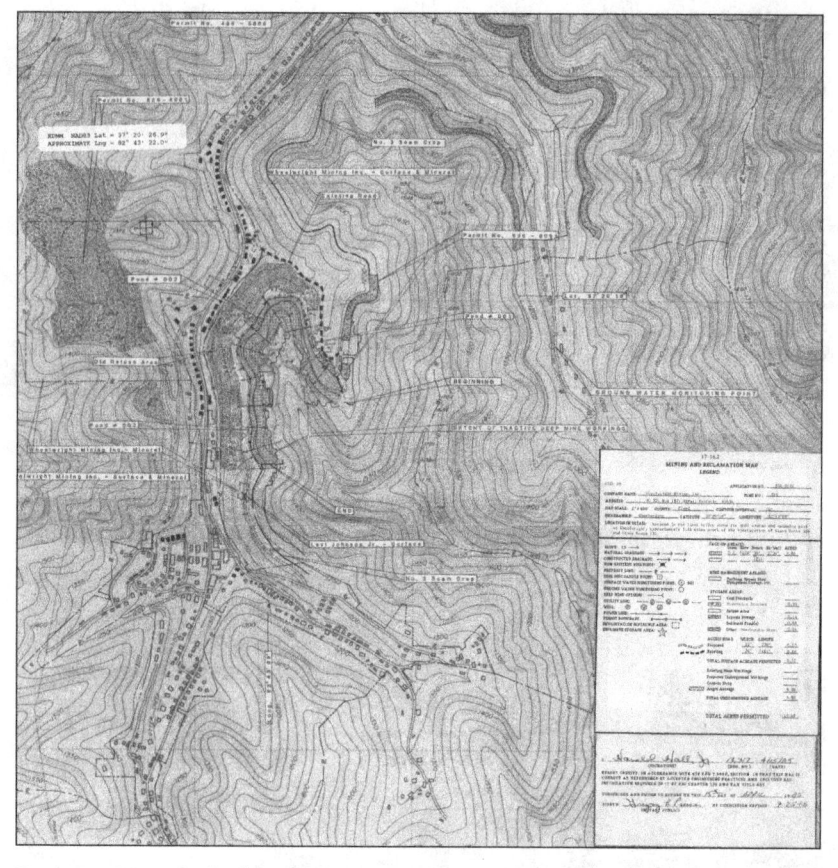

Figure 4.5. Map of Wheelwright. Box 363, Folder 20, Wheelwright Collection, 1916–1979, 88M6, Special Collections and Digital Programs, University of Kentucky Libraries, Lexington.

incarceration. The story of Otter Creek, in this more truncated and penological history, would thus begin in 1992, or perhaps just a few years earlier as the state began to consider a contract for a private prison. Instead, this chapter insists, Otter Creek cannot be understood in the narrow confines of explanatory frameworks that focus on corporate power and profit alone, nor in those that focus on mass incarceration, nor still in those that argue that the rural prison is just about jobs. Rather, the prison must be understood as reflective of changing state capacities and logics under neoliberalizing racial capitalism, and therefore as the state's primary approach in this moment to a much older project of producing and reproducing capitalist social order.

This chapter first examines the hundred-year history of Wheelwright through a focus on coal camps and company towns, police power, and corporate ownership in order to better explain the conditions of possibility for Otter Creek Correctional Center and its tumultuous twenty-year existence. The chapter then examines the prison's sordid history as well as the plans, in circulation at the time of my research, to reopen the prison as a state-run facility, leased by Kentucky from Core Civic. This likely future for the prison, driven by imperatives both to alleviate overcrowding in Kentucky state prisons and to address the economic woes of Wheelwright, instructs an acute reading of the contours of the historical moment.

Off the Farm and into the Mines: The Arrival of Wage Labor

Spend any amount of time in Wheelwright and one invariably hears the invocation of the community's old moniker, "Camelot," referring to the town's glory days under the control of Inland Steel, from 1930 to 1965. During this period in the long history of Wheelwright's corporate ownership, the town benefited from a vision of welfare capitalism and boasted theaters, a pool, a golf course, and a hotel. But Wheelwright's birth as a company town by the Elkhorn Coal Company in 1916 marks an important moment in the wider history of land consolidation and coal company expansion occurring around the turn of the twentieth century. Wheelwright's founding, as with the larger story of coal's role in fueling industrialization and war, is tied to the expansion of the railroad into the more remote parts of Appalachia. The Chesapeake and Ohio (C and O) Railroad's branch line extension into Floyd and Letcher counties opened up some of the richest areas of the coalfields to extraction and markets, a testament to the power of the railroad as "a key infrastructure of continental imperialism."[7] The railroad enabled the reach of large mining companies into this more isolated area of the coalfields, perhaps none larger than Maryland-based Consolidation Coal Company, with prior holdings in West Virginia and Pennsylvania. The Consolidation Coal Company quickly purchased multiple tracts of land from coal companies in Central Appalachia equaling close to 150,000

It soon built its own railroad to connect to the C and O from its holdings in the Elkhorn coalfields and began setting up mining operations elsewhere in the region, including in Virginia and McDowell County, West Virginia.[8] Consolidation Coal Company then expanded through the incorporation of an affiliated company, the Elkhorn Fuel Company, and gained control of its 285,000 acres. Elkhorn Fuel reorganized as the Elkhorn Coal Company as production demand rose due to the beginning of World War I. By 1916, Elkhorn Coal Company had established the Wheelwright Company Town, and Consolidation Coal Company had amassed close to a million acres of holdings. At that time, almost 80 percent of the mine workers in southern West Virginia and over two-thirds of the miners in eastern Kentucky and southern Virginia lived in one of the nearly five hundred company-controlled communities in the region. In contrast, there were fewer than one hundred independently incorporated towns.[9]

There are conflicting accounts of the first decade of Wheelwright's existence as an Elkhorn Coal Company town. Interviews with former miners who lived and worked in Wheelwright during those early years, for example, offer damning appraisals of life in the company town. Henry Armour, a Black miner who arrived in Wheelwright in 1923, observed that "Wheelwright . . . wasn't all that good because they didn't care how you lived or where you lived." Burt Crisp, who arrived toward the end of Elkhorn's ownership of the town, concurred: "Well, it was just a very, very bad camp. Houses weren't painted, run down, had outside bathrooms. . . . It was in an awful bad shape, no road."[10] These firsthand accounts of life in Wheelwright confirm assessments of coal camps during this period more generally: living conditions "among the worst in the nation," with houses suffering from poor construction, no heating, and rare indoor water or plumbing, resulting in communities where "sewage from open privies filled the creeks that ran through the center of town or drained into hollows and stood in stagnant pools."[11] These conditions produced considerable health problems in coal camps, including in Wheelwright, including "dysentery, venereal disease, typhoid, and tuberculosis," which all contributed to a "high infant mortality rate."[12]

At the same time, some sources point to Wheelwright's exceptionality among the hundreds of other company towns in the region, even before Inland Steel would develop the town into "Camelot." Lisa Perry, a historian who wrote a book about Wheelwright, notes that the argument that company towns were exceptionally extractive of their residents' labor and money—through high prices at company stores and high rents taken out of paychecks—ignores some reports that found that rents and utilities in the towns were less than those found in other places. Indeed, the 1925 report by the United States Senate Coal Commission named Wheelwright and a handful of other larger company towns in West Virginia and eastern Kentucky as being notable for the recreational opportunities afforded to miners, including Black and immigrant miners. Sam Little Jr., who today runs the town's historical society, noted to me that Wheelwright was one of the first towns in the region to receive indoor plumbing, and had the first Black foreman in the state.

That same report from the Coal Commission, however, noted that these "exceptional" camps constituted just 2 percent of all company towns in the region; the vast majority had neither sewage systems nor indoor plumbing.[13] Moreover, the opportunities and facilities for Black miners in Wheelwright were segregated and inferior even as the mines themselves were integrated.[14] Still, much historical work has made the important observation that coal company town life varied greatly and was often dire. More to the point, company towns, very much including the ones boasting better conditions, were foundationally about controlling labor toward maximizing profits. Some companies pursued this objective by pitting immigrant and Black miners against native-born highlanders and through reliance on mine guards and police, while others enacted seemingly benevolent community-building endeavors, like constructing theaters and pools or encouraging household gardening.[15] The garden was a particularly insidious and successful company strategy for both securing labor and unloading the costs of social reproduction. It produced in the worker, who of course was a tenant in the company-owned home, "an added attachment to the place which tends to offset the temptation of packing up and following vague rumors about steadier work, higher wages, [and] thicker seams" while also reproducing "the household with household labor during household hours."[16]

Companies actively attempted to thwart unionization and pacify potential labor unrest. As the 1925 report noted of company towns in the coalfields of West Virginia and eastern Kentucky specifically,

> These groups of villages dot the mountain sides down the river valleys and need only castles, drawbridges, and donjon-keeps to reproduce to the physical eye a view of feudal days. There were no public corporations in many places to provide for the public welfare or to maintain law and order, so the mine owner had one of his employees deputized by the local sheriff, and thus came into existence the much discussed "mine guard." As the employees were the only ones who were furnished homes and their occupancy was contingent upon their employment, the courts of that state have decided that the relation of landlord to tenant did not exist, but that it was the relation of master and servant, and when the employment ceased the mine owner came into possession of the house.[17]

Moreover, the report argued, the presence of armed mine guards and the property laws that could guarantee that a union organizer could not even enter certain camps without trespassing on property owned by the company, and thus was subject to ejection by the guards, resulted in a system resembling peonage.[18]

Oral histories from that period corroborate the report's conclusions. Eula Hall, who cofounded the Mud Creek Community health clinic in the 1970s in Floyd County, and who was part of health, labor, and environmental struggles in the region, grew up in Floyd County on a subsistence farm outside of a coal camp:

> Livin' in the coal camps you know if you missed a day's work the company were on you.... You know you was obligated to the company by living in their houses and a lot of times the people dreaded to live in coal camps because of the bosses coming.... Let's say if they had to miss a day because somebody got sick or they had to go out of town you know if they had reasons, the company was always investigating why you're not workin'. People didn't like that because it was too much interference with your own private life. 'Course people in the coal camps barely survived. They owed their soul to the company store.... They was under a dictatorship. The coal company thought they owned 'em.[19]

Hall was also unromantic about life on the farm. She worked constantly with her siblings for their own survival and attended only a few years in school, finishing the eighth grade having only started formal schooling when she was nine. However, she also argued,

> [People in the coal camp] didn't have the freedom we had either. We could raise our own food and we wouldn't have to spend money at a company store like they did. ... After you draw out all the scrip [you were owed], you couldn't draw out anymore scrip and could starve to death in a coal camp. ... You also didn't have to worry about getting thrown out of a company house. Oh, they whipped them, they used to go in to these coal camps and if a man didn't get out and work, the bosses would go in and whip them with switches.[20]

Hall's recollections and analyses indicate that to criticize coal company towns is not to say that life outside of them was easy or even preferable. Hall offers elsewhere in her interview that company housing was better than what she experienced on her farm, particularly during winters. But people actively leaving their family farms for the brutal life of coal company towns constitutes a pivotal historical moment in the development of capitalism in the coalfields.[21] Prior moments of enclosure and expropriation—the settler-colonial theft of sovereign indigenous territory and the broad form deed, for example—set the conditions for the early-twentieth-century process that turned farmers into wage-laboring miners for the coal companies, a transition that was also shaped by shifting commodity frontiers elsewhere in the country.[22] Other testimonies from people who grew up in eastern Kentucky during the prominence of coal camps bear this out even more explicitly, as evidenced by this exchange between an interviewer and a woman named Mae Frazier:

> INTERVIEWER: Why do you think people left the farms to move into coal camps?
> MAE FRAZIER: There was no money in farming. Farmers in Eastern Kentucky raised what they needed for themselves, not for market. The farms were small and [people] needed money and they could buy things with money, that's why they went to the coalmines.
> INTERVIEWER: Do you think they ate better in the mines?
> MF: No. Farmers had a more adequate diet than the miners.
> INTERVIEWER: Healthcare?

MF: [Miners] had better healthcare, they had compensation, company doctors, many people in eastern KY didn't go to doctors until they were critically ill.

INTERVIEWER: Housing?

MF: Mining camp houses were small but were kept in pretty good condition.

INTERVIEWER: What class of farmers would be most likely to move into coal camps?

MF: The poorest.[23]

Frazier's testimony profiles the appeal of the transition away from subsistence agriculture and toward wage labor during this period of capitalist transformation in the region. This transition off the farm and into the company town signaled the rise of a new social order in the coalfields, and with it the necessary partnership between capital and the state in the exercise of police power.[24]

From Coal Camp to Camelot: The Manufacture of Social Order in Wheelwright

Wheelwright's mythology as "Camelot" derives from the second stage of its life, 1930–1965, during which Inland Steel owned it, having bought the mines, and the town itself, from the Elkhorn Coal Company in 1930. The narrative of the town during this era is well established, drawing its strength from a number of sources, including former residents as well as the media and the company itself. One article in the *Louisville Courier-Journal* from 1950 noted that Wheelwright "is the shining star among coal camps in Kentucky, if not the nation."[25] As another article noted in particularly dramatic language twenty years later, in 1970, while covering the departure of Island Creek Coal Company from the community (after it had bought Wheelwright from Inland Steel), "A town is dying. And with it dies the last hope for a noble experiment in American capitalism—for a communal life in the benevolent custody of a great corporation."[26] Such baldly company-friendly narratives have some foundation in truth, at least concerning Inland Steel's treatment of workers and residents. While Wheelwright's origins are similar to those of many other company towns in the coalfields, under the stewardship

Figure 4.6. Harry Fain, coal loader, putting on one of the greens of the golf course. Inland Steel Company, Wheelwright #1 & 2 Mines, Wheelwright, Floyd County, Kentucky, 09/21/1946.

of town manager Edward "Jack" Price, who arrived in the town in 1928 while it was still owned by the Elkhorn Coal Company and who managed it through its tenure under Inland Steel, Wheelwright developed into the more modernized and developed town that current residents invoke in personal and collective memory as "Camelot." According to the *Courier-Journal*'s reporting, Price oversaw the town's transformation. When he arrived, the place was "a morass of mud in winter, a pall of dust in summer . . . [where] outdoor privies drained into Otter Creek . . . [and] the mines were dangerous, the people were sick all the time. . . . White children well enough to attend classes had only four teachers in one frame schoolhouse [and] Negro children went to one teacher in a one-room church." Under Price's management, it became a community described as having a "34 room hotel that competed with the best in Louisville, a 4000 volume free library . . . [and] down the street are a chic beauty shop, a modern air-conditioned theater, attractive stores with quality merchandise and a kitchen-equipped community hall. Up the street is a City Hall so modern that litigants in Police Court sit in swivel chairs upholstered in brown leather." Price also oversaw the expansion of both white and Black schools in the community and, as the paper noted, "Wheelwright has the only Negro high school in Floyd

Figure 4.7. Wading pool for small children, foreground, and main swimming pool, open during spring and summer months. Inland Steel Company, Wheelwright #1 & 2 Mines, Wheelwright, Floyd County, Kentucky, 09/22/1946.

County."[27] While there is historical truth here—Wheelwright was certainly one of the very few company towns to have amenities like a movie theater, a bowling alley, a golf course, a pool, and soda fountains—it is important to consider the ideological work performed by this narrative of an exceptional company town.

While there is ample evidence in the archives of Wheelwright's comforts, fitting them into a coherent narrative of exception that anchors the town to the fictional geography of Camelot requires the work of ideology. That is, following Stuart Hall, Wheelwright's status as a "model" company town must be understood within "the mental frameworks—the languages, the concepts, categories, imagery of thought, and the systems of representation—which different classes and social groups deploy in order to make sense of, define, figure out and render intelligible the way society works."[28] Consider, for example, two articles published in the *Wheelwright News* in 1963. The company, which published the newspaper "for the Employees of Inland Steel Co. Wheelwright, KY," narrated its own history for its readership:

> Back in April, 1930, Inland Steel Company acquired the coal mining properties at Wheelwright from the Elkhorn Coal Corporation which

had operated the mines for about fourteen years. They also acquired a town! ... Wheelwright is an incorporated town with a council and police court [and] it is owned entirely by Inland.... Inlanders at Wheelwright enjoy their community and take pride in its appearance. Hedges, lawns, shrubs, flowers and trees attest to their desire to make their rented property, a home. Outside patios and barbecue pits are common. Inland has been most generous in their role as landlord to a whole town.[29]

Following the death of Jack Price in 1962, the *Wheelwright News* eulogized that, under his leadership, "Wheelwright emerged from a squalid coal-mining town to a model community."[30] Lisa Perry notes the extent to which Price sought to manufacture a particular representation of the community, observing that he was "keenly aware of the importance of perception in steering public opinion, among both employees and the outside world. Through company publications, as well as features in mining and lifestyle magazines of the day, he ensured that depictions of conditions and life in Wheelwright were favorable."[31]

While most sources acknowledge that conditions in Wheelwright under Inland Steel were comparably better than in other company towns, the historical record is much more circumspect when it comes

Figure 4.8. Changing shifts at the mine portal in the afternoon. Wheelwright, Floyd County, KY, 9/23/46. Box 1, Item 6, Russell Lee Photographic Collection, 1979, 79PA103. Special Collections, University of Kentucky Libraries.

to the quality of life for the town's Black and immigrant miners. Wheelwright remained formally segregated into the 1960s, with separate boarding houses for Black, immigrant, and native white miners.[32] The separate facilities for Black miners were inferior, and work prospects for them were the first to suffer when changes in the industry hit the town,[33] as they did in the postwar years as many other coal camps closed and mechanization began to drive down employment, a trend that continues today.[34] Mechanization in the coalfields impacted Black miners particularly hard, including in Wheelwright. One former Black resident, Hilton Garrett, who operated a boarding house for Black miners in the town, noted that the house was full "until they put this machine in the coal mines."[35] By the end of the 1950s, Garrett's last boarder had left the town and few Black residents remained.

The ideological narrative of Wheelwright's exceptionality also works to mystify the motivations for Inland Steel's investments in the town. The company's amenities for miners reflected foundational concerns about business rather than benevolence. While the brutal reign of mine guards around the coalfields was by most accounts not present in Wheelwright, Inland Steel's welfare capitalist governance was motivated by the same need to secure a labor force and social order inherently and intimately tied to working for the company. Even as most people with whom I spoke during my trips to Wheelwright invoked its past as a Camelot in the mountains, the company's motivations for its investments in Wheelwright are not lost on some of the people who benefited. Ray Gibson, who lived and worked in Wheelwright for Inland Steel from 1950 to 1964, noted in an interview with Lisa Perry that even as he refers to the town as "Camelot" because of its amenities, he recognizes that "happy workers tend to be contented people and they're more productive and I think Inland learned that lesson. And tried to live it out. They wanted our people to work for them. They ... wanted a stable workforce, they wanted an efficient and effective workforce; they wanted a safe workforce."[36]

Prominent historians of the region and the industry concur on this point. Ronald Eller notes of this period and the approaches taken by coal camps that "the desire to attract workers, to resist the encroachment of unions, and to stem the appeal of other 'radical' movements pointed in the same direction."[37] John Alexander Williams observed of the model company towns, including Wheelwright, that they should be understood as "paternalistic towns, firmly in the control of authoritarian operators devoted to the care of 'their' people," and whose welfare capitalism was a company strategy "to blunt the appeal of the UMWA by providing good working and living conditions."[38] More directly, Steven Stoll concludes, "Everything about coal mining instigated class warfare."[39] Accordingly, we might consider Wheelwright less as a seemingly distinct or even exceptional manifestation of a coal camp than as embodying the "velvet glove" of police power or "the dreams of pacification."[40] Wheelwright underscores that in a more capacious definition of police as "the means through which order is achieved," we might understand explicit violence on the one hand and benevolent welfare capitalism on the other not as contradictions but rather as dual strategies for ensuring compliance.[41] As a result, the amenities of Wheelwright did not so much distinguish the town from other coal camps reliant on mine guards as express and execute an alternative strategy for securing the same social order centered around extraction, profit, poverty management, and company hegemony.

Coal executives and observers of the industry admitted as much during this period. As one coal baron noted of his company's investments in schools, roads, and recreational facilities, "We are doing this as a business policy. . . . A lot of this welfare work is done with that object in view. We think it is good business. We have had no strikes in seventeen years."[42] An article from the *Louisville Courier-Journal* praising Wheelwright's exceptionality noted, "Inland Steel Company, Chicago, owns the town of 3,000. It operates the 6,500-ton-a day workings primarily for its own use. The operation is Big Business, with two capital B's. *But the head man there is a lot like the friendly policeman who occasionally stops a long line of fast traffic to let a little girl and her doll buggy cross the street in safety.*"[43]

This sense of the company's orientation to the town and its residents is edifying. The police officer invoked by the reporter fits the "Officer Friendly" or community police construct that exists in the liberal imaginary as somehow outside of the violent and coercive power the police embody and distribute.[44] Moreover, the article explicitly collapses capital and police into the figure of Jack Price, the company's town manager, who in this configuration stands in as the "human-scale expression" of both the state and the corporation.[45] That is, Inland Steel is business *and* police, two social practices that were historically co-constitutive parts of creating order centered on markets, property, and poverty.[46]

Of course, the newspaper's comparison of Jack Price to a policeman is also significant because of the historically central role of sheriffs, police, and mine guards around the coalfields and in particular in the operation of the company town. Coal company executives focused on electing sheriffs, who then appointed deputy sheriffs, the salaries of whom coal operators often paid. These officers then served "as official mine guards in the company towns, protecting the company's property and payrolls, collecting rents, overseeing elections, and performing other services."[47]

A brief examination of the history of another town in the coalfields further elucidates the direct historical thread from coal to prison fastened through police power. Chapter 1 examined the construction of Wallens Ridge State Prison in Big Stone Gap, Virginia, one of two "supermax" prisons in Wise County. Nearly one hundred years before the prison, Big Stone Gap was also the site of considerable investment in police at the turn of the twentieth century. John Fox Jr., an early-twentieth-century developer and novelist whose writings circulated pernicious stereotypes about the people of Appalachia to a broad and urban readership, boasted about the development of a volunteer police guard in Big Stone Gap in order to exert "the sternest ideals of good law and order" as mining came to the county:

> In this town, certain young men—chiefly Virginians and blue-grass Kentuckians—simply formed a volunteer police guard. They enrolled themselves as county policemen and each man armed himself—usually with a Winchester, a revolver, a billy, a belt, a badge, and a whistle. . . . They were lawyers, bankers, real-estate brokers, newspaper men, civil and mining engineers, geologists, speculators and several men of leisure. Nearly all were active in business—as long as there was business—and most of them were college graduates representing Harvard, Yale, Princeton, the University of Virginia and other Southern Colleges. Two were great-grandsons of Henry Clay, several bore a like relation to Kentucky governors, and with few exceptions the guard represented the best people of the blue-grass of one State and the tide-water country of the other.[48]

There is a subtle racialization to the explicit geographical distinctions Fox makes in describing the class composition of the Big Stone Gap police force. The "bluegrass" and "tide-water" regional origins of the Kentucky and Virginia guardsmen distinguish them from the mountainous rabble they aimed to control, an example of what Cedric Robinson observed in Europe as the tendency of capitalism "to exaggerate regional, subcultural, and dialectical differences into 'racial' ones."[49] Examining the mission of this volunteer police force, and not just its aristocratic configuration, further clarifies the relationship between racial capitalist social order and police power. Fox notes that this volunteer police guard was first organized to put down a strike of workers at a newly established brick plant. They then turned their attention to guarding "the streets, day and night, when there was need; they made arrests, chased and searched for criminals, guarded jails against mobs, cracked toughs over the head with billies, lugged them to the 'calaboose,' and appeared as witnesses against them in court the next morning."[50] As Helen Lewis and her coauthors summarize Fox's argument, the police force "turned a mountain crossroads town where mountain boys frolicked and fought into a quiet, respectable outpost of high society."[51] Fox himself concludes that in Big Stone Gap, civilization—meaning the police—"was forged ahead of church, school, and railroad."[52]

The dynamics on display here illustrate the intimacies and interdependencies between class power and police power. The early writings and lectures of "father of capitalism" Adam Smith himself make this point, as he argued before he published *Wealth of Nations* that the principal task of the police was facilitating *bon marche*, or "good markets," and, perhaps more baldly, as "promoting the opulence of the state."[53] That the Appalachian nobility self-deputized in order to enforce the order dictated and required by the growing and powerful coal industry affirms the broader history of police power as it also foreshadows the role of the prison in the same coalfields, and same community, one hundred years later.[54] Importantly, these outside interests eventually won over local middle-class leaders, integrating them into the necessity of social-control efforts. It is important to recognize that the class dynamics at work in Big Stone Gap were unexceptional across coal camps in the region.[55]

From Welfare Capitalism to the Neoliberal Carceral State: Otter Creek Correctional Center, 1992–2012

Back in Wheelwright, Inland Steel sold the town to the Island Creek Coal Company in January of 1966. Just ten months later, on November 10, Island Creek turned around and resold the town to a local investment company called Mountain Investment. As one miner summarized life in Wheelwright under its three coal company benefactors,

> Well, it's like being in the darkest part of the night, the sun suddenly come out, and then it gets dark again. I compare the three companies that way. Elkhorn, because they were good to their people and they were good people to work for. But as far as modern facilities, there was no such thing here. When Inland Steel came in, they modernized the town. It was considered the most modern mining town in the world. When they left here Island Creek came in and they don't worry about anything other than getting the coal out [of the ground].[56]

The transfers of Wheelwright's and its residents' destinies across decades of corporate buy-outs, consolidations, and liquidations ultimately landed the town in the care of the Kentucky Housing Corporation, after it bought all of Mountain Investment's assets, including the town, in 1979. Kentucky Housing Corporation then turned all of the utilities over to the town for one dollar, and the Floyd County Development District purchased all of the residential buildings in order to render the community eligible for federal grants, funding from which they had been prohibited while under the ownership of the private companies.[57] The town's sixty-year history of corporate ownership was over, but its effects would linger for decades. Despite some attempts and even initial successes by local residents to build and attract businesses, the town faltered and, according to historian Lisa Perry, "By the mid 1980s, Wheelwright residents were on their own—Kentucky Housing and all the other federal agencies were gone, work programs had ended, and the town finally achieved independence."[58]

Then, on October 27, 1992, Kentucky governor Brereton Jones visited Wheelwright to announce that the struggling former company town would be receiving some much-needed economic development: a

Figure 4.9. The Wheelwright mine. Credit: Jill Frank.

new prison, to be built and operated by Louisville-based private prison company U.S. Corrections Corporation. Promising one hundred temporary construction jobs and eighty-five full-time prison positions, Jones did not hide the fact that the prison was something of a reward for the community. Floyd County, in which Wheelwright sits, had provided the governor with his highest margin of victory in the region in the gubernatorial election the year before: "Floyd county was the best to me in my election," he told reporters. "And I haven't forgotten it."[59]

Former Floyd County judge-executive Paul Hunt Thompson served as a county campaign chair for Jones's campaign in 1991. Thompson is a long-time Wheelwright resident who had been active in the community in trying to generate business development. He opened a grocery store in the early 1980s and by his own admission was instrumental in local efforts to land the prison. In an interview, Thompson acknowledged his role in bringing Otter Creek to Wheelwright, but was guarded about providing details. He did proudly discuss his own decision to remain in Wheelwright and try to make something for the town.

I interviewed Thompson, along with five other people, on a warm spring day in Wheelwright's city hall in 2015, three years after the prison had closed. Thompson and everyone else with whom I spoke during that visit, as well as on prior and subsequent trips, identified reopening the prison as a priority and as vital to the town's future prospects, even as such acknowledgment complicated any notion of Wheelwright's independence from relying on the whims of corporations. Thompson began our interview by saying, "Things have progressed up here—we've come a long way—you know, we have a prison up here. 'Course there's nobody in it, hard to have a payroll like that, though we do employ five people. And the private prison company cooperates with the town knowing the town depends on it."

The prison arrived in the middle of a particularly stark period for the region and the county. Between 1980 and 2005, mining jobs decreased in Floyd County by 82 percent and mining fell 84.5 percent as a percentage of the total jobs in the county.[60] The prison, which operated for twenty years between 1992 and 2012 before closing, may have provided some measure of stability for some Wheelwright families during this period, although the strength of that narrative locally is contradicted by the available data. While the prison's closure resulted in the immediate loss of 170 jobs, according to several residents I interviewed, the majority of those jobs were held by people living outside of Wheelwright.

But even if it were true that Wheelwright suffered major employment losses with the closing of Otter Creek, the larger historical changes to the coal industry and regional political economy have produced rather desperate on-the-ground realities that the prison had, at best, perhaps moderated. Census data from 2011, when the prison was still open, shows per capita income in Floyd County at $16,201, with 27 percent of the population living below the poverty line. In Wheelwright specifically conditions were dire, with a $7,447 per capita income and 42.3 percent of people living below the poverty line.[61]

Life inside of Otter Creek during its twenty-year life span was considerably worse, characterized by numerous documented abuses, particularly of women prisoners. Core Civic, then known as Corrections Corporation of America, had bought U.S. Corrections Corporation in 1998 and took over the administration of Otter Creek and several other private prisons in Kentucky. Under CCA's ownership, there were allegations of rampant inadequate medical care, significant security breaches, including a staff suicide with a smuggled gun, and a litany of sexual abuse cases. Perhaps the most infamous of Otter Creek's series of abuses concerned significant sexual violence, including allegations that Otter Creek employees had sexually assaulted nineteen women prisoners from Hawaii. According to *Prison Legal News*, an investigative report by the Kentucky Department of Corrections found that "Corrections Corporation of America officials had failed to report 11 incidents involving possible sexual misconduct to state officials. In four of those incidents there was 'sufficient evidence to warrant a PREA [Prison Rape Elimination Act] investigation . . .' and the accused CCA staff members in those cases were terminated. Criminal charges were brought against at least six Otter Creek employees, including the facility's chaplain."[62] In 2009, a former prisoner from Hawaii filed suit against both Hawaiian state officials and CCA for the rape she suffered at the hands of an Otter Creek prison guard, who would eventually be convicted of second-degree sexual assault.[63] It must also be noted that the state's monitoring system of Otter Creek was compromised throughout the prison's operation and Kentucky declined to fine CCA for breach of contract following any of the abuses.[64]

The prison's infamy is important to document in this story. The inherent violence of captivity in American prisons is central to the expansion of incarceration under racial capitalism.[65] The incarcerated at Otter Creek during the prison's twenty-year life span—Hawaiians, all women and mostly indigenous; men and women from Kentucky and Indiana, almost all poor and disproportionately people of color—are foundational to every element of the broader story: the connections between urban and rural underdevelopment, the racial, colonial, gender, and sexual violence at the heart of the carceral state, and the success of the ideological work of the prison to naturalize its place in our landscapes, such that it was morally defensible, legally permissible, and financially responsible for Hawaii to send its prisoners five thousand miles away to the mountains of Kentucky. This kind of distance resulted in what the *Louisville Courier-Journal* called "double punishment," as the Hawaiians' incarceration in the continental United States, and all the way in Kentucky, precluded any kind of visitation from family.[66] The newspaper's assessment from 2006 was offered before the revelations of sexual violence at the prison.

Following the scandal at Otter Creek, Hawaii ended its contract with CCA and removed its prisoners. But the prison remained open and Kentucky, with its own substantially bloated state prison system, began housing state prisoners at Otter Creek for several years. Finally, amidst increased critical attention to the role of private prison companies and, importantly, because of the state's growing reliance on county jails to house state prisoners, Kentucky ended its contract with CCA and began moving prisoners out of its facilities, including Lee Adjustment Center in 2010, Otter Creek in 2012, and Marion Adjustment Center in 2013. But, as we will see, the state's break from the prison company was short lived. In late 2017, Kentucky signed a new contract with Core Civic (formerly CCA) to reopen Lee Adjustment Center to house state prisoners. In October 2019, outgoing governor Matt Bevin visited Wheelwright and announced that Otter Creek would soon reopen as well.

Profit, Order, and the State

Corporate rule in the coalfields has a long history. From early speculators to industrialization, from company towns to the contemporary "Mountain Royalty" that several of my research participants noted exerts powerful influence over regional politics, there is no doubt that, as Elizabeth Catte has argued, "Corporate welfare runs Appalachia."[67]

It can be tempting, therefore, when examining a private prison in the region, to identify Core Civic as simply the next iteration of a company exerting control over the coalfields in order to extract profit. This understanding is not incorrect, but it is limited. The vast majority of Central Appalachia's prisons and jails are public. And even as companies—timber, salt, coal, and natural gas—have dominated Appalachia for centuries, scholars have emphasized the central historical role that the state has played in facilitating capitalist development "and the making of wealth and poverty," including its function to protect capital.[68] With this distinction in mind, it is important to offer a more precise analysis of the reconfiguration of the state, across scales, that was both backdrop to and provided the conditions for Otter Creek's construction and operation.

A one-day snapshot of reporting from the *Louisville Courier-Journal* in late December 1993, just one year after Otter Creek opened, offers telling insight into the broader political and economic context in which to situate Wheelwright and the prison. This particular day came to my attention while I was researching Wheelwright's history because the newspaper ran a number of articles—something of a miniseries—examining the state's growing relationship to private prisons, including the newly opened Otter Creek. But other articles in the newspaper on that same day, covering statewide and national issues unrelated to private prisons, point to developments around Kentucky and the country that help explain the building of Otter Creek and the numerous other state and federal prisons that would rise in Kentucky later in the decade and into the twenty-first century.

On the front page of the newspaper that day, located just above the main article about private prisons, was a story about a state commission that recommended the elimination of 203 college programs at Kentucky community colleges and universities.[69] The article reported that Governor Jones formed the commission as part of a broader approach toward restructuring higher education in order to save money. Indeed, the article notes that Jones acknowledged that the panel's biggest accomplishment was its proposal to link state funding—traditionally allocated on the basis of enrollments—to measures of performance as indicated by graduation and retention rates as well employer-satisfaction measures, hallmarks of the neoliberalization of higher education.[70]

Sharing the front page, just under the lead story about private prisons, was an article about the fight to build the state's first nursing home wing for HIV and AIDS patients.[71] EPI Corporation, a Louisville-based company that built and operated a number of different health facilities in Kentucky, proposed to build a 150-bed nursing home, with a wing of thirty beds designated for AIDS patients, on land it owned just outside of Louisville. The state Cabinet for Human Resources Staff had initially rejected the proposal, despite the fact that at the time there were only two nursing home beds designated for patients with AIDS in the entire state. While there were shelters that counted people with AIDS as residents, those facilities had neither the staff nor the training to provide necessary medical care. According to the story, at that time there were at least 1,619 Kentuckians living with HIV, 404 of whom had "full blown AIDS."[72]

The story about the nursing home continued onto page 12. Just adjacent to its second half was a story from the Associated Press titled "Programs for Poor Likely to Be Cut" and predicting, with sourcing from inside the White House, the elimination or restructuring of numerous federal programs providing housing and food to people in poverty in the United States. Just a few pages earlier, on page 6, was a story with the rather self-explanatory headline of "Federal Grants Boost Police Squads: Clinton Says More Forces on the Way." Both stories, about the Clinton administration's cutting of federal programs for the poor and increases to police forces, foreshadowed, respectively, what we now know as the Personal Responsibility and Work Opportunity Act of 1996 and the Violent Crime Control and Law Enforcement Act of 1994. These were signature pieces of legislation at the time and are now crucial pieces of evidence for analysts of the neoliberal state's bipartisan reorganization.[73] Both stories in the *Courier-Journal* show the incremental buildup toward ending welfare and fortifying the already rapidly growing carceral state.

To summarize, on one random day in December of 1993, the Louisville newspaper's reporting exposed significant contours of the neoliberal carceral conjuncture that characterized the 1990s. The coverage revealed the national imposition of a political vision that shrank and even eliminated elements of the social wage while fortifying the carceral state, seemingly dollar for dollar. In Kentucky, this dynamic played out similarly, with the state—like the country, under a Democratic executive—cutting educational programs and underfunding health care for marginalized citizens while throttling through the process to build prisons. An exclusive focus on the profit motive behind Otter Creek and driving Core Civic would miss all of the ways in which the prison's very .... of possibility relied heavily on the state, at various scales— government, the governor, the local judge-executive—and its ɔacities.

"I Don't Care If You Reopen It as a Donut Factory as Long as There's Jobs in There!!"

If corporate profit does not capture the complexity of why Otter Creek was built and why it was built in the moment when it was, neither does Core Civic fit neatly into a tempting analysis of the reincarnation of the company town. For a community created by one coal company and owned for decades by others, Core Civic's presence in Wheelwright offers a narrative arc of prisons replacing coal economically, physically, and ideologically. And many elements of such a storyline ring true; part of the analytical scaffolding for this book rests on the argument that, in some places, prisons have done just that. In Wheelwright, residents' longing for a return to the "Camelot" days of Inland Steel are sutured to a hope that the prison will reopen and revitalize the community through the jobs that would return and the businesses that the prison would support.

But that argument also has limitations in Wheelwright. In addition to the dubiousness of prison-based economic development, an analysis of the reincarnation of Wheelwright as a company town might mistake residents' support for the prison as allegiance to the company and to incarceration. The reality is more complex. Otter Creek and Core Civic do not seem to capture the imaginations of people in Wheelwright. In the same breath that residents enthusiastically hope for Otter Creek's reopening, they also admit that their real desire is for the semblance of stability and normalcy offered by the presence of reliable and living-wage work. Experiences from my trips to Wheelwright and numerous conversations with residents bear this out directly.

On my very first trip to the community in the late winter of 2013, a local city councilman named Don, who would later become mayor, drove Jill and me to the closed prison for a scheduled tour. I had been somewhat surprised by his assurances over the phone that we could enter the prison even in its closed state. Sure enough, upon arriving at Otter Creek, a voice crackled over the intercom denying our entrance. Don responded by asking if the person might call in to what I presumed was Core Civic's corporate headquarters to request permission to provide us with a tour. The company denied our entrance. Still, we were able to walk around the grounds. Eventually Mike, the voice from within, emerged from the prison to join us. With a soft-spoken and thoughtful demeanor, Mike told me that despite sitting completely empty, Core Civic continued to employ five former correctional officers to watch over the facility 24/7, a point former judge-executive Paul Thompson would make on a subsequent trip years later. But employing five local people to monitor an abandoned prison does not make up for the 170 jobs that were lost when the facility closed. When I pressed Mike on what it meant to lose the prison and what he would do next, he shrugged and said, "There just ain't no jobs in eastern Kentucky." He and Don noted that the prison's departure had significant economic implications beyond job loss. As they explained, the absence of the prison can be felt in the empty gas station, the low utilities payments (which, during the prison's operation, accounted for as much city revenue as the rest of the town combined, according to Don), and the money that 170 people working in Wheelwright then spent in Wheelwright. When the jobs left, the money followed. By Mike's estimates, 80 percent of the prison's workforce lived within just a few miles of the facility. When I asked about pay at the prison, both men scoffed. As enthusiastic as they were for the prison to return, the hourly wage had been particularly low. The jobs started at about $8.75 an hour, they said; in contrast, average miner work and jobs at federal prisons started at double that rate. But those jobs required long, sometimes multi-hour commutes. With this in mind, it is perhaps not hard to understand why Wheelwright residents were dedicated to recruiting another private prison company to the community.

A discussion on a subsequent trip to Wheelwright with two other residents bears this point out well. One woman, who had worked with both Mountain Investment and Kentucky Housing Corporation, noted of the prison, "I hope, we all hope, something will come back. I think everybody thinks the prison will come back and that there will be jobs. 'Cause they don't have anything else to be optimistic about. My daughter couldn't wait to leave and hasn't come back! There has to be *something* to keep people to stay, otherwise [Wheelwright] will die out." At this point in our conversation, Sam Little Jr., a city commissioner and my contact in Wheelwright, interjected with a telling story. The Republican primary for the governor's race had recently occurred. Just a couple of weeks before, Little began, "I got a call from the guy running for governor out of

Louisville asking to speak to a commissioner. I said 'Well, you got one, what do you need?' [The candidate] then said, 'Well how would you all like to have the prison reopened as a state prison?' I said, '*I don't care if you reopen it as a donut factory as long as there's jobs in there!* Whatever you feel you need to do!'"

Sam Little Jr. is a dedicated advocate for the community. He started and runs the Wheelwright Historical Society and town library, volunteers for two churches and the local fire department, and writes grants to fund the work of the WHS and to obtain books for the local school. On that visit, he mentioned that he had obtained a grant for two thousand dollars' worth of art books for the school only to find out that the school's art program had just been cut for budgetary reasons. The community center that Little operates out of the WHS hosts card tournaments, movie nights, story time, classes, and band practices.

On the one hand, there is simply no overlooking the fact that Wheelwright residents almost to a person longed for the prison's reopening. For them, reopening Otter Creek remains the most likely avenue toward reestablishing elements of the town that loom large in community memory; Little himself has noted that the prison paves the road back to Camelot.[74] But we might also consider Little's "donut shop" comment and other sentiments from Wheelwright residents in another way, as a glimpse into the alternative politics and geographies that are imaginable, and whose materialization is stored as potential energy. The receptivity and even enthusiasm of Wheelwright residents about the reopening of the prison in some form is not due to a heartfelt attachment to Core Civic, nor to a political identification with incarceration, nor because of a punitive spirit or racial animus. Rather, in the carceral conjuncture, it is simply the prison that was offered and available. Even as Otter Creek's presence clearly structures what can be imagined for the community, prisons do not guarantee their own reproduction; the existing social formation grants them a kinetic energy that positions them as the commonsense form of economic development. This is a contingency that can be undone through struggles for alternative economic approaches to the region.

For now, though, there are a number of indications that Otter C may reopen imminently as part of Kentucky's strategy for managi vere overcrowding in the state's prison system. Officials have di reopening the prison for a number of years, and the different iterations of proposals during that time offer further instruction about the prison's place in the region. First, added by the Kentucky House of Representatives to the state budget for 2014 was language directing the Department of Corrections to transfer at least one hundred prisoners sixty-five years old or over into the former prison, which was to be converted into "an assisted living and/or nursing facility." Administratively, the prisoners would be "paroled from state prison with the requirement that they live at the facility until their parole term ends. The facility would remain privately owned and operated."[75] Paul Thompson, the Wheelwright leader and former Floyd County judge-executive, spoke with characteristic hope about this possibility during our interview:

> What's going to happen up there . . . we have looked at this company in Georgia, there's this doctor who owns this company in Georgia and he came up to look at it. I took him over to Prestonsburg and had him look at the college, made sure that the nursing supply would be good, took him to the Pikeville hospital so that he could talk with [people there]. Took him to Macdowell Hospital, Martin Hospital. . . . See what they was talkin' about was a medical facility to treat parolees that were just incapacitated, either mentally or physically. It was a good idea because once those people reach sixty-five years old their Medicare kicks in but while they're in the state system the state has to pick that tab up so if the governor would parole 'em, but parole 'em to Wheelwright medical facility where they could be taken care of, then that medical facility could take 'em out of the state prison and bill the federal government and then it would be an expense off the state. Nobody's come up with a good definition of what it is. [It is] basically a nursing home for parolees. It was a great idea. I don't feel as optimistic about it as I once did. Still also a possibility to get out-of-state prisoners in.

In other words, this new iteration of Otter Creek would be a nursing home in name only; state prisoners would be paroled but required to live in a former medium-security prison. There was no pretense that this arrangement expressed some correctional policy or priority; Kentucky Department of Corrections spokespeople openly admitted that the agency had nothing to do with the proposal to reopen the prison. Indeed, the proposal came from former House speaker Greg Stumbo.[76] At that time, Stumbo represented the district in which Wheelwright and Otter Creek are located. Reopening Otter Creek as a carceral nursing home would adhere to, if also adjust, the economic strategy of prison-based development. The maneuver would offload the costs of incarceration to Medicare but contract an Atlanta-based company called CorrectHealth to manage the facility.[77]

More recently, as the state prison population has grown despite the passage of sentencing reform in 2011, Kentucky has contracted with Core Civic again and reopened Lee Adjustment Center to house eight hundred state prisoners; reopening Otter Creek appears to be imminent. Perhaps tellingly, the candidate who had called Wheelwright and spoken to Sam Little Jr. ahead of the 2015 Republican primaries to inquire about reopening the facility was, at that time, a relatively unknown and far-right businessman in Louisville named Matt Bevin. As part of the wave of Tea Party candidates to surge into elected offices that year, Bevin won the primary and eventually the election for governor. Before leaving office, in October of 2019, Governor Bevin traveled to Wheelwright to announce the reopening of Otter Creek to house Kentucky state prisoners and alleviate overcrowding. Andy Beshear's first proposed budget as governor in January 2020 included the requisite funding and the prison, renamed Southeast Correctional Complex, is set to open with Kentucky leasing the facility from Core Civic. But the reopening of the prison is oriented as much toward addressing Wheelwright's economic woes as it is toward alleviating the state's bloated prison system, with promises of two hundred stable jobs coming to the community and broader region. As the current judge-executive of Floyd County observed, "Two-hundred people, plus family members, that's going to be visiting our restaurants, our gas stations—it'll be housing for our community." Moreover, he noted, the prison would galvanize a broader "custodial" effort, noting that it would "clean the city up. Clean ditches up. You know, new infrastructure. So, all in all, it's a great thing."[78]

Both of these potential futures for Otter Creek and for Wheelwright demonstrate the tenacity of the prison to adapt to changing imperatives around punishment and its centrality, even when closed, to planning for the community's operations and future. The chronology is important— the prison's place in the community has driven, rather than followed, policy development and proposals. The current judge-executive's expectation that reopening Otter Creek would not only bring jobs to Wheelwright but also would improve area housing and roads, clean up the city, and assist in the renovation of infrastructure indicates that the prison is more than a site of work. In its centrality to numerous processes and objectives, from regional development to municipal planning to household management, the prison in the coalfields enacts what this book calls "carceral social reproduction," a material and ideological process of imagining and planning the future through the promise or presence of the prison. This takes on an additional valence in Wheelwright because of the town's history. Placed into the lineage of Inland Steel, welfare capitalism, company hegemony, and the threat of police around the coalfields, Otter Creek's past and probable future can be perceived as the contemporary expression of the state's strategy for reproducing capitalist social order amidst very real crises.

PART III

Carceral Social Reproduction

5

Planning the Prison

Development, Revenue, and Ideology

While the story of federal policy and multinational corporations is seductive, regions still matter. It is only through an examination of organized power in the region that regional institutions, relations, and movements can be understood and structures of inequality may be dismantled.
—Clyde Woods, *Development Arrested*

A crisis occurs, sometimes lasting for decades. This exceptional duration means that incurable structural contradictions have revealed themselves (reached maturity) and that, despite this, the political forces which are struggling to conserve and defend the existing structure itself are making every effort to cure them, within certain limits, and to overcome them. These incessant and persistent efforts (since no social formation will ever admit that it has been superseded) form the terrain of the "conjunctural" and it is upon this terrain that the forces of opposition organize.
—Antonio Gramsci, *Prison Notebooks*

Kentucky's swollen state prison population has shaped Wheelwright's opportunity to reopen Otter Creek Correctional Facility as Southeastern Correctional Complex. The state's incarcerated population grew by 45 percent in the first decade of the twenty-first century, far outpacing the 13 percent growth experienced on average in the United States during the same period. In 2011, Kentucky joined over thirty states in approving sentencing reform legislation, passing House Bill 463, the Public Safety and Offender Accountability Act, which was designed to reduce corrections spending and the number of people in prison. But as the previous chapter noted, the state's prison population has actually *grown* since then, by about 18 percent, largely due to the state's persistent felony offender (PFO) law, a tough-on-crime-era policy, as well as parole practices that sentencing reform did not amend.[1] Today, the state has the second highest rate of incarceration for women in the United States; if Kentucky were its own country, it would have the seventh highest incarceration rate in the world.[2] As mentioned previously, if the state were to continue incarcerating its residents at this same rate, a recent Vera Institute of Justice report concluded, everyone in Kentucky will be incarcerated in 113 years.[3] A criminal justice reform bill introduced in 2017 and featuring twenty-two recommendations from a Justice Reinvestment working group to reduce state prison populations failed even to make it out of committee.[4]

Kentucky now has 24,000 state prisoners but only 11,700 beds in state prisons. Because of this severe overcrowding, the Kentucky Department of Corrections has incarcerated close to half of the state prison population in county jails, a maneuver that saves money for the state while offering struggling rural counties some much-needed revenue. The average 2016 daily cost to incarcerate someone in a state prison was $66.82. By contrast, Kentucky pays county jails $31.34 per day for prisoner housing and medical costs. By housing state prisoners in county jails, the state is subsidizing and incentivizing a significant expansion of carceral capacity at the county level. Counties have turned toward jails, in addition to prisons, as seemingly reliable sources of revenue, jobs, and economic stimulus. The proliferation of rural jails in eastern Kentucky is a response to the twin and interrelated crises of overcrowding and severe revenue loss, as the per-diem payments from the state help to "keep the lights on," as one sheriff put it to the researcher Jack Norton.[5] On the one hand, Kentucky has joined the majority of states in passing reform legislation, forming sentencing commissions, and shifting some official rhetoric around incarceration. On the other hand, the state has continued unabated in building out state carceral capacity at multiple scales, evidenced by local jail expansions and the reopening of private prisons to house state prisoners, in addition to the efforts to build yet another federal prison in the coalfields, in ·r County.[6] What can we make of these contradictions?

ie conflicts point to the carceral state's adaptability and even te- midst some critical attention, reminding us that carceral expansion can occur through shifting imperatives around punitiveness and poverty management.[7] That is, while there is no doubt that criminal justice policy affects the numbers going in and staying in jail and prison, it is equally clear that the durability of the Kentucky carceral state is underwritten by its economic and affective importance to rural communities suffering through various elements of capitalist crisis. The previous chapter examined the reliance of coal companies on police power in the creation of a social order that managed poverty, militated against worker organizing, and fostered allegiance to and dependency on the industry. Today, that chapter began to suggest, in the neoliberal era of austerity, mass incarceration, and mechanization, the prison has become a central mechanism for maintaining capitalist social order and social relations in the coalfields.

Part 3 of this book takes that provocation as a point of analysis and a point of departure, focusing almost entirely on the process of siting, constructing, and operating United States Penitentiary (USP) Letcher in Letcher County, Kentucky. That process, which intensified during my research into the broader regional carceral geography, revealed the deep connections between prisons and rural political economies, including regional planning, questions of work, and social reproduction.

A central contradiction of the coal industry, and of capitalism more generally, has situated the region in a particularly precarious position. The expansion of coal production increased the accumulation of wealth for coal operators and at times provided for the social reproductive capacities of communities, as in the case of Wheelwright under Inland Steel's ownership. However, over time the industry necessarily divested from, and even destroyed, strategies for social reproduction in coalfield communities. The coal industry maximized profits specifically by and through contaminating water tables, polluting air, destroying streams, enclosing and devastating areas for hunting, foraging, and harvesting, and shifting production and cutting jobs through mechanization. Moreover, the decline of production has dramatically impacted once-reliable revenue-generating mechanisms. The focus of chapters 5 and 6 on the social reproduction strategies of and through the prison hinges on the ways this contradiction of capitalism played out in the region.[8] As the coal industry has departed the region, the "burden of social reproduction"—strategizing, planning, and paying for it—has been fully offloaded down scale, to cash-strapped counties and to their agencies and households.[9] In turning to prisons and jails to manage this crisis, the state's reorganization under racial capitalism is ongoing. In places like Central Appalachia, experiencing a still-expanding carceral infrastructure through both prison and jail building, public, quasi-public, and private entities that fund municipal development hedge and hinge their funding on the promises of carceral construction. In turn, prisons and jails become a source for communities to imagine not only an economy post-coal but also the very possibility of a future in the region.

Marxist feminists have long emphasized the importance of social reproduction theory to an acute understanding of capitalist social relations and formations. In trying to understand the changing nature of work in the coalfields, we must also ask how the prison worker—or "violence worker," to employ Micol Seigel's helpful term for understanding the core of police power—arrives at the gates of the prison and jail for work.[10] One answer to the most literal interpretation of that question itself demonstrates the importance of carceral social reproduction: they arrive on roads, some of which are only able to be paved, widened, or updated precisely because of the promise or presence of the prison and the ability to secure infrastructure funding that it can offer. Probing further, their arrival depends on being qualified, educated, healthy, and ideologically positioned for such work, contingencies that point to the importance of education, family, culture, and health. In other words, these chapters ask, what produces the conditions of possibility for the worker to arrive at the prison in a Central Appalachian community and, in turn, what does the prison produce in the worker and their community?[11]

These chapters in particular demonstrate the importance of a conjunctural analysis, or an approach to understanding the crisis that considers not only the objective economic changes that produced it but also the political, sociocultural, and ideological forces that coalesce through struggle to resolve it.[12] Relying on interviews, site visits, local media, histories of regional planning, and testimonies submitted to the Bureau of Prisons during the official National Environmental Policy Act (NEPA) process, these chapters examine the relationships among planning, work, education, and economy with a particular interest in how concerns about futurity are central to debates about prison siting in communities with considerable and warranted existential concerns. As the prisons become significant political strategies for navigating crises, they also reveal glimpses into what is at stake in Central Appalachia, as carceral social reproduction portends a racialized and gendered political and cultural renovation in the coalfields around imprisonment.

Crucially, organized opposition to USP Letcher destabilized the position of the prison as central to the county's future. Starting in 2013, the Bureau of Prisons accelerated the formal process as the agency commenced the federal scoping and siting period required under federal environmental law. In the ensuing years, a powerful and multiscalar coalition of organizers, landowners, national environmental activists, and movement lawyers began to coalesce to challenge the project, resulting in a truly historic defeat in the early summer of 2019. Chapter 7, coauthored with Sylvia Ryerson, concludes part 3's examination of Letcher County and carceral social reproduction by following and analyzing the work to defeat USP Letcher, as much of the activism offered speculative and concrete alternative and abolitionist visions for the county's future. While those years from 2013 to 2019 showcase the outsized role that the prison played in planning for the county's future, the period also reveals the contingency, rather than inevitability, of prison growth.

Planning, Development, and Revenue

As is characteristic of much of the area, coal companies developed Letcher County during the late nineteenth and early twentieth centuries. The names of many communities in the county reflect the influence of the industry, including those named after coal companies and others named after their executives.[13] The county's population grew significantly during the rise of the industry and the arrival, in 1911, of the railroad. The population more than doubled between 1910 and 1920, from 10,500 to more than 25,000, nearly doubling again by 1940. But the changes wrought by mechanization and fluctuations in demand dramatically impacted the county during the later decades of the twentieth century and certainly in the twenty-first. The population has declined to its levels of one hundred years ago, at just over twenty-three thousand; some places within the county, formerly coal camps, have seen most people move away. As one historian of the region summarized the state of the county in 1994, "The social and political costs of such convulsive change were nearly incalculable. Besides carting off billions of dollars' worth of lumber and coal on which they paid no taxes, corporations changed the basic social structure, gained control of county politics, and in effect turned the whole county to their own private uses."[14]

Today, county politics and planning continue to reflect this long history of intimacy, and interdependency, between industry and local configurations of state power. Examining planning requires some deft multiscalar work, paying attention to granular flows of money, ideas, and policy as they gesture toward, but also enact, broader trends of the capitalist state. This chapter follows such flows as they moved through local and regional private and quasi-public bodies in the pursuit of siting and building USP Letcher. Studying the movement and momentum of money and ideas in the community and region is another way to say studying power, including the political and economic power necessary to mobilize a major project like a federal prison, as well as the ideological power to render it acceptable.[15]

The funding source for a federal prison is congressional appropriations to the Department of Justice. In the case of USP Letcher, appropriations from Congress under the Obama administration originally funded the prison project with $444 million after years of lobbying from US Representative Hal Rogers, who represents the fifth congressional district, which is all of eastern Kentucky, and for whom prison building has been a central strategy of rural economic development. But the project hit an unexpected snag when the Trump administration zeroed out the funding for the prison in its proposed budget for 2018 as part of a larger austerity package that would cut federal programs designed to help people in poverty. This sparked an entertaining moment of political theater that pitted Rogers against Deputy Attorney General Rod Rosenstein during a House Appropriations Committee meeting, where Rosenstein said that due to the fact that "the federal prison population has declined precipitously over the last several years . . . a decline of about 30,000 or 14%," as well as budget restraints, the Department of Justice (DOJ) had opted against building the prison. Rogers countered by insisting that Congress's appropriation of the funds made it the DOJ's legal obligation to the prison the agency had just admitted it did not need. Ultimately, ess kept the funding, increasing the appropriation to $510 million, and the DOJ relented, passing an official Record of Decision in March 2018 that moved the project beyond environmental review and toward construction.[16] Sylvia Ryerson and I explore this contested process further in chapter 7.

While congressional appropriations to the DOJ constitute the most direct source of funding for federal prison building, there are other streams of support that are important to acknowledge as they feed directly into what we might think of as the "reservoir" of ideas and funds for the prison. Following these streams reveals that their "currents" change over time: while they might serve to fund and legitimate the planning of the prison, including the construction of an affective scaffolding to support the project, the presumption is that once the prison is built, the streams will change direction and carry money toward other areas of the county. These flows of money and ideas are central to a broader picture of the political economy of the prison. In Letcher County, they connect local ad hoc private bodies, such as the Letcher Planning Commission, organized under the mantle of economic development, to quasi-public regional and state funding sources, such as the Kentucky River Area Development District, or KRADD.

KRADD was established in 1969 and covers eight counties across twenty-five hundred square miles, or an area larger than Delaware. Following an executive order passed in 1971, the district—again, a quasi-public agency—is the official comprehensive planning and program development agency for eastern Kentucky. At the time of the inception of local development districts, community action councils, developed during the War on Poverty, lobbied for representation on the bodies in order to ensure that poor people had an adequate voice in decision making about funding and planning. This attempt at grassroots democracy was defeated, however, and the original composition of KRADD included the judge-executives from the eight counties, the mayors from each of the eight county seats, and other citizen members selected by the judge-executives. Moreover, in 1972, the bylaws changed and allowed "major industries of the area" to place representatives on KRADD. The rise and power of KRADD, as expressed through its first comprehensive plan for the region, revealed an underlying set of assumptions that "laissez-faire economic arrangements, conventional bureaucratic structures, and middle class 'facilities and services' were assumed to be absolute necessities for a civilized social order."[17]

During this same period there were substantial allegations that the ultimate plan of bodies like KRADD, the Letcher Planning Commission, and the Appalachian Regional Commission was in fact population transfer out of eastern Kentucky, leaving behind solely a "residual maintenance population" and bringing in miner work crews but otherwise turning the region formally over to the coal industry.[18] When challenged on the veracity of these allegations, the executive director of the planning commission said, "We're not talking anything like that *at this stage*." Famed Letcher County author Harry Caudill was convinced of an even broader strategy, saying in 1972 that "depopulation was part of the Appalachian Regional Commission's scheme, not because it will benefit people but because it will clear the land for a new round of exploitation by the absentee corporations." Tom Gish, founder and editor of the Letcher County–based newspaper the *Mountain Eagle*, agreed, stating, "Make no mistake about it. The [Appalachian Regional Commission] is planning genocide in the mountains. . . . No mountain residents, no mountaineers, no mountain poverty, no problem." Just two years later, in response to Gish and his wife's trenchant reporting and activism against county corruption, including revelations of collusion between local politicians and coal executives as well as police brutality and intimidation, the offices of the *Mountain Eagle* were firebombed by a retired police officer.[19] Importantly, these bold allegations by residents and journalists were not conspiracy theories unmoored from real events, but rather would seem to be educated political analyses based on close study and scrutiny of the patterns of investment as well as official economic policy strategy, especially by the ARC.[20]

As one scholar of planning in the county argued about controversies in the 1970s, "The unmistakable smell of coal dust hangs over the planning enterprise in eastern Kentucky, and especially in Letcher County, where strip-mining and the consequent control of the county by coal companies is virtually complete. Connections between coal, politics and planning pile upon one another in wearying profusion."[21] It was not just that the coal industry instrumentalized the planning commission and development district. In addition, the composition of the different political bodies by members of the local power structure, as well as the

Figure 5.1. Mining near the proposed site for USP Letcher. Credit: Jill Frank.

Figure 5.2. Mining near the proposed site for USP Letcher. Credit: Jill Frank.

Figure 5.3. Letcher County coal. Credit: Jill Frank.

personal and business relationships between them, both created a narrow range of (self-serving) economic development projects and lubricated the process by which such projects could be approved. [22]

KRADD continues to oversee the distribution of funds to municipalities existing within the district, which includes much of eastern Kentucky. KRADD funds a variety of projects, but often within the categories of infrastructure development, extension, and maintenance as well as planning for economic development. It does so through a number of state and federal grants, including significant monies from sources familiar with local planning such as Community Development Block Grants, the Economic Development Administration, and the Appalachian Regional Commission. Of particular importance, KRADD also receives and distributes funds from something called the Coal Severance Tax.

The Coal Severance Tax began in 1972, one of the victories notched by a broad Appalachian movement for welfare rights, environmental justice, and the regulation and abolition of strip mining.[23] In Kentucky, the tax extracts a 4.5 percent fee on the gross value of coal "severed," or extracted and processed, in the state. Historically, this produced hundreds of millions of dollars in annual revenue for the state of Kentucky, with millions funneled to the coal-producing counties. But as the coal severance tax is indexed to production levels, fluctuations in production affect the amount of tax monies returned. Coal production in the state has been steadily declining since 2000, and precipitously so since 2012, due to the growth of natural gas, diminishing coal reserves, expanding renewable energy markets, the rise of the Powder River Basin in Wyoming, and environmental regulations. The decline has been especially pronounced in the eastern Kentucky coalfields, where production was down 39 percent in 2016 from just the year before (and compared to a 22 percent decline in the state's western coalfields).[24] Kentucky's coal severance money fell from $310.5 million in 2011 to $298 million in 2012 to $212 million in 2013 to $191.3 million in 2014, a 38 percent drop in just four years.[25]

Compounding the overall reduction in the amount of money returned to the state through the tax is an additional problem for coal-producing counties with respect to the fund: its method of distribution. Specifically, there is no direct or proportional dispersal of the monies back to the coalfield counties from which the coal was extracted. In fact, between 1972 and 1992, only 7.6 percent of the total amount raised by the tax—$2.7 billion—went to coal-producing counties. Half of the revenue, 50 percent, goes straight into the state's general fund. The other half is split between two funds. Fifteen percent goes to the Local Government Economic Assistance Fund (to share revenue with counties), and 35 percent is allocated to the Local Government Economic Development Fund.

The reductions in the fund and the uneven distribution across the state have impacted eastern Kentucky particularly hard. With the area already entering into crisis because of the rapid decline of coal jobs, the regression of the severance tax monies has forced eastern Kentucky counties to lay off public employees, cut programs, and fail to complete the kinds of municipal projects for which the funds have characteristically been used.[26] Adding insult to injury, the state has used the dwindling coal-severance monies in the general fund for updates to Rupp Arena, the downtown Lexington stadium that hosts major concerts, conventions, and other large-scale events, and where the University of

Kentucky basketball teams play. In 2013, $2.5 million of coal severance money went to Lexington for the Rupp Arena renovations as communities in eastern Kentucky were seeing their municipal budgets suffer because of the loss of the same monies. During that same year, for instance, Letcher County received half that same amount.[27] In 2011, Letcher County received nearly $2 million in severance-tax payments; in 2016, the county received $637,000 in tax payments, leading the county to a particularly acute fiscal crisis of a $1.3 million budget deficit. According to Jim Ward, the county's judge-executive and a member of the planning commission, the shortfall left the county without the ability to fund essential services despite having stopped "funding for five senior citizens centers and reducing contributions to fire departments, the ambulance service and sheriff's department and cutting about 90 jobs."[28] His and others' proposal to increase revenue by instituting a licensing fee on all businesses engaged in extracting nonrenewables from the county was met with intense opposition from the natural gas industry and its representatives and ultimately failed, likely paving the way for increased property taxes. Ward was also a major supporter of the prison.

Local resident Tarence Ray noted the discrepancy between local budgetary shortfalls and the overly ambitious plan for serving the prison:

> The Letcher County Fiscal Court is financially broke. It has very little resources or money to devote to the prison: save a potential grant or two from the ARC, it certainly won't have the money to construct a sewage treatment facility at Roxana [the site ultimately chosen for the prison], much less maintain it over time. The Letcher County Water and Sewage District is unprepared to service the prison facility. The LCWSD accrued 22 Safe Drinking Water Act violations in 2015. This is much higher than many other parts of the state.

As one state representative who represents Letcher County observed, "It's a tough time to be in a small community that has relied for so many years on coal for its main economic driver.... They're cutting everything. We have laid off employees. Road maintenance, garbage service, water. Everything."[29] Other counties home to prisons and traditionally reliant on coal-severance-tax monies for revenue experienced similar crises. In Martin County, the use of coal severance money in the late

1990s and early 2000s for projects like an office park, government building upgrades, and infrastructure extension to attract USP Big Sandy directly took money out of updating the water treatment plant, the deterioration of which has contributed to the county's severe water crisis, detailed in chapters 1 and 2.[30] In early 2019, Martin County's sheriff announced that he would temporarily cease law enforcement services for the county because the budgetary shortfalls meant they could not pay their employees.[31] Martin County's annual revenue from the coal severance tax had declined by more than 80 percent just since 2012.[32]

What do declining coal-severance-tax revenues and contracting state and municipal budgets have to do with plans to build a prison? How does the flow of the money impact the planning process for the prison? A variety of official and semi-official documents, including KRADD's annual comprehensive economic plans, multiple iterations of the Bureau of Prison's (BOP) environmental impact studies, conducted as part of the National Environmental Policy Act (NEPA) process, and official notes kept and exchanged during early meetings between different officials, all reveal telling overtures from both KRADD and the Planning Commission to the BOP as well as the ways in which the growing prospect of the prison guided municipal planning decisions. The maneuvers of these bodies implicate the lingering influence of the coal industry in continuing to affect economic and social policy decisions in the region. Moreover, they illuminate that a federal prison, while financed and operated by the highest levels of the federal government, nonetheless relies on state and local municipal bodies, intertwined with private companies and private individuals, to perform the ideological, financial, and infrastructural work necessary to realize the project.[33]

The BOP retained Cardno, an Australia-based infrastructure and environmental services company, in order to conduct an Enhanced Utility Investigation Report and prepare the Environmental Impact Statement for USP Letcher as required under NEPA. But Cardno was only the latest in a series of companies to be engaged by the BOP to consult on infrastructure, engineering, and environment for the Letcher County prison.[34] These actors engage in a variety of national and international projects and at first glance might not figure into an analysis of prison expansion. But their work to assess and analyze the suitability of sites for prison construction and the adaptability of utilities to the large strain such a facility would pose on a rural county's infrastructure is essential to the credibility of the prison.

Members of the Letcher Planning Commission and other county executives met with representatives of the BOP and Cardno (then known as TEC Inc.) in the spring of 2011, a full seven years before the BOP would officially render its Record of Decision. Official notes from that meeting reveal important details of the courtship between the county and the BOP. At that moment in the history of the prison project, four sites remained under consideration within the county, including one, Meadow Branch, that was on the border with Virginia. Had it been chosen as the prison site, USP Letcher would have been serviced by Pound, Virginia, already home to Red Onion State Prison. Presumably as part of their pitch for the prison to be serviced by Letcher County, "Judge Ward and the Director of Letcher Co. Water and Sewer stated several times that water and sewer service would be extended to [Roxana, Van Fields, or Payne Gap, the sites that would be serviced by Letcher County] if one of those sites was selected." Moreover, the notes from the meetings observe that:

- The Whitesburg WWTP [waste water treatment plant] was recently upgraded, partly in anticipation of the BOP project, to handle 630,000 [GPD—gallons per day] and is currently receiving approximately half of the capacity. The plant was designed to be upgraded with additional modules to nearly 1,000,000 GPD.
- The County is considering providing a dedicated sanitary line and system for the facility
- Letcher County would prefer to know which site is preferred so they could focus their effort towards that location.
- The county does not have commercial rates, only residential, the connection fees are minimal and may be waived for the project.
- Mayor Wylie reiterated the planning commission's and Judge Ward's sentiments regarding provision of service to the selected site.[35]

Other official documents corroborate what federal officials heard from the Planning Commission. First, beginning in 2012–13, KRADD's annual Comprehensive Economic Development Strategy included planning for infrastructure for USP Letcher, just as the BOP would begin its formal scoping and environmental review process.[36] In the BOP's Revised Final Environmental Impact Study, released years later in 2016, the agency applauded the planning, noting that because of such foresight, "there is ample capacity to handle the flow from [Roxana], as wastewater flow from the proposed prison was incorporated into the design of the plant. The existing plant was designed to accommodate expansion in the future. The [waste water treatment plant] site was selected for its ample space for expansion. The timing of the future sewer projects and future planning for expansion of the Whitesburg WWTP would minimize the cumulative impacts of [Roxana]."[37]

At that point in the process, the site selection had been narrowed down to Roxana and Payne Gap, a small area on the other side of the county from Roxana. Not to be outdone, members of the governing body of Jenkins, the small town adjacent to the Payne Gap site, wrote in to the BOP to express their strong preference for their site, noting in their pitch that "we would expect City utility services to be extended to the Prison. Our water and sewer capacity should be more than adequate to meet the Prison needs. We already provide water to the Payne Gap area. Our Police and Fire Department are only a few miles away. Locale likewise benefits our site as it is a mere five miles to the Virginia state line."[38]

The Cardno report further illuminates some of the microeconomic processes at work in the county. The document notes that at the remaining sites under consideration for the prison, the wastewater utility had indicated its intentions to extend existing systems to the prison. Similarly, American Electric Power, the power company servicing both sites, indicated no costs to the BOP for connecting to the grid at either site. Tellingly, Cardno noted that at the Roxana site, the BOP would need to spend approximately $12.8 million to close multiple natural gas wells.[39]

These mundane county processes speak to the broader politics and economies of prison siting. In offering to pay for utilities extensions and in reminding federal officials that some infrastructural preparation was already underway in anticipation of the prison, the record shows all-out YIMBY-ism, including competition between very small communities within the same small rural county and the prominence of the prison in guiding and even enabling certain updates and projects.[40] Notably, waste plays an important role in these processes. KRADD's funding of the wastewater treatment plant expansion was one of the earliest concrete signs that the county was positioning itself for the prison long before the BOP's official Record of Decision. Keeping in mind that the Roxana site was subjected to mountaintop removal in the 1980s, the gas wells currently on the site signal both an additional layer of extraction and its dialectical nature. As the next iteration of development presented itself—the prison—the wells became an impediment to "progress." They became waste, in need of elimination.

The overtures by local officials to federal agencies are notable because they indicate complex operations of, and interactions between, the state at different scales. First, the appeals from local officials to the federal government are important because the prison was first raised as a possibility for Letcher County by the office of Hal Rogers, the region's representative in the United States Congress. That is, it was an office of the federal government that initiated the process of siting USP Letcher even as local officials would later lobby for the prison. Second, at both the local and federal scale, a collection of private actors helped to shape the contours of what was possible, from funneling money to the project to conducting on-site analysis to writing the assessment for the BOP to lobbying as part of a quasi-public entity. The labor of prison siting suggests that our analytical terms—the carceral state, the prison industrial complex, etc.—must be capacious in order to capture the state and private actors, agencies, and other entities whose rather banal collaborations actively remake and reorganize state power. In at least some cases, these actors are responding to the shifting ground, quite literally, occurring in their communities and look to the prison in order "to set the stage for ordinary working people to accept extraordinary measures in hope of securing livelihoods."[41] These efforts and collaborations suggest that the prison is not foundationally a form of profit-making tied, like slavery, to commodified human beings, but rather a racialized mechanism for managing, and altering, the conditions of profit *outside* the prison.[42] In these instances, prison building is not necessarily nefarious, it is even worse: it is insidiously quotidian.

The Work of Ideology

dominant ideological scaffolding for the prison consisted of claims jobs and economic development, a discourse that tried to evacuate

PLANNING THE PRISON | 171

Thank You

Thank you for Attending the Public Scoping Meeting Environmental Impact Statement For the Federal Bureau of Prisons

JOBS   JOBS   JOBS

SUPPORT THE LETCHER

PRISON PROJECT

Figure 5.4. Back page of the document distributed to attendees of the BOP's public scoping meeting, Letcher County, KY.

any meaning from the Roxana land outside of coal and incarceration. The historical, current, and projected uses for the site, as outlined by several people in chapter 1 and which included everything from hosting major community events to being a prime location for hunting, foraging, and recreation to potentially serving as a site for any number of other economic-development possibilities, were outside of the official discourse of "jobs, jobs, jobs."

What makes the widespread (although contested) success of this narrative particularly interesting is its contradiction by both national and regional data. Compelling sociological work has shown that prison building has both mixed economic results generally and negative ones specifically when the host county is already economically distressed.[43]

The evidence is convincing enough that, upon receipt of comments from sociologists submitted to the Environmental Impact Study report during the NEPA process, the Bureau of Prisons was forced to admit that the prison would not provide the kind of economic development that the agency had been boasting of for years. The BOP explicitly acknowledged the data that effectively rendered its earlier claims dubious at best: "The Bureau analyzed the effect of development of the proposed USP and FPC on the local (county level) economy and presented its conclusions in the 2016 Revised Final Environmental Impact Statement (Sections 4.3 and 5.3). The Bureau concluded that implementation . . . would have minor beneficial economic impact in terms of employment, income, and population trends. *However, the Bureau recognizes recent studies indicate no correlation between prison development and long-term economic growth*" (my emphasis).[44]

But eleventh-hour admissions by the BOP (and confined to the appendices of their report) do not offset more than two decades of investment in the logic of rural economic development through prison building in the region. Moreover, in the final iteration of the agency's EIS report, the Final Supplemental Revised Final Environmental Impact Statement (FSRFEIS), the BOP reverted back to its own reliable account of the prison's economic effects: "It is anticipated that . . . construction and operation of the proposed USP and FPC would generate economic productivity in terms of new construction jobs, new payrolls, induced personal income, purchasing of materials, supplies, and services, and potential purchasing of new homes by Bureau staff once the facility opens. The economic viability of the Letcher County, Kentucky region would experience long-term benefits by virtue of the approximately 300 new permanent jobs that would need to be filled at the USP and FPC."[45] The narrative of prisons as rural economic development moved across scale and space. Originating from the BOP and US Representative Hal Rogers, the narrative was circulated among area residents by regional and local officials and their organizational bodies like KRADD and the planning commission. The predominance of that account and its cut against the grain of the data reveals the important ideological struggle at work to naturalize the prison into the commonsense vision of the future of the county.[46] Importantly, the circulation of the narrative was wide enough that it reached major national media outlets, already primed for stories about the region in the scramble for explanations of the relative success of Donald Trump among the so-called white working class.

In 2018, just days before the Bureau of Prisons signed the Record of Decision, which officially propelled the prison project forward from the siting process, *NBC News* published an article about the prospect of USP Letcher titled "Does American Need Another Prison? It May Be This Rural County's Only Chance at Survival."[47] The story, including an embedded video, chronicled the hopes of some Letcher County residents that the prison could resurrect their community. The story's narrative arc positioned the prison as the key, however imperfect, to the recovery and revitalization of the community. The six-minute-long video allotted a total of nine seconds to mention that data on the economic impact of prison building is disputable and that some residents opposed the prison and were organizing against it. This token coverage of both empirical data and local opposition conveyed near-universal support, set within a kind of redemption narrative of the prison as the sole and rational choice for Letcher County. Because the story appeared on NBC News' website, the analysis was oriented toward a national audience even as its appearance on the site granted legitimacy to local officials' claims about the prison.

In her book, *What You Are Getting Wrong about Appalachia*, the historian Elizabeth Catte names the most recent trend of reporting on Appalachia as the "Trump Country" genre.[48] Such pieces, Catte argues, rely on representations of dysfunction and disaffection in Appalachia to explain the 2016 election of Donald Trump. This reporting often ignores strikingly germane pieces of information in order to work within the genre, including the fact that the median income of Trump voters was over seventy thousand dollars a year, or more than twice the median income of most counties in eastern Kentucky, as well as the long legacies and contemporary manifestations of an Appalachian radical tradition.[49] "Trump Country" pieces hinge on a particular narrative of the hope Trump symbolized amidst economic devastation. In the NBC News coverage of USP Letcher, the prison stands in for the president and symbolizes promise and redemption for the struggling region.

Such coverage ignores the sociological data mentioned above, which, if included, would undermine the very foundational claims made by prison boosters. Moreover, surrounding eastern Kentucky communitie that now host prisons provide an instructive lesson on the dubious promises of economic development. Hal Rogers worked to bring federal prisons to Clay, Martin, and McCreary counties in Kentucky in 1992, 2003, and 2004, respectively.[50] Today, they remain three of the poorest counties in one of the nation's poorest congressional districts in the United States. According to the US Census Bureau's 2016 estimates, over 39 percent of the population in each county lives below the poverty line, over triple the national average of 12.7 percent. Furthermore, the closing of Otter Creek Correctional Center in Wheelwright, in neighboring Floyd County, as well as the closing of rural prisons in other states like New York, explodes the myth often circulated by boosters that prisons are a "recession-proof" industry. But such concrete examples of the failures of prisons to stimulate rural economies are often no match for a well-crafted narrative that, after almost fifteen years in the making just in Letcher County, travels rather freely and independently from the people and offices from which it originated.

Federal support for the prison's economic benefit to the region came from other areas of the government besides the BOP. Letcher County is one of eight southeastern Kentucky counties that, along with the Kentucky Highlands Investment Corporation, formed the first rural Promise Zone as designated by President Barack Obama in early 2014. The broad mission of the Promise Zone was to bring needed economic and community development to high-poverty regions. As the president of the KHIC noted of USP Letcher,

> The Correction Facility fits into our Strategic Vision [of providing economic opportunities and developing workforces]. The Promise Zone designation can leverage the economic impact of the Correctional Facility. The designation comes with prioritization on certain federal grants, free technical support and possibly future tax credits. With these tools, entrepreneurs can provided [sic] the ancillary and support services necessary to support the Correction Facility, as well as any relocating personnel.... It is our strongest desire that the Bureau of Prisons add the Promise Zone designation to its list to justify the facility in this location.[51]

There are a few notable elements from this testimony. First, the prison's role in economic development is unquestioned; the data that counter this claim directly, as well as the ways in which prisons actually portend the "jobless future" for those they incarcerate, are excised in order to maintain the credibility of the narrative.[52] Second, in its ability to extend a certain kind of economic development through grants, technical assistance, and tax breaks, the Promise Zone designation installs a perverse incentive structure for prison building. Following this logic, not only might building prisons create jobs and stimulate surrounding economic development, but also it can trigger other funding streams that could amplify these economic effects. This is an important indication not only of the state's reorganization behind and through prison building but also of how prisons become accepted into the logics and operations of other agencies and initiatives, mobilizing needed resources and infrastructure whose capacities might otherwise be idled or directed elsewhere were it not for the carceral stimulus.

In one example, in late 2018, officials successfully secured $4.5 million of grant funding from the Abandoned Mine Lands (AML) Pilot Grants program for both the construction of a sewage plant and the extension of nine miles of water lines to the Roxana site in anticipation of USP Letcher. The AML fund, the product of years of organizing and lobbying by activists, is intended to support projects that assist in transitioning the region away from coal and that offer environmental remediation. But the application language for the funds is vague, and the water line extensions would also result in connecting one hundred additional residents to city water.[53] The aging infrastructure, polluted ground water, and needed extensions were not enough, on their own, to qualify for the funds. It was only when those needs could be grafted onto the prospect of the prison that the state was able to apply for and secure the funding.

The testimony from KHIC's president points toward the network of ideological support for USP Letcher that buttressed the project's more vociferous and visible supporters. This network can be partially seen through examining the record of comments on the prison. In submissions to the BOP during the public comment period on the various iterations of the Environmental Impact Study, many people offered their support and listed their places of employment or affiliation. Looking at expressions of support alongside the respective affiliation implicates the power of the narrative and the places from which it likely received important enhancements.

The language of support was considerably uniform, and in numerous cases it was clear that groups of people had coordinated their commentaries. Many comments from unaffiliated individuals simply said, "support—jobs." Others offering expanded commentary relied on planning commission and BOP talking points: jobs, economic development, and recession-proof stability. A number of people from Jeremiah, a small community in Letcher County, all wrote the line, "Total support from everyone in our area."

Other comments were notable because of who authored them. Members of KRADD and the planning commission, for example, noted their affiliations with those organizations in their support of the prison; a member of the Big Sandy Development District, which includes Martin County, also expressed support.[54] Then-governor Steve Beshear expressed his "full support" on the Draft Environmental Impact Study, writing in a letter that in addition to alleviating overcrowding, the prison would bring three hundred much-needed jobs to eastern Kentucky, "which would have a significant, positive impact on the economy of Letcher County and surrounding counties."[55] Someone who did not include their name but who listed their occupation as "Justice, Kentucky Supreme Court" noted, "The community would be very supportive and we need the jobs."[56] Another comment read, "I strongly support moving forward with the USP/FPC in Letcher County, KY. The placement of the facility here will provide a much-needed boost to the local economy and the FBOP has repeatedly proven to be a consciensious [sic] and desirable community neighbor." The person who offered this comment listed their affiliation as GRW Engineers/Architects/Planners, a company that is based in Lexington, and for which the person served as vice president. Among other projects, the company also builds prisons. Likewise, a member of the Kentucky Laborers District Council based in Lawrenceburg, which is further west of Lexington, commented, "We have been involved in the construction of several prisons with excellent results. We have found it is great for the local economy."[57]

It was not only people who might stand to benefit from planning and construction jobs who offered supportive comments that spoke to the prison's perceived importance to the local economy. One enthusiastic supporter who worked as a respiratory therapist in a clinic located in the county seat of Whitesburg noted, "This county needs this prison. It will provide many jobs to the citizens in our county and surrounding counties. This will be great for the laid off coal miners and oil and gas workers. This prison will benefit the Whitesburg Appalachian Regional Healthcare and Daniel Boone clinic, my workplace."

The support for the prison from healthcare workers in particular was overwhelming. This likely reflected the potential they saw in the prison to provide a new and reliable client base amidst the long decline in funding for rural healthcare, including hospitals. In Kentucky, research reveals considerable, if varying, financial stress and risk of closure for rural hospitals, with at least one report indicating that up to half of rural hospitals in the state are in poor financial health and another report noting that a quarter of rural hospitals are at high risk of closing.[58] There are complex financial reasons for this crisis in rural health care, but almost all of them are due to financial cuts from the federal government, including some consequences of the Affordable Care Act, the healthcare reform law enacted under the Obama administration in 2010. While the ACA had considerable successes in Kentucky, reducing the number of uninsured residents by 50 percent, it also reduced reimbursement payments to hospitals.[59] All told, these and other reductions amount to an expected $7 billion in federal cuts to Kentucky hospitals from 2010 through 2024, the brunt of which will impact rural hospitals particularly hard. These cuts reveal telling configurations of state power, as they actively threaten rural health care—the existence of which in eastern Kentucky is the product of women's struggle and organizing—at the expense, quite literally, of funding a federal prison.[60] In this scenario, the prison acts as both the location of federal investment and the perverse conduit through which the federal government (inadequately) subsidizes the hospitals.

But the support from healthcare workers may also have been due, in part, to direct pressure from planning commission members on others to express their support for the prison project. There was a large representation of people from certain local groups in the public comments, including from healthcare and education sectors. Multiple people had told me of the influence of the CEO of Mountain Comprehensive Health Corporation, who was also a member of the Letcher Planning Commission. Perhaps unsurprisingly, there were numerous comments from people who listed their affiliation as MCHC. Of the 113 individual comments (that is, those that were not made through a form letter or form email) expressing support for the prison in the Final Revised Environmental Impact Statement, thirty-one were from people who listed their organizational affiliation, that is, their employer, as MCHC. By comparison, there were just two MCHC employees who wrote in opposition to the prison and did so anonymously. The CEO himself offered a comment, and a bit of a cheap shot at local opposition, saying, "I fully support the construction and operation of a maximum-security prison in Letcher County at Roxana, KY. The project is universally supported by the residents of Letcher County. There are only a few that are in opposition and they are opposed to the building of prisons anywhere, not in opposition to this project more so than anywhere else." It is possible that his support, and his central role on the planning commission, had a strong influence on the turnout and opinions of his employees.

The dismissal of opposition expressed what appeared to be a coherent and at times successful strategy among supporters of the prison. Supporters often downplayed dissent, likely in order to assuage any concerns from the BOP that the siting and construction process would be met with resistance. When they did acknowledge opposition, they dismissed it as the work of outsiders and those "opposed to prisons anywhere," two tropes—the radical and the outsider—with a long history in the region and thus readily available for grafting onto various tensions.[61] Downplaying dissent at times translated into coverage of the issue, as in the NBC News story and its minimal discussion of opposition.

The volume, scope, and precision of oppositional comments expressed during the NEPA process would seem to contradict the sentiments from members of the planning commission and other boosters. I had been surprised by the presence of oppositional comments during my casual reviews of the various Environmental Impact Study documents during my research and decided to examine their prevalence more systematically. I conducted basic coding and counting of comments to the BOP on the Supplemental Revised Final Environmental Impact Statement, where I assigned a rating of either "approval," "against," or "expressed concerns" based on their content. Of the individual comments submitted to the BOP, there were 113 that expressed support for the prison proposal. There were 74 individual comments that explicitly expressed opposition to the prison and 62 more that expressed significant concerns and/or advocated for continued study before a decision was made. Combining those categories means that of the individual comments submitted directly to the BOP, 113 advocated building the prison and 136 expressed opposition or concern, which clearly contradicts assertions of near consensus for the prison. Moreover, while people from as far away as Massachusetts, Oregon, and Florida wrote in to submit comments against the prison, there were also numerous comments from local or regional residents opposing or cautioning against moving forward. Finally, looking beyond the personal comments and toward the form letters submitted revealed a much wider gulf between support and opposition. In addition to the 113 individual comments submitted in favor of the prison, there were 326 form letters and 28 names attached to a petition expressing support for USP Letcher. In contrast, *there were 6,489 form emails submitted to the BOP against the proposal.* In fact, according to Panagioti Tsolkas, the coordinator of the Prison Ecology Project, an organization that was central to the environmental challenges to the prison, the official record shows that more than 20,000 individual comments were submitted against the prison during the entire NEPA process, in addition to expert testimonies and form letters with hundreds of signatures.[62]

As this chapter and the next demonstrate, the prison was central to local strategies of economic development, revenue generation, infrastructure maintenance, and visions for the future. The purported elasticity of the prison to address all of these areas was manufactured over time by regional and local planning and development bodies, state and federal agencies, and even the coal industry, a collaboration that attempted to address various crises through a renovation of economic, cultural, and political life. The process of integrating prisons and jails into the everyday operations of the county and the visions of its residents reveals "not just the persistence of oppression, but also the modes and terms through which the 'common' in 'common sense' changes through struggle and compromise."[63] This approach has succeeded in other counties—in the sense that the prisons were built—even if the crises have not abated, and in some cases have worsened. But the existence of opposition in Letcher County, as we have begun to explore in the archive created by the NEPA process, shows that the ideological hold of the prison was incomplete. In fact, as chapter 7 will argue, it was the interventionist work of local organizers and landowners as well as national activists that disrupted what had been a dominant narrative about the prison in the county, and that eventually weakened the prison's grip on the community and defeated the plan for its construction.

6

"To Bring a Future and Hope to Our Children"

Renovating Education, Identity, and Work

If, in order to understand the prison fix, we must develop complex understandings of how prisoners became so massively available as carceral subjects, we must likewise figure out how the ground the prisons stand on becomes available for such a purpose. In both contexts, changing relations of power and belongingness, mixed with uneven capacities for mobility (another way to think about political economy in an everyday way) set the stage for ordinary working people to accept extraordinary measures in hope of securing livelihoods.
—Ruth Wilson Gilmore, *Golden Gulag*

Coal jobs have been declining in Central Appalachia since 1950. In Kentucky, employment in coal mines peaked in 1949 when there were 75,707 miners in the state and over 120,000 miners were employed in the region. By contrast, in 2016, there were 52,110 people employed by the coal industry in *the entire United States*, including fewer than 15,000 in Central Appalachia. In Kentucky, the number is at its lowest since the nineteenth century: there are 3,760 existing coal jobs in the state, down 38 percent from just the year before.[1] In the language of labor, value, and waste, these developments have rendered a large portion of the Appalachian population superfluous, or "humans relegated as the waste necessary for continued capital accumulation."[2]

Incarceration resolves this potential crisis in two ways. First, following recent research from the Vera Institute of Justice, there are significant increases in the number of people from rural communities entering jail and prison. In fact, Vera's report reveals that more people are incarcerated in rural jails in the United States than in urban jails, reflective of rising incarceration rates in rural America and declining incarceration rates in many big cities. In the United States in 2019, there were 166,979 people incarcerated in urban jails, a decrease of 36,000 people, or 18 percent, since 2013. By contrast, rural jails in 2019 had 184,295 people incarcerated within them, an increase of 39,000 people since 2013, or 27 percent.[3] As eastern Kentucky communities expand their jail capacities in order to incarcerate people for state and federal agencies as a revenue strategy, there will be substantial new bed space that may also ensnare growing numbers of local people.[4] Incarceration, then, sits as the ultimate solution for rural communities home to segments of the relative surplus population and increasingly subject to criminalization.

Second, in the assurances about the prison as a tool of economic development is an implicit promise of stabilization, largely through offering the potential of wage labor to a population that sits on the edge of, or actively experiences, economic precarity. In an instructive development, the number of correctional officer jobs in Kentucky has grown to 6,640, *eclipsing by the thousands* the 3,760 remaining coal-mining positions left in the state. In eastern Kentucky specifically, there are now 1,490 COs and just over 2,200 people employed by the mining industry there, a number that includes miners, plant workers, and office staff.[5]

One indication of the significance of this economic transition is the fact that multiple regional school systems have reorganized curricula and programs to try to prepare a new generation of workers for jobs in the prison economy. In anticipation of USP Letcher and in response to the surrounding carceral geography, local community colleges, vocational schools, and regional public universities have attempted to develop and implement new criminal justice tracks and degrees. These shifting educational priorities reveal the success of the prison economy in impacting the way residents imagine and prepare for a future in the county.

Significant changes to regional educational curricula and programming in anticipation of USP Letcher began in earnest just as the Bureau of Prisons began the scoping and siting period. In 2012–2013, the local vocational school, the Letcher County Area Technology Center (LCATC), pursued a Criminal Justice and Law track. The local newspaper, the *Mountain Eagle*, quoted the assistant superintendent for the county (who also served as a member of the Letcher Planning Commission) as noting that the new program, which included a mock courtroom and a firing range in addition to new classroom space, was necessary because "2,559 criminal justice–related positions now exist within a 40-mile radius of Letcher County, and more positions are expected to be created with the opening of a federal prison planned for Letcher County."[6] A county Board of Education member concurred, noting, "It's a program that we really need. Our kids can benefit from it. If and when a federal prison comes in kids will have a leg up of having a few courses there."[7] The development of the program was an early indication of the growing alignment in the county around the prison. The county was able to pursue the new program because of a grant from the coal industry. In late 2012, Kentucky River Properties LLC, a mineral holding company that leases coal-bearing properties to coal-mine operators in exchange for royalty payments, awarded forty thousand dollars to the Letcher County school district to help fund the new program.[8] In addition, drafting students from the school designed the classroom, courtroom, and firing range spaces. Moreover, the county secured an agreement from Eastern Kentucky University for the LCATC students to receive dual credit.[9]

During the siting and scoping process, various actors testified to the importance of the prison for students as well as for educational systems. Before the BOP had decided on the Roxana site for USP Letcher, the agency entertained six different location possibilities, eventually narrowing the choice to the areas of Roxana and Payne Gap. The intracounty competition between jurisdictions that played out through overtures about infrastructure described in chapter 5 also occurred on the terrain of education. In the public comments offered during early iterations of the Environmental Impact Studies conducted during the NEPA process, a number of people who identified themselves as employees of the Jenkins Independent School District, including the superintendent, offered strong support for the prison to be built at the Payne Gap site, which would be served by the Jenkins municipality. One characteristic comment argued that "[the prison at Payne Gap] would help to bring in additional students for our school system and jobs for dislocated/unemployed miners."[10] There were several other comments that were almost identical. One teacher from the county put it this way: "Our county really needs this. The enrollment in all of our schools really needs a boost. This opportunity is perfect for our school system, employment of others in the county and would also give families an opportunity to come back to a community with more promising job opportunities."[11] A program coordinator at the Hazard Community and Technical College also invoked the prison's provision of "a job market for young people" in his endorsement. Another unaffiliated writer offered a similar sentiment when saying that the prison might bring family back to the area that have moved away while also noting, "Our children would be able to stay here because of more job opportunity."

Students themselves testified to the important link between higher education degrees in criminal justice and the prospect of work in the prison. A local criminal justice student at the community and technical college argued in a comment submitted to the Bureau of Prisons that the prison would "bring a whole new atmosphere" to the county. She continued,

> Eastern Kentucky University has agreed to allow criminal justice students to achieve a Bachelor's degree at Southeast Community College and are in talks to allow a Master's degree there. This is the perfect combination for our future generations to change the trajectory of their lives! To bring a future and a hope to our children. The construction jobs would allow financial independence for a lot of the coal miners that have lost their jobs. We have many hard working, God fearing, men and women in this area that really need this opportunity to support themselves and their families.... With this opportunity, our community could produce a whole new generation of law enforcement in many different fields.[12]

Even elementary schools in Letcher County officially advocated for the prison. One school posted to its Facebook page, which has more than a thousand followers, the following message during the final stages of the NEPA process:

> The Federal Bureau of Prisons has prepared a Draft Supplemental Revised Final Environmental Impact Statement for the proposed prison to be located in Letcher County. As part of the process, there will be another public meeting on April 12, 2017 from 5:30 p.m. to 8:00 p.m. at Letcher

County Central High School. You are encouraged to drop by the meeting to show your support for this project. This prison will not only help the citizens of Letcher County, but it will positively impact our school system. We are closer than we have ever been but we need this final push to make it happen. We need a large showing of support to help ensure success, so please stop by for a few minutes.

This post stood in sharp contrast to the rest of the school's social media page, which was otherwise characterized by reminders to parents about spring break and student picture day.

The prison loomed large in these accounts. Districts hoped that the prison would boost their enrollments, while high schools, vocational schools, and universities developed and implemented programs to prepare students for work in the carceral economy. In turn, students invested an optimism and a sense of futurity in the prison. This testifies to the significance of the prison not only to the economic vision of the county but also to its powerful operation in the realm of culture. The prison, in other words, "is felt, subjectively, as a profound process of learning: it is the organization of the self in relation to the future."[13]

Researchers have recorded similar patterns and testimonies in other parts of Central Appalachia where rural communities have sited and built prisons.[14] As the scholar Sylvia Ryerson discovered during her research in eastern Kentucky, Martin County officials working in the late 1990s to site USP Big Sandy harnessed concerns about the future for young people in the region and attached them to the promises of employment in the Bureau of Prisons if they were successful in building the prison.[15] During a visit to the county in 1996, the chief of site selection for the BOP met with educators and local officials to discuss preparations for a correctional workforce. He advocated for the implementation of "curricula dealing with law enforcement or corrections" for "students, especially those at the high school level," noting the importance of planting early seeds of interest before students arrived at universities where they could then pursue criminology and criminal justice degrees.[16]

A similar message was conveyed directly to young people two years later when Martin County officials invited employees from Federal Correctional Institution (FCI) Manchester, in Clay County, to address local high school students. The BOP employees implored Martin County students to begin laying the foundation for jobs at the prison, years before the facility would even open. As Ryerson describes, one of the officials from FCI Manchester told the students that in order to prepare for the coming prison jobs, they "can't get in any type of trouble with the authorities or involved in drug use," should participate in "volunteer work or community-based activity," and ultimately should plan to "work on taking college courses in law enforcement or criminology."[17] The advice here approximates the logic of the infamous Scared Straight approach to juvenile delinquency, except its deployment is designed to coerce young people's law abidance in order to *enter*, rather than *avoid*, the prison. The advice from the BOP employee reveals the distinctiveness of the prison from other forms of work and economic development. For teenagers hoping to stay in their home communities, they must first and foremost obey the law. Moreover, the BOP employee told them, volunteer work is instrumental: it increases their chances of obtaining formal work in the prison. Finally, students were encouraged to pursue the education that would underwrite their credibility for employment with the Federal Bureau of Prisons: a degree in criminology or criminal justice.[18]

The prison's role as a central strategy not only for economic development but also for broad attempts at social reproduction is revealing for the value elites place on the kinds of experiences available for residents of low-income communities, particularly children.[19] This calculation about the prison as the best investment in and plan for a future for the children of the region is particularly troublesome when considered against the data about whether prisons actually bring rural jobs to local residents. Significant work nationally and in Central Appalachia has shown that prison jobs do not necessarily go to local residents.[20] This occurs for a number of reasons. First, some applicants may not be able to pass credit and criminal background checks. Second, the BOP has certain requirements regarding minimum level of education as well as minimum age requirements. At the time when USP Big Sandy was built, for example, only 6 percent of Martin County residents had a bachelor's degree.[21] Third, the BOP often transfers employees between institutions.

This has occurred in eastern Kentucky communities with prisons even when school districts have developed educational opportunities to prepare a local workforce for the new carceral economy. Ryerson noted in 2010 that the judge-executive of McCreary County, Kentucky, reported that after five years of operation, USP McCreary did not employ more than twenty-five to thirty local people, despite having more than three hundred employees in total.[22] In Martin County, the coordinator of the Big Sandy Community and Technical College's (BSCTC) criminal justice program admitted that while 250 students had graduated over the decade that the program had been in existence, no more than ten to fifteen had acquired jobs at USP Big Sandy. Graduates who wished to work in prisons typically had to leave the area.[23] Crucially, and in anticipation of USP Letcher's opening, BSCTC would announce in 2018 a partnership with Eastern Kentucky University to offer four-year degrees in criminal justice. The director of college relations noted in the college's press release, "In addition to the federal penitentiary in Martin County, we have federal facilities in Ashland and Manchester, as well as a facility set to be constructed in Letcher County.... These programs will allow students to earn the credentials needed to have a rewarding career in law enforcement, corrections and support agencies."[24]

Despite the pattern of prison jobs often circumventing local residents, Letcher County residents saw the prison as key to the future viability of the county, even beyond its perceived role in stimulating new job growth. A director of a local community center expressed her support for the prison through the hope that the BOP might be able to offer financial support for the center and the nascent theater program housed there.[25] A current BOP employee who lives in Harlan County, Kentucky, and commutes more than an hour each way to his job at USP Lee in southwestern Virginia described the broad impact USP Letcher would have, including

> new careers with great benefits, local business with more income.... [The] local housing market will prosper.... Local schools will have more students and with more students comes a better budget and better opportunities for learning. Local hospitals will be able to sign contracts with the prison to provide care for prison staff members and inmates in the occurrence of an emergency. Also prospering will be the local police force, fire departments, EMS that also will be offered contracts by the BOP in the need of an emergency situation.[26]

A member of the Letcher County Chamber of Commerce wrote to the BOP of her "100% support" for the prison, noting, "We are having families have to be separated for the husband to find work. Worse than that we have had families have to leave the area permanently. This affects every business and school. We need 'hope' for our families and our schools and businesses. . . . You will be very welcome here. Let us show you our southern hospitality and give us the opportunity to save our county and provide jobs for our family."[27]

A particularly comprehensive and consequential statement about the broad effects USP Letcher would have on the county came from the *Mountain Eagle* when the newspaper officially endorsed the prison in 2013. The newspaper's trenchant reporting and political stances in the 1970s had put it in the crosshairs of the coal companies; readers might remember that its offices were firebombed after the paper reported about corruption, collusion, and police brutality. But decades later and experiencing circulation declines and revenue loss, the paper also looked to the prison as a possible solution for its own problems as well as the county's broader crises:

> The average pay for a Bureau of Prisons employee has jumped to about $65,000 annually since the local group first discussed the idea of a prison as a source of new jobs. In addition to the good pay offered, prospective prison employees would have to be 38 years or younger, meaning the families of those who are hired would remain in the area for a number of years. As a result, student populations in local school systems would grow, as would the local economy. Prison workers would eat at local restaurants, shop at local stores, and be treated at local healthcare facilities. For the prison to work, scores of other workers would also have to be involved—construction workers, electricians, doctors, dentists, . . . groundskeepers, etc. If we ever had any reservations about the thought of having to depend on a prison to provide well-paying jobs here, those reservations have been erased after watching the damaging effect the loss of about 200-plus well-paying coal jobs has done to the local economy over the last few months.[28]

In all of these testimonies, the prison provides more than just immediate relief in the form of jobs. Rather, the prison signals an enduring and extensive investment in the stability of the community, from producing the next generation of workers to bringing more students to schools, patients to healthcare facilities, support to social services, and updates and expansions to infrastructure. The prison's centrality to the survivability or resurgence of families, schools, hospitals, community centers, and small businesses reveals it to be both a site of "production," or work, and crucial to social reproduction—"the fleshy, messy, and indeterminate stuff of everyday life"—across scales of household, community, and county.[29] It is exploring the racialized and gendered contours and consequences of prison-based work and social reproduction to which this chapter now turns.

Racialized and Gendered "Dirty Work"

The efforts to attract and build USP Letcher were bound tightly to work. As this book has established, the collapse of the coal industry has generated a very real need for work, and prison supporters consistently invoked the jobs that the prison would offer. But in addition to evaluating the dubious claims about the number of positions that the prison might provide, it is also important to consider the functions and consequences of such jobs in and outside of the facility. In other words, we must explore the material and symbolic significance of work in the carceral economy being positioned to replace work in the coal industry.

Returning briefly to a consideration of waste as it functions within racial capitalism helps to unpack the significance. Some scholarship on waste and work suggests that we understand both the populations residing in prisons and the populations guarding them as operating within the logic of disposal and disposability. Writing of the category of what they call "officially valued labor," Collard and Dempsey argue that "there are clearly also huge variances within the waged category, with some workers far freer than others, far more valued . . . and despite being crucial for value production many are still often entirely disposable, wasted and expended."[30] Michelle Yates concurs, writing, "Those who still have access to wage labor are also embedded in a logic of disposability. The body of the laborer is used up or wasted at accelerated rates in order to secure the most profit. Those who have work could easily be disposed of and end up as part of the permanent surplus population as well."[31]

Similarly, Nancy Isenberg argues, "Modern America's reserve army of the poor are drummed into the worst jobs, the worst-paid positions, and provide the labor force that works in coal mines, cleans toilets and barn stalls, picks and plucks in fields as migrant laborers, or slaughters animals. Waste people remain the 'mudsills' who fill out the bottom layer of the labor pool on which society's wealth rests."[32] While I raise these treatments of wage labor and disposability in reference to prison work, it also bears noting that even as regional coal jobs dwindle, the violence of the coal industry—in the form of both injury and illness—has not abated, including record numbers of cases of black lung disease identified in the region recently.[33] The point is that disposability is not necessarily what distinguishes the prisoner from the prison guard. In the Appalachian context, disposability in fact characterizes wage labor across numerous employment sectors.

Of course, the processes that bring people to prisons on different sides of the cell bars—criminalization on the one hand and employment in corrections on the other—place those who may otherwise share much in common under capitalism on opposing sides of class struggle and state violence. These processes of differentiation are *fundamentally* gendered and racialized, although they manifest differently in different geographies. In Central Appalachia, they build on, and alter, existing hegemonic masculinities as well as racial formations.[34]

While rural prison towns in the United States are often multiracial,[35] Letcher County is 98 percent white. Martin County, the home of USP Big Sandy is, technically, 92 percent white. Dwelling for a moment on this latter figure from Martin County is revealing. Taken from the 2018 census, the figure of 92 percent white is misleading, concealing in its inaccuracy the very work of capitalism to naturalize race and produce a racialized social order through criminalization and incarceration. The 2000 census for Martin County noted that the county was 99.25 percent white; by the 2010 census, the percentage was down to 92 percent, largely due to the dramatic increase in the African American population from a total of four Black residents in 2000 to 892 ten years later.[36] What could possibly be the reason for such a massive demographic shift—*a growth of 22,200 percent in the Black population in a decade*—in a county of thirteen thousand people? The answer, of course, is the construction of USP Big Sandy in 2003, the subsequent imprisonment within it of hundreds and hundreds of Black people, and the counting of them as residents of the county in which they are incarcerated. This latter maneuver, known as prison-based gerrymandering, has garnered considerable and warranted attention by scholars and activists who rightly decry the injustice that even as prisoners are denied the right to vote, their "residency" in the rural community leads to political and economic benefits in the form of increased political representation as well as eligibility for state and federal grant monies and expenditures, including for infrastructure, schools, and other areas outside of corrections.[37] This insidious practice, particularly in places like eastern Kentucky, is a form of racialized expropriation. Not only are people of color extracted from their communities and disposed of in Appalachian prisons but also the political power and investment that should go to their home communities is, instead, extracted through them and deposited in the prison town.[38] These processes confirm Laura Pulido's point that "it is essential to remember that racial processes also produce the environmental landscapes of white people as well."[39] In eastern Kentucky, the coal ash dumps, trash landfills, and incinerators—quite literally repositories of capitalism's waste—sit proximate to the prison, threatening the health and environment of Central Appalachia as they also reproduce the environmental racism of low-income urban communities of color in places where there are few Black people outside of the prison.[40] Land, even in predominantly white spaces, is "thoroughly saturated with racism."[41]

The racial dynamics of Appalachian prisons—and in particular the absent presence of hundreds of incarcerated Black men in places like USP Big Sandy—should be considered within the long history of Black experiences in the region. The cultural imaginary of a uniform white Appalachia constitutes what Karida Brown calls a "double erasure": Black people rarely appear in representations of the region, and the history of their contributions to places like eastern Kentucky, to say nothing of their history of migrations into and out of them, is largely ignored.[42] Appalachia's whiteness, where it does exist, is not some primordial feature of the region but rather has been produced over time by specific historical patterns of mobility, themselves structured by racialized practices of capital and the state. In 1900, Black people accounted for 24 percent of the more than nine thousand miners in eastern Kentucky. But as the industry went through various iterations of mechanization in the first half of the twentieth century, Black miners were the first to lose their jobs, a practice that accelerated as the industry shifted from deep mining to surface mining. This led to what historians have called "an outright exodus" from the mountains, which completed one generational chapter of the Great Migration for many African American families.[43] By the peak of coal employment in 1950, Black people accounted for just 4.6 percent of the 64,000 miners in eastern Kentucky, their share of the total jobs having dropped by several percentage points in the intervening decades. By 1960, mining jobs had dropped in eastern Kentucky to 37,519, with Black miners accounting for just 3 percent of the workforce. The number of coal jobs rebounded briefly in the late 1970s and early 1980s because of the oil crisis, but Black employment in the industry never recovered, as by then many families had left. Black miners accounted for just 1.6 percent of the mine workforce in 1980 in eastern Kentucky. The forced migration of African Americans back to the region in the 1990s and 2000s—transported in and for captivity, counted by the census but otherwise stripped of official recognition, and omitted from representations—enacts a third erasure.

The prospect and provision of prison jobs to mostly white Central Appalachian residents takes on a definitively gendered valence as well. The severe decline of coal employment has produced what we might call a "crisis of surplus masculinities" in the coalfields.[44] The coal industry has had to develop particularly compelling propaganda in order to maintain a hegemonic masculinity that orbits closely around coal mining while the mechanization of production has directly depleted the material avenues for achieving it.[45] In this way, the structural economic crisis triggered by the precipitous decline of coal employment and production has deeply racialized and gendered affective and cultural contours. The prison offers a path toward repairing and renovating the region's racialized and gendered social order through transforming once and would-be white (and largely male) miners into white (and largely male) prison guards.[46]

What is the broader sociocultural, political, and economic significance of the shifting social order? One analytic that helps in conceptualizing the connections between employment in coal and incarceration as well as the ways in which working in a prison is importantly distinct, is the concept of "dirty work." Both industries employ the same people, sometimes literally, to do their "dirty work" in places that elude any kind of democratized gaze: under the ground, inside the mountain, and behind the barbed wire and walls.[47] Dirty work also can refer to the labor of collecting, managing, storing, moving, and disposing of waste. In Central Appalachia, where prisons and jails proliferate and their edges interface in space and time with landfills, incinerators, and slurry ponds in addition to active and closed mining sites, racialized and gendered dirty work constitutes a predominant category of labor in the region.[48]

The dialectical relationships in operation here, not only between coal and incarceration in Appalachia but also between urban and rural geographies, further reveals the significance of dirty work. In the organized abandonment of cities, criminalization and policing—what Ruth Wilson Gilmore and Craig Gilmore call "organized violence"— became predominant and commonsense approaches to the remaking of urban social order.[49] One way this practice has been discussed by other theorists and historians is as the management of "social dirt." "Dirt," the anthropologist Mary Douglass famously argued, "is matter out of place . . . the byproduct of a systematic ordering and classification."[50] Obstructions to order, the political theorist William Connolly expands, "become . . . abnormality, waste, sickness, perversity, incapacity, disorder, madness, unfreedom. They become material in need of rationalization, normalization, moralization, correction, punishment, discipline, disposal, realization, etc."[51] In industrializing England, writes Mark Neocleous, the project of removing dirt from the street became indistinguishable from the project of removing "moral filth" as the poor and working classes became the commonsense source of the waste and thus "the subversion of all order."[52] The work of managing and removing this threat to social order was foundationally a police objective. Neocleous writes, "As crime came to be one of the strongest reminders of disorder, so it came to be thought of in terms of dirt and garbage. The dirt—that is, the crime—needs to be removed in order to deny the disorder which it produces. The removal of the dirt/crime is a reimposition of order, a re-placement of matter into an ordered system."[53] When police or politicians invoke the phrase "cleaning up the streets" during campaigns, they are inherently making claims about crime, dirt, and order, confirming police power as a form of sanitation or waste work, a mantle some police officers themselves embrace.[54]

As chapters 1 and 2 explored in detail, at approximately the same historical moment when cities began sending their solid waste to new landfills and trash incinerators in Appalachia, they were also sending their populations "wasted" by capitalism to the same mountains for disposal in newly built prisons next door. This "spatial reorganization of waste" reveals that the disappearance of work in many places, particularly urban although increasingly rural, became the condition of possibility for work in others.[55] The disposability of criminalized populations—quite literally, the racialized political and economic processes that make them into surplus or waste—itself produces opportunity, this "dirty work," for others, who, unmoored from former sources of stable employment, are newly available to refashion themselves as prison guards.[56]

We might further understand the relationship between prisoner and the dirty work of being a prison guard as an example of the racialized difference between exploitation and expropriation. As Nancy Fraser helpfully clarifies, "The subjection of those whom capital expropriates is a hidden condition of possibility for the freedom of those whom it exploits."[57] Expropriation confiscates capacities and resources and conscripts them—in the case of the prison, by idling—into capital's circuits of self-expansion. In Appalachian prisons, these expropriated individuals are the conditions of possibility for the promises of exploitation: former miners and their children hoping to sell their labor power to guard them. In the production of this relationality between the expropriated and the exploited, we see a core function of racial capitalism: what Jodi Melamed calls the "manufacturing of densely connected social separateness."[58]

Details about the prison in Letcher County contribute an additional and important—if complicating—layer to this analysis. Attention to the prison project from both supporters and critics largely focused on USP Letcher due to its size and the projected twelve hundred individuals it would incarcerate. But the Bureau of Prisons had planned to construct *two* prisons on the Roxana site: the maximum security USP and, adjacent to it, a minimum-security federal prison camp designed to hold 256 additional prisoners. In a close reading of the BOP's Environmental Impact Study, activist and attorney Emily Posner found that the agency appeared to offer neither any kind of correctional justification for the FPC's existence nor rationale for its size. In fact, Posner argued in a comment to the BOP, all of the FPCs adjacent to other regional USPs had population capacities in the low one hundreds, half the size of the FPC proposed for Letcher County. In a particularly revealing response to Posner's comments, the BOP justified the FPC neither in correctional-capacity considerations nor in criminal-legal system processes, but rather in the administrative needs of the maximum-security prison that would reside next door: "A USP is not a stand-alone facility and typically includes additional supporting facilities that are integral to its operation. Such facilities, for example, include an FPC, staff training center, warehouse, and powerhouse. The FPC for the proposed project, just like FPCs at existing USPs, *is an integral part of the USP because it houses minimum-security inmates that provide a work cadre needed to help maintain the USP facilities and grounds*" (my emphasis).[59] This admission by the BOP is as plain as it is instructive. The agency justified the FPC, and 256 additional incarcerated individuals, on the grounds that they would provide necessary maintenance work for the very carceral system that would imprison them and their neighbors in the USP. That is, they would perform what Craig Gilmore has called "the reproductive labor of the prison itself."[60]

It is important to pause here and consider this in light of official arguments for constructing the USP, existing tensions within scholarship on the relationship between prisons and racial capitalism, and this chapter's discussion about work. In admitting the need for minimum-security prisoners to perform various duties associated with the operation of the maximum-security prison, the BOP and its local supporters in the Planning Commission and elsewhere would seem to undermine their own arguments about the jobs the prison would bring to the county. At least some of the labor those captive individuals in the FPC would be forced to perform might otherwise fall within the work promised to local residents. What we should infer from this is that the reliance on prisoners to maintain and service both their own and an adjacent prison enables the BOP to avoid having to adhere to federal minimum wage laws and provide federal benefits to free workers.

This affirms arguments from critical prison studies scholars about the nature of work inside prisons as well as the ways in which the prison is woven into capitalist social relations beyond profit.[61] The prisoners intended for the FPC would not be incarcerated in order to serve as a slave-wage force for corporations. Rather, by the BOP's own admission, their incarceration is instrumental to the very maintenance of the system. While in the final analysis it may be that those whom capital expropriates are guarded by those whom it exploits, there are nonetheless examples where the state actively creates divisions *within* the expropriated class to meet the requirements it sets for itself, while also rather plainly trying to cut costs. In this case, we should recognize, prisoners are "deployed" to perform the custodial dirty work of maintaining their own custody.

The precarity of Appalachian residents on the edges of the relative surplus population serves two important political functions for the carceral state. First, the prospect and possible realization of "guard labor" jobs offer to stabilize life for those on the precipice of, or experiencing, unemployment.[62] But second, and more insidiously, work in a prison must be understood as fundamentally different from the kinds of work that have disappeared in Appalachia (and the United States more generally). The coal mine, manufacturing plant, factory, and farm, while sites of profound exploitation at times, have also been locations of multiracial class struggles.[63] In contrast, jobs in the carceral economy foundationally rest on, and continue to manufacture, racism, understood here as "the state-sanctioned and/or extra-legal production and exploitation of group-differentiated vulnerabilities to premature death, in distinct yet densely interconnected political geographies."[64] This is one place from which to view the relationship between the political economy of the carceral state—i.e., the centrality of prisons and jails to the mundane operations of rural municipalities—and the force of its ideological work to inscribe subjectivities.[65] It is not just that the prison may provide some jobs, but rather that it threatens to deputize hundreds of people into one of the central institutional sites of racialized class war.[66] While the prison attempts to replace the coal mine spatially, psychically, and economically in the community, it also functions to fuse the police powers in operation in the twentieth-century coal camps and company towns into the new form of work. That is, miner on the one hand and mine guard/sheriff/state police officer on the other, at bloody odds with each other periodically during the twentieth century, might be best understood now in some areas of the coalfields as a single individual: the prison guard.[67]

Conclusion

The long decline of coal jobs and the significant downturn in coal production created two elements of crisis: structural unemployment and severe revenue shortages, the latter due to the rapid loss of coal-severance-tax receipts. These dramatic changes in the realm of production have stark effects on the cultural and material work of social reproduction. Some residents have moved out of Central Appalachia; those who stay have to seek out alternative forms of reproducing themselves and their region. The mobility of capitalist production, as seen in the reorganization of the coal industry, is not matched by an equally mobile or flexible social reproduction, a process that is much more closely committed and accountable to place.[68] As discussed in the previous chapter, for example, there are not only very few jobs in Letcher County, but also local government had to withdraw the funding for five senior citizens centers in addition to reducing allocations to fire departments, the ambulance service, and the sheriff's department, and cutting about ninety jobs.[69] This is the crisis—the very real threat to the reproduction of the county—for which the prison and jail serve as putative solutions. At a more distanced level of abstraction, the role of USP Letcher reveals the carceral state—at the federal scale—investing in the county in order to address the crisis at the scale of its most acute expression, where it is experienced most severely by both organizations and people. In the process, this form of state investment threatens to produce a "racialized and gendered geography of . . . securitized social reproduction," or a renovation of county politics, economy, and culture through the prison.[70]

It is important to recognize the contributions of various actors within the county and region who worked to create hospitable material and ideological conditions to recruit and site the prison. Members of the county school system, individual community schools, the planning commission, a major public university, and various businesses each indicated their aspirations, and their intention to realize them, for the reproduction of the county as a prison town. This was not conspiratorial, although there was certainly coordination. Rather, the work of these actors aligns with what Stuart Hall and coauthors meant when arguing that in periods of crisis, it is "*politics* which provides the key mechanism of *consent*: and it is through the political system that the dominant economic class exercises its hegemony."[71] Of course, it is also politics—in the form of organizing, activism, and political education—that actively challenges consent and the exercise of hegemony. In would-be prison towns in the coalfields, this would seem to require a political vision for the future that takes seriously the prison's role—at least at the level of ideology—in providing for the reproductive capacities of the area. As Hall notes elsewhere, hegemony is achieved when "ideology captures or 'hegemonises' common sense; when it becomes so taken-for-granted that its ways of looking at the world seem to be the only ways in which ordinary people can calculate what's good and what's not, what they should support and what they shouldn't, what's good for them and what's good for society."[72] The campaign against USP Letcher fought for both a different common sense and a noncarceral future. It is this political fight to which we now turn.

7

The Plot of Abolition

Solidarity Politics across Scale, Strategy, and Prison Walls

WITH SYLVIA RYERSON

But if prison abolition requires creating a world where prisons are no longer needed, then the real work of abolition must be done away from prisons—in shelters, health clinics, schools, and in battles over government budget allocations.
—Alexander Lee, *Abolition Now: Ten Years of Strategy and Struggle against the Prison Industrial Complex*

I am an abolitionist. Abolition is a plot against racial capitalism, which is all capitalism, not just some of it. It is a plot in a narrative sense. It is a plot in which the arc of change is always going resolutely towards freedom. It is a plot in a geographic sense. It is a plot in which we aim to make all space, not just some space, free in two senses. Free in the sense it cannot be alienated which is to say it cannot be sold by anybody to anybody, and free in the sense of non-exclusion—no boundary, no border, which would keep somebody in or keep somebody out.
—Ruth Wilson Gilmore, Rustbelt Abolition Radio

The narrative arc of the carceral state has shown a remarkable flexibility in integrating new characters (such as carceral humanists advocating benevolent expansion), shifting to accommodate what may have seemed like plot twists (such as bipartisan reform), and yet staying the course on its trajectory of and toward unfreedom.[1] The geographic plot of the carceral state is equally tenacious, continuing to consume people from the urban and largely Black and Brown underclass but also stretching its amoeba-like form to ensnare those from suburban and rural communities as well.[2] Moreover, the carceral state's real estate is expansive in both territory and form, including prisons that have expanded across rural communities; various kinds of boutique-sounding institutions proposed for or built in places as diverse as Indianapolis and Bloomington, Indiana, Illinois, Colorado, California, Iowa, and New York City; and increasingly technologized forms of control that "e-carcerate" residents where they live.[3]

As we have seen, in Central Appalachia the rise of the carceral state has been largely successful. This has been due, in part, to its diversification across scales and jurisdictions. Even as there are a disproportionate number of federal prisons in eastern Kentucky, there are also state and private prisons as well as an expanding jail system, all of which have risen in response to the severity of the crises in the region. But if the history and operations of the coal industry set the political economic and spatial conditions of possibility for a carceral geography to shape and take shape in Appalachia, it is equally true that the history of resistance to the coal industry in the region has helped to shape opposition to the prisons today. Coal's expropriation and exploitation of land and people produced militant organizing and insurrection to defend both from an industry whose immense profits depended on the literal sacrifice of the region's residents, as black lung cases, mine collapses, polluted water tables, and cancer rates make clear. Appalachian organizing against the coal industry is a history of struggling for life and democracy, and for the abolition of the practices that preclude both. There is thus a history of *abolitionist* politics in Appalachia, and that history includes building support for grassroots democracy, for environmental protection, for a restoration of commons, and for full employment.[4]

That history has been carried into the present by a coalition that coalesced to oppose USP Letcher and its federal prison camp neighbor, the prison complex at the center of the previous two chapters, sited for a former mountaintop removal site in Letcher County, Kentucky. The coalition included local organizers fighting for a just economic transition away from coal and prisons, local landowners opposed to selling their property to the US Bureau of Prisons, national activists fighting prison building on abolitionist and environmental-justice grounds, and federal prisoners who signed on as plaintiffs in a lawsuit opposing the construction. Working across scales and strategies, these groups fought the prison project and built important counternarratives to weaken its ideological foundations.

The fight against USP Letcher in Appalachia is important on its own but also offers insights for the broader abolitionist political movement. In particular, it demonstrates that abolitionists must take seriously the places, like Appalachia, where prisons and jails proliferate and where a growing political, economic, and cultural realignment around incarceration can take hold.[5] At the same time, the fight against the prison, and the radical genealogies of which it is a part, reveals the region as home to abolitionists—of fossil fuel extractivism, racial capitalism, and the carceral state alike. Locating this particular fight within the long history of Appalachian resistance to the captivity and disposability of land and people demonstrates how the region must also be understood as a critical site of emergent abolitionist analysis and strategy.

Focused on the opposition to USP Letcher, this chapter draws from interviews, local archives, and official government documents in order to examine the dialectical space of overlapping carceral and abolitionist geographies, read as both the narrative terrain and the cartographic landscape on which visions for Appalachia are projected and contested. Coauthored with the scholar and activist Sylvia Ryerson, whose extraordinary undergraduate thesis, local reporting, and other work on and against prison growth in Appalachia has been foundational for those of us who have come after her, this chapter examines and reflects on the coalitional politics that led to the defeat of this prison as it also considers what the defeat means for the future of the region and the US carceral state. In the tradition of political and intellectual collaborations among organizers, scholar-activists, journalists, and others, this chapter draws heavily on, and learns primarily from, many of the actors who were intimately involved in the fight against USP Letcher.[6] We were also both a part of this story in different ways, and we felt strongly that the people with whom we spoke for the research were our interlocutors and cotheorists, deeply informing our own understandings of what lessons can be learned from this fight.

Defeating a Prison in the Coalfields

On Thursday, June 20, 2019, the US Bureau of Prisons posted a "Notice of Withdrawal" in the Federal Register, announcing its reversal of the previously issued "Record of Decision" (ROD) to build the United States penitentiary and federal prison camp in Letcher County, Kentucky. The ROD is considered the end of the environmental review process for all new BOP projects, providing the greenlight for land acquisition and construction to commence. When the ROD was originally announced just over a year prior, on April 12, 2018, it came as a devastating blow to activists who had long been fighting the prison. After almost fifteen years in various stages of planning, the half-billion-dollar project seemed inexorably poised to begin on the former mountaintop removal mining site in Roxana, and to become the sixth federal prison built in Central Appalachia since 1992. And yet, with the announcement of the withdrawal, the entire project came to an abrupt halt, marking the first time in BOP history that the building of a federal prison has been stopped after the ROD was issued, effectively defeating what was slated to become the most expensive federal prison ever built in US history. What happened? What does this tell us about the future of prison expansion and the carceral state in Central Appalachia? And what lessons can be taken forward from this fight, in the *making* of abolitionist geographies?

Foundations for Opposition

As previous chapters noted, the prison was first proposed to the Letcher County Planning Commission by US Representative Harold "Hal" Rogers's office in 2003, following the exact pattern of the way federal prisons were brought to the neighboring eastern Kentucky counties of Clay, Martin, and McCreary in 1992, 2003, and 2004. In 2006, Rogers's office secured $5 million for an initial site planning and selection process, and six possible prison sites were identified within the county. After nearly a decade of bureaucratic stops and starts, the project began to gain momentum in 2013, with the commencement of the Bureau of Prison's official scoping period, the first stage in a federal agency's movement through the environmental impact process required under the National

Environmental Protection Act (NEPA). Following the 1969 passage of NEPA, all federal agencies must conduct such a process, culminating in a series of Environmental Impact Statements (EIS), public comments on those statements, and an official Record of Decision.

And yet, over the course of the decade in which the prison took root in elite-driven local planning efforts, there was another simultaneous history unfolding. Letcher County has long played a central role in the cultivation of critical political analysis and regional radical organizing against injustice in the coalfields. Harry Caudill, whose best-selling book *Night Comes to the Cumberlands* is credited with catalyzing President Kennedy's early efforts in what would eventually become the War on Poverty, was from Letcher County. And while Caudill would eventually embrace eugenicist ideas about the region, his work in the 1960s elicited significant national attention, resulting in increases of both progressive activism and federal investment in the county and region. Many Letcher Countians were deeply involved in the movement against strip mining in the 1960s and 1970s. And in 1969, the nationally recognized Appalachian media arts and education center Appalshop was founded in Letcher County. Appalshop was originally one of nine community film workshops across the country funded by the Office of Economic Opportunity (OEO) during the War on Poverty, as a jobs training program for underserved youth. Politicized by the flood of derogatory national coverage of Appalachia during the years of the War on Poverty, Appalshop's young filmmakers became deeply engaged in the politics of representation, producing local media to counter pathologizing dominant narratives of the region by "tell[ing] stories the commercial cultural industries don't tell, challenging stereotypes with Appalachian voices and visions," and to "support communities' efforts to achieve justice and equity and solve their own problems in their own ways."[7] Appalshop incorporated as a nonprofit organization in 1975, and has since expanded to produce documentary film, theater, and radio, including Appalshop's community radio station, WMMT-FM 88.7, and is also home to an important regional archive, youth media program, and traditional music program.

Letcher County was also a site in the foundational 1981 Appalachian Landownership Study, organized at the Highlander Research and Education Center in New Market, Tennessee, an iconic social movement organization. Many Letcher County activists were leaders in the multiyear participatory land study, which documented both the staggering rates of absentee corporate land ownership across the region and the minuscule property taxes being paid by these companies. The findings from the study resulted in the formation of the Kentucky Fair Tax Coalition, a direct-action organizing campaign dedicated to progressive land and tax reform. As their organizing expanded to statewide issues, the group renamed itself Kentuckians for the Commonwealth (KFTC) in 1987.[8] Today, KFTC is a member-led and chapter-based force for progressive statewide organizing, playing a central role in the more recent movements against mountaintop removal coal mining, oil and gas extraction, the campaign to restore voting rights to formerly incarcerated people, and fights for a living wage. Until 2017, there was an active KFTC chapter in Letcher County. Thus, the county has long been home to deeply rooted local institutions committed to narratively contesting and politically organizing against the dominant deficiency discourses of needed "cultural progress" and "economic growth" that have defined corporate/state planning processes in Appalachia, and it has been a central site of multi-issue organizing campaigns. It was within this historical and political context that abolitionist rural anti-prison activism unfolded against USP Letcher.

Relational Abolitionism: Coalition Building across Scale and Strategy

The issue of prison expansion first emerged in Letcher County in the 1990s, with the proposal and construction of two identical super-maximum-security Virginia state prisons in adjacent Wise County, Virginia, just over the state line from Kentucky. In 2006, Appalshop filmmakers Amelia Kirby and Nick Szuberla released the documentary film *Up the Ridge*, following the opening of, and horrific and deadly abuse within, one of these facilities, the Wallens Ridge State Prison. In the late 1990s, Kirby and Szuberla started the nationally recognized weekly radio show *Holler to the Hood* (now *Hip Hop from the Hill Top and Calls from Home*) on Appalshop's community radio station, WMMT-FM. For over two decades, the show has broadcast toll-free messages and music dedications from family members to their loved ones incarcerated in the seven regional prisons that exist within

WMMT's airwaves. In late 2001, Kirby connected with Critical Resistance (CR), as the national abolitionist organization began planning for its 2003 conference, CR South. The following year, CR organizers and conference coordinators Ashley Hunt and Melissa Burch traveled to Whitesburg to meet with Kirby and local young people. As Burch's notes state from that meeting, "*September 27 Whitesburg, KY. Excellent event with young people who work with Appalshop. 10–15 young people who had had direct experiences with the system. Folks who had been locked up for fighting and had first-hand experience with guards and the idea that people don't care about you in prison. (Someone's Aunt had killed her batterer and went to prison; another person had a brother who was a prison guard and quit). They had a real direct understanding of the PIC's (Prison Industrial Complex) impact on local community.*"[9] CR cofounder and long-time community organizer and educator Rachel Herzing noted that CR later screened *Up the Ridge* as part of its organizing efforts in California.

Thus, when the USP Letcher prison project began to gain momentum in the summer of 2013, many local actors had been closely following the proposal for years, their analyses of the harms that prisons create in rural and urban communities alike informed by the effects seen and experienced firsthand in neighboring rural counties as well as by national abolitionist organizing. One of us (Sylvia) had conducted extensive archival research and interviews in the neighboring federal prison–hosting eastern Kentucky counties of Martin, McCreary, and Clay, which starkly revealed the lies about jobs and economic growth that local, state, and federal officials had touted to these communities during the site selection processes, as well as their accompanying social harms.[10] The record in these eastern Kentucky counties demonstrates what has now been documented across Appalachia as well as in other rural communities, namely, that prison building works to uphold local hierarchies of wealth and power, furthering the dispossession of the county's most vulnerable residents. Even as the presence or promise of a prison can drive infrastructure project proposals and generate some employment, the jobs often go to residents living outside of the host community or county and the prison consumes funding that might otherwise finance needed community investment, in addition to bringing a plethora of social harms.[11] These case studies from the region offered a road map of how the process had unfolded right next door, helping local organizers to plan and strategize while also revealing the contradictions of rural prison growth.

Activists worked to mobilize this regional data and analysis, and to connect it to the growing body of research demonstrating the negative impacts of rural prison growth nationwide. As the local newspaper, the *Mountain Eagle* (reliant on pro-prison county elites for advertising revenue), ran stories supportive of the prison and officially endorsed the project in 2013, Sylvia, then working as a reporter for WMMT-FM and codirecting the *Calls from Home* radio show, reached out to leading scholars in the emergent subfield of rural prison studies, including Anne Bonds, Gregory Hooks, and Ruth Wilson Gilmore.[12] All immediately offered to share their research, which was then broadcast in a radio documentary on WMMT.[13] In 2004, Gregory Hooks and colleagues published the first national study on prison building and rural job growth, observing employment trends in every prison-hosting county in the United States from 1969 to 2004.[14] As Hooks summarized this landmark work over the local airwaves,

> The overarching finding was that we found that [having] a prison present in a county had very little impact whatsoever, positive or negative. And then we pursued that question in greater detail, looking at the counties that were supposed to benefit the most. . . . We really focused our attention on those counties that were lagging in terms of employment growth before the prison came. And what we found is that—we did find a statistically significant impact, but that impact was negative. The counties in which a new prison was built we found actually had slower employment growth not faster. So, we concluded that, to the extent that prisons are doing *anything* in rural counties in the United States, they were doing more harm than good. . . . The counties that are more likely to be *harmed* by prisons, are more likely to divert scarce resources toward capturing prisons.[15]

And as Ruth Wilson Gilmore summarized, speaking directly to the radio station's rural audience,

> My grandmother was from the country, from rural Connecticut. And they used to talk about flim flam artists coming through rural New

England, persuading farmers and others to do things that were not in the farmers' interest ... that was never going to bring them anything but heartache and greater poverty.

The way that rural counties have been *persuaded* to put up money in order to prepare the ground, quite literally, putting in roads and sewers and water systems and so forth, is really flim flam, because the numbers that are used to persuade *well-meaning* county executives and county managers to do what they do, never ever, *ever* cost out, in real life, to real income for the county—they don't do it.... So the county gets stuck with the cost of building the infrastructure for the prison. And really, to think of this in other words—the county makes itself poorer than it already *was*, in order to try to get an economic benefit that will not benefit the county. And this we have seen happen over and over and over throughout the United States.[16]

With the support of these scholars, the independent airwaves of WMMT provided a crucial local media outlet that was able to directly counter the dominant pro-prison narrative saturating the local press. And—through the *Calls from Home* radio show—it created the space for an alternative political imaginary that included those incarcerated within WMMT's broadcast area as a *part of* the community.

Elizabeth Sanders and Sylvia worked with the Letcher County KFTC chapter to add opposition to prison building as economic development to the statewide KFTC platform. In 2013, anticipating the coming environmental review process as required under NEPA, the two of us (Sylvia and Judah) reached out to Rachel Herzing and Craig Gilmore, founding members, respectively, of Critical Resistance and the California Prison Moratorium Project, who have extensive experience using environmental review processes to delay prison building in California. Gilmore shared with us his archive of official documents, articles, and field notes from prison scoping meetings, and gave invaluable advice on how to navigate the NEPA process and anticipate the BOP's moves.

In February 2015, the BOP released its Draft Environmental Impact Statement (DEIS), opening the first public comment period on the project, and local and national activists rallied to submit hundreds of comments against the project. Five months later the BOP published a Final

Environmental Impact Statement (FEIS), opening a second public comment period.

Still in the midst of this environmental review process and years before the issuance of the Record of Decision that would propel the project forward, the United States Congress and President Obama approved the 2016 federal budget on December 18, 2015, in which $444 million of funding was allocated for the construction of USP Letcher. This federal funding allocation catalyzed local opposition with a heightened sense of urgency. In the winter of 2015–2016, a group of primarily young people in the county came together to form the Letcher Governance Project (LGP). The LGP began formally organizing and holding weekly meetings as a response to the closed planning process for the proposed prison, which according to them had "largely been done by wealthy and powerful people in the county, without the input of local landowners and citizens," and which stood to directly benefit members of the Letcher County Planning Commission. Situating itself in both an Appalachian-justice and prison-abolitionist framework, LGP explicitly stood "against the racist systems that lead to mass incarceration, as well as mass incarceration itself," and "for a just and diversified regional economy that is not built on fossil fuel industries and prisons."[17] The majority of LGP's original members were regular hosts of Appalshop's *Calls from Home* radio show, members of the Letcher County KFTC chapter, seasoned organizers in the fight against mountaintop removal mining, and deeply rooted in the region's social-justice-movement landscape. Importantly, as the small group worked to mobilize public comments against the prison for the NEPA process, it also articulated a broader intervention into the long history of undemocratic and corporate-friendly local government in the region. The choice of the Letcher Governance Project as a name was a deliberate and strategic move to establish its credibility and commitment to the future of the county. From the beginning, LGP's larger vision centered on challenging regional power structures and organizing for grassroots democratic decision making and local self-determination. In this crucial sense, we understand LGP as pursuing the project of abolition democracy, where local planning expresses both "the promise of new social relations based on economic redistribution, environmental sustainability, and the full realization of basic human and cultural rights" and multiracial solidarity against the carceral state and corporate power.[18]

With this name, they also connected themselves to prior battles against local political corruption and extraction. They took the name from a local citizen-led group that formed in the 1990s to oppose rampant gas drilling and the collusion between outside gas companies and local leaders. Thus, the LGP aimed to explicitly frame its opposition to USP Letcher as locally based and locally committed in order to counter inevitable accusations of opposition solely coming from "outside agitators."

In what would become a central and impactful part of its strategy, the LGP developed the social media hashtag #our444million in order to disavow the prison and simultaneously demand meaningful, community-controlled investment in Letcher County. LGP founding member Tanya Turner described how the group developed this framing:

> We just personally in our meetings had been dreaming about what that money could have been spent on. It's hard not to go there—when you are just seeing so intimately everyday what your community lacks, it's hard not to dream about what that much money could do. . . . And we landed on #our444mil and that hashtag campaign generated hundreds of local people sharing ideas that they had, for what they would spend that money on. And they were really big dreams, it was pretty incredible. People talked about rehab facilities, art centers, big maker spaces, all kinds of stuff. There were local high school teachers, local artists, kids, and punk rockers all using the hashtag.

Turner also conveyed how LGP's arrival at the hashtag and framing was developed in study and struggle with other organizers in the South. In 2015, as the prison project was accelerating but before funding had been allocated, she and other activists who would soon form LGP had traveled to New Orleans for a gathering commemorating the tenth anniversary of Hurricane Katrina. Sitting with organizers from Project South and the Highlander Research and Education Center, two leading southern movement organizations, Turner and others shared their growing concerns about the prison, and both organizations promised critical support. Later, LGP would learn from these organizers of a campaign in Atlanta led by young African American youth affiliated with Project South. These young people, who spoke of being subjected to daily criminalization and harassment by the police, had discovered that the Atlanta school district was about to contract with the Atlanta Police Department for $10 million to fund additional police in schools, metal detectors, and more. According to Turner,

> The kids created a campaign that we ended up basing ours on, called "Ten Mil 4 Real?" Like with a question mark, like "What the fuck?" It was very youthful and very clear. . . . It's always hard to organize around budget issues and money. These aren't easy things to organize around. But we thought that was so clever from the kids, like "Is this for real? Are you kidding us? You're gonna spend ten million dollars on *police* for our schools?!" One thing led to another and we landed on #our444mil.

Ash-Lee Woodard Henderson, codirector of the Highlander Center in Tennessee and who was a part of these conversations, also spoke of the meeting between young Black Atlanta organizers and LGP members at a Southern Movement Assembly. Henderson remembered the youth describing not only their daily encounters with the police but also their underfunded schools:

> [The youth had said,] "Our books are like two decades old, our school band is using musical instruments that our grandmothers marched with, and [the school board is] gonna give ten million dollars to the police? . . . We're gonna start this campaign, called '10 Mil 4 Real?' and we're gonna tell them all the ways they could spend those ten million dollars differently." And these hillbillies from Appalachia were like "That's a really good idea. Let me tell you what we could do with all this money they're about to spend on this federal prison."

Developed through southern movement work with Black organizers, #our444million opened up a discursive and political space in Letcher County for imagining alternative material proposals, powerfully disrupting and recharting the terms of local debate. Putting this framing into action, in the summer of 2016, LGP members physically and narratively interrupted a regional economic development and "innovation summit" hosted by Congressman Hal Rogers's office holding signs that read "Prisons Are Not Innovation" and "#our444million."

Figure 7.1. US Representative Hal Rogers is at the podium as LGP members and supporters hold signs and disrupt his address. Credit: Mimi Pickering

As LGP launched an organized local front against the prison, national abolitionist activists and movement lawyers around the country had also been closely following its development, including Panagioti Tsolkas with the Prison Ecology Project/Fight Toxic Prisons (PEP/FTP), and attorneys Dustin McDaniel and Emily Posner with the Abolitionist Law Center (ALC). All three had extensive experience using the NEPA process to challenge extractive or expropriative projects. The Abolitionist Law Center and the Prison Ecology Project reached out to their networks across the country to rally activists nationwide to submit public comments against the prison. Importantly, they did not see the commenting process as an end in and of itself, but rather as accomplishing several instrumental purposes. First, comments raised legitimate environmental concerns ignored by the BOP. Writing in from around the country following outreach from ALC and PEP, experts warned of light pollution, threats to local biodiversity and old-growth forest at the nearby Lilley Cornett Woods, and numerous public health issues for future prisoners, and also emphasized the importance of local biologist Jonathan Hootman's observations of endangered Indiana bat habitat on site. These extensive comments successfully delayed the prison by years, since the BOP had to submit revisions that addressed each issue raised by commenters. Generally, the strategy of delaying serves to hold off the project as long as possible, ideally weakening its "demonstrated need" and overall feasibility. The lawyers and activists all hoped for the possibility that the prison could be delayed long enough for political conditions to shift, making the project no longer viable. Furthermore, the filing of administrative comments in the NEPA process is required in order to participate in any future litigation, akin to a legal exhaustion requirement. In other words, the movement lawyers soliciting and organizing the comments during this stage assumed that the BOP would eventually deliver a Record of Decision, moving the prison project past the NEPA phase and toward construction. As they engaged with the NEPA process, they were simultaneously creating standing for a lawsuit that would follow.

The hundreds of oppositional public comments submitted to the BOP throughout the EIS process also generated a kind of counterhegemonic archive from which to read the proposal, discrediting dominant assertions of universal support for the prison from the Letcher County Planning Commission and in mainstream coverage of the project.[19] As LGP member Tarence Ray stated in his comments on the final version of the EIS, "More than anything, I hope this document exists in 200 years to show that there was an organized group of people here who resisted not only this prison, but prisons in general, that they were morally and spiritually repulsed by the idea of locking people up and discarding them; and that they believed human beings to be generally decent and good and worthy of compassion and capable of incredible things if given the chance."[20] Opposing comments ranged from critical analyses by antiprison LGP activists to other local residents expressing reservations about the economic promises, water contamination, and broader public health implications of prison construction to regional and national biologists voicing concern over the prison's threats to habitat and old-growth forest to sociologists who study prisons and economic development in the region who questioned the foundational logics of economic development. Against the grain of the prison boosters' insistence on jobs and economic development, the comments offered incisive, multifaceted, and passionate rejections of official logic and process. As one longtime Letcher County resident wrote,

> We have enough poverty, we do not need more and all research proves more poverty comes with prisons. This is a total insult to Letcher County people and the hardworking coalminers. A prison is all they can give us for the economy. Shame on all people involved. We get poverty and officials get cash. . . . If the prison comes in the children has no future. Why the government would bring prisoner[s] and family to this area is stupid. We have the highest cancer rate in the nation. Also the most prejudice[d] people. Contaminated water. This prison will destroy our environment and our beautiful mountains. It has already divided the people. People in the head of hollers with no transportation, no communication to outside world has not had their opinions used and that's not fair to them. There needs to be a more comprehensive survey on [the old-growth forest area] Lilley Cornett Woods. Too much damage to the woods. . . . It will be destroyed. Our county will be destroyed only because politicians want more money. We pay the high price of poverty for them. The health issue to the staff and prisoners is enough to not build prison. Again, shame on everyone involved in destroying Letcher Co. Stop this prison!!!

This particular testimony challenged central tenets of support for the prison. The commenter identified the way local elites stood to materially benefit from the prison and emphasized that people in the more remote areas of the county had not been able to participate in the process. In a direct challenge to those who saw in the prison a strategy for social reproduction (as discussed in chapter 6), this resident argued, "If the prison comes in the children has no future."

Other local comments offered similar challenges to the prison's purported role as a site of both production and reproduction, aiming squarely at claims about jobs but also recognizing the prison's negative impact on broader elements of the community. As one resident noted, "I think this prison will be a burden on our land, our people and our efforts to build new, sustainable economies. I'm not fooled for a second that this prison will create many jobs in our region and I question [why] this [is] what we are giving to our young people in the region—'stay [here] and you can work in a prison.' No person's aspirations are to work for an industry that puts humans in cages."[21] Another writer from Pound, Virginia, a community just across the border from Letcher County, wrote,

> We should be spending our tax dollars, human resources and political capital on creating innovative, healthy alternatives to [the] failed, crumbling infrastructure of this inhumane prison system. We could be creating cutting edge facilities geared toward true reconciliation, justice and reintegration that would provide an example for the country. Instead, this project replicates ... a failed, inefficient and ultimately costly system that in no way addresses the needs of our society. ... Prisons destroy families, communities, and shatter individual lives. We can and should do better and the rejection of this project is a step in the process of redefining our goals and values as a human community.[22]

Another resident who spent much of their comment questioning the Christian values of people who would support more prisons, noted the relevance of an analysis of waste: "Prisons, to me, are beginning to look like spill containers for people our society refuses to take care of, or thoughtfully acknowledge the value of."[23]

An architect in Portland, Oregon, offered a long and personal testimony that offered numerous interventions. The commenter first connected the prison to the legacy of destruction caused by mountaintop removal mining before going on to note how the rise of carceral Appalachia in the 1990s shifted the nature of work in the region:

> I lived in Appalachia in the 1990's in Wise County, VA and even then the social and economic damage of mountaintop removal and prison building in the region far outweighed any perceived economic benefit. Crossing into Letcher County the scars on the land are plain to see, and they affect everything downstream of them. It may seem like a shortsighted win-win to pair these sites with new corrections facilities, but the sum total of the message is "stay away." ... All other options should be explored first and the $444 million dollars that would be spent on this would be better put to other uses in the region: real environmental restoration, improved public infrastructure (including high speed data), job training, education and health initiatives. My personal story of leaving Appalachia

dates back to when my architecture and engineering company shifted from building schools to prisons and detention centers. I can't blame them for pursuing what work was available, but given the choice, I would not have staked my career on that shift. I couldn't be proud to participate in what seemed to be an unjust and self-defeating cycle. Wishing the best for Letcher County, all of Appalachia, and all involved in its governance and development.

A pastor from the Germantown Mennonite Church in Philadelphia offered this measured view of the prison:

> As someone who has spent most of my life in rural areas, I know that prisons can create jobs. However, I also know from personal experience that prisons do not meaningfully address rural poverty, they provide some jobs (and in this case, jobs with serious health costs attached) to a few people, but leave many people behind. I know that community members in Eastern Kentucky have generated a list of programs that would have a greater positive impact on the region, where the $444 million set aside for the prison could be better put to use. Please consider some of these alternatives:
>
> - Build a cutting-edge community healing facility and needle exchange programs across the region
> - Fund "maker spaces" for skill sharing, community training, and re-tooling
> - Organize participatory budgeting to drive civil engagement and governing transparency
> - Run fiber optic internet to homes and businesses to support digital literacy and economic growth
> - Grow local food economies and health by supporting farmers and farmer's markets
> - Create an endowment for young people to run and use to invest, keeping them there

As the pastor's comments demonstrate, LGP's #our444million framing created a discursive and political space for alternative material proposals, revealing the influence and amplification of organizers bas

Letcher County through their collaborations with national abolitionist lawyers and activists.

While the NEPA process was still underway, local landowner Mitch Whitaker, whose opposition to and analysis of the prison was discussed in chapter 1, reached out to national activists Panagioti Tsolkas and Emily Posner as well as to LGP members. Whitaker had felt alone in his steadfast refusal to sell his land to the BOP and was looking for someone whom he might "hook his wagon to." As Whitaker put it to us, "I told Emily up front [that] the reason I'm doing this is that this is in my back yard. I don't want this. This is as bad as having one of those incinerator plants come. It's something you just fight against." It might be tempting to interpret Whitaker's opposition here solely as NIMBYism, a rejection of the prison based on the proximity of the unsightly and unpleasant institution to his property. Crucially, however, there is a long history of fights over his back yard, which informed and intensified his opposition. As discussed in chapter 1, decades earlier, a coal company had tried to force his grandfather to allow it to use the land to haul coal away from a nearby mine, under the hugely contested broad form deed.[24] Had the company succeeded, the process would have split through a pasture where his grandfather kept cattle. His father and uncle assisted his grandfather in defeating the efforts, but the experience shaped Whitaker's resolute commitment to protecting his land from predatory outside interests, which is how he understood the BOP as well: "This was to me a flashback of that heyday [of mineral rights acquisition and land destruction by coal companies].... And had it not been for dad telling [grandpa] 'you've got the *right*'—it would have busted right through my grandfather's cow pasture and just been the awfullest mess there ever was.... It would have been terrible to have seen it split down the middle—and that's what I thought was gonna happen again." For Whitaker, rejecting the BOP was the continuation of a long struggle against outside interests.

Moreover, partnering with the emerging coalition deepened Whitaker's understanding of mass incarceration: "The more I got to research with them, [the more I realized that] once a person is put into prison they're no longer a citizen hardly anymore. Then they lost *all* their rights. They're felons now and they have no rights. I'm sixty years old, so to see that possibly our government could put *a whole group of people* in there just to sort of get rid of them." Coalitional organizing expanded

Whitaker's analysis; his deepened analysis further cemented his opposition both to USP Letcher and to mass incarceration more broadly.

By all accounts, Whitaker's unwavering refusal to sell his land to the BOP was essential to the defeat of the project. While his property comprised only fifteen acres of the proposed seven-hundred-acre prison site, the parcel's inclusion in the official site map made his opposition a problem for the BOP. Whitaker's consistent repudiation forced the agency to redraw the boundaries of the proposed site. Redrawing the site map required another revision of the EIS. This alone significantly delayed the project. As attorney Dustin McDaniel told us, "The number of [EIS] redo's was . . . thanks to the way that we organized. It was thanks to . . . the involvement of local folks, in particular Mitch Whitaker. He bought us like a year or two. When he refused to sell his land, they changed the footprint [of the prison] and [therefore] had to redo the process. Mitch Whitaker was a big deal." Tsolkas agreed, saying, "Mitch came out swinging, saying that he was not willing to hand over his land. . . . That really forced them back to the drawing board. They withdrew the EIS and put out a revised EIS that didn't include his land. So that gave us another round of organizing and petition signing and online campaigning."

All told, the challenges during the NEPA process resulted in a record number of EIS revisions, which succeeded in delaying the project for three years, even *after* funding had been allocated for construction. After the BOP was forced to withdraw its original Final EIS in July 2015, the agency issued a Revised Final EIS in April 2016, a Draft Supplemental Revised Final EIS in March 2017, and a Final Supplemental Revised Final EIS in September 2017. Meanwhile, during these same years the political context at the highest level of the federal government dramatically shifted: Donald Trump was elected president and, with him, the contradictions of the carceral state intensified. Even as the Bureau of Prisons handed down a Record of Decision (ROD) in March 2018, officially moving the prison project into the construction phase, there were noticeable and widening cracks in the foundation of support.

The Lawsuit

NEPA statute requires public notice and invitation to participation from all who stand to be affected by a given federal project determined to significantly impact human environments. For movement lawyers, including Posner and McDaniel, centering the voices of those who stood to be most affected by the construction and operation of USP Letcher was of paramount importance. This included nearby communities and their residents, those who might work at the prison, and federal prisoners who would be eligible to be transferred and incarcerated there. These are three populations often assumed to be on opposing sides of prison siting. While the NEPA fight was still underway against USP Letcher, the Prison Ecology Project/Fight Toxic Prisons was simultaneously working on a campaign to push for the EPA to recognize prisoners as members of environmental justice communities. Once recognized as such, prisoners would have the very basic right to comment on a NEPA process, which would require the BOP to make all EIS documents available in all federal prison libraries. The agency failed to do this for USP Letcher, and so the legal team believed the prisoners had standing to sue. Posner reached out to federal prisoners across the country to solicit their public comments on the EIS and to invite them to join in the coming lawsuit against its construction, as part of her commitment to pursuing all administrative remedies available to federal prisoners. After the ROD was handed down in 2018, twenty-one prisoners retained Posner as their lawyer to represent them as plaintiffs in a lawsuit against the BOP. Their claim was that they were unlawfully excluded from the NEPA process because the agency had failed to provide them personally or their prison law libraries with copies of the EIS. Individually, as federal prisoners they would have no legal standing to oppose being transferred to USP Letcher once the new prison was built. And so, they made a collective claim, the only one available to them, to fight the construction of the prison itself. They argued that the prison was unnecessary according to the BOP's own projections and thus did not meet the "stated purpose and need" required for construction, that it would cause extreme and unnecessary environmental harm, and that everyone incarcerated within the federal prison system had been unjustly excluded from the public review process. As Manuel Gauna, one of the incarcerated plaintiffs who joined the lawsuit from a federal prison in Arizona, stated, "I believe that construction of this particular prison is neglecting the people in Letcher and the people in the prison ≥m. We as prisoners should have had the opportunity to participate in this public comment period for this project."[25] Posner and her team filed the lawsuit in November of 2018.

During and after the NEPA process, activists were carefully attuned to the widening contradictions of the federal government. The previous year, in the spring of 2017, the Trump administration proposed a budget for 2018 that omitted the funding for USP Letcher. Then–deputy attorney general Rod Rosenstein publicly feuded with US Representative Hal Rogers over the allocation and stated openly that the prison was unnecessary: "The FBOP population has precipitously declined over the last years [by] 30,000 inmates or 14% over the last four years. . . . Given the projections and needs the FBOP just didn't feel that we needed that facility at this time."[26] Ultimately, Rogers, from his perch on the House Appropriations Committee, succeeded in negotiating for the funds to be reinstated, and Congress *increased* the allocation from $444 million to $510 million, making USP Letcher the recipient of the largest prison-building allocation in US history. And yet the political terrain on which the prison proposal had sat comfortably for years was significantly destabilized.

Adding to these contradictions, in May 2018, just over a month after the BOP delivered the official ROD, the House passed the criminal justice reform bill known as the First Step Act; six months later, on December 21, 2018, the Senate passed the act and President Trump signed it into law. The very next day, at midnight on December 22, Trump shut down the federal government, beginning the longest government shutdown in US history, as his demand for $5.7 billion in federal funding for a US-Mexico border wall reached an impasse with Congress. When Trump finally delivered his 2019 State of the Union address on February 5, delayed a week due to the shutdown, he celebrated his historic passage of "groundbreaking criminal justice reform" in the First Step Act, while also openly criminalizing "illegal" migrants as murderers, sex traffickers, and "savage" gang members in the next breath.[27] While maintaining his racist obsession with massively funding a southern border wall, Trump simultaneously championed himself as a criminal justice reformer. In the spring of 2019, his administration again proposed cutting the funding for USP Letcher in the fiscal year 2020 federal budget.

Seizing on this lack of support from the White House, the ALC legal team moved forward with an amended complaint to strengthen and resubmit their lawsuit. They argued that the Department of Justice itself had now consistently and numerously contradicted the statutory requirement under NEPA that the purpose and need of the proposed prison project be legitimate. As the lawyers prepared the amended complaint, they also cultivated a local plaintiff to add to the lawsuit. Several individuals, including one of us (Judah), worked with the ALC legal team to form Friends of the Lilley Cornett Woods and North Fork River Watershed (FOLC), a nonprofit organization dedicated to "conserving and strengthening the environmental integrity of Letcher County and the human and natural environments of the broader Appalachian region." As Prison Ecology Project/Fight Toxic Prisons (PEP/FTP) organizer Panagioti Tsolkas explained to us, this strategy was derived directly from the campaign against the Delano II prison in California, led by Critical Resistance and the CA Prison Moratorium Project, which successfully delayed that prison by six years.[28] As Tsolkas described,

> The Letcher County fight is another example of resistance to prison expansion built on the model of the Delano II campaign. The named plaintiff in the Delano II lawsuit was actually the Tipton kangaroo rat. The kangaroo rat led the fight in a way and brought to the table environmentalists and others who had not engaged directly with prison abolition or prisoner rights organizing. That was a huge piece that we wanted to build on. We wanted to open the door for environmental activists to engage; to bring their skillset, their networks and their tools into the fight around incarceration. That was the inspiration for us to include concerns around the endangered Indiana bat in our public comments, to coordinate with biologists and to conduct extensive wildlife research.[29]

As a local organization comprised mostly of local residents who stood to be adversely impacted by the prison, the FOLC constituted a traditional NEPA plaintiff and thus added legal legibility to the lawsuit built around the federal prisoners' complaints. Posner described this to us as the enactment of a "solidarity politics" in which local landowner Mitch Whitaker, twenty-one incarcerated federal prisoners, concerned local citizens, and other concerned Kentucky residents all joined together as plaintiffs in the lawsuit. In March 2019, the attorneys filed the amended complaint, in which they argued that the passage of the First Step Act, the White House's open defection, and former deputy attorney general Rosenstein's public admission that the prison was unnecessary, all established a clear lack of the legally required "demonstrated purpose and need" for the project, coupled with the additional adverse environmental impacts the prison would have on the local community, as claimed by FOLC. Within a month, DOJ attorneys had contacted the ALC attorneys to enter into discussions to settle. Then, in early June, the BOP officially withdrew its Record of Decision, effectively, if not permanently, ending the fifteen-year attempt to build USP Letcher.

"When a Win Isn't a Win": The Re-formation of the Carceral State and the Plot of Abolition

The news of the defeat of USP Letcher and its adjacent FPC was rightly heralded as a historic victory by abolitionists. Never before has a US federal prison project been stopped after both funding was secured for construction and a Record of Decision to build was delivered. And while it is a historic triumph that stopped twelve hundred new prison beds from being built, the histories of both the carceral state and the region warrant caution and analysis as to what the defeat means for Appalachia and what it might portend about the carceral state. For many organizers in Letcher County, while a huge relief after a hard-fought campaign, the defeat of the prison did not exactly feel like a victory. Even as the BOP was forced to admit that its claims of prison-driven economic development were dubious, in the wake of the withdrawal of the ROD, there remains no alternate regional reinvestment strategy for the federal money. LGP's demand for redirecting #our444million toward other forms of desperately needed community support remains unmet. This starkly reveals how the prison was never intended or structured as a true rural employment program; rather, the rhetoric of "jobs" has long been used to secure consent for a prison-building regime primarily deployed to resolve urban and rural crises of "organized abandonment."[30] The fifteen years of pro-prison organizing and boosterism required local officials to disguise and deny the very real and urgent social needs of Letcher County, in order to entice the BOP to come. County elites tirelessly promoted Letcher County to BOP officials as having excellent and available housing, health care, and education. Yet by all measures, these systems are failing local residents, and Letcher County's needs remain, dire and unmet, exacerbated in recent years by declining revenues from the coal severance tax. LGP founding member Elizabeth Sanders summarized the defeat of USP Letcher as feeling like "when a win isn't a win."

The history of USP Letcher serves as a weathervane from which we can observe the national incoherence of the carceral state. The contradictions at the highest level of the federal government created an impasse of political importance that extends far beyond eastern Kentucky. Part of the reasoning given by the Trump administration for the rescinding of the ROD was that the half-billion dollars could be better used elsewhere, namely, to help pay for the architecture of racialized immigration enforcement. Within weeks of the BOP withdrawing its ROD for USP Letcher, Congress approved the Emergency Supplemental Appropriations for Humanitarian Assistance and Security at the Southern Border Act, providing $4.5 billion for "humanitarian assistance and security to respond to migrants attempting to enter the United States at the southern border."[31]

In August of 2019, Immigration and Customs Enforcement arrested 680 people in Mississippi, in the largest ICE raid in US history. The synchronism of such events chillingly reveals how Trump's violent and criminalizing immigration practices demanded resources at the same time that the BOP had to admit it lacked justification for USP Letcher.[32] In Kentucky, despite state sentencing reform, the state prison population continues to grow and with it, new and expanded jail and prison space. As discussed in previous chapters, Kentucky has shifted the locus of carceral power to the county jail, where almost half of the state prison population is incarcerated, in addition to prisoners held for federal agencies, including ICE. Moreover, the state has just reopened Otter Creek, the prison at the center of chapter 4's analysis, renamed as the Southeastern Correctional Complex, leasing the facility from Core Civic and housing state prisoners. This ability to move money, capacities, and cages demonstrates the amoeba-like nature of the carceral state: defeated in one place and at one scale of the state, it can reorganize and re-form itself in others, including through reopening decommissioned sites or expanding the interlocking systems of local jail capacities and border enforcement. Indeed, in the testimony from Deputy Attorney General

Rosenstein defending the Department of Justice's initial decision to withdraw funding for USP Letcher, he offered that "the FY2018 budget does request 80 million dollars to open a prison that has already been built and this will add 2,500 high-security beds. So, what we are doing Congressman [Rogers] is prioritizing our spending given the tight budget."[33] In other words, the Bureau of Prison's withdrawal of the funding was driven by an austerity calculus of maximizing carceral capacity and minimizing spending. Still, as of this writing, as US Representative Hal Rogers and Senator Mitch McConnell continue to insist on funding USP Letcher and the Trump administration insists on not building it, the $510 million remain suspended in legal limbo, appropriated specifically for the project within the Department of Justice budget and thus not able to be spent elsewhere, resulting in the funds going towards neither a federal prison in Appalachia nor another concentration camp at the southern border.

It is crucial to recognize that this stalemate is not just the product of contradicting priorities within the Republican Party but also the result of strategic and visionary coalitional politics. The NEPA strategy delayed the prison for years, buying time for organizers to disrupt and directly challenge the legitimacy of the project, as political conditions did dramatically change. LGP's #our444million campaign created a powerful local counternarrative to rural prison building, demanding transparent state investment in initiatives that address harm rather than perpetuate it, and building towards a future forged in solidarity politics between urban and rural geographies of dispossession.[34] The coalition this visioning enabled—multisited and multiscaler—exploited the moment, forcing the BOP to rescind the ROD. Thus, even in a region characterized by prison and jail building and a growing political alignment around incarceration, abolitionist challenges to the logics and practices of the carceral state offer important interventions. What unfolded in Letcher County, a place often dismissed as "Trump country," is precisely where strategies against prison building, crafted and enacted in other geographies and contexts of the long prison abolitionist movement, were adjusted to regional conditions and successfully deployed. The campaign against USP Letcher was grounded in and informed by the persistent quest for an abolition democracy, connecting st across time and space, and committed to racial, environment economic justice rooted in demands for liberating and healing the land and people, not furthering layers of toxicity that foreclose the possibility of restoration.

This historic defeat raises important questions about political, narrative, and geographic strategies for abolitionists. If prisons (and, increasingly, jails) remain entrenched in places like Appalachia because of their growing centrality to municipal strategies for revenue and infrastructure and broader claims for jobs in the midst of severe crises and abandonment, then abolitionist struggle must take seriously the plight of rural communities under racial capitalism—as places ensnared by carceral logics but *also* as insurgent spaces where consent to this regime can be, and is being, radically challenged. At the same time, the contest over the funding for USP Letcher demonstrates the elasticity of the carceral state, and therefore the need for rural anti-prison campaigns to align with struggles for migrant justice, campaigns against new jails, e-carceration, and other forms of increased carceral capacity, as well as efforts to defund and dismantle the police. The lawsuit by twenty-one incarcerated plaintiffs offers a concrete strategy for claiming the legitimate standing prisoners should have on questions of carceral expansion. The alignment of their legal challenge with the broader work conducted throughout the NEPA process, including environmental challenges stewarded by the Abolitionist Law Center and Fight Toxic Prisons, and the LGP's organizing efforts on the ground to claim #our444million, rooted in deep grassroots connections among Kentuckians for the Commonwealth, Appalshop, Critical Resistance, the Highlander Center, Project South, and other movement organizations, underscores the political power of coalition building across time, scale, race, space, strategy, and prison walls.

According to organizer, scholar, and educator Rachel Herzing, the early work in the 2000s against the prison industrial complex in Appalachia was occurring while Critical Resistance was expanding nationally, and these efforts helped to shape the organization's strategy. These enactments of mutual learning built important personal ties, political solidarities, and organizational connections, which would prove to be critically helpful to the efforts against USP Letcher almost two decades later. Just as Appalshop's *Up the Ridge* film informed organizing in California, so the fight against Delano II informed the on-the-ground organizing and legal strategy against USP Letcher.[35] USP Letcher's defeat occurred in a conjunctural moment characterized by both the shifting terrain of the carceral state *and* the work of a coalition to *plot*—that is, to imaginatively narrate and map—a future without a prison. In turn, we hope this radical history will help to inform the next site of struggle, as we continue to build as we fight.

Conclusion

The Long, Violent History and the Struggle for the Future

One of the questions I get asked when talking about prisons in Appalachia is, "Well, what are people there supposed to do instead?" It is a reasonable question, but one that also reveals important contours of the ideological fixture of the prison. It is a variation of the question every abolitionist has encountered on the issue of responses to crime—"What do you propose instead?" These questions, posed by critics and would-be allies alike, reveal an inherent premise that something must be in place to fill the footprint of the prison—as a response to harm or as a strategy of economic development—before incarceration can or should be opposed.[1] When asked specifically about Appalachia, the question seems to reveal the solidity of the prison in the imagination of what rural places can expect, as it also perhaps discloses something about what we believe they deserve.

Despite its persistence in both imagination and material landscape, the prison is neither inevitable nor indefinite. Moments of crisis create openings for new social relations and political formations. In the late-nineteenth-century Tennessee coalfields, the state responded to worker insurrections by at once meeting their demands to abolish the convict lease system and creating a new carceral regime in the footprint of the old by building Brushy Mountain State Penitentiary. One hundred years later, all over the region, local officials working in partnership with state and federal agencies turned to prisons to try to navigate crises of production and reproduction generated by the decline and departure of the coal industry. That process continues today, as counties look to expand jails and the state of Kentucky reopens Otter Creek Correctional Facility as Southeastern Correctional Complex.

But as that process arrived in Letcher County, organizers and activists stalled, insisted, impugned, reframed, and fought until the prison project lost its footing under the weight of both opposition and the newly shifting and unstable terrain of contradictory positions within the carceral state. The opposition to USP Letcher was fueled by a capacious vision of environmental justice, grassroots democracy, and antiracist class solidarity. The #our444million campaign and the comments to the Bureau of Prisons generated an archive that countered the notion of total support and that offered visions of alternative economic and political futures. In an interview during my first trip to Letcher County, Letcher Governance Project cofounder Elizabeth Sanders spoke honestly about the tension she felt between the desire for jobs that "feed your soul" and the material necessity of "jobs that feed your family now." Ultimately, she told me, there is "no one silver bullet" for a transition away from coal and prison economies, but rather "1,000 silver BB's."

The win against USP Letcher "wasn't a win," as Sanders later observed of the dialectics of the campaign and the lack of an alternative plan for the county's economy in the wake of the prison's defeat. But stopping USP Letcher notched a victory in what is a much broader struggle. It is the dimensions of that struggle, and the relationships—between urban and rural, between fights against police and fights against prisons, and between abolition and anticapitalism—that define it to which this chapter turns to conclude.

Crises of 2020

The conditions under which I am writing this conclusion bear heavily on the arguments that have unfolded in this book. It is currently October 2020 and the pandemic known as Severe Acute Respiratory Syndrome Coronavirus 2 (SARS-CoV-2), or simply as "coronavirus," continues to rage through the United States and around the world. Globally, fifty-two million people have had the illness and more than a million have died from it. In the United States alone, more than ten million people have contracted the virus just since the beginning of the calendar year; more than two hundred thousand of them have died because of it. The pandemic has completely altered the rhythms of daily life for everyone. I am writing this sentence, for example, at 5:38 a.m. Like many children, my two daughters are attending school remotely this fall, and I assist with their work and other needs between the hours of 8:30 a.m. and

2:00 p.m., while my wife works. The predawn hours provide some of the only time to write, edit, prepare classes (which I teach entirely online, like millions of other educators in this moment), and do other work. Both my wife and I now fit our full-time jobs into the seams of daily life organized around making this period work in some semifunctional way for our children. And of course, we have it better than most as two relatively privileged people whose jobs have some built-in flexibility. So many others—facing evictions, lack of health care, unemployment, and other forms of precarity during the hyperausterity that defines the United States' response to a global pandemic—have it so much worse.

Coronavirus is highly contagious, spreading through respiratory droplets and particles, which has produced an acute need for social distancing and mask wearing, practices that some Americans, including President Donald Trump, have flouted. But these practices, which are essential to public health, are also structurally very difficult to maintain in certain places, most importantly in prisons and jails. As Dylan Rodríguez puts it in characteristically brilliant prose, "[The] Pandemic is neither universal in its consequences nor common in its scales and intensities of coerced misery, suffering, and mourning."[2] Prisons and jails around the country have seen horrifying outbreaks of coronavirus. As of late October 2020, 161,349 people in prison have tested positive for the virus.[3] Some states, under pressure from advocacy groups and organizers, have taken measures to release some people from both prisons and jails to alleviate overcrowding.

This has occurred in Kentucky, where close to two thousand people have been released since the beginning of 2020 because of the pandemic. But that number is woefully insufficient, as it constitutes less than 10 percent of the state's prison population, and is not even close to enough to alleviate overcrowding. Moreover, even as the state's Democratic governor, Andy Beshear, has received considerable praise for his handling of coronavirus in the early months of the pandemic, he also has reopened Otter Creek Correctional Facility in Wheelwright, purportedly as a way to ease overcrowding in the existing state prisons. Overcrowding is a problem produced by criminalization and the state's ongoing investment in prisons; reopening a decommissioned prison evidences and enacts the same structural problems. Reopening a prison in this particular moment of the pandemic is an unconscionable act of what Rodríguez calls the "genocidal logic of pandemic in a Civilizational order that is—and has always been—a state of asymmetrical war."[4] In California, there have been just under sixteen thousand coronavirus cases amongst state prisoners, a number higher than the entire prison populations of more than a dozen states. Almost half of South Dakota's prison population has tested positive for coronavirus. In Kentucky, several prisons, including Little Sandy, have had outbreaks of coronavirus, with hundreds of prisoners and dozens of staff becoming ill.[5] The ongoing reliance on and investment in cages, including in the coalfields, demonstrates more than just an ideological attachment to incarceration. With over twenty-five hundred coronavirus-related deaths among prisoners, including hundreds across Kentucky and other Central Appalachian states, the lives lived—and cut short—in cages in 2020 demonstrate an acceleration and intensification of the "slow violence" of imprisonment.[6]

The coronavirus pandemic is not the only contemporary crisis that bears heavily on the analyses offered in this book. A searing insurrection and a movement against police have also characterized 2020. In response to police killings of Breonna Taylor in Louisville, George Floyd in Minneapolis, Jacob Blake in Kenosha, Walter Wallace in Philadelphia, and so many others, protests have occurred in all fifty states in possibly the largest movement in United States history.[7] The 2020 uprising builds on the emergence and prominence of Black Lives Matter, the movement that materialized in the wake of high-profile vigilante and police killings of Trayvon Martin, Eric Garner, Mike Brown, Tamir Rice, Freddie Gray, Renisha McBride, Sandra Bland, John Crawford, Rekia Boyd, and hundreds of others during the preceding years. Moreover, decades of abolitionist organizing and intellectual production have shifted the commonsense analysis of police in this moment. While there are various orientations adjusted to the political contexts of different regions and communities, there is no doubt that a central political tendency of the 2020 movement centers on defunding and abolishing, rather than reforming and retraining, the police.

A shallow political analysis might see police violence and the movement for defunding as only tangentially related to the work of understanding, and upending, the rise of prisons in Central Appalachia. Criminology, for example, often abstracts analyses of cops from those of cages by segmenting scholars and students, as if police and prisons are not fundamentally mutually constituting forces and technologies. The arrest, for example, as David Correia and Tyler Wall clarify, "is a euphemism for captivity. . . . To be arrested is to be captured, to be caught and deprived of bodily autonomy, however temporarily or prolonged captivity might last. Arrest is not only a mode of state violence, but an initial and primary site of incarceration."[8] Moreover, some on the left have disparaged defunding the police as both enacting and portending austere neoliberal changes, shrinking the state further and opening up spaces for privatized forces to fill.[9] This analysis entirely misses foundational political claims of abolition. Defunding the police, like defeating USP Letcher, is an *anti-austerity* politics, a demand both *against* the quotidian and spectacular violence of police and prisons and *for* political formations that fund and value life-giving and -sustaining institutions, capacities, and individuals. In Los Angeles, for example, organizers with Black Lives Matter–LA convened the People's Budget based on grassroots participatory budgeting with twenty-five thousand residents across the city. In the words of their report, "Our document and data both reveal a clear referendum: invest in universal needs (e.g., housing security, public health/health care, mental health and wellness, etc.) and divest from traditional forms of policing."[10] In Minneapolis, organizers with MPD150, one of the organizations that pushed that city's council to pass a resolution defunding the police, note that abolition is "a process of strategically reallocating resources, funding, and responsibility away from police and toward community-based models of safety, support, and prevention. . . . We want to create space for more mental health service providers, violence prevention specialists, social workers, victim/survivor advocates, elders and spiritual leaders, neighbors and friends—all of the people who really make up the fabric of a community—to look out for one another."[11] These and many other calls arising out of the 2020 movement, grounded in the visionary work of decades of abolitionist praxis, reject outright the neoliberal logics of privatization, state retrenchment, and austerity.

Demands to defund the police align with the calls from Letcher County to defeat the prison. On the most fundamental level, defunding the police implicates incarceration; no cops mean no cages. Beyond that, the work of the coalition to defeat USP Letcher, and in particular the call from the Letcher Governance Project for #our444million, had sights set beyond the prison itself. As Sylvia Ryerson and I argued in chapter 7, #our444million was a claim for grassroots democratic planning, a rejection of extractivism and incarceration, and a demand for economies organized around restorative and regenerative practices for land and people. It was also a politics that understood the prison "as a key component in the entirety of capitalist social relations," connecting rural and urban communities through criminalization and incarceration practices.[12] The LGP's rejection of the prison, then, was both a call for something different for rural Appalachia and also a stance of class solidarity with racialized and criminalized communities in and outside of the region. As we observed in chapter 7, members of the LGP were radicalized through experiences with WMMT 88.7's *Calls from Home* show, the history of activism in the region, and the emergent Black Lives Matter movement in the early years of the 2010s. Indeed, the decision to use #our444million was forged in LGP's analysis of material conditions on the ground in Letcher County *and* in the group's conversations with Black grassroots organizers in the South fighting a campaign against police in schools. Defunding the police and defeating prisons are not just aligned. Rather, they are two fronts of the same struggle.

The twin crises of this moment are exceptional in the scale of their expression (in the case of the violence of the pandemic and the uprisings against police). But preventable deaths due to poverty, criminalization, arrest, imprisonment, and disinvestments in public health are ordinary and central components of the banal configurations of state power that has invested so heavily in cops and cages quite literally at the expense of care. As it has built prisons, Central Appalachia has seen hospital closures, part of the broader and disturbing pattern of decline in rural hospitals across the country. The hospital in Pennington Gap, Virginia, the community surrounded by three prisons and where Beth Davies worked as a substance abuse counselor, closed in 2013 due to the confluence of low use, a lack of physicians, and the state government's refusal to expand Medicaid coverage under the Affordable Care Act. This latter maneuver left the hospital without a path to reimbursement for patients without insurance. In Martin County, Kentucky, the Bureau of Prisons opened the most expensive federal prison in history in 2003 while residents were still digging out from the coal sludge spill that the EPA identified at the time as the worst environmental disaster in southern United States history. In Letcher County, health workers looked to the prison as a method to bring more patients, and thus stability, to their clinics. Police, pollution, and prisons—the "three P's" identified by Craig Gilmore and Rose Braz as central environmental threats to rural and urban communities in California, to which we might add a fourth, public health crises—continue to configure the carceral state across urban and rural communities, shaping in the process the terrain on which struggles occur and abolition is practiced.[13]

The Long, Violent History and the Struggle for the Future

In the late summer of 2020, eastern Kentucky musician Tyler Childers released the song "Long Violent History," the final track off his eponymous album. On an otherwise bluegrass and country instrumental album by the eastern Kentucky native, "Long Violent History" is oriented toward Childers's fellow white Appalachians and offers a reflection on positionality and a call for multiracial class solidarity in the historical moment of uprisings against police:

> Now what would you get if you heard my opinion, conjecturin' on matters that I ain't never dreamed
> in all my born days, this white boy from Hickman, based on the way that the world's been to me?
> It's called me belligerent, it's took me for ignorant, but it ain't never once made me scared just to be.
> Could you imagine just constantly worrying, kicking and fighting, begging to breathe?
> How many boys could they haul off this mountain, shoot full of holes, cuffed and laying in the streets
> 'til we come into town in stark raving anger, looking for answers and armed to the teeth?
> Thirty-aught-sixes and Papaw's old pistol, how many, you reckon, would it be four or five?
> Or would that be the start of a long violent history, of tucking our tails as we tried to abide?

Childers's reflexive questions recognize a legacy of Appalachian opposition to state violence. Contemporary fights in and against carceral

Appalachia are a part of this much longer struggle in the coalfields, which includes everything from labor organizing and insurrection to fights for the abolition of strip mining, welfare rights, full employment, community health, black lung benefits, and political and economic self-determination.

Mitch Whitaker made this argument, connecting his opposition to the Bureau of Prisons to his grandfather's fight against coal companies as part of a multigenerational struggle for his family's land and for the broader region. Beth Davies and Mickey and Nina McCoy offered similar analyses of land expropriation and toxicity, linking extraction, waste, pharmaceuticals, and prisons. Members of the Letcher Governance Project, who in other parts of their lives conduct sex education workshops for Appalachian youth, host anticapitalist podcasts, join laid-off miners in direct actions against coal companies, and work in community media, environmental conservation, drug treatment, and voting rights, understood the campaign against USP Letcher as part of a radical genealogy of political work in the region.

But while these are unquestionably Appalachian struggles, it would be a mistake to see them as provincial or separate. The long, violent history blazing in the streets in 2020 is *also a history of Appalachia*. It includes settler-colonial expropriation, anti-Black racism, spectacular and quotidian displays of state and corporate violence, environmental devastation, the not-so-slow deaths hastened by cancer and black lung, and the rise of the prison. Tyler Childers's sublime poetry is a call for white Appalachians to join the struggle for Black lives, but it is also a reminder to remember their own history.

To end where we began, Central Appalachia is a place with a distinct history and is also a set of relationships and interfaces, including the meeting of historical forces that created it and continue to remake it through struggle. As extraction and incarceration are fundamental to both global racial capitalism and state formation, so too are the fights against strip mining and mountaintop removal, for unionization and black lung benefits, and for a future without prisons and police central to the work of imagining and realizing something radically different, for Appalachia and beyond.

ACKNOWLEDGMENTS

I started the preliminary research that eventually would lead to this book in 2011. I am writing the acknowledgments in the first weeks of 2021. It has taken me *a while* to figure out what to make of prison growth in Central Appalachia. Many people have shaped and sharpened my analysis along the way.

Comrades in the Critical Prison Studies Caucus of the American Studies Association have created intellectual, political, virtual, and physical spaces for dynamic and committed work to flourish. I am grateful for the opportunities created by, and the collaborations and conversations with, Andrea Morrell, Anoop Mirpuri, Annie Spencer, Anne Bonds, Ashley Hunt, Brett Story, Bronwyn Dobchuk-Land, Christina Heatherton, Craig Gilmore, Dan Berger, David Stein, Dylan Rodríguez, Elissa Underwood Marek, Emily Thuma, Erica Meiners, Garrett Felber, Jack Norton, James Kilgore, Jen Manion, Jenna Loyd, Jordan Camp, Judy Rhorer, Katy Ryan, Laura McTighe, Laurel Mei-Singh, Liat Ben-Moshe, Lucia Trimbur, Lydia Pelot-Hobbs, Marisol LeBrón, Melissa Burch, Michelle Brown, Micol Seigel, Naomi Murakawa, A. Naomi Paik, Orisanmi Burton, Patrick DeDauw, Rashad Shabazz, Sarah Haley, Shana Agid, Stuart Schrader, Sylvia Ryerson, Rebecca Hill, Ruth Wilson Gilmore, Toussaint Losier, and Tyler Wall.

My friends, colleagues, and comrades at Eastern Kentucky University and in the insurgent pockets of criminology offer valuable spaces of support, respite, and inspiration. My thanks to Alessandro De Giorgi, Alex Vitale, Avi Brisman, Bill McClanahan, Brendan McQuade, Bronwyn Dobchuk-Land, Chris Magno, Corina Medley, Eamonn Carrabine, Dawn Rothe, Luis Fernandez, Gary Potter, Jeff Ferrell, Justin Piché, Justin Turner, Kaitlyn Selman, Ken Tunnell, Kevin Walby, Megan McDowell, Michael Coyle, Michelle Brown, Phil Parnell, Randy Myers, Reuben Miller, Rob Werth, Stefania De Petris, Stephanie Kane, Tammi Arford, Tony Platt, Travis Linnemann, Victor Kappeler, Victoria Collins, and Viviane Saleh-Hanna. In addition, EKU's School of Justice Studies Research Program, administered by Peter Kraska and Amy Eades, offered generous internal funding and support for numerous years of research for this project.

Conversations with people in, of, and about Central Appalachia, and the region's relationship to extraction, incarceration, racial capitalism, and abolition, have led to crucial expansions and refinements of the analysis found in the book. I am forever grateful to both early and ongoing discussions and strategy sessions with Amelia Kirby, Ann Kingsolver, Annie Stilz, Ash-Lee Woodard-Henderson, Ashley Hunt, Avery Kolers, Beth Davies, Beth Howard, Betsy Taylor, Brett Story, Craig Gilmore, Dustin McDaniels, Elizabeth Sanders, Emily Posner, Jacob Kang-Brown, Jack Norton, Jasmine Heiss, Jordan Mazurek, Karen Rignall, Lee Bullock, Lydia Pelot-Hobbs, Lill Prosperino, Lindsay Shade, Michelle Brown, Mickey McCoy, Mitch Whitaker, Mizari Suarez, Naomi Murakawa, Nina McCoy, Panagioti Tsolkas, Rachel Herzing, Robert Perdue, Robin Bird, Ruth Wilson Gilmore, Shannon Bell, Sylvia Ryerson, Tanya Turner, Tarence Ray, Tom Sexton, Tyler Wall, and Zhandarka Kurti. Many of these people, and many more not named here, are part of organizations whose work on and analysis of these issues have shaped my own, especially as someone not from the region. These organizations include the Abolitionist Law Center, California Prison Moratorium Project, Critical Resistance, the Highlander Research and Education Center, Fight Toxic Prisons, Kentuckians for the Commonwealth, the Letcher Governance Project, and the Vera Institute of Justice's In Our Backyards (IOB) project. Researching and writing in conversation with Jack Norton, whose work with IOB on rural jail growth is mapping the new terrain of the carceral state, was particularly generative and affirming.

Graduate student research assistants and students have contributed significant support and insight over the years, from helping to conduct background research to editing, coauthoring, and engaging in ongoing discussions. My thanks to Casey Bertone, Elizabeth Bailey, Jerome Williams, Jordan Frazier, Jordan Mazurek, Kyra Martinez, Macey Hall, Melissa Pujol, Molly Dunn, Natalie Cranfill, Rossana Diaz, and Savannah Sublette.

Michelle Brown has been in my corner for so long that her support and encouragement is baked into everything I do. She is mentor, friend, colleague, and comrade par excellence. My friendship with Tyler Wall has deeply impacted my thinking on racial capitalism, the carceral state, and the Left; I can only hope that our friendship has had a similar effect on his understanding of NBA basketball. Our conversations—in bars, over texts, and once upon a time in our shared office—consistently push me to think harder and further in order to get the analysis right. Sylvia Ryerson's work on prison expansion in Central Appalachia is foundational and her support for this book has been energizing and steadying. Sylvia shared her personal archive to help with my research and has been a brilliant interlocutor for the entirety of the project. Coauthoring the final chapter of this book together, grounded in conversations with the organizers and activists responsible for the defeat of USP Letcher, was a true experience of collaborative and committed abolitionist scholarship. I consider myself incredibly lucky to have been able to learn from the work of Ruth Wilson Gilmore and Craig Gilmore for the last two decades, ever since a summer internship in 2000 provided me with a front-row seat to abolitionist organizing in California. Their work—studying, analyzing, educating, writing, and organizing—has deeply influenced my own, very much including this book, and I am thankful to and for them.

Numerous campuses and organizations have invited me to speak on carceral expansion and opposition over the years. I am honored by the opportunities to have been in conversation with students, scholars, and activists at Gannon University (Department of Criminal Justice); Kansas State University (Department of Sociology, Anthropology, and Social Work); Old Dominion University (Critical Intersections conference); Princeton University (Students for Prison Education and Reform conference); the University of Kentucky (the Appalachian Center; Department of Community and Leadership Development; Department of Geography); the University of Louisville (Department of Philosophy; Princeton-Kentucky Institute); and the University of Tennessee (Department of Sociology; Criminalizing the Mountain South series).

Collaborating with Jill Frank on this book was an inspiring experience. We have been friends for more than two decades, the latter half of which included our work together on this project. Our research trips somehow always managed to be focused and productive and yet underwritten with a kind of lightness and ease that comes with long-lasting friendship. Her photographs in the book offer both a visual story of the carceral geographies of Central Appalachia as well as an intervention into dominant representations of the region. Crucially, I *learned* from her images—seeing the interfaces of the prison definitively shaped my analysis. "Seeing comes before words," John Berger has noted. Jill's images helped me to find the words.

One hears stories about bad experiences with reviewers. My own experience was emphatically different. Reviews of earlier versions of this manuscript by Shannon Bell, Jordan Camp, Christina Heatherton, Brett Story, and other anonymous reviewers have improved the clarity, sharpened the analysis, and otherwise deeply improved the book. I am so grateful for their thorough, generous, and rigorous suggestions and critiques.

I am thankful to be working with NYU Press again. Ilene Kalish, Eric Zinner, and Sonia Tsuruoka have offered enthusiastic support for this project for years. Alexia Traganas and Emily Wright provided crucial final editing. I am deeply appreciative of the encouragement, patience, and trust I received from the entire team.

Finishing this book in the beginning of 2021 has meant that some of the final pieces came together during the most difficult year of many of our lives. Despite going far too long without seeing them in person because of the need for social distancing, my parents, Ken and Susan, and my sister extraordinaire, Rebecca, manage to convey heartfelt support and excitement for this book over virtual gatherings, texts, and phone calls. I am beyond thankful for them and cannot wait to share a hug. I also always appreciate the support from my "other" family, especially April Dickey, Becky Denham, Clayton Gentile, and Frances Strickland.

The COVID-19 pandemic's impact on the world has sharpened many contradictions; in my own home, it forced important shifts for my partner and me in what work looks like and when it occurs. Much of my writing and editing during the last year of the project have happened in the seams of the days as part of our attempt to support everyone's needs, in particular those of our children. My predawn and late afternoon writing sessions bookended days filled with baking projects, hikes, games, bike rides, dog walks, virtual school, homework, and lots of conversations, both light and heavy. In other words, moments of adventure, boredom, hardship, hilarity, and fierce feelings of loss and love configured my life outside of this book, and therefore also shaped every word within it. My eternal thanks and love to Brooke, Talula, and Rhea for all of it.

NOTES

INTRODUCTION

1 There are important exceptions here. See Adler-Bell 2019; Che 2005; Davis 2012; Perdue and Sanchagrin 2016; Ryerson 2010, 2013; Ryerson and Schept 2018; Szuberla and Kirby 2006.
2 Huling 2002, 1–2, quoting Beale 2001.
3 Nicholas Mirzoeff 2011a, 2011b. Following Jacques Rancière, Mirzoeff relies on this phrase to identify visuality's presence and to demarcate what he calls the "right to look." It is notable that this line is a literal command of police. I am grateful to Tyler Wall for making this point.
4 Stewarding this iterative process here has been work from scholars like Ruth Wilson Gilmore. Early on in her foundational *Golden Gulag*, Gilmore notes all of the urgent social issues that prisons both generate and putatively resolve. She then argues, "Such breadth belies the common view that prisons sit on the edge—at the margins of social spaces, economic regions, political territories, and fights for rights. This apparent marginality is a trick of perspective because, as every geographer knows, edges are also interfaces" (2007, 11). It also bears mentioning that the dominant tendency within criminology is not to say that there is a complete absence of criminological scholarship that understands crime and punishment as central to the operations of racial capitalism. In particular, see Christie 2001; De Giorgi 2006; Greenberg 1981; Melossi and Pavarini 2018; Rusche and Kirchheimer 2017; Platt et al. 1982; Reiman and Leighton 2013; Lynch and Michaloski 2006.
5 For a helpful discussion on the periodization of the carceral state, see Benson 2019.
6 Brown 2009; Smith 2013.
7 Stuart Hall 1981, 238. More broadly, see Hall 1982, 1996; Hall et al. 2013. Other scholars have made similar arguments. For Judith Butler, the photograph does not sit idly awaiting interpretation, but rather actively interprets because "it is constituted fundamentally by what is left out, maintained outside the frame within which representations appear. We can think of the frame, then, as active, as both jettisoning and presenting, and as doing both at once, in silence, without any visible sign of its operation" (Butler 2009, 73). Katherine Biber makes a similar argument, writing of Susan Sontag that the author "urges us to remember that, for everything we look at, there is something else we have failed to notice" (Biber 2007, 16). Eamonn Carrabine likewise has written of Roland Barthes that "from the outset he sets himself the task of unmasking bourgeois 'common sense'

and disturbing the 'what goes without saying' to reveal how the seemingly innocent representations and conventions of everyday life shore up power relations" (Barthes 1993, 11, in Carrabine 2017, 32). As Jones and Wardle explain in their treatment of the visual construction of Maxine Carr, "A photograph imbued and read within the dominant ideology will itself become expressive of those ideas; will solidify them, then seem to connote them inherently" (Jones and Wardle 2010, 56). As Phil Carney notes, the photograph "is not primarily a semiotic spectacle. It is not a static picture but a dynamic power. As a social force, the photograph performs in a field where the material realities of cultural practices in the field of power and desire are at stake" (Carney 2010, 31).

8 Fowler 2015. See also Garringer 2020.
9 Benjamin 1969a, 1969b; Buck-Morss 1991; S. M. Smith 2013.
10 Spoken to the writer Eric Reece, in Reece 2006, 61.
11 See Norton and Stein 2020 for a crucial corrective to this kind of scholarship.
12 See Bonds 2013, 2012, 2009; Che 2005; Eason 2016; Gilmore 2007; Huling 2002; King, Mauer, and Huling 2003; Lynch 2010; Morrell 2021, 2012; Norton 2016; Schoenfeld 2018; Walker et al. 2017; Williams 2011.
13 Lewis, Johnson, and Askins 1978; Lewis and Knipe 1978; House 2016.
14 Billings and Blee 2000; Dunaway 1995; Marley 2016a; Stoll 2017; Walls 1978.
15 Eller 2008; Scott 2010.
16 See Bell 2016 for important examination of this particular campaign and discourse. See also Ray 2019; Ryerson 2020.
17 Dunaway 1995, 67.
18 Billings and Blee 2000, 36.
19 Neeson 1993, 329. See also Linebaugh 2014, 144, on the same point, albeit with a slightly different periodization.
20 Dunbar-Ortiz 2014, 52–54.
21 Wolfe 2016, 22–23.
22 Dunaway 1995, 68.
23 Richard Kirby, quoted in Appalachian Land Ownership Task Force 1983, 10.
24 Appalachian Land Ownership Task Force 1983.
25 Stoll 2017, 7.
26 Perdue and Sanchagrin 2016 note that the region is home to twenty-nine prisons. They use a larger regional geography for Central Appalachia than is typical.
27 Clear and Frost 2014, 177–86; Gottschalk 2015, 98–116; Tucker and Cadora 2003.
28 Austin et al. 2013; Gottschalk 2015; Story 2016a.
29 De Giorgi 2017; Miller 2014.
30 Cheves 2014a, 2019.
31 Cheves 2019; Norton and Schept 2019.
32 Camp 2016; Gilmore 2007; Lichtenstein 2011; Linebaugh 1976; Peck 2003; Peck and Theodore 2008; Rusche and Kircheimer 2017; Wacquant 2009.
33 Kentucky Energy and Environment Cabinet, Kentucky Quarterly Coal Report 2020; Kentucky Energy and Environment Cabinet, "Kentucky Coal Facts—2017";

Bureau of Labor Statistics, Occupational Employment and Wages, May 2017: Correctional Officers and Jailers, https://www.bls.gov.
34 "Occupational Employment Statistics," U.S. Bureau of Labor Statistics, https://www.bls.gov.
35 *Correctional Building News*, 1999, quoted in Christie 2001, 136.
36 See for example Hall et al. 2013; Hall and Massey 2010.
37 On the 1950 National Bituminous Coal Wage Agreement and its effects on employment, see Eller 2008; Marley 2016b; Williams 2002, 318.
38 Linebaugh 1976.
39 Hallett 2012. On the relationship between the prison and the labor market, see also Gilmore 2007; Lichtenstein 2011; Peck and Theodore 2008; Purser 2012; Stein 2014; Thompson 2010; Wacquant 2009; Western and Beckett 1999.
40 See Eason 2016 for a close examination of how this transition unfolded in a different region. See also Bonds 2013; Huling 2002, 1998; Thorpe 2014; Walker et al. 2017.
41 Katz 2001; Schept 2015.
42 Du Bois 1998; Gilmore 2007; Roediger 1999; Singh 2019, 2014. On this issue regarding prison siting specifically, see Bonds 2013 and Ooten and Sawyer 2016.
43 Estes and Dunbar-Ortiz 2020; Petitjean and Gilmore 2018; Melamed 2015; Robinson 2000. Robinson notes at the very beginning of *Black Marxism*, for example, that racism "was not simply a convention for ordering the relations of European to non-European people, but has its genesis in the 'internal' relations of European peoples" (2). Melamed also reads this history specifically back through Marx and in particular primitive accumulation, noting the racializing work of vagabondage laws during the enclosing of the commons and the transition from feudalism to capitalism. J. M. Neeson's book on the enclosure of the commons also observes the centrality of racialization to the expropriation of land: "Critics of commons loathed commoners with a xenophobic intensity. They were a 'sordid race,' as foreign and uncultivated as the land that fed them. Like commons, they were wild and unproductive. They were lazy and dangerous" (1993, 32).
44 Fields and Fields 2014.
45 Norton and Stein 2020. See Adolph Reed and Merlin Chokwayun (2012, 150) on what they call the "interpretive pathologies" of some social science research in the measurement of disparity.
46 Melamed 2015; Singh 2005, 223; Gilmore 2002, 261.
47 Catte 2018, 52.
48 Pollard and Jacobsen 2020, 22–29.
49 On the double erasure of Black people in Appalachia, see Brown 2018. Ronald L. Lewis notes that at the height of African American mining in in the United States, Black people accounted for over 650,000 workers in the industry in 1920. By 1970, there were fewer than 130,000 (R. Lewis 1987, xii). Both Lewis and Turner and Cabbell (1985) discuss these dynamics across the Appalachian region, including in West Virginia, where they were particularly pronounced. For how they played out

in certain specific contexts, see Billings and Blee 2000, in particular 208–40, for a focus on Clay County, Kentucky, and Brown 2018 for a focus on Harlan County, Kentucky.
50 Nyden 1974, 3.
51 Nyden 1974, 6. On the role of Black miners in the formation of the NMU see also 44–45.
52 Bianca Spriggs notes that Walker found a definition of Appalachians in Webster's dictionary that defined them as "white residents from the mountains." It was this literal writing of race into region that prompted his original coinage of "Affrilachian." See Spriggs 2011. For more on Affrilachian poetry and other literature see Walker 2000, 2006; Spriggs and Paden 2017.
53 This process, known as prison-based gerrymandering, has been roundly examined and criticized by many scholars and organizations. See Huling 2002; Hunter and Wagner 2008; Wagner 2002; Walker et al. 2017, especially their discussion of state expenditures in rural prison towns; and the work of the Prison Policy Initiative on the issue: "Prison Gerrymandering Project," Prison Policy Initiative, http://www.prisonersofthecensus.org.
54 Pulido 2016, 13. See also Pulido 2000.
55 On hegemonic masculinity and coal mining, see Bell 2016; Bell and York 2010; and Bell and Braun 2010. Also see Daggett 2018 for a broader analysis of what she calls "petro-masculinities."
56 Cowen and Siciliano 2011.
57 See Robinson 2007. Also see Camp and Heatherton 2017. On prisons and the racialization of white prison guards, see Morrell 2021.
58 Melamed 2015, 81.
59 Wray 2006; McCarroll 2018.
60 Stoll 2017, 24.
61 See for example Fields 1990; Robinson 2000; Wolfe 2016.
62 In recognizing the centrality of racialization, it is important not to flatten out the difference in racism's applications, which tends to reflect the different orientation or position between a given racialized group and capitalism. See Patrick Wolfe 2016 especially on this point generally. For a concise discussion of this point in the Appalachian context vis-à-vis "the Black south" and "white Appalachia," see Klotter 1985.
63 Dunbar-Ortiz 2014; Andrea Smith 2012; Wolfe 2016; Bonds and Inwood 2015; Reardon and TallBear 2012; N. Estes 2019.
64 Robinson 2000; Gilmore 2007.
65 Wolfe 2016, 5.
66 See HoSang and Lowndes 2019 for a particularly compelling discussion of contemporary racialization of white poverty. In noting increases in phenomena like deaths of despair, a growing white incarceration rate, and ongoing dispossessions, HoSang and Lowndes note that the "wages of whiteness" no longer underwrite a guaranteed avoidance of crisis: "We need to reevaluate the assumption that

whiteness reliably provides a kind of material and social floor below which those marked as white cannot fall" (56).

67 While differentiating between the terms can be an important intellectual and political project in order to trace their respective cultural histories, it is equally important to note that they are sometimes used interchangeably and to perform social differentiation. As Nancy Isenberg writes in her history of the term "white trash," "Waste people. Offscourings. Lubbers. Bogtrotters. Rascals. Squatters. Crackers. Clay-eaters. Tackis. Mudsills. Scalawags. Briar hoppers. Hillbillies. Low-downers. White niggers. Degenerates. White trash. Rednecks. Trailer trash. Swamp people. . . . They are renamed often, but they do not disappear" (2016, 320). Alternatively, see 255–66, where Isenberg parses "red neck," "white trash," and "hillbilly." Similarly, Anthony Harkins notes in his cultural history of the term "hillbilly" that in its primary role as a signification of inferior cultural traits (rather than a specific geography), the term is

> no different than dozens of similar labels and ideological and graphic constructs of poor and working class southern whites coined by middle- and upper-class commentators. . . . These derisive terms were intended to indicate a diet rooted in scarcity ("clay eater," "corn cracker," "rabbit twister"), physical appearance and clothing that denoted hard and specifically working class laboring conditions ("red neck," "wool hat," "lint head"), an animal-like existence on the economic and physical fringes of society ("brush ape," "ridge runner," "briar hopper"), ignorance and racism, and in all cases, economic, genetic and cultural impoverishment (best summed up by the label "poor white" or more pointedly "poor white trash"). (Harkins 2004, 5)

68 On "white trash," see Isenberg 2016; Linnemann 2016; Linnemann and Wall 2013; Murakawa 2011; Wray and Newitz 1997; Wray 2006.
69 Wray 2006, 2.
70 Harkins 2004, 5.
71 Isenberg 2016, 320. We can also see how the terms for marking racial difference and deficiency move across spaces and nestle into specific contexts. Carl Zimring writes of the ways in which skin was a technology of power servicing the management of waste in industrializing Chicago and other cities: "In nineteenth-century constructions of race, white supremacists stained Native Americans, Asian Americans and African Americans with assumptions that their skin, bodies and behaviors were somehow dirtier than the skin, bodies and behaviors of 'white' people. Similar pejoratives were used against Jews, Slavs, Italians, Hungarians, and a host of people Americans now uncritically identify as being white. These were people who were entrusted to keep American society clean; these were the people who got their hands dirty to do so" (2015, 6).
72 Isenberg 2016, 320.
73 See McIntyre and Nast 2011 on the dehumanization and "de-naturing" of surplus people and places. See Linnemann 2016, especially 46–84, on the mobility of white trash from urban to rural contexts. See Allen 2012 on distinctions between

racial and national oppressions. Carl Zimring has written extensively on the ways in which waste, as a social process, shaped industrializing cities and their rapidly growing populations of immigrants and Black Americans. He makes a number of points germane to a discussion of Appalachian topography and residents, as well as to their conflation. First, he notes, "Immigrants living near the stockyards were subject to noxious odors and polluted water. Jewish and Italian immigrants who worked in the waste trades were blamed by local reformers such as Jane Addams and the Chicago Juvenile Protection Association for being 'moral menaces' to urban children" (Zimring 2015, 144). The spatial proximity between immigrants, not yet considered white, and industries considered dirty assisted in their conflation. The noxious odors and dirty work polluted environment and person alike. Writing of Homeowners Loan Corporations in urban areas during the New Deal and their practices that came to be known as "redlining," Zimring notes that the HOLC's work "conflated physical attributes of the built environment with racial and economic attributes of the people living in the buildings. This model equated physical deterioration and demographic change. . . . The mere presence of undesirable people was enough social pollution to downgrade an entire neighborhood as an unfit investment" (2015, 155). In the first passage, we see the proximity to dirty industry polluting the bodies of those immigrants in the vicinity; here we see the direction change and the racial characteristics of the residents contaminate the surrounding urban ecology. Looking back to the enclosures of the commons in Europe reveals similar patterns of conflation between common lands and common peoples. J. M. Neeson notes, "Critics of commons loathed commoners with a xenophobic intensity. They were a 'sordid race,' as foreign and uncultivated as the land that fed them. Like commons, they were wild and unproductive. They were lazy and dangerous" (1993, 32). While a central task of this book is to locate prison growth in Appalachia in the specific history of the region, it also must be acknowledged that representational practices deployed to produce difference—including conflations of "dirty" people and "dirty" land—in the service of managing order connect Appalachia across time and space to many other areas and people. In fact, processes of criminalization and state violence help to forge that connection. The history of the foundational period of land enclosures and consolidation of bourgeois class power occurred, in part, through processes of criminalization, imprisonment, and execution reliant on new classifications of crime. As Peter Linebaugh observes of this period characterized by expropriations and hangings of the newly urban poor, it's a "history of the neck," and as Marx noted, this "history of . . . expropriation is written in the annals of mankind in blood and fire" (Linebaugh 2006, xxiii; Marx 1990, 875; see also Linebaugh 2014).
74 Stoll 2017, 21.
75 Harkins 2004, 30; see also Catte 2018, esp. 35–38.
76 In Gaventa 1980, 65.
77 Shapiro 1986, 115; for a broader theorization and history of the production of knowledge about mountains and mountaineers, see Debarbieux and Rudaz 2015.

78 Billings and Blee 2000, 28–30.
79 Kephart 1922, 446, quoted in Billings and Blee 2000, 29.
80 Catte 2018, 74; Du Bois 1998, 17–31; Harkins 2004, 110–11.
81 Scott 2010, 37. See more broadly 31–64.
82 Harrington 1997.
83 Harrington 1997, 46.
84 Williamson 2013; J. D. Vance 2016.
85 Williamson 2020.
86 J. D. Vance 2016; Catte 2018; see also Harkins and McCarroll 2019.
87 Stoll 2017, 20.
88 On this process of crafting race, see Fields and Fields 2014; Linnemann 2016; HoSang and Lowndes 2019. On this process in Appalachia, see McCarroll 2018.
89 Camp and Heatherton 2017, 101.
90 HoSang and Lowndes 2019, 159.
91 Scott 2010, 139. See also Eller 1982. Scott quotes from a *Mine Workers Journal* article found in Robert Shogan's *Battle of Blair Mountain* that comments on the deaths of thirteen miners in a mine explosion: "These local boys died in the interests of democracy, they were exerting their manpower in the production of coal with which to help win the war." See Shogan 2004, 50–51, in Scott 2010, 139.
92 Batteau 1990.
93 Williams 1978, 353. See also HoSang and Lowndes 2019, in particular 48–55.
94 Stewart 1996, 117. Stewart expands that "'Appalachia,' like the inner city, became a symbolic pocket of poverty in an affluent society and an unassimilated region in an otherwise united nation. . . . It was at once an absence that marked the gains of 'our' material wealth, education, literacy, and sophistication and a living folk-ways that marked the hope of redemption lodged in culture or tradition itself" (118).
95 Helen Lewis et al. 1978; House 2016. See Anglin 2016; Billings and Blee 2000; and Fisher and Smith 2016 for concise critiques of the colonialism model and Walls 1978 for a more in-depth critical treatment.
96 See Neel 2018.
97 Anglin 2016.
98 Gilmore 2007, 27.
99 Gordon 2017, 202.

CHAPTER 1. "THIS IS A PLACE FOR TRASH"
1 Reece 2006, 55. See also Rebecca Scott 2010, whose research participants offered similar reactions to MTR.
2 See Story 2016b, 2019.
3 Reece 2006, 35.
4 McNeil 2012, 2.
5 Scott 2013, 43.
6 Haney 2011.
7 Reece 2006; Davis 2017; Cooper n.d.

8 Reece 2006, 60.
9 Lockwood 2002; "Thanks for Nothing" 2002; Hickman 1998.
10 Story 2016b.
11 Garland 2001; Miller 1991; Post 2017; Zoukis 2017.
12 Cheves 2015.
13 Newman 2018.
14 See Bernd, Loftus-Farren, and Metri 2017, for example, who note, "Additionally, [prisons] are built on some of the least desirable and most contaminated lands in the country, such as old mining sites, Superfund cleanup sites, and landfills. According to a GIS analysis of a 2010 dataset of state and federal prisons by independent cartographer Paige Williams, at least 589 federal and state prisons are located within three miles of a Superfund cleanup site on the National Priorities List, with 134 of those prisons located within just one mile."
15 Lockwood and Evans 2014.
16 Thill 2015.
17 Thill 2015, especially 79–80, where he writes that even as photography and waste seem made for each other, "We should consider the possibility that our longstanding tradition of privileging the image may have outlived some of its usefulness. If we consider that nearly all of what we would call waste is being churned up in places that are well guarded and closed to the public, powerful images might not be the smartest thing to be looking for." More generally, see Paglen 2010a and 2010b, as well as Jobey 2015 and Van Tomme 2014.
18 Cheves 2015; personal conversation with the McCoys.
19 Hallinan 2001, 203.
20 Szuberla and Kirby 2006.
21 Meier 2019, 2003; Macy 2018.
22 See Meier 2019.
23 Achenbach 2019; Achenbach et al. 2019.
24 Buer 2020, 46.
25 Eller 2008; Appalachian Land Ownership Task Force 1983.
26 Clark 2007.
27 Clark 2007.
28 "Kings Creek Volunteer Fire Department (KCVFD)," Letcher County Culture Hub, https://www.letcherculture.org.
29 Ginseng harvesting has a long history in the region and is intimately connected to processes of enclosure and commoning as well as social reproduction. See for example Hufford 2003. See also Marley 2016a.
30 Gidwani 2013; Gidwani and Story 2012; Collard and Dempsey 2017. Scott (2010) writes about this historical process in Appalachia specifically, noting that "pro MTR discourse evacuates the land of meaning in a way that is reminiscent of the erasure of Native Americans in the colonizing discourse of early European settlers and of Manifest Destiny. In this case, not only is much of the local forest-based *human* activity ignored but the nonhuman life on the unmined mountains is

rendered completely invisible" (180). In pro-industry discourse, she writes, "the land is often construed as useless or empty."
31 Bureau of Prisons 2017, appendix J 303–6. On the enclosure of air space, see Shaw 2017.
32 See "Who We Are," Friends of Coal, https://www.friendsofcoal.org. For compelling analyses of coal industry propaganda generally and this campaign specifically in West Virginia, see Bell 2016, esp. 89–108. See also Ray 2018, 2019; and Ryerson 2020.
33 Interview with Sylvia Ryerson, for Ryerson and Schept 2021.
34 H. Paul Douglass 1909, 339–40, in Whisnant 1994, 240.
35 Montrie 2003; see also Goldstein 2013.
36 Interview with Sylvia Ryerson, for Ryerson and Schept 2021.
37 Thill 2015, 78.
38 See Simon 1993; Hernández 2017; Katz 2011. Michelle Yates 2011 notes the importance of considering human-produced waste (residing in landfills and burned in incinerators) and humans-as-waste (those caged in prisons and, to a lesser extent, those paid to guard them) within the capitalist mode of production. As she writes, "These two modalities of by-product—the redundant worker and the residuals from the production process itself—demonstrate the necessary relation between the generation of (surplus) value and the generation of surplus populations (as a form of waste)" (1681).
39 Simon 1993, 2007.
40 Davis 2003, 16.
41 Katz 2011.
42 Hernandez 2017.
43 Bauman 2004, 27.
44 Bauman 2004, 84–86.
45 Lerman and Weaver 2014; Price 2015.
46 See Hetherington 2004 for an important discussion on disposal, including a critical treatment of theories that equate disposal with waste. As he notes, disposal is about "placing absences," which is consequential for thinking about social relations (159).
47 Berger 2014a, 2014b; James 2005; Meiners 2009.
48 See for example, "Hot 88.7—Hip Hop from the Hilltop/Calls from Home," WMMT 88.7, https://www.wmmt.org. More broadly, see Jackson 1994; James 2005; Law 2012.
49 On the prison as a spatial fix for the crises of racial capitalism, see Gilmore 2007, 1999.

CHAPTER 2. WARS, LAWS, LANDSCAPES

1 On conjunctural analysis, see Gramsci 1971; Hall 2017; Hall et al. 2013; Hall and Massey 2010; Camp 2016. As Hall et al. write in their preface to *Policing the Crisis* (2013),

Conjuncture is a concept . . . that designates a specific moment in the life of a social formation and refers to a period when the antagonisms and contradictions, which are always at work in society, begin to *"fuse"* into a *"ruptural unity."* Conjunctural analysis deploys a type of periodization based on a distinction between moments of relative stability and those of intensifying struggles and unrest, which may result in a more general social crisis. The concept covers the development of contradictions, their fusion into a crisis and its resolution. Resolutions to the crisis can take different forms: there is no preordained result. (xiv–xv)

2 Adam Yarmolinsky quoted in Eller 2008, 88. See also Catte 2018, 82; Eller n.d. This directive about representation contradicts the record of testimonies heard in House hearings and floor debate, most of which were offered by spokespersons from urban areas (Whisnant 1994, 92–126). On the migration and erasure of Black Appalachians, see Turner and Cabbell 1985 and Lewis 1987.
3 Eller 2008, 53–89; Williams 2002, 339–49; Catte 2018, 78–83.
4 Catte 2018, 81.
5 Eller 2008; Williams 2002; Cheves and Estep 2012.
6 Bigart 1963.
7 Caudill 1963, 13.
8 Cheves and Estep 2012. See also Catte 2018, 78–89.
9 Appalachian Regional Commission 2011, 2013, 2015.
10 Vance 2016; K. Williamson 2013.
11 Appalachian Regional Commission 2011, 4.
12 Interview with Charles (Buck) Maggard, November 29, 1990, Louie B. Nunn Center for Oral History, University of Kentucky Libraries, Thomas Kiffmeyer, Appalachia Oral History Collection, War on Poverty Oral History Project. See also Cheves 2015, who notes that in Martin County, "The judge-executive in the late 1960s [stole relief money] and went to prison. He quickly was pardoned by President Richard Nixon and was re-elected to office, where he hired several of his relatives."
13 Arnett 1978, 172, quoted in Eller 2008, 107.
14 Eller 2008; Hinton 2016, see especially 27–62; Whisnant 1994, 98–101.
15 Report from Appalachian Committee for Full Employment, Box 1, Folder 3, Everette Tharp Collection, 1958–1976, 87M13, Special Collections and Digital Programs, University of Kentucky Libraries, Lexington.
16 Report from Appalachian Committee for Full Employment.
17 Lyndon B. Johnson, "Statement by the President on Establishing the President's Commission on Law Enforcement and Administration of Justice," July 26, 1965. Online by Gerhard Peters and John T. Woolley, the American Presidency Project, http://www.presidency.ucsb.edu, PID number 27110. See also Hinton 2016.
18 Historians and other analysts of state violence and social movements have tended to refer to Watts as an uprising or rebellion, rather than as a "riot," the term gener-

ally deployed by the police. See for example Camp 2016; Davis and Wiener 2020; Hinton 2016; and Horne 1995. Gerald Horne (1995, 3) argues that the evidence suggests that the "Watts Uprising was no mindless riot but rather a conscious, though inchoate, insurrection." Similarly, Ruth Wilson Gilmore (2007, 39) argues that "the 1965 Watts Rebellion was a conscious enactment of opposition (even if 'spontaneous' in a Leninist sense) to inequality in Los Angeles, where everyday apartheid was forcibly renewed by police." Mike Davis and Jon Wiener (2020, see especially 203–5) offer crucial detail into what kinds of organization, spontaneity, and other dynamics characterized the uprising, noting that its composition and character changed over the course of the days. See Clover 2019 and Osterweil 2020 for compelling arguments for retaining and embracing "riot."

19 Lyndon B. Johnson, Statement on the Watts Riots, History Central, http://www.historycentral.com.
20 See Camp 2016 broadly on this point and 21–42 in particular on Watts. See also Murakawa 2014, especially 69–112; and Hinton 2016.
21 Hinton 2016; Murakawa 2014; Camp 2016. Murakawa (2014, 76) notes, for example, that

> modernization of law enforcement was not incidental to Johnson's Great Society. Following in the tradition of Kennedy's 1961 Juvenile Delinquency Act, Johnson advocated federal funding for local crime prevention and control programs. But there was a more fundamental way in which his vision of criminality was enmeshed in his Great Society agenda. Johnson understood the Great Society as crime prevention, its resources a balm to the kind of deprivation that compels criminal acts. At the same time, Johnson imbued black people with the kind of violence and criminality structured in a place too personal for policy to touch.

As Jordan Camp 2016 makes clear, concerns about crime and violence were components of broader moral panics surrounding challenges to capitalist social order in urban America. Framing these challenges in the discourse of crime enabled the expanded use of police and prisons as the commonsense response by the state to crises of legitimacy.

22 Lyndon Johnson, quoted in Murakawa 2014, 78.
23 Lyndon Johnson, quoted in Murakawa 2014, 79.
24 Hinton 2016, 14.
25 Hinton 2016, 14.
26 A sample of this work includes Alexander 2010; Camp 2016; Camp and Heatherton 2017; Clear and Frost 2014; Gilmore 2007; Goodman, Page, and Phelps 2017; Gottschalk 2006, 2015; Hinton 2016; Lynch 2010; Murakawa 2014; Platt 2018; Schoenfeld 2018; Simon 2007.
27 Hallinan 2001, 205.
28 Appalachian Land Ownership Task Force 1983, 120.
29 Eller 2008, 162.
30 Eller 2008, 129–76; Fisher 1993; Bingman 1993; Montrie 2003.

31 Interview with Charles (Buck) Maggard, November 29, 1990, Louie B. Nunn Center for Oral History, University of Kentucky Libraries, Thomas Kiffmeyer, Appalachia Oral History Collection, War on Poverty Oral History Project. See also Eller 2008; Montrie 2003.
32 Eller 2008, 228. In eastern Kentucky, see Kentucky Energy and Environment Cabinet 2017.
33 Geredien 2009.
34 Reece 2006, 60.
35 Eller 2008; Haney 2011; Reece 2006.
36 Eller 2008, 228. In eastern Kentucky, see Kentucky Energy and Environment Cabinet 2020 and Reece 2006.
37 Eller 2008, 252; Haney 2011; Perks and Wetstone 2002.
38 Dunaway 1995, 61, citing the *Kentucky State Journal*, 1828.
39 Wright 1978.
40 Eller 1982, 55.
41 Eller 1982, 56.
42 Eller 2008, 38.
43 The precipitous drop in coal production since 2012 (which itself has important implications for prisons as it has led to significant losses in the coal-severance-tax receipts that provide a significant revenue stream for coalfield communities) nonetheless is a separate phenomenon from the much longer downward spiral in coal jobs.
44 Reece 2006, 52.
45 Newman 2018.
46 Hickman 1998.
47 See Catte 2018, 13–14. See also Appalachian Land Ownership Task Force 1983, 38, and Eller 2008, 199–200. As the land study would make clear, Harvard's absenteeism and ability to avoid property taxes was indicative of the broader pattern of land ownership in the region. The study found that corporations controlled 40 percent of the land and 70 percent of the mineral rights and that the vast majority of these corporations were located outside of the areas they controlled. Moreover, the study found that 75 percent of the companies owning the mineral rights paid less than twenty-five cents per acre.
48 Montrie 2003, 294; Hickman 1997a.
49 Reece 2006, 33.
50 Reece 2006, 33; Eller 2008, 251.
51 Appalachian Voices 2015; Crist 2018; "Black Lung Returns" 2012.
52 Haney 2011.
53 Salyer 2005.
54 Scott et al. 2005; McSpirit, Scott, and Welch 2005; Spadaro 2005.
55 Martin County Concerned Citizens and Appalachian Citizens Law Center event, May 29, 2019, Lexington, KY; Wright 2018.
56 In Hey Kentucky! 2018.

57 See Union of Concerned Scientists 2009; Spadaro 2005; Salyer 2005. Specifically, a spill in 1994 from the same Martin County reservoir resulted in nine recommendations to the company from a MSHA engineer, including that the reservoir should not be raised unless the recommended changes were implemented. According to reports and testimony, the Martin County Coal Company and the local MSHA office ignored these changes and knew of the possible risks. The post-spill investigation was cut short and severely compromised by the incoming Bush administration. MSHA is an agency under the Department of Labor, whose new head, Elaine Chao, was married to Kentucky senator Mitch McConnell, a recipient of major campaign contributions from MCCC's parent company and industry giant Massey Energy.

58 On the cultural and political work of Friends of Coal see Bell 2016, Bell and York 2010, and Ryerson 2020. See Ray 2019 on the ideological work of CEDAR in regional schools.

59 Bureau of Prisons 2017.

60 Allen 1890, 568, quoted in Gaventa 1980, 62.

61 Scott 2010, 177. See also Berry 2013.

62 Scott 2010, 177. See also Berry 2013.

63 Blomley 2003, 134.

64 Blomley 2003, 134.

65 Gidwani 2016, 277. Elsewhere, Gidwani (2013, 776) expands on the relationship between commons-as-waste and capitalist value,

> Nevertheless, at certain historical moments, projects of capitalist value come to view commons as an impediment and construct it as "waste," weighted down by the double pejorative, moral, and economic that attaches to the term. In these moments (the colonization of America, the parliamentary enclosures in England, land settlement operations in British India, "civilizing" ventures in Mandate Palestine, development projects in postcolonial Indonesia, or "urban renewal" and "urban reform" programs today), commons-as-waste becomes, in the words of historian J. M. Neeson, "an enemy to be engaged and beaten" (1993: 30–31). This antithetical aspect of waste, as a logic that stymies the accumulation of property qua capital, is mirrored in the various ways it comes to connote not only merely the uncultivated or untended but also the pointless, the misdirected, and the futile; the ineffectual, the foolish, and the worthless; the idle and the improvident; the excessive, prodigal, the improper, the inefficient. As history reveals: time, money, words, things, actions, and nature—all may be wasted, and are disciplined accordingly.

66 Indeed, as recent scholarship has recovered, there is seemingly very little that falls outside of the police power. See Correia and Wall 2018a; Dubber 2005; Seigel 2018. On waste and police power, see especially Neocleous 2000.

67 On the work of capital to seek out and transform such spaces, see Smith 2008; Goldstein 2013. On commons and waste see Gidwani and Reddy 2011; Linebaugh 2014, 2008; Neeson 1993.

68 Scott 2010, 37. More broadly, see Catte 2018; Stoll 2017. On the way that photography and sight have been implicated in this very process, see S. M. Smith 2013, 167.
69 See for example Gilmore 2007; Harvey 1996; D. Mitchell 1996, 2003; W. J. T. Mitchell 2005, 2002; Smith 2008.
70 D. Mitchell 1996, 17.
71 W. J. T. Mitchell 2002, 2. Importantly, the idea of landscape as a way of seeing is intimately tied to the commodification and expropriation of land during the rise of capitalism in Europe. As Don Mitchell observes of Denis Cosgrove's body of work, "The very idea of landscape as a 'way of seeing,' as a particular kind of view rendered through a rationalization and mathematical ordering of perspective, has a history that is inextricably bound up to the hyper-commodification of land that came with the capitalist transformation in Europe" (1996, 26).
72 See also Berger 1972; Guenther 2015; Mirzoeff 2011a, 476, 2011b.
73 Neocleous 2003, 101.
74 Scott 2010, 2–3.
75 Reece 2006, 4.
76 The historian Barbara Jeanne Fields, in her investigation of the production of race as ideology, writes, instructively, "A commonplace that few stop to examine holds that people are more readily oppressed when they are already perceived as inferior by nature. The reverse is more to the point. People are more readily perceived as inferior by nature when they are already seen as oppressed" (1990, 106).
77 On the relationship between site and sight vis-à-vis prison building, see Armstrong 2014.
78 Bell 2016; Corbin 2011; Dreiser et al. 2008; Fisher 1993; Harris 2017; Montrie 2005.
79 For an important intervention into the idea that these forms of "slow violence" are invisible, see Davies 2019, who rightly raises the question of "to whom?"
80 Zimring 2015, 139; Melossi 2005. See also Lawson, Jarosz, and Bonds 2010; Thorpe 2014.
81 Eller 2008, 254.
82 Zimring 2015, 139; Douglass 2002; Connolly 1988. On police power and its role in/as "sanitation," see Neocleous 2000; Correia and Wall 2018a; Smith 2001.
83 Stewart 1996. As she writes of West Virginia, "These hills—at once occupied, encompassed, exploited, betrayed, and deserted—become a place where the effects of capitalism and modernization pile up on the landscape as the detritus of history, and where the story of 'America' grows dense and unforgettable in remembered ruins and pieced-together fragments" (1996, 4).
84 Rubin and York 2018.
85 Harvey 1996, 48–68.
86 Joshua Reno writes of landfills that "this common reliance on the uneven distribution of mass waste is what connects most North American 'backyards.' But landfills are designed to make clues of this imbalance vanish, to clean up the scene of the crime so completely that we don't suspect one has even been committed. All that remains is the productive absence of what was once there.

When that redistributed waste comes from and goes to distant places, the challenge to recognize waste management as a social relationship is even greater" (2016, 209).

CHAPTER 3. "WHAT A MAGNIFICENT FIELD FOR CAPITALISTS!"

1. On prison tourism see for example Brown 2009; Ferguson et al. 2014; Ferguson, Piché, and Walby 2015; Fiander et al. 2016.
2. Morris and Arford 2018, 430.
3. Cotham 1995, 59.
4. Cotham 1995, 58; Williams 2002.
5. Cotham 1995, 58. Du Bois also notes that crime during this period was "above all . . . used in the South as a source of income for the state" (1998, 698).
6. Woodward 1981, 234.
7. Mcghee 1991, 28. See also Cotham 1995; Hutson 1935.
8. Hutson 1935.
9. On the Coal Creek War see Cotham 1995, 55–77; Gaventa 1980, 73–76; Hutson 1935, 1936; Lane 2003; Lichtenstein 1996, 73–104; Williams 2002, 263–64.
10. On this period, see especially Hutson 1935.
11. Cotham notes of the shift to property damage by the miners that "the miners, now more militant, did not want to destroy human life. On the other hand, they wanted to render it impractical and unlikely for the state to resume the old convict lease system—at least in their area. Thus, facilities were destroyed" (1995, 70).
12. Cotham 1995, 56. More broadly on this period, see Cotham 1995, 55–77; Lane 2003; Lichtenstein 1996, 73–104; Williams 2002, 263–64.
13. Quoted in Lichtenstein 1996, 100.
14. Cotham 1995, 76; Hutson 1936.
15. On prisons as "spatial fixes" for capital's crises, see Gilmore 2007, 1999.
16. Cotham 1995; Eller 1982, 153; Williams 2002.
17. Shelden 1981.
18. Brushy Mountain Mines, Statement of Operations for the Year 1917 and Six Months of 1918, Ending July 1st, in *Second Biennial Report of Tennessee Board of Control, 1915–1916* (Nashville, TN: Baird-Ward Printing Company), 14.
19. Brushy Mountain Mines, Statement of Operations for the Year 1917 and Six Months of 1918, Ending July 1st, in *Second Biennial Report of Tennessee Board of Control, 1915–1916* (Nashville, TN: Baird-Ward Printing Company), 14.
20. WBIR 2018.
21. WBIR 2018.
22. Walby and Piché 2015a, 2015b, 2011.
23. See "Paranormal Tours," Tour Brushy, https://tourbrushy.com.
24. On hauntology and other "ghostly matters," see Derrida 2006; Gordon 2008; Fiddler 2019; Fiddler, Kindynis, and Linnemann 2022; Fisher 2014; Saleh-Hanna 2015. On haunting and prison tourism specifically, see Luscombe, Walby, and Piché 2017; Hodgkinson and Urquhart 2017; Schept 2014.

25 On the confluence of this nexus of knowledge, power, and representation, see Hall et al. 2013; Foucault 1980; Schept 2015, 125–61.
26 Brown 2009; Moran 2015, 132–41; Piché and Walby 2010; Schept 2014; Walby and Piché 2011. Indeed, the way that a site depicts the past shapes the messages that tourists receive (Wilson 2011). As Barton and Brown (2011, 485) argue, "[W]hen a discourse of dangerousness is used to represent prisoners, it creates a public and official indifference to their mistreatment."
27 WECO Radio 2013.
28 Brown 2009, 87.
29 See Wall 2014, 2016, and Wall and McClanahan forthcoming for more developed analyses on the animalization of capitalist natures in the service of police power, including "the teeth of power" and "carnivorous capitalism," through critical treatments of the police dog.
30 Gidwani 2016, 2013; Gidwani and Reddy 2011. In the words of Francoise Vergés, "Capitalist production is waste production" (2017, 81).
31 Stoll 2017, 20.
32 Scott 2010, 139; Eller 1982, 2008; Debarbieux and Rudaz 2015, 126–30; Stewart 1996; Williams 2002.
33 Walby and Piché 2011, 465.
34 Caleb Smith 2013, 167. As Smith argues, perhaps we should "think of the shops, museums, and parks of Manhattan in the early-twenty-first century as sites violently carved out of the urban landscape by the penal state." More broadly on this point, see Brett Story 2016a, 2016b, 2019.
35 Mitchell 1996, 27, emphasis in the original.
36 Hoelscher and Alderman 2004, 348.
37 Brett Story and I extend the idea of the ideology of punishment further in Story and Schept 2018.
38 Broadly see Rusche and Kirchheimer 2017.
39 Petchesky 1981.
40 See Gilmore 2017a, 227.
41 White 2002, 85.
42 WECO Radio 2013.
43 Smith and Phillips 2001, 458.
44 See also Leebrick 2015.
45 See Pellegrin 2019. The total number of incarcerated Tennesseans is much higher—in fact, it is doubled—when accounting for those under federal and local jurisdictions.

CHAPTER 4. THE COMPANY TOWN

1 Haley 2016; Lewis 1987; Lichtenstein 1996; Oshinsky 1996.
2 The play was created in a year-long writing workshop led by teaching artist Julia Taylor, through Appalshop, the nonprofit media arts center in Whitesburg, KY.
3 Ryerson 2010, 73.

4 Kang-Brown et al. 2018; Norton and Schept 2019.
5 Ronald Eller notes of the complete reliance on the company in these towns that the miner "lived in a company house, he worked in the company mine, and he purchased his groceries and other commodities from the company store. He sent his children to the company school and patronized the company doctor and company church. The company deducted rent and school, medical, and other fees from his monthly wage. . . . He had no voice in community affairs or working conditions, and he was dependent upon the benevolence of the employer to maintain his rate of pay" (Eller 1982, xxii–iii).
6 See Smith 2008, 6–11, 196–206. Smith argues that development of a particular area leads to development of productive forces, in turn leading to lower unemployment, an increase in wages, and development of unions, all lowering the rate of profit and taking away the impetus for development in the first place. At the opposite pole, he argues, lack of capital leads to high unemployment, low wages, and reduced worker organization. Thus,

> The underdevelopment of specific areas leads, in time, to precisely those conditions that make an area highly profitable and hence susceptible to rapid development. Underdevelopment, like development, proceeds at every spatial scale and capital attempts to move geographically in such a way that it continually exploits the opportunities of development without suffering these economic costs of underdevelopment. That is, capital attempts to seesaw from a developed to an underdeveloped area, then at a later point back to the first area which is by now underdeveloped . . . [Capital] resorts to complete mobility as a spatial fix; here again, spatial fixity and spacelessness are but prongs of the same fork. Capital seeks not an equilibrium built into the landscape but one that is viable precisely in its ability to jump landscapes in a systematic way. This is the seesaw movement of capital, which lies behind larger uneven development practices. (Smith 2008, 198)

7 Karuka 2019, 54.
8 Almost exactly one hundred years later, McDowell County would become the epicenter of journalistic pieces looking to understand the phenomenon of Donald Trump, as the small county voted for him in particularly large numbers. The Appalachian historian Elizabeth Catte observes that these articles formed a distinct genre she labels as "Trump Country" pieces, which rely on and reactivate tropes organized around difference and deficiency.
9 Eller 1982, 162–63.
10 Henry Armour, interview by Sonny Houston and Lyn Adams, August 8, 1973, Tape 1914, Appalachian Oral History Program, Alice Lloyd College, Pippa Passes, KY; and Burt Crisp, interview by Patti Rose, June 22, 1971, transcript, Appalachian Oral History Program, Alice Lloyd College, Pippa Passes, KY, in Perry 2014, 65.
11 Eller 1982, 182–85; Trout 1950. See also United States Congress. Senate 1925.
12 Perry 2014, 85. See also United States Congress. Senate 1925.
13 United States Congress. Senate 1925.

14 R. Lewis 1987, 148.
15 On company towns in the Appalachian coalfields, see Eller 1982; H. Lewis, Johnson, and Askins 1978; R. Lewis 1987; and Williams 2002. On Wheelwright's specific history as a coal camp, see especially Perry 2014. On Black miners in company towns, see R. Lewis 1987 as well as Turner and Cabbell 1985, especially 79–113. On company towns and labor, see Banks 1995, who quotes extensively from the 1925 congressional report by the US Coal Commission, which noted the significant efforts of coal companies to control the post and the roads in their towns in an attempt to prevent communications and collaboration between unions and nonunion miners in the camps.
16 Whisnant 1974, 199, quoting from a 1921 manual from the coal industry; Stoll 2017, 222.
17 United States Congress. Senate 1925, 169.
18 United States Congress. Senate 1925, 173. Sociologist Alan Banks expands further, noting that "law officials were frequently paid directly from corporate coffers. This gave additional incentive for local law officers to pay careful heed to the wishes and likes of company officials. When asked by one researcher what his major responsibility was, one local sheriff frankly stated, 'It is my job to keep the union out of [the] county'" (Banks 1995, 339). Some of the more infamous bouts of violence in the coalfields were at their foundation about this same project of police power exercised to thwart unionization. In Harlan County, Kentucky, the Harlan County Coal Operators Association hired members of Chicago organized crime families to work alongside sheriffs, deputies, and others to terrorize miners who were suspected of joining the UMWA. According to Eric Reece, "The [HCCOA] paid the salaries of all the sheriff's 164 armed deputies, 64 of whom had been indicted and 27 convicted of felonies, including murder" (2006, 165).
19 Eula Hall, interview by Glenna Graves, June 18, 1988. Family and Gender in the Coal Community Oral History Project, Louis B. Nunn Center for Oral History, University of Kentucky. For more on Hall, and the work of the Community Health movement, see Wilkerson 2019.
20 Eula Hall, interview by Glenna Graves, June 18, 1988. Family and Gender in the Coal Community Oral History Project, Louis B. Nunn Center for Oral History, University of Kentucky.
21 As Marx observed, this process of primitive accumulation "can be nothing other than the process which divorces the worker from the ownership of his own labour; it is a process which operates two transformations, whereby the social means of subsistence and production are turned into capital, and the immediate producers are turned into wage-labourers" (1990, 874).
22 Marley 2016a; Stoll 2017. It is important to note that the rise of the midwestern "bread basket" contributed to the decline in agriculture in Appalachia, including livestock, ginseng, and other agricultural commodities, accelerating the process of enclosure and accumulation that saw farms shrink in size and close and farmers move to coal camps to become the region's first wage workers. This shift in

commodity frontiers—the rise of agriculture in the Midwest and its effect on the eventual rise of the coal frontier in Appalachia—was, like the rise of prisons in the region a hundred years later, predicated in part on the way capital seizes, uses, and enervates the landscape. Livestock, once a reliable agricultural commodity in Appalachia, moved to the Plains states because the vast amounts of flat land—stolen from First Nations peoples, eliminated of buffalo, and divided up for settlers following the 1862 Homestead Act—could accommodate large feedlots (Marley 2016a, 233). See also Estes 2019.

23 Mae Frazier, interview by Glenna Graves, December 8, 1988. Family and Gender in the Coal Community Oral History Project, Louis B. Nunn Center for Oral History, University of Kentucky

24 See Neocleous for an explanation of understanding police less as an institution than as an activity. He writes that across centuries and the development of new social formations, there is "a consistency that resides in the centrality of police to not just the *maintenance* or *reproduction* of order, but to its *fabrication*, and that at the heart of this fabrication is work and the nature of poverty. This presents police as a far more productive force than many assume, in the sense that the police project is intimately connected to the fabrication of an increasingly *bourgeois* order, achieved through the *exercise of state power*" (2000, 5, italics in the original). Similarly, David Correia and Tyler Wall 2018b have argued that "historically, however, police was a term used *to explain the means through which order is achieved*. When we talk about police, in other words, we're talking about order, and the ways order is produced and reproduced in highly unequal ways." For a concise example of how order was achieved in the coal camps of the time, see Stoll 2017, 212–43, where he uses the concept of the "Captured Garden" to discuss the ways that mining companies encouraged home gardens for the dual purposes of pacification and social reproduction.

25 Trout 1950.
26 Hawpe 1970.
27 Trout 1950.
28 Hall 1986.
29 *Wheelwright News*, July–August 1963, Box 37, folder 5, Wheelwright Collection, 1916–1979, 88M6, Special Collections and Digital Programs, University of Kentucky Libraries, Lexington.
30 *Wheelwright News*, Fall 1962, Box 37, folder 5, Wheelwright Collection, 1916–1979, 88M6, Special Collections and Digital Programs, University of Kentucky Libraries, Lexington.
31 Perry 2014, 97.
32 As Paul Nyden observed in his analysis of unionization in the coalfields at this time, "Black and white miners have nearly always stood together in building their union. But their solidarity sometimes evaporates once the miners leave the mines." A Black miner he interviewed explained, "Underground the white and the black get along fine. We would eat right out of each other's buckets. But the

minute we got outdoors, and we washed the coal dust off our faces, some white miners would become different men. They remembered they were white and we were black" (Nyden 1974, 6). Other observers of this period arrive at somewhat different conclusions, going as far as noting an interracial class solidarity between white and Black miners in company towns. For example, see Corbin 1981.

33 On September 26, 1955, John Brock, who leased the two soda fountains in Wheelwright—one for white people and one for Black people—sent a letter to the company, care of Harry Zimmerman, the manager of coal properties:

> Dear Mr. Zimmerman,
>
> I know you hear a lot of complaints and I really hate to mention this but; due to business conditions I'm having a tough time meeting my expenses. Business in the soda fountain is about the same but; the colored fountain is off about fifty percent. For the past six or seven months I've had to take the profits from the soda fountain to pay the expense on the colored fountain. The business in the colored fountain has always been based on the men going and coming from work and as you know during the past three or four years the men going in at Wheelwright has been getting smaller and smaller. My rental expenses on both places are as follows: Rent: $300; Sanitation: 7$; Water: 7$; Power: $142.02.
>
> I'm not telling you this in order to try and get something for nothing. I'm really grateful to Inland Steel for the opportunity they gave me and I've done very well but right now I'm not doing so good. If there is any way you could help me on the rent or by a cheaper power rate it would be deeply appreciated.
>
> Respectfully yours, John R. Brock

A little under four years later, on May 26, 1959, Harry Zimmerman confirmed in an interoffice memo that the lease to Brock had been terminated and the "colored soda fountain" was being converted into a "youth or teenage center," presumably for white young people. Box 37, folder 6, Wheelwright Collection, 1916–1979, 88M6, Special Collections and Digital Programs, University of Kentucky Libraries, Lexington.

34 On this process in Wheelwright during this time, see Perry 2014 and R. L. Lewis 1987, esp. 147–48 and 180. On mechanization and labor in Appalachia more broadly, see Eller 2008. Marley 2016b, 94, makes the crucial point that mechanization in this period expressed industry strategy to avoid the costs incurred by significant labor victories. After the signing in 1950 of the National Bituminous Coal Wage Agreement, which was the product of decades of struggle by the UMWA and which resulted in wage increases and improvements to retirement and health care, the industry immediately began reorganizing production toward mechanization.

35 Hilton Garrett, quoted in Lewis 1987, 180.
36 Perry 2014, 88.
37 Eller 1982, 220.

38 Williams 2002, 260.
39 Stoll 2017, 212.
40 Platt et al. 1982; Neocleous 2013 notes, "Capital and police dream of pacification: a dream of workers available for work, present and correct, their papers in order, their minds and bodies docile, and a dream of accumulation thereby secure from resistance, rebellion, or revolt" (18).
41 Correia and Wall 2018b. It may be equally important to parse what we mean by violence. That is, there was the everyday violence of police in the coalfields and then there was also what the historian Steven Stoll calls "the slow violence" wrought by the constant threat of starvation and eviction by coal companies. In addition to the coal camps that "operated like small police states . . . where company rule functioned as martial law," coal companies also "wielded subsistence as a weapon" (Stoll 2017, 213).
42 See Eller 1982, 220, fn 67. This sentiment confirms important historical and etymological work on the connections among police, welfare, and policy. See Neocleous 2000, 9.
43 Trout 1950, my emphasis.
44 On community policing as a strategy of social order, see Abolition Research Group 2017; Correia and Wall 2018a, 129–31; Hansford 2016; Heatherton and Camp eds. 2016; McQuade 2015; Platt et al. 1977; Vitale 2017. On Officer Friendly, see especially Correia and Wall 2018a, 141–44.
45 See Seigel 2018, 9, where she argues that state and police are separated by degree and that police are the "human-scale expression" of the state.
46 Correia and Wall 2018a; Neocleous 2000; Harcourt 2010.
47 Eller 1982, 215.
48 John Fox Jr. 1994, 210–11, quoted in Eller 1982, 210.
49 Robinson 2000, 26.
50 Fox, Jr. 1994, 211.
51 Lewis, Kobak, and Johnson 1978, 121.
52 Fox, Jr. 1994, 2010.
53 See Harcourt 2010, in particular 81–84. See also Neocleous 2000, 23. See also Smith 1869.
54 This is not to say that the prison and jail didn't figure into these primary forms of police power. In fact, during early fights for labor protections, wages, and rights, the jail and the prison operated as central sites of what several authors have called the "terrorism" in the coalfields waged by coal companies and the police working on their behalf. See Dreiser 2008.
55 Eller 1982, 210. There is a long history of the role of police in securing the dominance of the coal companies. It was during the West Virginia mine wars, for example, that deputy sheriffs and private mine guards operated interchangeably and the state itself, prompted by the coal industry, established its police force. See Scott 2010, 139; Williams 2002, 261. In Kentucky during what came to be known as the Harlan County War, the infamous sheriff J. H. Blair, immortalized in the

folk song "Which Side Are You On?" oversaw and deputized the private mine guards who fought unionizing miners and protected scabs. See Hevener 2002; Eller 1982, 213–16; Dreiser 2008. A 1935 US congressional report would label this collusion a "reign of terror" and conclude, "It appears that the principal cause of existing conditions is the desire of the mine owners to amass for themselves fortunes through the oppression of their laborers, which they do through the sheriff's office" (United States Congress 1935, 639).

56 Mountain Community Television n.d.
57 Lisa Perry details this history, but also see a number of articles in the *Louisville (KY) Courier-Journal*, including Hawpe 1970; Sparrow 1979a, 1979b; and Vance 1972, 1968, 1966.
58 Perry 2014, 125. See also Sparrow 1979a, 1979b.
59 Voskuhl 1992. See also Perry 2014.
60 See "Floyd County," Kentuckians for the Commonwealth, http://www.kftc.org.
61 U.S. Bureau of the Census, Floyd County, Kentucky, Census 2010 Demographic Profile Highlights, http://factfinder2.census.gov.
62 Prison Legal News 2011. The abuses at Otter Creek over the years were reported in numerous outlets, including prison watchdog organizations like *Prison Legal News* but also extensively documented in the *Louisville Courier-Journal* and the Lexington *Herald-Leader*. See Dunlop 2010a, 2010b, 2010c; Wynn 2013.
63 Musgrave 2009.
64 Dunlop 2010b.
65 By violence I mean, of course, the violence of medical neglect and sexual assault but also the quotidian and inherent violence of imprisonment even under seemingly humane conditions and benevolent regimes.
66 Wolfson 2006.
67 Catte 2018, 13.
68 Dwight Billings and Kathleen Blee note, for example, that "coercion and command by the state, even in the relatively laissez-faire economy of antebellum Appalachian Kentucky, also were essential to capitalist development and the making of wealth and poverty" (2000, 105). Moreover, they note that while the state was largely absent from some areas of local governance, including redistribution of wealth, "state force was necessary to en-*force* contracts, adjudicate disputes, and to build the necessary infrastructures that economic development demanded, especially roads and passable waterways." "Even more importantly," the authors continue, "centralized and legitimate 'public' force was necessary to protect various forms of commodified private property, none more essential to the wealth, prosperity and class privilege of antebellum Appalachian elites than land and slaves" (2000, 105).
69 Schaver 1993.
70 Giroux 2014; Olssen and Peters 2007.
71 Shafer 1993.
72 Shafer 1993.

73 See for example Beckett and Western 2001; Gilmore 2002, 2007; Gilmore and Gilmore 2008; Peck 2003; Wacquant 2010, see 204 in particular, and 2009, 55–86.
74 See for example in Story 2016b.
75 Cheves 2014.
76 Cheves 2014.
77 According to reporting in the Associated Press and covered in the *Louisville Courier-Journal*, CorrectHealth is owned by Georgia doctor Carlo Musso, who received some critical attention for opening a similar facility in Georgia where he stood to make millions of dollars off the deal and for importing sodium thiopental from overseas in order to aid Georgia's execution protocol.
78 Forbes 2020.

CHAPTER 5. PLANNING THE PRISON

1 The state's PFO law significantly increases the sentence of someone who commits any felony (including writing a bad check, failure to pay child support for a period of time, theft of over five hundred dollars, etc.) who already has at least one prior felony. In addition, since 2015 the average parole rate dropped from around 60 percent to around 40 percent of those eligible. A 20-percentage-point drop during that window meant that around twenty-four hundred people who would have been paroled in a year remained in prison.
2 Spalding 2019; Wagner and Sawyer 2018.
3 Kang-Brown et al. 2018.
4 On the original promises and eventual pitfalls of Justice Reinvestment, see Austin et al. 2013; Story 2016a. On the fallacies of the fiscal logic built in to so-called smart-on-crime initiatives, see Cate and HoSang 2017.
5 Norton and Schept 2019. See also Cheves 2019.
6 On the concept of state capacity and carceral expansion, see Schoenfeld 2018.
7 Kang-Brown et al. 2018; Schept 2015; Story and Schept 2018.
8 On production and reproduction, see Bhattarcharya 2017; Fraser 2017; Giménez 2018; Katz 2001; Norton and Katz 2017. On social reproduction and care work in Appalachia, see Wilkerson 2019. Fraser 2016a offers a clear take on this contradiction of capitalism: "[E]very form of capitalist society harbours a deep-seated social-reproductive 'crisis tendency' or contradiction: on the one hand, social reproduction is a condition of possibility for sustained capital accumulation; on the other, capitalism's orientation to unlimited accumulation tends to destabilize the very processes of social reproduction on which it relies. This social-reproductive contradiction of capitalism lies at the root of the so-called crisis of care."
9 I use "burden" here deliberately, invoking both Ruth Wilson Gilmore and Jessie Wilkerson. Gilmore writes, "Organized abandonment—the removal of jobs, factories, benefits, schools, you name it—sums up to a general burden that households and communities bear," reminding us of who pays for capital's quest for profit and the state's reorganization. Wilkerson's understanding of the "burden

of social reproduction" expertly points us at once to the gendered histories of care work in the coalfields and beyond as well as the ways that such work, such as the creation of rural health clinics in eastern Kentucky, connected in certain conjunctures to antipoverty organizing and militant labor insurrections. See Wilkerson 2019, 145.

10 Seigel writes, "It is the potential use of force that constitutes the quotidian power of policing. . . . Police realize —they *make real*—the core of the power of the state. That is what I mean to convey by calling police 'violence workers.' It is not intended to indict police officers as bad people, vicious in their personality or in their daily routines. . . . It takes work to represent and distribute state violence" (2018, 9-11, emphasis in original).

11 Seigel 2018.

12 As Hall et al. 2013 write in *Policing the Crisis*, "Hegemony, in Gramsci's sense, involves the 'passage' of a crisis from its material base in productive life through to 'the complex spheres of the superstructures.' Nevertheless, what hegemony ultimately secures is the long-term social conditions for the continuing reproduction of capital. The superstructures provide that 'theatre' where the relations of class forces, given their fundamental form in the antagonistic relations of capitalist production, appear and work themselves through to a resolution" (215). On conjunctural analysis, see in addition Camp 2016; Hall 2017; Hall and Massey 2010. Writing of Gramsci, for example, Hall 2017 notes we must demand of ourselves this kind of approach: "When a conjuncture unrolls, there is no 'going back.' History shifts gears. The terrain changes. You are in a new moment. You have to attend, 'violently,' with all the 'pessimism of the intellect' at your command, to the 'discipline of the conjuncture.'"

13 Whisnant 1994, 240.

14 Whisnant 1994, 240.

15 Gaventa 1980; Woods 2017.

16 Estep 2017c, 2018. See also House Appropriations Committee, Hearing, Department of Justice Budget, June 13: https://www.youtube.com/watch?v=dSsF5vNndes&feature=youtu.be.

17 Whisnant 1994, 244. See also Whisnant 1974.

18 Whisnant 1994, 248.

19 Whisnant 1994, 248-49; Farley 2017.

20 The ARC's economic strategy in its first decade was to invest in the growth of urban "poles" as well as the infrastructures, like highways, that would allow residents in the more remote areas of the region to commute to—or move away for—jobs and other amenities. "Growth pole theory," as this strategy was called, implied a long-term vision of urbanization and depopulation of the rural hinterlands of Appalachia, a strategy that some executives within the ARC, like cochair John Sweeney and Executive Director Ralph Widner, made rather explicit. See Eller 2008, especially 177-220.

21 Whisnant 1994, 254.

22   As Clyde Woods notes about planning in the Mississippi Delta, "Regional planning has always held the promise of creating new social relations based on economic redistribution, environmental sustainability, and the full realization of basic human and cultural rights. Yet, without a thoroughgoing critique of regional power and culture based on indigenous conceptions of development, these efforts often create more repressive social relations" (Woods 2017, 3–4).
23   Eller 2008.
24   Kentucky Energy and Environment Cabinet 2017.
25   Kentucky Energy and Environment Cabinet 2017, 35.
26   Baumann 2016; Cheves 2013.
27   Cheves 2013.
28   Estep 2017a.
29   Rep. Angie Hatton, quoted in Adams 2019b.
30   Day 2018; Hickman 1997a; McCoy 2018.
31   Wright 2018; Adams 2019b.
32   Boles 2019.
33   See Pelot-Hobbs 2018 on the sometimes-contradictory relationships between the state at different scales when it concerns prison and jail construction. More generally, this suggests the need for an understanding of the ruling class across scales. County-level elites were instrumental to the circulation of and support for the prison proposal, but also did so in coordination with the US representative for the region. It is helpful to remember Marx's imploration from *The German Ideology* that the ruling ideas of an age are the ideal expressions of dominant material relationships, i.e., that the members of the ruling class "rule also as thinkers, as producers of ideas, and regulate the production and distribution of the ideas of their age" (1998, 64). Crucially, however, this chapter and the next show that while this principle may govern social relationships as a tendency, it doesn't do so indefinitely or without struggle. In the very same county where local elites were able to sell the idea of a prison for fifteen years, a coalition of activists coalesced to disrupt it.
34   As the company itself noted in the beginning of its Enhanced Utility Investigation Report for the BOP, "Prior to the initial Utility Investigation Report, several studies had previously been performed in support of the potential construction of a new federal correctional facility at the three potential sites. These studies include: Site Reconnaissance Study prepared by the Louis Berger Group (November 2008); Mine History Reports (each site) prepared by Summit Engineering (August 2010); Site Investigation Trip Memo prepared by KCI Technologies (October 2010). Information from each of these studies was utilized in developing background information, baseline data starting points, initial contact information, and additional evaluation criteria" (Cardno 2014, 2).
35   Cardno 2014, appendix 2.
36   Kentucky River Area Development District (KRADD) 2012.
37   Bureau of Prisons 2016, 8–6. See also Cardno 2014; KRADD 2012, 2015, 2017.

38 Bureau of Prisons 2017. See Ryerson 2010 for substantial analysis of this same dynamic in other eastern Kentucky communities with prisons.
39 Cardno 2014.
40 As Anne Bonds notes, "As neoliberal rural restructuring leads communities to pursue development strategies that put places in direct competition with one another for scarce resources (e.g. community block grants, industrial development) and employment opportunities, poverty is denied and invisibilized by community officials seeking to remain competitive for investment" (2009, 433). On YIMBY-ism see Bonds 2013; Eason 2016; Huling 2002.
41 Gilmore 2007, 131.
42 I am thankful to Jack Norton and his work for helping to clarify this point.
43 Hooks et al. 2004; Hooks et al. 2010; Huling 2002; Glasmeier and Farrigan 2007; Mosher, Hooks, and Wood 2005; Perdue and Sanchagrin 2016. See Eason 2016 for important ethnographic examination and complication of this phenomenon.
44 Bureau of Prisons 2017, appendix J.
45 Bureau of Prisons 2017, 6–1.
46 On the relationship among ideology, class position, and social formations, see Hall 1986. On ideology and planning, see Woods 2017; Gilmore 2017b.
47 Schuppe 2018.
48 Catte 2018.
49 Catte 2019.
50 See Ryerson 2013.
51 Bureau of Prisons 2017, appendix E1–60. See also Peak 2015.
52 Hallett 2012. See also Story and Schept 2018.
53 Kase 2018; Dodson 2019; Stine 2019.
54 See Bureau of Prisons 2017, appendix E1–64 and E1–201, for examples.
55 Bureau of Prisons 2017, appendix E1–33.
56 Bureau of Prisons 2017, appendix J, 204. This statement most likely came from Justice Samuel T. Wright III, a Supreme Court justice who is from Letcher County.
57 Bureau of Prisons 2017, appendix J-67.
58 Mosley and DeBehnke 2019; Thomas, Pink, and Reiter 2019; Kentucky Hospital Association 2015; Patrick 2019. On the broader relationship between rural hospital closures and incarceration expansion, see Norton and Heiss 2020.
59 Kentucky had a particularly successful roll-out of the ACA, with Medicaid expansion and the state's online marketplace healthcare exchange, known as Kynect, leading to the insurance of over four hundred thousand Kentuckians, or a reduction by 50 percent in the number of uninsured residents. But some of the funding mechanisms behind the ACA have led directly to considerable revenue shortages for rural hospitals. The act imposed reductions in Medicaid and Medicare payments to rural hospitals. Both programs provide just over 80 percent of the cost of care to hospitals and have not adjusted for inflation. As the majority of newly insured Kentuckians are insured through Medicaid (75 percent) rather than private insurance, the reductions in payments have impacted the hospitals especially

hard. In rural Kentucky, more than 70 percent of patients have Medicaid or Medicare, which means that the hospitals are consistently delivering care at a net loss. Moreover, the funding mechanism designed to help rural hospitals compensate for the discrepancy between cost of care and Medicare and Medicaid reimbursement, known as Disproportionate Share Hospital payments, has also been cut. Unsurprisingly, as wages and benefits account for a large share of a given hospital's expenses, the costs of the reductions have been offloaded onto staff in the form of layoffs, wage freezes and reductions, reductions in benefits, attrition, and the elimination of both positions and programs. See Kentucky Hospital Association 2015; Edelen 2015.
60 See Wilkerson 2019, especially 120–45; see also Eula Hall, interview by Glenna Graves, June 18, 1988. Family and Gender in the Coal Community Oral History Project, Louie B. Nunn Center for Oral History, University of Kentucky.
61 Catte 2018.
62 Personal communication, April 14, 2018.
63 Gilmore 2017b, xii, writing of Clyde Woods's examination of the regional power blocs in the Mississippi Delta. For Woods, the hegemony of the plantation class across different historical moments was not a given, but rather required material and ideological adjustments and shifts to maintain.

CHAPTER 6. "TO BRING A FUTURE AND HOPE TO OUR CHILDREN"

1 Kentucky Energy and Environment Cabinet 2020.
2 Yates 2011, 1689.
3 Kang-Brown and Subramanian 2017.
4 Norton and Schept 2019.
5 Kentucky Energy and Environment Cabinet 2020; Bureau of Labor Statistics 2019. The number of correctional officers listed here is conservative, as it does not include those who will work in Southeastern Correctional Complex, in the former Otter Creek prison in Wheelwright.
6 Mountain Eagle Staff 2013a.
7 Mountain Eagle Staff 2013b.
8 Mountain Eagle Staff 2013b.
9 Mountain Eagle Staff 2012.
10 Bureau of Prisons 2017, E1–101.
11 Bureau of Prisons 2017, appendix J, 181.
12 Bureau of Prisons 2017, E1–155.
13 Willis 1977, 172.
14 See for example Che, who records supporters of a federal prison in Appalachian Pennsylvania in the 1990s framing the need for the prison in familiar ways: "This is our last chance, folks, to bring a dying town back to life. To make a better living for ourselves and our children. To see new businesses, lower prices, improved roads, something to be proud of and the ability to say we did it. Just say 'yes,' to the prison" (2005, 823). See also Ryerson 2010 for examinations of this process

in other eastern Kentucky counties that built prisons in the late 1990s and early 2000s.
15 Ryerson 2010.
16 Hickman 1997c.
17 Ball 1998a, quoted in Ryerson 2010.
18 The role of criminology and criminal justice degrees in underwriting the work-readiness of would-be correctional officers is unmistakable, confirming many criticisms of the prosthetic work of the discipline in its role in providing the veneer of credibility to the violence work of police and prisons. As a science of crime and punishment, criminology both is subordinate to the terms and ideologies of the state and continually reproduces and reifies those terms by providing the gloss of scientific objectivity. Michel Foucault (1980) has offered forceful critiques of criminology, noting its intimacy with the state. Calling criminology a "set of garrulous discourses," full of "endless repetitions," Foucault notes that the discipline was integral to the growth of systems of punishment in the nineteenth century and that it remains "indispensable in enabling judges to judge" (1980, 47–48). That is, criminology offers to judges (read here more broadly as those possessing juridical or political power) the minimum credibility necessary to pass sentences, remand to treatment, arrest, imprison, and execute—in short, to engage in what Robert Cover calls "organized, social practices of violence" (1986, 1601). As Mark Neocleous concludes, "Criminology has become little more than ideology" (2000, ix). See also Agozino 2003; Brown and Schept 2017; Cohen 1998, 26; Morrison 2004, 343; Morrison 2010, 191; Loader and Sparks 2010 and Piché 2016 on the complicity of well-intentioned "public criminology"; Polsky 1967, 141–42; Schept 2016; Schept, Wall, and Brisman 2015; Seigel 2018; Young 2011. On similar connections between burgeoning prison growth and state investments in community colleges and universities to produce a new slate of working-class jobs as correctional officers, see Gilmore 2007, 116–20.
19 Cindi Katz writes, "The settings in which children grow up speak volumes about their value as present and future members of particular societies. For instance, the increase in prison construction in the US over the past two decades at the expense of schools and playgrounds suggests a particular (and horrifying) valuation of certain classed, raced, and gendered young people there, since less skilled manufacturing jobs dried up in so many places during the 1970s" (2001, 715). In the focus in these counties on the benefits to both children and schools afforded by prison building lies important insight into Katz's claims about the variable and contested distance between childhood and the capital relation as it also affirms the foundational point about the disciplinary and social reproductive work of schools. Ruth Wilson Gilmore makes a similar point when asking, "When people talk about the kids, about 'saving' a place, what are they talking about? Far from freezing a landscape in time and place, the desire seems to be quite the opposite—one of pursuing particular kinds of change in order to produce the conditions under which social and cultural reproduction might happen" (2007, 178).

20 Hooks et al. 2004; Hooks et al. 2010; Glasmeier and Farrigan 2007; Perdue and Sanchagrin 2016.
21 Ball 1998b.
22 See Ryerson 2010; Ooten and Sawyer 2016.
23 See Ryerson 2010; Ooten and Sawyer 2016.
24 Big Sandy Community and Technical College 2018.
25 Bureau of Prisons 2017, E1–164.
26 Bureau of Prisons 2017, E1–166.
27 Bureau of Prisons 2017, E1–158.
28 Mountain Eagle Staff 2013b.
29 On the dialectical nature of production and reproduction, see Katz 2001; Norton and Katz 2017.
30 Collard and Dempsey 2017, 85.
31 Yates 2011, 1680.
32 Isenberg 2016, 315.
33 Berkes 2016; Berkes and Lancianese 2018; Raby 2018.
34 Broadly, see Mitchell, Marston, and Katz 2003; Fraser 2016b; McIntyre and Nast 2011; Bhattercharya 2017. On this process and rural prison construction, see especially Bonds 2013 and Morrell 2021.
35 See Eason 2016, 2012, 2010; Gilmore 2007; Braz and Gilmore 2006.
36 See "Population of Martin County, Kentucky," Census View, http://censusviewer.com; and "QuickFacts: Martin County, Kentucky," United States Census Bureau, https://www.census.gov.
37 On prison gerrymandering see Huling 2002; Hunter and Wagner 2008; Wagner 2002; Walker et al. 2017, especially their discussion of state expenditures in rural prison towns. See also Prison Policy Initiative's Prisoners of the Census Project: https://www.prisonersofthecensus.org.
38 As Gilmore writes,
> Today's prisons are extractive. What does that mean? It means prisons enable money to move because of the enforced inactivity of people locked in them. It means people extracted from communities, and people returned to communities but not entitled to be of them, enable the circulation of money on rapid cycles. What's extracted from the extracted is *the* resource of life—time. If we think about this dynamic through the politics of scale, understanding bodies as places, then criminalization transforms individuals into tiny territories primed for extractive activity to unfold—extracting and extracting again *time* from the territories of selves. The process opens a hole in a life, furthering, perhaps to our surprise, the annihilation of space by time. A stolen and corrupted social wage flies through the time-hole to prison employees' paychecks. To vendors. To utility companies. To debt service. The cash takes many final forms: wages, interest, rent, and sometimes profit. (Gilmore 2017, 227)

On "the prison town," see Pyle and Gilmore 2005.

39 Pulido 2016, 13; see also Pulido 2000.
40 Bernd, Loftus-Farren, and Mitra 2017; Markowitz 2015; McDaniel et al. 2014; Rakia 2015; Waters 2018. Broadly, see Pulido 2016, who argues that environmental racism is fundamental to racial capitalism. On the history and migration of Black people out of Appalachia, see Brown 2018.
41 Pulido 2016, 5.
42 Brown 2018. See also Lewis 2009.
43 Lewis 2009, 181. As Lewis continues, the exodus out of the mountains "was part of a general demographic pattern whereby one generation moved out of the Deep South to Central Appalachia, and their children or grandchildren completed the trek north."
44 Cowen and Siciliano 2011.
45 Cowen and Siciliano 2011; Bell 2016, especially 89–108, for a discussion of the Friends of Coal campaign, the industry's primary avenue for circulating a particular ideological program; Bell and York 2010; Bell and Braun 2010; Ray 2019; Scott 2010.
46 See Robinson 2007. Also see Camp and Heatherton 2017.
47 See Platt 1969 for an early analysis of prison guards as dirty workers, "technicians of behavior" (37).
48 Ashforth and Kreiner 1999; Hughes 1962. Ashforth and Kreiner's conceptual updating of Hughes's foundational work offers a typology that explicitly connects the miner with the prison guard. Writing of similar dynamics that they observe of e-waste workers in Bangalore and waste-pickers in Delhi, Gidwani and Reddy write of "two ecology sets: on the one side, a way of life that churns out growing quantities of 'waste'; on the other, lives that live off this commodity detritus . . . valuable lives, wasted lives; and mapped onto these, valuable spaces and spaces designated as wasteful. Colonizing and re-making wasted spaces as valuable spaces, excluding from political citizenship those whose labors are not counted" (2011, 1652). Crucially, these authors recognize that this process of what they call "eviscerating urbanism" is fundamental to the violent "order of police." Within this order, they write, "excess matter—waste—is either expelled or else violently absorbed through primitive accumulation when it becomes a threat to the liberal social order of 'property' and 'economy.' Often the excess matter is 'surplus humanity' that is *superfluous* to a regime of capitalist value. When it cannot be easily expelled it is simply abandoned, thrust into a zone of indistinction where it is regulated but not considered worth redeeming" (1653).
49 Gilmore and Gilmore 2016; Peck and Theodore 2008; Neocleous 2000; Camp 2016.
50 Douglass 2002, 35.
51 Connolly 1988, 13.
52 Neocleous 2000, 86.

53 Neocleous 2000, 86–87. See also Vinay Gidwani and Rayjashree Reddy, who argue that waste is "that which must be continuously acted upon and improved, first to enable passage from the state of 'nature' to the state of 'civil society' and subsequently to preserve that order of society" (2011, 1628).
54 See Neocleous 2000, 87, where he notes that police officers see themselves as "refuse collectors, sweeping up the human dross." See Vesely-Flad 2017 for a related argument regarding police power, racial purity, and pollution; Ashforth and Kreiner 1999. As Neil Smith observed of New York City's "Broken Windows" strategy, "Zero tolerance was passed off as an anticrime program. Actually, it is a social cleansing strategy" (Smith 2001, 69). David Correia and Tyler Wall similarly note, "Police logic is the logic of sanitation, the logic of 'polishing' and making 'polite' those 'dirty' populations that threaten order" (Correia and Wall 2018a, 102).
55 Zimring 2015, 139.
56 Gilmore 2007, 1999; Ashforth and Kreiner 1999; Hughes 1958. As Gilmore notes elsewhere, "The rise in security work, therefore, is the natural outcome of the renovation and deepening of uneven development throughout the world." (Gilmore 2011, 251–52).
57 Fraser 2016b, 166. Importantly, in Fraser's account, we find a helpful conceptual updating of expropriation that can account not only for its most obvious manifestations in slave labor, colonial conquest, and enclosure but also in more subtle ways: prisoner labor, certainly, but also the "commandeered capacities" that characterize life in neoliberal deindustrialized communities: fines and fees, debt, foreclosure, civil asset forfeiture.
58 Melamed 2015, 81.
59 Bureau of Prisons 2016, appendix J, 36.
60 Gilmore 2014, 6.
61 Kilgore 2013; Gilmore and Kilgore 2019; Norton and Stein 2020; Story and Schept 2018.
62 Jayadev and Bowles 2006.
63 Camp 2016; Huber 2006; Kelley 1999; Mann 2001; Nyden 1974.
64 Gilmore 2002, 261.
65 Katz 2001; Schept 2015.
66 Ignatiev 2009, 2003; Singh 2014; Roediger 2017, 1999. On this issue regarding prison siting specifically, see Bonds 2013; Morrell 2021; and Ooten and Sawyer 2016.
67 Dreiser et al. 2008.
68 See Katz 2001. On the tight relationship between production and reproduction in the coalfields, see Stoll 2017.
69 Estep 2017a.
70 Cowen and Siciliano 2011, 1519.
71 Hall et al. 2013, 207. See also Gilmore 1999, 2007; Camp 2016.
72 Hall and Massey 2010, 62.

CHAPTER 7. THE PLOT OF ABOLITION

1. On carceral humanism, see Braz 2006; Kilgore 2014; Kurti and Martin 2018; Schept 2015, 2013. On the perils and deceptions of bipartisan reform, see Whitlock and Heitzeg 2021. On the tenacity of the carceral state broadly, see Gottschalk 2015.
2. Gottschalk 2015; Kang-Brown and Subramanian 2017; Walters, Heiss, and Norton 2020.
3. Cullors-Brignac and Zuñiga 2014; Kilgore 2022, 2014; Kurti and Martin 2018; Parks 2013; Schept 2015. See also https://www.challengingecarceration.org/.
4. Bell 2016; Black 1990; Harris 2017; Corbin 2011, 1981; Fisher 1993; Fisher and Smith 2012; McNeil 2012; Montrie 2003; Stein 2014.
5. Norton and Schept 2019.
6. Camp and Heatherton 2017; Hale 2008; Fisher 1993.
7. "About Us," Appalshop, https://www.appalshop.org.
8. Szakos 1993.
9. Rachel Herzing, personal communication, September 2019; Melissa Burch, personal communication, October 2019.
10. Ryerson 2010.
11. Ryerson 2010, 2013; Hooks et al. 2010; Huling 2002; Perdue and Sanchagrin 2016; Bonds 2013, 2012, 2009.
12. Mountain Eagle Staff 2013b.
13. Ryerson 2011.
14. Hooks et al. 2004.
15. Gregory Hooks, interview with Sylvia Ryerson, September 16, 2011. In Ryerson 2011.
16. Ruth Wilson Gilmore, interview with Sylvia Ryerson, September 19, 2011. In Ryerson 2011.
17. See Letcher Governance Project, www.letchergovproject.com. See also Ryerson and Schept 2018.
18. Woods 2017, 2–4. On abolition democracy, see Davis 2005; Du Bois 1998; Lipsitz 2004. See also Heynen 2018 for an argument for "abolition ecology."
19. Schuppe 2018. For a critique, see Ryerson and Schept 2018.
20. See for example Bureau of Prisons 2017, J-166.
21. Bureau of Prisons 2017, J-167.
22. Bureau of Prisons 2017, J-186–87.
23. Bureau of Prisons 2017, J-168.
24. On the broad form deed see Eller 2008, 1982.
25. See Fight Toxic Prison 2018. See also *Barroca et al. v. Bureau of Prisons* 2018.
26. *Barroca et al. v. Bureau of Prisons* 2018, 41.
27. Trump 2019, available at the White House, "President Donald J. Trump's State of the Union Address," https://www.whitehouse.gov.
28. See Braz and Gilmore 2006.

29 In Gilmore et al. 2019. See also Braz and Gilmore 2006.
30 Gilmore and Gilmore 2016.
31 House of Representatives, "H.R. 3401—Emergency Supplemental Appropriations for Humanitarian Assistance and Security at the Southern Border Act, 2019," 2019–2020, https://www.congress.gov.
32 One of the central explicit arguments on which the credibility of the prison hinged was a claim about the need for more prison space in order to alleviate overcrowding at other federal prisons. In her comments on the supplemental final EIS, Emily Posner argued that this justification for the facility dated to 2005 and the respective prison population at that time. As she noted (in Bureau of Prisons 2017, appendix J, 38),

> The BOP confined 145,780 people in 2005, and its facilities were 37 percent over-capacity. As of May 4, 2017, the BOP incarcerates 153,937 people in 122 facilities. . . . Since its determination in November 2005 that building a new prison in Letcher County was the best means of managing its population, the BOP has built 20 new prisons and increased its overall capacity by 28,559 prisoners, a 26.7 percent increase. On the other hand, the BOP only incarcerates 8,157 more people in 2017 than it did in 2005, an increase of 5.6 percent. Overall, the federal prison population declined by more than 30,000 prisoners since its peak in 2013, a 14 percent reduction, and the overcapacity rate has fallen from 37 percent to 13 percent during the same time period.

Posner continued that there were any number of alternative mechanisms by which the BOP could accommodate the supposed need for more maximum-security beds at existing facilities where there are empty beds or where renovation could occur. These parsings of the numbers, including the rates of incarceration, overcapacity, and prison building, strike at the core of the prison's correctional justification.
33 *Barroca et al. v. Bureau of Prisons* 2018, 41.
34 See Gilmore 2008.
35 Braz and Gilmore 2006.

CONCLUSION

1 Davis 2003.
2 Rodríguez 2020.
3 The Marshall Project, "A State-by-State Look at Coronavirus in Prisons," March 19, 2021, https://www.themarshallproject.org.
4 Rodríguez 2020
5 Ferguson 2020; Lee and Greene 2020; see also Department of Corrections, "Covid-19 Response," Commonwealth of Kentucky, https://corrections.ky.gov.
6 On coronavirus deaths among people in prison, see The Marshall Project 2021 and Turcotte, Sherman, Griesbach, and Klein 2021. On slow violence, see Nixon 2013. On slow violence and toxic landscapes, see Davies 2019. On the slow violence of earlier eras in the coalfields, see Stoll 2017.

7   Buchanan, Bui, and Patel 2020.
8   Correia and Wall 2018a, 217.
9   See for example End Notes 2020.
10 The People's Budget 2020.
11 MPD150 2020.
12 Norton and Stein 2020.
13 Braz and Gilmore 2006.

BIBLIOGRAPHY

Abolition Research Group. 2017. "The Problem with Community Policing." For a World without Police. Available at http://aworldwithoutpolice.org.
Achenbach, Joel. 2019. "A Remote Virginia Valley, Flooded by Prescription Opioids." *Washington Post*, July 18.
Achenbach, Joel, Joyce Koh, Dalton Bennett, and Melina Mara. 2019. "Flooded with Opioids, Appalachia Is Still Trying to Recover." *Washington Post*, July 24.
Adams, Mason. 2020. "Without Serious Help, COVID-19 Could Mean the End for Already-Struggling Rural Hospitals." *100 Days in Appalachia*, March 24. Available at https://www.100daysinappalachia.com.
———. 2019a. "$44,000 for an Ambulance, Hour-Long Drives to an ER: The Impossible Cost of Healthcare in Appalachia." *In These Times*, November 21. Available at https://inthesetimes.com.
———. 2019b. "'They're Cutting Everything': As Coal Disappears, Appalachians Lose Access to Basic Services." *Southerly Magazine*, February 27.
Adler-Bell, Sam. 2019. "Appalachia vs. the Carceral State." *New Republic*, November 25.
Agozino, Biko. 2003. *Counter-colonial Criminology: A Critique of Imperialist Reason*. London: Pluto Press.
Alexander, Michelle. 2010. *The New Jim Crow: Mass Incarceration in the Age of Colorblindness*. New York: New Press.
Allen, James Lane. 1890. "Mountain Passes of the Cumberlands." *Harpers New Monthly Magazine*, September.
Allen, Theodore. 2012. *The Invention of the White Race*. Volume 1, *Racial Oppression and Social Control*. Second edition. New York: Verso.
Anglin, Mary. 2016. "Toward a New Politics of Outrage and Transformation: Placing Appalachia within the Global Political Economy." *Journal of Appalachian Studies* 22(1): 51–56.
Appalachian Land Ownership Task Force. 1983. *Who Owns Appalachia? Landownership and Its Impact*. Lexington: University of Kentucky Press.
Appalachian Regional Commission. 2015. *Appalachia Then and Now: Examining Changes to the Appalachian Region since 1965*. February 23. Available at http://www.arc.gov.
———. 2013. *County Economic Status in Appalachia, Fiscal Year 2014*. Available at http://www.arc.gov.
———. 2011. *Economic Overview of Appalachia—2011*. September 29. Available at https://www.arc.gov.

Appalachian Voices. 2015. "Communities at Risk from Mountaintop Removal." Available at https://appvoices.org.

Armstrong, Sarah. 2014. "Siting Prisons, Sighting Communities: Geographies of Objection in a Planning Process." *Environment and Planning A* 46(3): 550–65.

Arnett, Douglass. 1978. "Eastern Kentucky and the Politics of Dependency and Development." PhD diss., Duke University.

Ashforth, Blake E., and Glen E. Kreiner. 1999. "'How Can You Do It?': Dirty Work and the Challenge of Constructing a Positive Identity." *Academy of Management Review* 24(3): 413–34.

Austin, James, Eric Cadora, and Todd R. Clear, et al. 2013. "Ending Mass Incarceration: Charting a New Justice Reinvestment." Washington, DC: Sentencing Project.

Ball, Gary. 1998a. "'Prepare for Jobs Now': Manchester Prison Officials Visit, Give SCHS Students a Lesson to Remember." *Mountain Citizen*, April 8.

———. 1998b. "Prison Housing Survey Says County Lags Behind Rest of State in Education." *Mountain Citizen*, January 28.

Banks, Alan. 1995. "Class Formation in the Southeastern Kentucky Coalfields, 1890–1920." In *Appalachia in the Making: The Mountain South in the Nineteenth Century*, edited by Mary Beth Pudup, Dwight B. Billings, and Altina Waller, 321–46. Chapel Hill: University of North Carolina Press.

Barroca v. Bureau of Prisons (1:18-cv-02740-JEB (D.D.C.), November 26, 2018).

Barthes, Roland. 1993/1957. *Mythologies*. London: Village.

Barton, Alana, and Alyson Brown. 2011. "Dartmoor: Penal and Cultural Icon." *Howard Journal of Criminal Justice* 50(5): 478–49.

Batteau, Allen W. 1990. *The Invention of Appalachia*. Tempe: University of Arizona Press.

Bauman, Zygmunt. 2004. *Wasted Lives: Modernity and Its Outcasts*. Malden, MA: Blackwell.

Baumann, Anna. 2016. "Coal County Services Harmed by Severance Tax Collapse at Time of Transition." February 24. Kentucky Center for Economic Policy. Accessed at https://kypolicy.org.

Beale, Calvin. 2001. "Cellular Rural Development: New Prisons in Rural and Small-Town Areas in the 1990s," paper prepared for presentation at the annual meeting of the Rural Sociological Society, Albuquerque, New Mexico, August 18.

———. 1998. "Rural Prisons: An Update." *Rural Development Perspectives* 11(2): 25–27.

Beckett, Katherine, and Bruce Western. 2001. "Governing Social Marginality: Welfare, Incarceration, and the Transformation of State Policy." *Punishment and Society* 3(1): 43–59.

Bell, Shannon. 2016. *Fighting King Coal: The Challenges to Micromobilization in Central Appalachia*. Cambridge, MA: MIT Press.

Bell, Shannon, and Yvonne Braun. 2010. "Coal, Identity, and the Gendering of Environmental Justice Activism in Central Appalachia." *Gender & Society* 24(6): 794–813.

Bell, Shannon Elizabeth, and Richard York. 2010. "Community Economic Identity: The Coal Industry and Ideology Construction in West Virginia." *Rural Sociology* 75(1): 111–43.

Benjamin, Walter. 1969a. "Theses on the Philosophy of History." In *Illuminations*, edited by Hannah Arendt, 253–64. New York: Shocken Books.

———. 1969b. "The Work of Art in the Age of Mechanical Reproduction." In *Illuminations*, edited by Hannah Arendt, 217–52. New York: Shocken Books.

Benson, Sara. 2019. *The Prison of Democracy: Race, Leavenworth, and the Culture of Law*. Oakland: University of California Press.

Berger, Dan. 2014a. *Captive Nation: Black Prison Organizing in the Civil Rights Era*. Chapel Hill: University of North Carolina Press.

———. 2014b. *The Struggle Within: Prisons, Political Prisoners, and Mass Movements in the United States*. Oakland, CA: PM Press.

Berkes, Howard. 2016. "Advanced Black Lung Cases Surge in Appalachia." National Public Radio, December 15. Available at https://www.npr.org.

Berkes, Howard, and Adelina Lancianese. 2018. "Black Lung Study Finds Biggest Cluster Ever of Fatal Coal Miners' Disease." National Public Radio, February 6. Available at https://www.npr.org.

Bernd, Candice, Zoe Loftus-Farren, and Maureen Nandini Mitra. 2017. "America's Toxic Prisons: The Environmental Injustices of Mass Incarceration." *Earth Island Journal*. Available at https://earthisland.org/.

Berry, Wendell. 2013. "Contempt for Small Places." Science and Environmental Health Network, August 5. Available at https://www.sehn.org.

Bhattacharya, Tithi, ed. 2017. *Social Reproduction Theory: Remapping Class, Recentering Oppression*. London: Pluto Press.

Biber, Katherine. 2007. *Captive Images: Race, Crime, Photography*. New York: Routledge.

Bigart, Homer. 1963. "Kentucky Miners: A Grim Winter; Poverty, Squalor, and Idleness Prevail in Mountain Area; Poverty Grips Kentucky Miners with Winter's Ordeal Looming." *New York Times*, October 20.

Big Sandy Community and Technical College. 2018. "BSCTC Announces Partnership with EKU to Offer Classes towards Bachelor's Degree on Prestonsburg, Pikeville Campuses!" Eastern Kentucky University Regional Criminal Justice Campuses and Sites. Available at https://cjregional.eku.edu.

Billings, Dwight, and Kathleen M. Blee. 2000. *The Road to Poverty: The Making of Wealth and Hardship in Appalachia*. New York: Cambridge University Press.

Bingman, Mary Beth. 1993. "Stopping the Bulldozers: What Difference Did It Make?" In *Fighting Back in Appalachia: Traditions of Resistance and Change*, edited by Stephen Fisher, 17–30. Philadelphia: Temple University Press.

Black, Kate. 1990. "The Roving Picket Movement and the Appalachian Committee for Full Employment, 1959-1965: A Narrative." *Journal of the Appalachian Studies Association* 2: 110–27.

"Black Lung Returns to Coal Country: Special Series." 2012. National Public Radio. Available at https://www.npr.org.

Blomley, Nicholas. 2003. "Law, Property, and the Geography of Violence: The Frontier, the Survey, and the Grid." *Annals of the Association of American Geographers* 93(1): 121–41.

"Board Won't Fund Teacher for Program." 2013. *Mountain Eagle*, June 26.

Boles, Sydney. 2019. "First These Kentuckians Couldn't Drink the Water: Now They Can't Afford It." National Public Radio, October 31.

Bonds, Anne. 2013. "Economic Development and Relational Racialization: 'Yes in My Backyard' Politics and the Reinvention of Madras, Oregon." *Annals of the Association of American Geographers* 103(6): 1389–1405.

———. 2012. "Building Prisons, Building Poverty: Prison Sitings, Dispossession, and Mass Incarceration," In *Beyond Walls and Cages: Prisons, Borders, and Global Crisis*, edited by Jenna Loyd, Matt Mitchelson, and Andrew Burridge, 129–42. Athens: University of Georgia Press.

———. 2009. "Discipline and Devolution: Constructions of Poverty, Race, and Criminality in the Politics of Rural Prison Development." *Antipode: A Radical Journal of Geography* 41(3): 416–38.

Bonds, Anne, and Joshua Inwood. 2015. "Beyond White Privilege: Geographies of White Supremacy and Settler Colonialism." *Progress in Human Geography* 40(6): 715–33.

Braz, Rose. 2006. "Kinder, Gentler, Gender Response Cages: Prison Expansion Is Not Prison Reform." *Women, Girls, and Criminal Justice*, October/November: 87–88, 91.

Braz, Rose, and Craig Gilmore. 2006. "Joining Forces: Prisons and Environmental Justice in Recent California Organizing." *Radical History Review* 96: 95–111.

Brown, Karida. 2018. *Gone Home: Race and Roots through Appalachia*. Chapel Hill: University of North Carolina Press.

Brown, Michelle. 2009. *The Culture of Punishment: Prisons, Society, Spectacle*. New York: NYU Press.

Brown, Michelle, and Judah Schept. 2017. "New Abolition, Criminology, and a Critical Carceral Studies." *Punishment & Society* 19(4): 440–62.

Buchanan, Larry, Quoctrung Bui, and Jugal Patel. 2020. "Black Lives Matter May Be the Largest Movement in U.S. History." *New York Times*, July 3.

Buck-Morss, Susan. 1991. *The Dialectics of Seeing: Walter Benjamin and the Arcades Project*. Cambridge, MA: MIT Press.

Buer, Lesley-Marie. 2020. *Rx Appalachia: Stories of Treatment and Survival in Rural Kentucky*. Chicago: Haymarket Press.

Bureau of Labor Statistics. 2019. "Occupational Employment and Wages: Correctional Officers and Jailers." May. Available at https://www.bls.gov/.

Bureau of Prisons. 2017. *Final Supplemental Revised Final Environmental Impact Statement for Proposed United States Penitentiary and Federal Prison Camp Letcher County, Kentucky*. United States Department of Justice.

———. 2016. *Revised Final Environmental Impact Statement for Proposed United States Penitentiary and Federal Prison Camp Letcher County, Kentucky*. United States Department of Justice.

Butler, Judith. 2009. *Frames of War: When Is Life Grievable?* London: Verso.
Camp, Jordan. 2016. *Incarcerating the Crisis: Freedom Struggles and the Rise of the Neoliberal State.* Berkeley: University of California Press.
Camp, Jordan, and Christina Heatherton. 2017. "The World We Want: An Interview with Cedric and Elizabeth Robinson." In *Futures of Black Radicalism*, edited by Gaye Theresa Johnson and Alex Lubin, 95–107. New York: Verso.
Cardno. 2014. *Enhanced Utility Investigation Report, Federal Bureau of Prisons Letcher County, Kentucky.*
Carney, Phil. 2010. "Crime, Punishment, and the Force of Photographic Spectacle." In *Framing Crime: Cultural Criminology and the Image*, edited by Keith Hayward and Mike Presdee, 17–35. New York: Routledge.
Carrabine, Eamonn. 2017. "Social Science and Visual Culture." In *The Routledge International Handbook of Visual Criminology*, edited by Michelle Brown and Eamonn Carrabine, 23–39. New York: Routledge.
Cate, Sarah, and Daniel HoSang. 2017. "'The Better Way to Fight Crime': Why Fiscal Arguments Do Not Restrain the Carceral State." *Theoretical Criminology* 22(2): 169–88.
Catte, Elizabeth. 2019. "Finding the Future in Radical Rural America." *Boston Review*, July 11. Available at http://bostonreview.net.
———. 2018. *What You Are Getting Wrong about Appalachia.* Cleveland, OH: Belt Publishing.
Caudill, Harry. 1963. *Night Comes to the Cumberlands: A Biography of a Depressed Area.* New York: Little, Brown.
Che, Deborah. 2005. "Constructing a Prison in the Forest: Conflicts over Nature, Paradise, and Identity." *Annals of the Association of American Geographers* 95(4): 809–31.
Cheves, John. 2019. "Caged: How Kentucky Dangerously Overcrowds Its County Jails with State Prisoners." *Lexington (KY) Herald-Leader*, August 21.
———. 2015. "Fifty Years of Night, Chapter 11: 'A Lot of People Here Have Just Given Up.'" *Lexington (KY) Herald-Leader*, November 12.
———. 2014a. "After 3 Years, Overhaul of Kentucky's Drug-Crime Laws Hasn't Created Expected Savings." *Lexington (KY) Herald-Leader*, February 15. Available at http://www.kentucky.com.
———. 2014b. "House Adds Nursing Home for Felons to Kentucky Budget: Likely Location is in Stumbo's District." *Lexington (KY) Herald-Leader*, March 12. Available at http://www.kentucky.com.
———. 2013. "State Using Coal Taxes for Rupp Arena Project, Upsetting Coal-County Leaders." *Lexington (KY) Herald-Leader*, June 11. Available at https://www.kentucky.com.
Cheves, John, and Bill Estep. 2012. "Fifty Years of Night, Chapter 4: Disillusioned, Harry Caudill Blames 'Genetic Decline' in Eastern Kentucky." *Lexington (KY) Herald-Leader*, December 21.
Christie, Nils. 2001/1993. *Crime Control as Industry: Toward Gulags, Western Style.* New York: Routledge.

Clark, Amy. 2007. "Two Catholic Sisters: Working in the Web of Life." *Appalachian Voices*, February 1. Available at http://appvoices.org.
Clear, Todd, and Natasha Frost. 2014. *The Punishment Imperative: The Rise and Failure of Mass Incarceration in America*. New York: NYU Press.
Clover, Joshua. 2019. *Riot, Strike, Riot: The New Era of Uprisings*. New York: Verso.
Cohen, Stanley. 1998. *Against Criminology*. New Brunswick, NJ: Transaction Publishers.
Collard, Rosemary-Claire, and Jessica Dempsey. 2017. "Capitalist Natures in Five Orientations." *Capitalism Nature Socialism* 28(1): 78–97.
Connolly, William. 1988. *Political Theory and Modernity*. Oxford: Blackwell.
Cooper, Dave. N.d. "Mountaintop Removal Driving Tour." The Mountaintop Removal Road Show. Available at http://www.mountainroadshow.com.
Corbin, David Allen. 2011. *Gun Thugs, Rednecks, Radicals: A Documentary History of the West Virginia Mine Wars*. Oakland, CA: PM Press.
———. 1981. *Life, Work, and Rebellion in the Coal Fields: The Southern West Virginia Miners, 1880–1922*. Champaign: University of Illinois Press.
Correia, David, and Tyler Wall. 2018a. *Police: A Field Guide*. New York: Verso.
———. 2018b. "Response by David Correia and Tyler Wall." *Society and Space*, October 30. Available at https://www.societyandspace.org.
Cotham, Perry C. 1995. *Toil, Turmoil, and Triumph: A Portrait of the Tennessee Labor Movement*. Franklin, TN: Hillsboro Press.
Cover, Robert. 1986. "Violence and the Word." *Yale Law Journal* 95(8): 1601–29.
Cowen, Deb, and Amy Siciliano. 2011. "Surplus Masculinities and Security." *Antipode* 43(5): 1516–41.
Crist, Carolyn. 2018. "Resurgence of Crippling Black Lung Disease Seen in US Coal Miners." *Reuters*, August 23. Available at https://www.reuters.com.
Cullors-Brignac, Patrisse, and Diana Zuñiga. 2014. "A Mental Health Jail Is an Oxymoron: Diversion Is What's Needed; Guest Commentary." *Los Angeles Daily News: Opinion*, June 24.
Daggett, Cara. 2018. "Petro-Masculinity: Fossil Fuels and Authoritarian Desire." *Millenium: Journal of International Studies* 47(1): 25–44.
Davies, Thom. 2019. "Slow Violence and Toxic Geographies: 'Out of Sight' to Whom?" *Environment and Planning C: Politics and Space*, 1–19. Article available in OnlineFirst.
Davis, Angela Y. 2005. *Abolition Democracy: Beyond Empire, Prisons, and Torture*. New York: Seven Stories Press.
———. 2003. *Are Prisons Obsolete?* New York: Seven Stories Press.
Davis, Dee. 2012. "Living in the Fixer-Upper." *Daily Yonder*, October 29. Available at https://dailyyonder.com.
Davis, Mike. 2017. *Buda's Wagon: A Brief History of the Car Bomb*. New York: Verso.
Davis, Mike, and Jon Wiener. 2020. *Set the Night on Fire: L.A. in the Sixties*. New York: Verso.
Day, Noah. 2018. "Martin County Water Crisis." *Hey Kentucky!*, January 31.

Debarbieux, Bernard, and Gilles Rudaz. 2015. *The Mountain: A Political History from the Enlightenment to the Present*. Chicago: University of Chicago Press.

De Giorgi, Alessandro. 2017. "Back to Nothing: Prisoner Reentry and Neoliberal Neglect." *Social Justice* 44(1): 83–120.

———. 2006. *Re-thinking the Political Economy of Punishment: Perspectives on Post-Fordism and Penal Politics*. Aldershot, UK: Ashgate.

Derrida, Jacques. 2006. *Specters of Marx: The State of the Debt, the Work of Mourning, and the New International*. New York: Routledge.

Dodson, Willie. 2019. "KY Plans to Spend Abandoned Mine Land Pilot Funds on a Federal Prison." *Appalachian Voices*, April 24. Available at https://appvoices.org.

Douglass, H. Paul. 1909. *Christian Reconstruction in the South*. Boston: Pilgrim Press.

Douglass, Mary. 2002/1966. *Purity and Danger: An Analysis of Concepts of Pollution and Taboo*. New York: Routledge Classics.

Dreiser, Theodore, et al. 2008/1932. *Harlan Miners Speak: Report on the Terrorism in the Kentucky Coalfields*. Lexington: University of Kentucky Press.

Dubber, Markus Dirk. 2005. *The Police Power: Patriarchy and the Foundations of American Government*. New York: Columbia University Press.

Du Bois, W. E. B. 1998/1935. *Black Reconstruction in America, 1860–1880*. First Free Press edition. New York: Free Press.

Dunaway, Wilma A. 1995. "Speculators and Settler Capitalists: Unthinking the Mythology about Appalachian Landholding, 1790–1860." In *Appalachia in the Making: The Mountain South in the Nineteenth Century*, edited by Mary Beth Pudup, Dwight B. Billings, and Altina Waller, 50–75. Chapel Hill: University of North Carolina Press.

Dunbar-Ortiz, Roxanne. 2014. *An Indigenous Peoples' History of the United States*. Boston: Beacon Press.

Dunlop, R. G. 2010a. "Behind the Bars at Otter Creek: Complaints Went Unanswered at Prison." *Louisville (KY) Courier-Journal*, July 4.

———. 2010b. "Behind the Bars at Otter Creek: Monitoring at Troubled Prison Flawed." *Louisvile (KY) Courier-Journal*, July 4.

———. 2010c. "Behind the Bars at Otter Creek: Suit, Secretary's Suicide Raise Red Flags." *Louisville (KY) Courier-Journal*, July 4.

Eason, John M. 2016. *Big House on the Prairie: Rise of the Rural Ghetto and Prison Proliferation*. Chicago: University of Chicago Press.

———. 2012. "Extending the Hyperghetto: Towards a Theory of Punishment, Race, and Rural Disadvantage." *Journal of Poverty* 16(3): 274–95.

———. 2010. "Mapping Prison Proliferation: Region, Rurality, Race, and Disadvantage in Prison Placement." *Social Science Research* 39: 1015–28.

Edelen, Adam. 2015. *Special Report on the Strength of Kentucky's Rural Hospitals*. Auditor of Public Accounts. Accessed at http://apps.auditor.ky.gov.

Eller, Ronald. 2008. *Uneven Ground: Appalachia since 1945*. Lexington: University of Kentucky Press.

———. 1982. *Miners, Millhands, and Mountaineers: Industrialization of the Appalachian South, 1880–1930*. Knoxville: University of Tennessee Press.

———. N.d. "The War on Poverty in Appalachia." Institute for Rural Journalism and Community Issues. Available at http://www.uky.edu.

End Notes. 2020. "Onward Barbarians." *End Notes*. Available at https://endnotes.org.uk.

Estep, Bill. 2018. "New Federal Prison in Eastern Kentucky Wins Final Approval: 300 Jobs Expected." *Lexington (KY) Herald-Leader*, March 30.

———. 2017a. "Crippled by Coal's Decline, County's Leaders Deadlock on Fee to Fix Revenue Drop." *Lexington (KY) Herald-Leader*, April 10.

———. 2017b. "Kentucky Returning Inmates to For-Profit Prison Four Years after Dumping Company." *Lexington (KY) Herald-Leader*, November 16.

———. 2017c. "Programs That Help Poor Kentuckians Face Big Cuts under Trump's Budget Plan." *Lexington (KY) Herald-Leader*, May 23.

———. 2016. "Coal Jobs in Kentucky Fall to Lowest Level in 118 Years." *Lexington (KY) Herald-Leader*, May 2.

Estes, Nick. 2019. *Our History Is the Future: Standing Rock versus the Dakota Access Pipeline, and the Long Tradition of Indigenous Resistance*. New York: Verso.

Estes, Nick, and Roxanne Dunbar-Ortiz. 2020. "Examining the Wreckage." *Monthly Review: An Independent Socialist Magazine*, July 1. Available at https://monthlyreview.org.

Farley, William. 2017. *A Stubborn Courage: Mean and Ornery Journalists in Eastern Kentucky*. PhD diss., University of Kentucky Department of History.

Ferguson, Danielle. 2020. "Almost Half of South Dakota's Inmates Have Tested Positive for COVID-19." *Sioux Falls Argus Leader*, October 26. Available at https://www.argusleader.com.

Ferguson, Matthew, Elizabeth Lay, Justin Piché, and Kevin Walby. 2014. "The Cultural Work of Decommissioned Carceral Sites: Representations of Confinement and Punishment at Kingston Penitentiary." *Scapegoat: Landscape, Architecture, Political Economy* 7: 83–98.

Ferguson, Matthew, Justin Piché, and Kevin Walby. 2015. "Bridging or Fostering Social Distance? An Analysis of Penal Spectator Comments on Canadian Penal History Museums." *Crime, Media, Culture* 11(3): 357–74.

Fiander, Sarah, Ashley Chen, Justin Piché, and Kevin Walby. 2016. "Critical Punishment Memorialization." *Critical Criminology* 24(1): 1–18.

Fiddler, Michael. 2019. "Ghosts of Other Stories: A Synthesis of Hauntology, Crime, and Space." *Crime, Media, Culture* 15(3): 463–77.

Fiddler, Michael, Theodore Kindynis, and Travis Linnemann, eds. 2022. *Ghost Criminology: The Afterlife of Crime and Punishment*. New York: NYU Press.

Fields, Barbara Jeanne. 1990. "Slavery, Race, and Ideology in the United States of America." *New Left Review* 1(181): 95–118.

Fields, Barbara Jeanne, and Karen Elise Fields. 2014. *Racecraft: The Soul of Inequality in American Life*. London: Verso.

Fight Toxic Prisons. 2018. "Prisoners File Unique Environmental Lawsuit against New Federal Facility on Strip Mine Site in Kentucky." Available at https://fight-toxic-prisons.org.

Fisher, Mark. 2014. *Ghosts of My Life: Writings on Depression, Hauntology, and Lost Futures*. Winchester, UK: Zero Books.

Fisher, Stephen., ed. 1993. *Fighting Back in Appalachia: Traditions of Resistance and Change*. Philadelphia: Temple University Press.

Fisher, Stephen, and Barbara Ellen Smith. 2016. "Internal Colony: Are You Sure? Defining, Theorizing, Organizing Appalachia." *Journal of Appalachian Studies* 22(1): 45–50.

———, eds. 2012. *Transforming Places: Lessons from Appalachia*. Urbana: University of Illinois Press.

Forbes, Buddy. 2020. "'This Is Regional': How Gov. Beshear's Proposed Budget Benefits Eastern Kentucky." *Mountain News WYMT*. Available at https://www.wymt.com.

Foucault, Michel. 1980. *Power/Knowledge: Selected Interviews and Other Writings, 1972–1977*. New York: Random House.

Fowler, Kate. 2015. "Interrogating the Notion of Documentary Truth: Stacey Kranitz, 'As It Was Give(n) to Me.'" *ASX: American Suburb X*. Available at http://www.americansuburbx.com.

Fox, John, Jr. 1994. *Bluegrass and Rhododendron: Outdoors in Old Kentucky*. Lexington: University of Kentucky Press.

Fraser, Nancy. 2017. "Crisis of Care? On the Social Reproductive Contradictions of Contemporary Capitalism." In *Social Reproduction Theory: Remapping Class, Recentering Oppression*, edited by Tithi Bhattacharya, 21–36. London: Pluto Press.

———. 2016a. "Contradictions of Capital and Care." *New Left Review*, July/August. Available at https://newleftreview.org.

———. 2016b. "Expropriation and Exploitation in Racialized Capitalism: A Reply to Michael Dawson." *Critical Historical Studies* 3(1): 163–78.

Garland, David. 2001. *The Culture of Control: Crime and Social Order in Contemporary Society*. Chicago: University of Chicago Press.

Garringer, Rae. 2020. "The Media's Extractive Telling of Appalachia." *Scalawag*, December 15. Available at https://scalawagmagazine.org.

Gaventa, John. 1980. *Power and Powerlessness: Quiescence and Rebellion in an Appalachian Valley*. Urbana: University of Chicago Press.

Geredien, Ross. 2009. "Post-Mountaintop Removal Reclamation of Mountain Summits for Economic Development in Appalachia." Prepared for Natural Resources Defense Council, December 7. Available at http://ilovemountains.org.

Gidwani, Vinay. 2016. "Waste/Value." In *The Wiley-Blackwell Companion to Economic Geography*, edited by Trevor J. Barnes, Jamie Peck, and Eric Sheppard, 275–88. Malden, MA: Blackwell.

———. 2013. "Six Theses on Waste, Value, and Commons." *Social & Cultural Geography* 14(7): 773–83.

Gidwani, Vinay, and Rayjashree Reddy. 2011. "The Afterlives of 'Waste': Notes from India for a Minor History of Capitalist Surplus." *Antipode* 43(5): 1625–58.

Gidwani, Vinay, and Brett Story. 2012. "In Conversation: On Waste as the Political Other of Value." *Garage Sale Standard* 2: 7–9.

Gilmore, Craig. 2014. "An Interview with James Kilgore." *Abolitionist* 23: 6–7.
Gilmore, Craig, Emily Posner, Sylvia Ryerson, Judah Schept, and Panagioti Tsolkas. 2019. "Fighting Toxic Prisons: Restoring Land and Lives. *Abolitionist*, May 16. https://abolitionistpaper.wordpress.com.
Gilmore, Ruth Wilson. 2017a. "Abolition Geography and the Problem of Innocence." In *Futures of Black Radicalism*, edited by Gaye Theresa Johnson and Alex Lubin, 225–40. New York: Verso.
———. 2017b. "Introduction." In Clyde Woods, *Development Arrested: The Blues and Plantation Power in the Mississippi Delta*. New York: Verso.
———. 2011. "What Is to Be Done?" *American Quarterly* 63(2): 245–65.
———. 2007. *Golden Gulag: Prisons, Surplus, Crisis, and Opposition in Globalizing California*. Berkeley: University of California Press.
———. 2002. "Race and Globalization." In *Geographies of Global Change: Remapping the World*, edited by R. J. Johnson, Peter J. Taylor, and Michael J. Watts. Second edition. Malden, MA: Blackwell.
———. 1999. "Globalization and U.S. Prison Growth: From Military Keynesianism to Post-Keynesian Militarism." *Race and Class* 40(2–3): 171–88.
Gilmore, Ruth Wilson, and Craig Gilmore. 2016. "Beyond Bratton." In *Policing the Planet: Why the Policing Crisis Led to Black Lives Matter*, edited by Jordan T. Camp and Christina Heatherton, 173–99. New York: Verso.
———. 2008. "Restating the Obvious." In *Indefensible Space: The Architecture of the National Insecurity State*, edited by Michael Sorkin, 141–62. New York: Routledge.
Gilmore, Ruth Wilson, and James Kilgore. 2019. "Some Reflections on Prison Labor." *Brooklyn Rail*, June. Available at https://brooklynrail.org.
Giménez, Martha E. 2018. *Marx, Women, and Capitalist Social Reproduction*. Chicago: Haymarket Books.
Giroux, Henry. 2014. *Neoliberalism's War on Higher Education*. Chicago: Haymarket Books.
Glasmeier, Amy K., and Tracey Farrigan. 2007. "The Economic Impacts of the Prison Development Boom on Persistently Poor Rural Places." *International Regional Science Review* 30: 274–99.
Goldstein, Jesse. 2013. "Terra Economica: Waste and the Production of Enclosed Nature." *Antipode* 45(2): 357–75.
Goodman, Philip, Joshua Page, and Michelle Phelps. 2017. *Breaking the Pendulum: The Long Struggle over Criminal Justice*. New York: Oxford University Press.
Gordon, Avery. 2017. "The Bruise Blues." In *Futures of Black Radicalism*, edited by Gaye Theresa Johnson and Alex Lubin, 194–205. New York: Verso.
———. 2008. *Ghostly Matters: Haunting and the Sociological Imagination*. Minneapolis: University of Minnesota Press.
Gottschalk, Marie. 2015. *Caught: The Prison State and the Lockdown of American Politics*. Princeton, NJ: Princeton University Press.
———. 2006. *The Prison and the Gallows: The Politics of Mass Incarceration in America*. New York: Cambridge University Press

Gramsci, Antonio. 1971. *Selections from the Prison Notebooks*. New York: International Publishers.
Greenberg, David. 1981. *Crime and Capitalism: Readings in Marxist Criminology*. Palo Alto, CA: Mayfield.
Guenther, Lisa. 2015. "Protected: A Critical Phenomenology of the Trousdale Turner Correctional Facility." *Tennessee Students and Educators for Social Justice*, March 31. https://tnsocialjustice.wordpress.com/tag/critical-phenomenology/.
Hale, Charles, ed. 2008. *Engaging Contradictions: Theory, Politics, and Methods of Activist Scholarship*. Berkeley: University of California Press.
Haley, Sarah. 2018. *No Mercy Here: Gender, Punishment, and the Making of Jim Crow Modernity*. Chapel Hill: University of North Carolina Press.
Hall, Stuart. 2017. "Gramsci and Us." *Verso Blog*. Available at https://www.versobooks.com/blogs/2448-stuart-hall-gramsci-and-us.
———. 1996. "Encoding/Decoding." In *Culture, Media, Language*, edited by Stuart Hall, Dorothy Hobson, Andrew Lowe, and Paul Willis, 128–38. New York: Routledge.
———. 1986. "The Problem of Ideology: Marxism without Guarantees." *Journal of Communication Inquiry* 10(2): 28–44.
———. 1982. "The Rediscovery of 'Ideology': Return of the Repressed in Media Studies." In *Culture, Society, and the Media*, edited by Michael Gurevitch, Tony Bennett, James Curran, and Janet Woollacott, 52–86. London: Methuen.
———. 1981. "The Determination of News Photographs." In *The Manufacture of News: Social Problems, Deviance, and the Mass Media*, edited by Stan Cohen and Jock Young. London: Constable Sage.
Hall, Stuart, Chas Critcher, Tony Jefferson, John Clarke, and Brian Roberts. 2013/1978. *Policing the Crisis: Mugging, the State, and Law and Order*. 35th anniversary edition. New York: Palgrave Macmillan.
Hall, Stuart, and Doreen Massey. 2010. "Interpreting the Crisis." *Soundings* 44(Spring): 57–71.
Hallett, Michael. 2012. "Reentry to What? Theorizing Prisoner Reentry in the Jobless Future." *Critical Criminology* 20(3): 213–28.
Hallinan, Joseph T. 2001. *Going Up the River: Travels in a Prison Nation*. New York: Random House.
Haney, Bill. 2011. *The Last Mountain*. Los Angeles: Uncommon Productions.
Hansford, Justin. 2016. "Community Policing Reconsidered: From Ferguson to Baltimore." In *Policing the Planet: Why the Policing Crisis Led to Black Lives Matter*, edited by Jordan T. Camp and Christina Heatherton, 215–25. New York: Verso.
Harcourt, Bernard. 2010. "Neoliberal Penality: A Brief Genealogy." *Theoretical Criminology* 14(1): 74–92.
Harkins, Anthony. 2004. *Hillbilly: A Cultural History of an American Icon*. New York: Oxford University Press.
Harkins, Anthony, and Meredith McCarroll, eds. 2019. *Appalachian Reckoning: A Region Responds to "Hillbilly Elegy."* Morgantown: West Virginia University Press.

Harrington, Michael. 1997/1962. *The Other America: Poverty in the United States.* 50th anniversary edition. New York: Simon & Schuster.
Harris, Wess, ed. 2017. *Written in Blood: Courage and Corruption in the Appalachian War of Extraction.* Oakland, CA: PM Press.
Harvey, David. 1996. *Justice, Nature, and the Geography of Difference.* Malden, MA: Blackwell.
Hawpe, David. 1970. "Agony at Wheelwright, KY: Noble Experiment Is Dying with Town." *Louisville (KY) Courier-Journal,* May 31.
Hernández, Kelly Lytle. 2017. *City of Inmates: Conquest, Rebellion, and the Rise of Human Caging in Los Angeles, 1771–1965.* Chapel Hill: University of North Carolina Press.
Hetherington, Kevin. 2004. "Secondhandedness: Consumption, Disposal, and Absent Presence." *Environment and Planning D: Society and Space* 22: 157–73.
Hevener, John W. 2002. *Which Side Are You On? The Harlan County Coal Miners, 1931–39.* Champaign: University of Illinois Press.
Hey Kentucky! 2018. "Martin County Water Crisis." Available at https://www.youtube.com/watch?v=gnx5i6AeMr8.
Heynen, Nik. 2018. "Toward an Abolition Ecology." In *Abolishing Carceral Society,* edited by Abolition Collective, 240–47. Brooklyn, NY: Common Notions.
Hickman, Ronnie. 1998. "Prison Gets Official Go-Ahead." *Mountain Citizen,* February 11.
———. 1997a. "BOP Prefers Site in Martin County." *Mountain Citizen,* October 15.
———. 1997b. "Honey Branch Leads Race for State $$." *Mountain Citizen,* September 3.
———. 1997c. "Prison Jobs in Martin County? Education Is the Key." *Mountain Citizen,* June 25.
———. 1997d. "71 Attend Public Hearing on Prison." *Mountain Citizen,* July 9.
Hinton, Elizabeth. 2016. *From the War on Poverty to the War on Crime: The Making of Mass Incarceration in America.* Cambridge, MA: Harvard University Press.
Hodgkinson, Sarah, and Diane Urquhart. 2017. "Ghost Hunting in Prison: Contemplating Death through Sites of Incarceration and the Commodification of the Penal Past." In *The Handbook of Prison Tourism,* edited by Jacqueline Z. Wilson, Sarah Hodgkinson, Justin Piché, and Kevin Walby, 559–82. London: Palgrave-Macmillan.
Hoelscher, Steven, and Derek Alderman. 2004. "Memory and Place: Geographies of a Critical Relationship." *Social and Cultural Geography* 5(3): 347–55.
Hooks, Gregory, Clay Mosher, Shaun Genter, Thomas Rotolo, and Linda Lobao. 2010. "Revisiting the Impact of Prison Building on Job Growth: Education, Incarceration, and County-Level Employment, 1976–2004." *Social Science Quarterly* 91(1): 228–44.
Hooks, Gregory, Clay Mosher, Linda Lobao, and Thomas Rotolo. 2004. "The Prison Industry: Carceral Expansion and Employment in U.S. Counties, 1969–1994." *Social Science Quarterly* 85: 37–57.
Horne, Gerald. 1995. *Fire This Time: The Watts Uprising and the 1960s.* Charlottesville: University of Virginia Press

HoSang, Daniel Martinez, and Joseph E. Lowndes. 2019. *Producers, Parasites, Patriots: Race and the New Right-Wing Politics of Precarity*. Minneapolis: University of Minnesota Press.

House, Silas. 2016. "The Road Back: Appalachia as Internal Colony." *Journal of Appalachian Studies* 22(1): 65–68.

Hoy, Suellen. 1996. *Chasing Dirt: The American Pursuit of Cleanliness*. New York: Oxford University Press.

Huber, Patrick. 2006. "Red Necks and Red Bandanas: Appalachian Coal Miners and the Coloring of Union Identity, 1912–1936." *Western Folklore* 65(1/2): 195–210.

Hufford, Mary. 2003. "Knowing Ginseng: The Social Life of an Appalachian Root." *Cahiers de Littérature Orale* 53(4): 265–91.

Hughes, Everett C. 1962. "Good People and Dirty Work." *Social Problems* 10(1): 3–11.

Huling, Tracy. 2002. "Building a Prison Economy in Rural America." In *Invisible Punishment: The Collateral Consequences of Mass Imprisonment*, edited by Marc Mauer and Meda Chesney-Lind. New York: New Press.

———. 1998. *Yes, in My Backyard*. Freehold, NY: Galloping Girls Productions.

Hunter, Gary, and Peter Wagner. 2008. "Prisons, Politics, and the Census." In *Prison Profiteers: Who Makes Money from Mass Incarceration*, edited by Tara Herivel and Paul Wright, 80–89. New York: New Press.

Hutson, A. C., Jr. 1936. "The Overthrow of the Convict Lease System." *East Tennessee Historical Society's Publications* 8: 82–103.

———. 1935. "The Coal Miners' Insurrections of 1891 in Anderson County, Tennessee." *East Tennessee Historical Society's Publications* 7: 103–21.

Ignatiev, Noel. 2009. *How the Irish Became White*. New York: Routledge Classics.

———. 2003. "Whiteness and Class Struggle." *Historical Materialism* 11(4): 227–35.

Isenberg, Nancy. 2016. *White Trash: The 400-Year Untold History of Class in America*. New York: Viking.

Jackson, George. 1994. *Soledad Brother: The Prison Letters of George Jackson*. New York: Coward-McCann

James, Joy. 2005. *The New Abolitionists: (Neo)Slave Narratives and Contemporary Prison Writings*. Albany: State University of New York Press.

Jayadev, Arjun, and Samuel Bowles. 2006. "Guard Labor." *Journal of Development Economics* 79: 328–48.

Jobey, Liz. 2015. "Trevor Paglen: What Lies Beneath." *Financial Times Magazine*, December 31. Available at https://www.ft.com.

Jones, Philip J., and Claire Wardle. 2010. "Hindley's Ghost: The Visual Construction of Maxine Carr." In *Framing Crime: Cultural Criminology and the Image*, edited by Keith Hayward and Mike Presdee, 53–67. New York: Routledge.

Kang-Brown, Jacob, Oliver Hinds, Jasmine Heiss, and Olive Lu. 2018. "The New Dynamics of Mass Incarceration." Vera Institute of Justice. Available at https://www.vera.org.

Kang-Brown, Jacob, and Ram Subramanian. 2017. "Out of Sight: The Growth of Jails in Rural America." Vera Institute of Justice. Available at https://www.vera.org.

Karuka, Manu. 2019. *Empire's Tracks: Indigenous Nations, Chinese Workers, and the Transcontinental Railroad*. Berkeley: University of California Press.

Kase, Justin. 2018. "Multi-Million-Dollar Grant Moves Letcher Co. Prison Project Forward." *WYMT Mountain News*, September 4. Available at https://www.wymt.com.

Katz, Cindi. 2011. "Accumulation, Excess, Childhood: Toward a Countertopography of Risk and Waste." *Documents d'Anàlisi Geogràfica* 57(1): 47–60.

———. 2001. "Vagabond Capitalism and the Necessity of Social Reproduction." *Antipode* 33(4): 709–28.

Kelley, Robin D. G. 1999. "Building Bridges: The Challenge of Organized Labor in Communities of Color." *New Labor Forum* 5: 42–58.

Kentucky Energy and Environment Cabinet. 2020. "Kentucky Quarterly Coal Report, 2020—Q2." Available at https://eec.ky.gov.

———. 2017. "Kentucky Coal Facts—2017." Available at https://eec.ky.gov.

Kentucky Hospital Association. 2015. "Code Blue: Many Kentucky Hospitals Struggling Financially Due to Health System Changes." April.

Kentucky River Area Development District. 2017. "Comprehensive Economic Development Strategy." Available at https://www.kradd.org.

———. 2015. "Comprehensive Economic Development Strategy." Available at https://www.kradd.org.

———. 2012. "Comprehensive Economic Development Strategy." Available at https://www.kradd.org.

Kephart, Horace. 1922. *Our Southern Highlanders: A Narrative Adventure in the Southern Appalachians and a Study of Life among the Mountaineers*. New York: Outing.

Kilgore, James. 2022. *Understanding E-Carceration: Electronic Monitoring, the Surveillance State, and the Future of Mass Incarceration*. New York: New Press

———. 2014. "Repackaging Mass Incarceration." *Counterpunch*, June 6. Available at https://www.counterpunch.org.

———. 2013. "The Myth of Prison Slave Labor Camps in the U.S." *Counterpunch*, August 9. Available at https://www.counterpunch.org.

King, Ryan S., Marc Mauer, and Tracy Huling. 2003. "Big Prisons, Small Towns: Prison Economies in Rural America." The Sentencing Project, February 1. Available at https://www.sentencingproject.org.

Klotter, James C. 1985. "The Black South and White Appalachia." 1985. In *Blacks in Appalachia*, edited by William Turner and Edward J. Cabbell, 51–67. Lexington: University of Kentucky Press.

Kurti, Zhandarka, and William Martin. 2018. "Cuomo's 'Carceral Humanism.'" *Jacobin*, November 16. Available at https://jacobinmag.com.

Lane, Stonney Rae. 2003. *Building Time at Brushy*. Self-published.

Law, Victoria. 2012. *Resistance behind Bars: The Struggles of Incarcerated Women*. Oakland, CA: PM Press.

Lawson, Victoria, Lucy Jarosz, and Anne Bonds. 2010. "Articulations of Place, Poverty, and Race: Dumping Grounds and Unseen Grounds in the Rural American Northwest." *Annals of the Association of American Geographers* 100(3): 655–77.

Lee, Iris, and Sean Greene. 2020. "Tracking the Coronavirus in California State Prisons." *Los Angeles Times*, October 29. Available at https://www.latimes.com.
Leebrick, Rhiannon. 2015. *Environmental Gentrification and Development in a Rural Appalachian Community: Blending Critical Theory and Ethnography*. PhD diss., University of Tennessee, Knoxville.
Lerman, Amy, and Vesla Weaver. 2014. *Arresting Citizenship: The Democratic Consequences of American Crime Control*. Chicago: University of Chicago Press.
Lewis, Helen Matthews, Linda Johnson, and Donald Askins. 1978. *Colonialism in Modern America: The Appalachian Case*. Boone, NC: Appalachian Consortium.
Lewis, Helen Matthews, and Edward Knipe. 1978. "The Colonialism Model: The Appalachian Case." In *Colonialism in Modern America: The Appalachian Case*, edited by Helen Matthews Lewis, Linda Johnson, and Donald Askins. Boone, NC: Appalachian Consortium.
Lewis, Helen Matthews, Sue Easterling Kobak, and Linda Johnson. 1978. "Family, Religion, and Colonialism in Central Appalachia." In *Colonialism in Modern America: The Appalachian Case*, edited by Helen Matthews Lewis, Linda Johnson, and Donald Askins. Boone, NC: Appalachian Consortium.
Lewis, Ronald. 2009. *Black Coal Miners in America: Race, Class, and Community Conflict, 1780–1980*. Lexington: University of Kentucky Press.
Lichtenstein, Alex. 2011. "A 'Labor History' of Mass Incarceration." *Labor: Studies in Working-Class History of the Americas* 8(3): 5–14.
———. 1996. *Twice the Work of Free Labor: The Political Economy of Convict Labor in the New South*. New York: Verso.
Linebaugh, Peter. 2014. *Stop, Thief! The Commons, Enclosures, and Resistance*. Oakland, CA: PM Press.
———. 2008. *The Magna Carta Manifesto: Liberties and Commons for All*. Berkeley: University of California Press.
———. 2006. *The London Hanged: Crime and Civil Society in the Eighteenth Century*. Second edition. New York: Verso.
———. 1976. "Karl Marx, the Theft of Wood, and Working-Class Composition: A Contribution to the Current Debate." *Crime and Social Justice* 6: 5–16.
Linnemann, Travis. 2016. *Meth Wars: Police, Media, Power*. New York: NYU Press.
Linnemann, Travis, and Tyler Wall. 2013. "'This Is Your Face on Meth': The Punitive Spectacle of White Trash in the Rural War on Drugs." *Theoretical Criminology* 17(3): 315–34.
Lipsitz, George. 2004. "Abolition Democracy and Global Justice." *Comparative American Studies* 2(3): 271–86.
Loader, Ian, and Richard Sparks. 2010. "What Is to Be Done with Public Criminology?" *Criminology and Public Policy* 9(4): 771–81.
Lockwood, Alan H., and Lisa Evans. 2014. "Ash in Lungs: How Breathing Coal Ash Is Hazardous to Your Health." Earthjustice. Available at https://earthjustice.org.
Lockwood, Frank E. 2002. "Kentucky Federal Prison Sinking Even before It's Finished." *Lexington (KY) Herald-Leader*, July 24.

Luscombe, Alex, Kevin Walby, and Justin Piché. 2017. "Haunting Encounters at Canadian Penal History Museums." In *The Handbook of Prison Tourism*, edited by Jacqueline Z. Wilson, Sarah Hodgkinson, Justin Piché, and Kevin Walby, 435–55. London: Palgrave-Macmillan.

Lynch, Michael, and Ray Michalowski. 2006. *Primer in Radical Criminology: Critical Perspectives on Crime, Power, and Identity*. Monsey, NY: Criminal Justice Press.

Lynch, Mona. 2010. *Sunbelt Justice: Arizona and the Transformation of American Punishment*. Palo Alto, CA: Stanford University Press.

Macy, Beth. 2018. "'They Were All Lawyered Up and Rudy Giuliani'd Up.'" *Politico Magazine*, August 5. Available at https://www.politico.com.

Mann, Eric. 2001. "'A Race Struggle, a Class Struggle, a Women's Struggle All at Once': Organizing on the Buses of L.A." *Socialist Register* 37: 259–73.

Markowitz, Eric. 2015. "Poison Prison: Is Toxic Dust Sickening Inmates Locked Up in Coal Country?" *Prison Legal News*, May 27.

Marley, Ben. 2016a. "The Coal Crisis in Appalachia: Agrarian Transformation, Commodity Frontiers, and the Geographies of Capital." *Journal of Agrarian Change* 16(2): 225–54.

———. 2016b. "From War on Poverty to War on Coal: Nature, Capital, and Work in Appalachia." *Environmental Sociology* 2(1): 88–100.

Marx, Karl. 1998/1932. *The German Ideology*. Amherst, NY: Prometheus Books.

———. 1990/1867. *Capital*. Volume 1. New York: Penguin Classics.

Mbembe, Achille. 2017. *Critique of Black Reason*. Durham, NC: Duke University Press.

McCaroll, Meredith. 2018. *Unwhite: Appalachia, Race, and Film*. Athens: University of Georgia Press.

McCoy, Nina. 2018. "A Victim of Official Abuse, Martin County Says 'Time's Up.'" *Lexington (KY) Herald-Leader*, February 11. Available at https://www.kentucky.com.

McDaniel, Dustin, Bret Grote, Ben Cigarillo, Devon Cohen, Quinn Cozzens. 2014. "No Escape: Exposure to Toxic Coal Waste at State Correctional Institution Fayette." Abolitionist Law Center. Available at https://abolitionistlawcenter.org.

Mcghee, Marshall. 1991. *Briceville: The Town That Coal Built*. Jacksboro, TN: Action Printing.

McIntyre, Michael, and Heidi J. Nast. 2011. "Bio(necro)polis: Marx, Surplus Populations, and the Spatial Dialectics of Reproduction and 'Race.'" *Antipode* 43(5): 1465–88.

McNeil, Bryan T. 2012. *Combating Mountaintop Removal: New Directions in the Fight against Big Coal*. Champaign: University of Illinois Press.

McQuade, Brendan. 2015. "Against Community Policing." *Jacobin*, November 18.

McSpirit, Stephanie, Shaunna L. Scott, Sharon Hardesty, and Robert Welch. 2005. "EPA Actions in Post-Disaster Martin County, Kentucky: An Analysis of Bureaucratic Slippage and Agency Recreancy." *Journal of Appalachian Studies* 11(1/2): 30–63.

Meier, Barry. 2019. "A Nun, a Doctor, and a Lawyer—and Deep Regret over the Nation's Handling of Opioids." *New York Times*, August 18. Available at https://www.nytimes.com.

———. 2003. *Pain Killer: A "Wonder" Drug's Trail of Addiction and Death*. New York: St. Martin's.
Meiners, Erica. 2009. "Resisting Civil Death: Organizing for Access to Education in Our Prison Nation." *DePaul Journal for Social Justice* 3(1): 79–96.
Melamed, Jodi. 2015. "Racial Capitalism." *Critical Ethnic Studies* 1(1): 76–85.
Melossi, Dario, and Massimo Pavarini. 2018/1981. *The Prison and the Factory: Origins of the Penitentiary System*. 40th anniversary edition. London: Palgrave Macmillan.
Melossi, Martin. 2005. *Garbage in the Cities. Refuse, Reform, and the Environment*. Pittsburgh: University of Pittsburgh Press.
Mezzadra, Sandro, and Brett Neilson. 2017. "On the Multiple Frontiers of Extraction: Excavating Contemporary Capitalism." *Cultural Studies* 31(2–3): 185–204.
Miller, Jerome G. 1991. *Last One over the Wall: The Massachusetts Experiment in Closing Reform Schools*. Columbus: Ohio State University Press.
Miller, Reuben Jonathan. 2014. "Devolving the Carceral State: Race, Prisoner Reentry, and the Micro-Politics of Urban Poverty Management." *Punishment & Society* 16(3): 305–35.
Mirzoeff, Nicholas. 2011a. "The Right to Look." *Critical Inquiry* 37(3): 473–96.
———. 2011b. *The Right to Look: A Counterhistory of Visuality*. Durham, NC: Duke University Press.
Mitchell, Don. 2003. "Dead Labor and the Political Economy of Landscape: California Living, California Dying." In *Handbook of Cultural Geography*, edited by Kay Anderson, Mona Domosh, Steve Pile, and Nigel Thrift, 233–49. London: Sage.
———. 1996. *The Lie of the Land: Migrant Workers and the California Landscape*. Minneapolis: University of Minnesota Press.
Mitchell, Katharyne, Sallie A. Marston, and Cindi Katz. 2003. "Introduction: Life's Work; An Introduction, Review, and Critique." *Antipode* 35(3): 415–42.
Mitchell, W. J. T. 2005. *What Do Pictures Want? The Lives and Loves of Images*. Chicago: University of Chicago Press.
———, ed. 2002. *Landscape and Power*. Chicago: University of Chicago Press.
Montrie, Chad. 2005. "To Have, Hold, Develop, and Defend: Natural Rights and the Movement to Abolish Strip Mining in Eastern Kentucky." *Journal of Appalachian Studies* 11(1/2): 64–82.
———. 2003. *To Save the Land and People: A History of Opposition to Surface Coal Mining in Appalachia*. Chapel Hill: University of North Carolina Press.
Moran, Dominique. 2015. *Carceral Geography: Spaces and Practices of Incarceration*. Burlington, VT: Ashgate.
Morrell, Andrea R. 2021. "Hometown Prison: Whiteness, Safety, and Prison Work in Upstate New York State." *American Anthropologist*. Available in OnlineFirst.
———. 2012. "The Prison Fix: Race, Work, and Economic Development in Elmira, New York." CUNY Academic Works. Available at https://www.academicworks.cuny.edu.
Morris, Patricia, and Tammi Arford. 2018. "'Sweat a Little Water, Sweat a Little Blood': A Spectacle of Convict Labor at an American Amusement Park." *Crime, Media, Culture* 15(3): 423–46.

Morrison, Wayne. 2010. "A Reflected Gaze of Humanity: Cultural Criminology and Images of Genocide." In *Framing Crime: Cultural Criminology and the Image*, edited by Keith Hayward and Mike Presdee, 189–206. New York: Routledge.

———. 2004. "Reflections with Memories: Everyday Photography Capturing Genocide." *Theoretical Criminology* 8(3): 341–58.

Mosher, Clayton, Gregory Hooks, and Peter Wood. 2005. "Don't Build It Here: The Hype versus the Reality of Prisons and Local Employment." *Prison Legal News*, January 15. Available at https://www.prisonlegalnews.org.

Mosley, David, and Daniel DeBehnke. 2019. "Rural Hospital Sustainability: New Analysis Shows Worsening Situation for Rural Hospitals, Residents." Navigant Consulting, Inc. Available at https://guidehouse.com.

Mountain Community Television. N.d. "Wheelwright: Coal Mining Town." *Internet Archive*. Available at https://archive.org.

Mountain Eagle Staff. 2013a. "Board Won't Fund Teacher for Program." *Mountain Eagle*, June 26.

———. 2013b. "Prison Would Bring Needed Jobs." *Mountain Eagle*, August 7.

———. 2012. "Training for Prison Jobs Coming." *Mountain Eagle*, December 19.

MPD150. 2020. "Enough Is Enough: A 150-Year Performance Review of the Minneapolis Police Department." Summer. Available at https://www.mpd150.com.

Murakawa, Naomi. 2014. *The First Civil Right: How Liberals Built Prison America*. New York: Oxford University Press.

———. 2011. "Toothless: The Methamphetamine 'Epidemic,' 'Meth Mouth,' and the Racial Construction of Drug Scares." *Du Bois Review* 8(1): 219–28.

Musgrave, Beth. 2009. "Victim Sues Otter Creek Prison Owner." *Lexington (KY) Herald-Leader*, October 8.

Neel, Phil A. 2018. *Hinterlands: America's New Landscape of Class and Conflict*. London: Reaktion Books.

Neeson, J. M. 1993. *Commoners: Common Right, Enclosure, and Social Change in England, 1700–1820*. Cambridge: Cambridge University Press.

Neocleous, Mark. 2013. "The Dream of Pacification: Accumulation, Class War, and the Hunt." *Socialist Studies* 9(2): 7–31.

———. 2003. *Imagining the State*. Philadelphia, PA: Open University Press.

———. 2000. *The Fabrication of Social Order: A Critical Theory of Police Power*. Sterling, VA: Pluto Press.

Newman, Katelyn. 2018. "Hope for Change in Appalachia." *U.S. News and World Report*, September 25. Available at https://www.usnews.com.

Nixon, Rob. 2013. *Slow Violence and the Environmentalism of the Poor*. Cambridge, MA: Harvard University Press.

Norton, Jack. 2016. "Little Siberia, Star of the North: The Political Economy of Prison Dreams in the Adirondacks." In *Historical Geographies of Prisons*, edited by Karen M. Morin and Dominique Moran, 168–84. New York: Routledge.

Norton, Jack, and Jasmine Heiss. 2020. "Prioritizing Jails over Hospitals Has Made Rural US More Vulnerable to COVID-19." *Truthout*, April 12. Available at https://truthout.org.

Norton, Jack, and Cindi Katz. 2017. "Social Reproduction." In *The International Encyclopedia of Geography*, edited by Douglas Richardson, Noel Castree, Michael F. Goodchild, Audrey Kobayashi, Weidong Liu, and Richard Marston. Hoboken, NJ: Wiley.

Norton, Jack, and Judah Schept. 2019. "Keeping the Lights On: Incarcerating the Bluegrass." Vera Institute of Justice. Available at https://www.vera.org.

Norton, Jack, and David Stein. 2020. "Materializing Race: On Capitalism and Mass Incarceration." *Spectre Journal*, October 22.

Nyden, Paul. 1974. *Black Coal Miners in the United States*. New York: American Institute of Marxist Studies.

Olssen, Mark, and Michael A. Peters. 2007. "Neoliberalism, Higher Education, and the Knowledge Economy: From the Free Market to Knowledge Capitalism." *Journal of Education Policy* 20(3): 313–45.

Ooten, Melissa, and Jason Sawyer. 2016. "From the Coal Mine to the Prison Yard: The Human Cost of Appalachia's New Economy." In *Appalachia Revisited: New Perspectives on Place, Tradition, and Progress*, edited by William Schumann and Rebecca Adkins Fletcher, 171–84. Lexington: University of Kentucky Press.

Oshinsky, David. 1996. *Worse Than Slavery: Parchman Farm and the Ordeal of Jim Crow Justice*. New York: Free Press.

Osterweil, Vicky. 2020. *In Defense of Looting: A Riotous History of Uncivil Action*. New York: Bold Typer Books

Paglen, Trevor. 2010a. *Blank Spots on the Map: The Dark Geography of the Pentagon's Secret World*. New York: New American Library.

———. 2010b. *Invisible: Covert Operations and Classified Landscapes*. New York: Aperture Foundation.

Parks, Kiera. 2013. "'Reflection Cottages': The Latest Spa Getaway or Concrete Solitary Confinement Cells for Kids?" American Civil Liberties Union of Colorado. Available at https://www.aclu.org.

Patrick, Melissa. 2019. "Study Concludes 16 Rural Hospitals in Ky. at High Risk of Closing: Another Found 35 in Poor Financial Health; Remedies Proposed." *Kentucky Health News*, October 6. Available at https://kyhealthnews.blogspot.com.

Peak, Chris. 2015. "Inside the Big Plan to Get One Appalachian Community Back on Track." *Nationswell*, June 11. Available at https://nationswell.com.

Peck, Jamie. 2003. "Geography and Public Policy: Mapping the Penal State." *Progress in Human Geography* 27(2): 222–32.

Peck, Jamie, and Nik Theodore. 2008. "Carceral Chicago: Making the Ex-Offender Employability Crisis." *International Journal of Urban and Regional Research* 32(2): 251–81.

Pellegrin, Mandy. 2019. "Incarceration in Tennessee: Who, Where, Why, and How Long?" Sycamore Institute, February 14. Available at https://www.sycamoreinstitutetn.org.

Pelot-Hobbs, Lydia. 2018. "Scaling Up or Scaling Back: The Pitfalls and Possibilities of Leveraging Federal Interventions for Abolition." *Critical Criminology* 26(3): 423–41.

People's Budget. 2020. "The People's Budget Los Angeles, 2020–2021." *People's Budget*. Available at https://peoplesbudgetla.files.wordpress.com.

Perdue, Robert T., and Kenneth Sanchagrin. 2016. "Imprisoning Appalachia: The Socio-Economic Impacts of Prison Development." *Journal of Appalachian Studies* 22(2): 58–71.

Perks, Robert, and Gregory Wetstone. 2002. "Rewriting the Rules: Year-End Report 2002; The Bush Administration's Assault on the Environment." National Resources Defense Council. Available at https://www.nrdc.org.

Perry, Lisa. 2014. *Reimagining Camelot: Wheelwright, Kentucky, in Memory and Folklore*. Self-published.

Petchesky, Rosalind. 1981. "At Hard Labor: Penal Confinement and Production in Nineteenth-Century America." In *Crime and Capitalism: Readings in Marxist Criminology*, edited by David F. Greenberg, 341–57. Palo Alto, CA: Mayfield.

Petitjean, Clément, and Ruth Wilson Gilmore. 2018. "Prisons and Class Warfare: An Interview with Ruth Wilson Gilmore." Verso, August 2. Available at https://www.versobooks.com.

Piché, Justin. 2016. "Assessing the Boundaries of Public Criminology: On What Does (Not) Count." *Social Justice: A Journal of Crime, Conflict, and World Order* 42(2): 70–90.

Piché, Justin, and Kevin Walby. 2010. "Problematizing Carceral Tours." *British Journal of Criminology* 50(3): 570–81.

Platt, Tony. 2018. *Beyond These Walls: Rethinking Crime and Punishment in the United States*. New York: St. Martin's.

———. 1969. *The Child Savers: The Invention of Delinquency*. Chicago: University of Chicago Press.

Platt, Tony, et al. 1982. *The Iron Fist and the Velvet Glove*. Third edition. San Francisco: Crime and Social Justice Associates.

Pollard, Kelvin, and Linda A. Jacobsen. 2020. "The Appalachian Region: A Data Overview from the 2014–2018 American Community Survey." Appalachian Regional Commission. Available at https://www.arc.gov.

Polsky, Ned. 1967. *Hustlers, Beats, and Others*. New York: Lyons Press.

Post, Paul. 2017. "Closed Prisons in Rural Areas Are a Tough Sell." *New York Times*, April 10.

Price, Joshua. 2015. *Prisons and Social Death*. New Brunswick, NJ: Rutgers University Press.

Prison Legal News. 2011. "Female Prisoners Removed from CCA Facility in Kentucky." Available at https://www.prisonlegalnews.org.

"Prison Would Bring Needed Jobs." 2013. *Mountain Eagle*, August 7.

Pulido, Laura. 2017. "Geographies of Race and Ethnicity II: Environmental Racism, Racial Capitalism, and State-Sanctioned Violence." *Progress in Human Geography* 41(4): 524–33.

———. 2016. "Flint, Environmental Racism, and Racial Capitalism." *Capitalism, Nature, Socialism* 27(3): 1–16.

———. 2000. "Rethinking Environmental Racism: White Privilege and Urban Development in Southern California." *Annals of the Association of American Geographers* 90(1): 12–40.
Purser, Gretchen. 2012. "'Still Doin' Time': Clamoring for Work in the Day Labor Industry." *WorkingUSA: The Journal of Labor and Society* 15: 397–415.
Pyle, Kevin, and Craig Gilmore. 2005. "Prison Town: Paying the Price." Northampton, MA: Real Cost of Prisons Project.
Raby, John. 2018. "Coal Mining Deaths Surge in 2017 after Hitting Record Low." *AP News*, January 2. Available at https://apnews.com.
Rakia, Raven. 2015. "Coal Ash May Be Making Pennsylvania Inmates Sick, and Now They're Fighting to Shut Their Prison Down." *Vice*, May 18.
Ray, Tarence. 2019. "Hollowed Out: Against the Sham Revitalization of Appalachia." *Baffler* 47. Available at https://thebaffler.com.
———. 2018. "A Way Out: An Activist with an Ulcer Asks, 'Why Do Nonprofits Exist?'" *Popula*, November 18. Available at https://popula.com.
Reardon, Jenny, and Kim TallBear. 2012. "'Your DNA Is *Our* History': Genomics, Anthropology, and the Construction of Whiteness as Property." *Current Anthropology* 53(S5): S233–45.
Reece, Eric. 2006. *Lost Mountain: A Year in the Vanishing Wilderness*. New York: Penguin Group Riverhead Books.
Reed, Adolph, and Merlin Chokwayun. 2012. "Race, Class, Crisis: The Discourse of Racial Disparity and Its Analytical Discontents." *Socialist Register* 48: 149–75.
Reiman, Jeffrey, and Paul Leighton. 2013/1979. *The Rich Get Richer and the Poor Get Prison: Ideology, Class, and Criminal Justice*. 10th edition. New York: Routledge.
Reno, Joshua O. 2016. *Waste Away: Working and Living with a North American Landfill*. Berkeley: University of California Press.
Robinson, Cedric. 2007. *Forgeries of Memory and Meaning: Blacks and the Regimes of Race in American Theater and Film before World War II*. Chapel Hill: University of North Carolina Press.
———. 2000. *Black Marxism: The Making of the Black Radical Tradition*. Chapel Hill: University of North Carolina Press.
Rodríguez, Dylan. 2020. "Covid-19 Pandemic as Carceral Revelation: Toward Abolitionist Counter-War." In "Post-Covid Fantasies," edited by Catherine Besteman, Heath Cabot, and Barak Kalir. American Ethnologist website, July 27. Available at https://americanethnologist.org.
Roediger, David R. 2017. *Class, Race, and Marxism*. New York: Verso.
———. 1999. *The Wages of Whiteness: Race and the Making of the American Working Class*. Revised edition. New York: Verso.
Rubin, Sally, and Ashley York, dirs. 2018. *Hillbilly*. Holler Home Productions.
Rusche, Georg, and Otto Kirchheimer. 2017/1939. *Punishment and Social Structure*. New York: Routledge.
Ryerson, Sylvia. 2020. "Precarious Politics: Friends of Coal, the UMWA, and the Affective Terrain of Energy Identification." *American Quarterly* 72(3): 719–47.

———. 2013. "Prison Progress?" *Daily Yonder*, February 20. Available at https://dailyyonder.com.

———. 2011. "Prison Progress? A Three-Part WMMT Radio Documentary." *Making Connections News*. WMMT-FM 88.7 Mountain Community Radio. Whitesburg, KY, October. Available at https://www.makingconnectionsnews.org.

———. 2010. *Prison Progress . . . Neocolonialism as a Relocation Project in "Post Racial" America: An Appalachian Case; or, Listening to the Canaries in the Coal Mine*. Honors thesis, Wesleyan University, Middletown, CT.

Ryerson, Sylvia, and Judah Schept. 2021. "'Prisons Are Not Innovation': Abolitionist Interventions for a Just Transition." In *Just Transitions*, edited by Shaunna Scott and Kathryn Engle. Forthcoming.

———. 2018. "Building Prisons in Appalachia." *Boston Review*, April 28. Available at https://bostonreview.net.

Saleh-Hanna, Viviane. 2015. "Black Feminist Hauntology: Rememory the Ghosts of Abolition?" *Champ Pénal/Penal Field* 12. Available at https://journals.openedition.org.

Salyer, Robert. 2005. *Sludge*. Appalshop. Film available at https://appalshop.org.

Schaver, Mark. 1993. "Panel Wants 203 College Programs Cut." *Louisville (KY) Courier-Journal*, December 21.

Schept, Judah. 2016. "Visuality and Criminology." In *The Oxford Encyclopedia of Crime, Media, and Popular Culture*, edited by Nicole Rafter and Michelle Brown, 599–620. New York: Oxford University Press.

———. 2015. *Progressive Punishment: Job Loss, Jail Growth, and the Neoliberal Logic of Carceral Expansion*. New York: NYU Press.

———. 2014. "(Un)seeing like a Prison: Countervisual Ethnography of the Carceral State." *Theoretical Criminology* 18(2): 198–223.

———. 2013. "'A Lockdown Facility . . . with the Feel of a Small, Private College': Liberal Politics, Jail Expansion, and the Carceral Habitus." *Theoretical Criminology* 17(1): 71–88.

Schept, Judah, Tyler Wall, and Avi Brisman. 2015. "Building, Staffing, and Insulating: An Architecture of Criminological Complicity in the School-to-Prison Pipeline." *Social Justice* 41(4): 96–115.

Schoenfeld, Heather. 2018. *Building the Prison State: Race and the Politics of Mass Incarceration*. Chicago: University of Chicago Press.

Schuppe, Jon. 2018. "Does America Need Another Prison? It May Be This Rural County's Only Chance at Survival." NBCNews, March 22. Available at https://www.nbcnews.com.

Scott, Rebecca. 2013. "From Appalachia to the Globe: Translations in Space and Place." In Meredith McCarroll et al., "Roundtable Discussion of Transforming Places: Lessons from Appalachia." *Appalachian Journal* 41(1/2): 43–45.

———. 2010. *Removing Mountains: Extracting Nature and Identity in the Appalachian Coalfields*. Minneapolis: University of Minnesota Press.

Scott, Shaunna L., Stephanie McSpirit, Sharon Hardesty, and Robert Welch. 2005. "Post-Disaster Interviews with Martin County Citizens: 'Gray Clouds' of Blame and Distrust." *Journal of Appalachian Studies* 11(1/2): 7–29.

Seigel, Micol. 2018. *Violence Work: State Power and the Limits of Police.* Durham, NC: Duke University Press.

Shafer, Sheldon. 1993. "Proposed Care Home to Have 30 AIDS Beds." *Lousville (KY) Courier-Journal*, December 21.

Shapiro, Henry. 1986. *Appalachia on Our Mind: The Southern Mountains and Mountaineers in the American Consciousness, 1870–1920.* Chapel Hill: University of North Carolina Press.

Shaw, Ian. 2017. "The Great War of Enclosure: Securing the Skies." *Antipode* 49(4): 883–906.

Shelden, Randall. 1981. "Convict Leasing: An Application of the Rusche-Kircheimer Thesis to Penal Changes in Tennessee, 1830–1915." In *Crime and Capitalism: Readings in Marxist Criminology*, edited by David F. Greenberg, 358–66. Palo Alto, CA: Mayfield.

Shogan, Robert. 2004. *The Battle of Blair Mountain: The Story of America's Largest Labor Uprising.* Boulder, CO: Westview Press.

Simon, Jonathan. 2007. *Governing through Crime: How the War on Crime Transformed American Democracy and Created a Culture of Fear.* New York: Oxford University Press.

———. 1993. *Poor Discipline: Parole and the Social Control of the Underclass.* Chicago: University of Chicago Press.

Singh, Nikhil Pal. 2019. *Race and America's Long War.* Berkeley: University of California Press.

———. 2014. "The Whiteness of Police." *American Quarterly* 66(4): 1091–99.

———. 2005. *Black Is a Country: Race and the Unfinished Struggle for Democracy.* Cambridge, MA: Harvard University Press.

Smith, Adam. 1869. *Lectures on Justice, Police, Revenue, and Arms.* Oxford: Clarendon. Available at https://oll.libertyfund.org.

Smith, Andrea. 2012. "Indigeneity, Settler Colonialism, White Supremacy." In *Racial Formation in the Twenty-First Century*, edited by Daniel Martinez HoSang, Oneka LaBennett, and Laura Pulido, 66–90. Berkeley: University of California Press.

Smith, Caleb. 2013. "Spaces of Punitive Violence." *Criticism* 55(1): 161–68.

Smith, Darren, and D. A. Phillips. 2001. "Socio-cultural Representations of Greentrified Pennine Rurality." *Journal of Rural Studies* 17(4): 457–69.

Smith, Neil. 2008. *Uneven Development: Nature, Capital, and the Production of Space.* Third edition. Athens: University of Georgia Press.

———. 2001. "Global Social Cleansing: Postliberal Revanchism and the Export of Zero Tolerance." *Social Justice* 28(3): 68–74.

Smith, Shawn Michelle. 2013. *At the Edge of Sight: Photography and the Unseen.* Durham, NC: Duke University Press.

Spadaro, Jack. 2005. "Mountaintop Removal and the Destruction of Appalachia." *Appalachian Heritage* 33(2): 37–40.
Spalding, Ashley. 2019. "Kentucky Needs to Reverse Course on Criminal Justice Trends." Kentucky Center for Economic Policy, May 16.
Sparrow, Herbert. 1979a. "Housing Board Approves State Efforts to Purchase Town of Wheelwright." *Louisville (KY) Courier-Journal*, June 15.
———. 1979b. "Wheelwright Sale Closing Set for Today." *Louisville (KY) Courier-Journal*, September 21.
Spriggs, Bianca. 2011. "Frank X. Walker: Exemplar of Affrilachia." *Appalachian Heritage* 39 (4): 21–25.
Spriggs, Bianca, and Jeremy Paden. 2017. *Black Bone: 25 Years of the Appalachian Poets*. Lexington: University of Kentucky Press.
Stein, David. 2014. "Full Employment for the Future." *Lateral* 3. Available at http://csalateral.org.
Stewart, Kathleen. 1996. *A Space on the Side of the Road: Cultural Poetics in an "Other" America*. Princeton, NJ: Princeton University Press.
Stine, Allison. 2019. "The Phantom Promise: How Appalachia Was Sold on Prisons as an Economic Lifeline." *Yes! Magazine*, November 9. Available at https://www.yesmagazine.org.
Stoll, Steven. 2017. *Ramp Hollow: The Ordeal of Appalachia*. New York: Hill and Wang.
Story, Brett. 2019. *Prison Land: Mapping Carceral Power across Neoliberal America*. Minneapolis: University of Minnesota Press.
———. 2016a. "The Prison in the City: Tracking the Neoliberal Life of the 'Million Dollar Block.'" *Theoretical Criminology* 20(3): 257–76.
———, dir. 2016b. *The Prison in Twelve Landscapes*. 90:00. Grasshopper Films.
Story, Brett, and Judah Schept. 2018. "Against Punishment: Centering Work, Wages, and Uneven Development in Mapping the Carceral State." *Social Justice* 45(4): 7–34.
Szakos, Joe. 1993. "Practical Lessons in Community Organizing in Appalachia: What We've Learned at Kentuckians for the Commonwealth." In *Fighting Back in Appalachia: Traditions of Resistance and Change*, edited by Stephen Fisher, 101–21. Philadelphia: Temple University Press.
Szuberla, Nick, and Amelia Kirby, dirs. 2006. *Up the Ridge*. 53:16. Appalshop
"Thanks for Nothing: Mountaintop Prison Site a Lemon of a Gift." 2002. Editorial, *Lexington (KY) Herald-Leader*, July 26.
Thill, Brian. 2015. *Waste*. New York: Bloomsbury Academic.
Thomas, Sharita R., George H. Pink, and Kristin Reiter. 2019. "Geographic Variation in the 2019 Risk of Financial Distress among Rural Hospitals." North Carolina Rural Health Research Program. Available at https://www.shepscenter.unc.edu.
Thompson, Heather Ann. 2010. "Why Mass Incarceration Matters: Rethinking Crisis, Decline, and Transformation in Postwar American History." *Journal of American History* 97(3): 703–34.
Thorpe, Rebecca. 2014. "Urban Divestment, Rural Decline, and the Politics of Mass Incarceration." *Good Society* 23(1): 17–29.

Trout, Allen. 1950. "To Know What Makes Wheelwright Tick, You Have to Know about Jack Price." *Louisville (KY) Courier-Journal*, August 27.
Tucker, Susan B., and Eric Cadora. 2003. "Justice Reinvestment: To Invest in Public Safety by Reallocating Justice Dollars to Refinance Education, Housing, Healthcare, and Jobs." *Ideas for an Open Society* 3(3). Available at http://opensocietyfoundations.org.
Turcotte, Maura, Rachel Sherman, Rebecca Griesbach, and Ann Hinga Klein. 2021. "The Real Toll from Prison: Covid Cases May Be Higher Than Reported." *New York Times*, July 7.
Turner, William, and Edward J. Cabbell, eds. 1985. *Blacks in Appalachia*. Lexington: University of Kentucky Press.
Union of Concerned Scientists. 2009. "Coal Slurry Spill Investigation Suppressed: Political Interference, Whistleblower Retaliation, and Lack of Transparency at the Mine Safety and Health Administration." Union of Concerned Scientists, May 26. Available at https://www.ucsusa.org.
United States Congress. 1935. *Stabilization of the United States Bituminous Coal Mining Industry: Hearings before a Subcommittee of the Committee on Ways and Means*. Washington, DC: Government Printing Office.
United States Congress. Senate. 1925. *Report of the United States Coal Commission*. Senate document 125, 68th congress, 2nd session. Washington, DC: Government Printing Office.
Vance, J. D. 2016. *Hillbilly Elegy: A Memoir of a Family and Culture in Crisis*. New York: HarperCollins.
Vance, Kyle. 1972. "Mine Closures May Close Town Too." *Louisville (KY) Courier-Journal*. September 20.
———. 1968. "Out from under Company Control, Wheelwright Now Running Its Town." *Louisville (KY) Courier-Journal*, February 11.
———. 1966. "The Wheelwright Purchase." *Louisville (KY) Courier-Journal*, November 21.
Van Tomme, Niels. 2014. *Visibility Machines: Harun Farocki and Trevor Paglen*. Baltimore, MD: Center for Art, Design, and Visual Culture.
Vergés, Françoise. 2017. "Racial Capitalocene." In *Futures of Black Radicalism*, edited by Gaye Theresa Johnson and Alex Lubin, 72–85. New York: Verso.
Vesely-Flad, Rima. 2017. *Racial Impurity and Dangerous Bodies: Pollution and the Criminalization of Blackness in US Society*. Minneapolis, MN: Fortress Press.
Vitale, Alex. 2017. *The End of Policing*. New York: Verso.
Voskuhl, Jake. 1992. "Coalfield Town Gets Prison to Be Run by Louisville Firm." *Louisville (KY) Courier-Journal*, October 28.
Wacquant, Loic. 2010. "Crafting the Neoliberal State: Workfare, Prisonfare, and Social Insecurity." *Sociological Forum* 25(2): 197–220.
———. 2009. *Punishing the Poor: The Neoliberal Government of Social Insecurity*. Durham, NC: Duke University Press.
Wagner, Peter. 2002. "Importing Constituents: Prisoners and Political Clout in New York." Prison Policy Initiative, May 20.

Wagner, Peter, and Wendy Sawyer. 2018. "States of Incarceration: The Global Context 2018." Prison Policy Initiative. Available at https://www.prisonpolicy.org.

Walby, Kevin, and Justin Piché. 2015a. "Making Meaning out of Punishment: Penitentiary, Prison, Jail, and Lock-Up Museums in Canada." *Canadian Journal of Criminology and Criminal Justice* 57(4): 475–502.

———. 2015b. "Staged Authenticity in Penal History Sites across Canada." *Tourist Studies* 15(3): 231–47.

———. 2011. "The Polysemy of Punishment Memorialization: Dark Tourism and Ontario's Penal History Museums." *Punishment and Society* 13(4): 451–72.

Walker, Frank X. 2006. *Black Box*. Lexington, KY: Old Cove Press.

———. 2000. *Affrilachia*. Lexington, KY: Old Cove Press.

Walker, Hannah L., Rebecca Thorpe, Emily K. Christensen, and J. P. Anderson. 2017. "The Hidden Subsidies of Rural Prisons: Race, Space, and the Politics of Cumulative Disadvantage." *Punishment and Society* 19(4): 393–416.

Wall, Tyler. 2016. "'For the Very Existence of Civilization': The Police Dog and Racial Terror." *American Quarterly* 68(4): 861–82.

———. 2014. "Legal Terror and the Police Dog." *Radical Philosophy* 188: 2–7.

Wall, Tyler, and Bill McClanahan. *Bestial Acts*. Forthcoming.

Walls, David S. 1978. "Internal Colony or Internal Periphery? A Critique of Current Models and an Alternative Formulation." In *Colonialism in Modern America: The Appalachian Case*, edited by Helen Lewis, Linda Johnson, and Donald Askins, 319–40. Boone, NC: Appalachian Consortium.

Walters, Jonah, Jasmine Heiss, and Jack Norton. 2020. "Mass Incarceration Is a Rural Problem, Too." *Jacobin*, January 25. Available at https://jacobinmag.com.

Waters, Michael. 2018. "How Prisons Are Poisoning Their Inmates." *Outline*, July 23. Available at https://theoutline.com.

Watkins, Morgan. 2016. "Private Prisons: Crowded Jails Have Officials Considering Temporary Return." *Louisville (KY) Courier-Journal*, October 9.

WBIR. 2018. "Back to Brushy Mountain, Part 1: Prison's Coal Roots." WBIR 10News, May 13. Available at https://www.wbir.com.

WECO Radio. 2013. "Brushy Mountain Group." WECO FM, July 30. Available at wecoradio.com.

Western, Bruce, and Katherine Beckett. 1999. "How Unregulated Is the U.S. Labor Market? The Penal System as a Labor Market Institution." *American Journal of Sociology* 104(4): 1030–60.

Whisnant, David. 1994. *Modernizing the Mountaineer: People, Power, and Planning in Appalachia*. Revised edition. Knoxville: University of Tennessee Press.

———. 1974. "Revolt! Against the Planners in the Kentucky Area River Development District." *Southern Exposure* 2(1): 84–102.

Whitaker, Mitch. 2016. "Will Federal Prison Keep E. Ky. Locked in Cycle of Poor Choices?" *Lexington (KY) Herald-Leader*, April 1. Available at https://www.kentucky.com.

White, Rob. 2002. "Environmental Harm and the Political Economy of Consumption." *Social Justice* 29(1–2): 82–102.
Whitlock, Kay, and Nancy Heitzeg. 2021. *Carceral Con: The Deceptive Terrain of Criminal Justice Reform*. Berkeley: University of California Press.
Wilkerson, Jessie. 2019. *To Live Here You Have to Fight: How Women Led Appalachian Movements for Social Justice*. Urbana: University of Illinois Press.
Williams, Eric. 2011. *Big House in a Small Town: Prisons, Communities, and Economies in Rural America*. Santa Barbra, CA: Praeger.
Williams, John Alexander. 2002. *Appalachia: A History*. Chapel Hill: University of North Carolina Press.
———. 1978. "Henry Shapiro and the Idea of Appalachia: A Review/Essay." *Appalachian Journal* 5(3): 350–57.
Williamson, Kevin. 2020. "Big White Ghetto." *National Review*, November 17. Available at https://www.nationalreview.com.
———. 2013. "The White Ghetto." *National Review*, December 16. Available at https://www.nationalreview.com.
Willis, Paul. 1977. *Learning to Labor: How Working-Class Kids Get Working-Class Jobs*. New York: Columbia University Press.
Wilson, Jacqueline Z. 2011. "Australian Prison Tourism: A Question of Narrative Integrity." *History Compass* 9(8): 562–71.
Wilson, Jacqueline Z., Sarah Hodgkinson, Justin Piché, and Kevin Walby, eds. 2017. *The Handbook of Prison Tourism*. London: Palgrave-Macmillan.
Wolfe, Patrick. 2016. *Traces of History: Elementary Structures of Race*. New York: Verso.
Wolfson, Andrew. 2006. "Hawaiian Women Incarcerated in KY: Double Punishment." *Louisville (KY) Courier-Journal*, February 20.
Woods, Clyde. 2017. *Development Arrested: The Blues and Plantation Power in the Mississippi Delta*. New York: Verso.
Woodward, C. Vann. 1981. *Origins of the New South*. Revised edition. Baton Rouge: Louisiana State University Press.
Wray, Matt. 2006. *Not Quite White: White Trash and the Boundaries of Whiteness*. Durham, NC: Duke University Press.
Wray, Matt, and Annalee Newitz, eds. 1997. *White Trash: Race and Class in America*. New York: Routledge.
Wright, Warren. 1978. "The Big Steal." In *Colonialism in Modern America: The Appalachian Case*, edited by Helen Lewis, Linda Johnson, and Donald Askins, 161–75. Boone, NC: Appalachian Consortium Press.
Wright, Will. 2018. "'Tip of the Spear': As Customers Beg for Clean Water, Is a Crisis Looming in Appalachia?" *100 Days in Appalachia*, December 21.
Wynn, Mike. 2013. "Private Prisons' Legacy in Kentucky Mixed." *Louisville (KY) Courier-Journal*, September 15.
Yates, Michelle. 2011. "The Human as Waste: The Labor Theory of Value and Disposability in Contemporary Capitalism." *Antipode* 43(5): 1679–95.

Young, Jock. 2011. *The Criminological Imagination*. Boston: Polity Press.
Zimring, Carl. 2015. *Clean and White: A History of Environmental Racism*. New York: NYU Press.
Zoukis, Christopher. 2017. "New York State Closes 14 Prisons amid Decline in Crime Rates." *Prison Legal News*, February 8.

INDEX

Abandoned Mine Lands Pilot Grants, 175
abolition, 33–34, 56, 159, 199–234, 236, 261n44, 272n18; and defunding the police, 33, 224, 230–232; geography, 33, 201–202, 223; of strip mining, 74, 80, 164; of the Convict Lease System, 96–97
Abolition democracy, 208, 223, 272
Abolitionist Law Center, 211, 219–221, 224
activism: against strip mining, 40–41, 62, 73–74, 159, 162, 175, 203; against prisons, 86, 159, 198, 199–225, 227–228, 232, 265n33. *See also* Abolitionist Law Center; Appalachian Committee for Full Employment; insurrection; Letcher Governance Project; organizations; social movements
addiction, 51–52. *See also* Oxycontin
Affrilachia, 19, 244n52
African Americans: population of in Appalachia, 9, 19, 25, 93–97, 128–129, 133, 136, 270n40, 270n42; and coal mining, 19, 129, 136, 192, 243n49, 244n51, 244n52, 244n62, 258n15; 259n32, 260n33; erasures of, 19–20, 66, 191–192, 243n49; Great Migration of, 192, 250n2, 270n40; and organizing, 209–210, 244n51; and prison growth, 190–192, 199–200, 209–210, 230–232, 234, 270n40; and uprisings, 71, 250n18. *See also*: Black Lives Matter, race; racialization; racism
agriculture, 56, 129, 132, 258n16, 258n22
AIDS, 145–146, 297

airport, 42, 48–49
Akhmetov, Rinat, 8, 13, 75
Allen, James Lane, 24, 82–83
Appalachia: and America, 24–28, 247n94; "bourgeois imaginary" of, 28, 87; cultural accounts of 7, 21–28, 66–69, 82–83, 138–139, 173, 245n67, 245n71, 247n94; data on, 12, 15, 19, 68–69, 171; Frozen Head Mountain, 102–103, 107, 114; history of activism in, 73–74, 200, 251n30, 272n4; Cumberland Mountains, 82, 92, 95, 102; ecosystems, 78; theories of, 10, 28, 247n95. *See also*: mountaintop removal; cultural representation; prison construction
Appalachian Citizens Law Center, 80
Appalachian Committee for Full Employment, 69–70, 250n15, 277
Appalachian Land Ownership Task Force, 12, 78, 203–204, 251–252n47
Appalachian Regional Commission, 12, 19, 101; and the War on Poverty, 66, 68–72, 77; and allegations of population transfer, 162–164, 264n20
Appalshop, 203–205, 208, 224, 256n2, 272n7. *See also* Calls from Home/Hip Hop from the Hilltop; WMMT-FM
attorneys. *See* lawyers
austerity, 33, 157, 160, 223, 231. *See also* neoliberalism

Beale, Calvin, 72, 241n2
Beshear, Andy, 151, 229

304 | INDEX

Beshear, Steve, 123, 176
Bevin, Matt, 144, 151
Big Stone Gap, VA, 50, 86, 138–139
Bigart, Homer, 67, 250n6
Billings, Dwight, 11, 244–245n49, 247n95, 262n68
bipartisan reform, 199, 272n1
Black Lives Matter, 230–232, 234
black lung disease, 78, 190, 200, 234, 252n51
Blee, Kathleen, 11, 244–245n49, 247n95, 262n68
bluegrass music, 54, 233
Bonds, Anne, 206, 242n12, 243n40, 243n42, 244n63, 266n40, 269n34, 271n66
Braz, Rose, 233, 269n35, 272n1, 272n28, 273n29, 273n35, 274n13,
Briceville, TN, 94–95. *See also* Coal Creek War
broad form deed, 59–61, 76–77, 131, 216, 272n24
Brown, Karida, 191, 243n49, 270n40
Brushy Mountain Development, 31, 91–93, 100–106, 109–119; brand campaign of, 100–101, 110, 115–116; haunting of, 105–106, 255n23, 255n24; and punishment, 109–110, 113, 117; representations of Appalachia, 112–115; touring of, 102–110. *See also* Brushy Mountain State Penitentiary; Coal Creek War
Brushy Mountain State Penitentiary, 31; and the Coal Creek War, 96; and coal mining, 96–100;
purchase of by developers, 100–101; violence of, 105–108
building, see: prison construction
Bureau of Prisons: lawsuit against, 217–221; and relationships with the coal industry, 42, 59–60, 78, 232, 234; and relationships with local leaders, 13, 167–170; and rural development, 43, 54, 170–172, 185–189, 194–196, 221; and site considerations and contestations, 37, 53–56, 82, 159, 182, 200, 207–208, 216–217; and its withdrawal of the Record of Decision, 33, 202, 217–221, 223. *See also* Abolitionist Law Center; development; Environmental Impact Statements; Fight Toxic Prisons; Letcher Governance Project; United States Penitentiary, Big Sandy; United States Penitentiary, Letcher
Bush, George W, 75–76, 80, 253

California, 205, 207, 220, 224, 230, 233
California Prison Moratorium Project, 207, 220
Calls from Home/Hip Hop from the Hilltop, 204, 206–208, 232. See also Appalshop; Letcher Governance Project; WMMT-FM
cancer, 51, 61, 78, 200, 213, 234
capital: accumulation of: 83, 91, 94, 157, 181, 243n43, 253n65, 258n21, 258n22, 261n40, 263n8, 270n48; and labor, 93–96, 115; mobility of, 8, 75, 88, 117–118, 125, 257n6, 259n22; and the state, 16, 70, 132, 137, 145, 261n40. *See also* capitalism; corporations; crisis; profit.
capitalism: contradictions of, 29; 65, 81, 155–159; and crisis, 15–16, 20, 70, 91–96, 157–158, 165–166, 181, 192, 197; and natures, 64, 82–83, 256n29, 271n53; and racialization, 18; 21–28; 190–192; 243n43; 244n66, 245n67, 245n73; as racial capitalism, 9–11, 18–20, 28–29, 71, 100, 117, 143, 158, 194–195, 199, 201, 224, 234; and social reproduction, 157–159, 197, 263n8, 263–264n9, 264n12, 268n19; value and waste, 30, 40, 49, 63–64, 82, 100, 117, 182, 189–191, 245n67, 245n71, 245–246n73, 249n38, 253n65, 256n30, 270n48
carceral geography, 1, 29, 33, 56, 86, 116–119, 182, 200–201; and extraction, 6–8, 30, 41,

44, 62–64, 82–87, 114, 121–124, 200; photography of, 7, 55, 114. *See also* abolition
carceral social reproduction, 5, 17–18, 31, 152–153, 158–159, 181–189; racialized and gendered contours of, 32, 159, 189–196
carceral state: analyses of, 2, 9, 116; and racial capitalism, 63–64, 88, 92–93, 117, 146, 189–190, 195–197; contradictions within, 217, 222–223, 228; and local political economies, 5, 17, 65, 84, 157–170, 185–186, 189–197; growth of in Central Appalachia, 30, 70, 72, 87, 119, 146, 200, 214, 224; and ideology, 17, 30, 62, 81–87, 117, 197–198; opposition to, 201, 208, 224, 233–234; shifting capacities of, 13–14, 31, 72, 92–93, 151, 155–157, 199–202, 222–223, 228; violence of, 114, 117, 143. *See also* capitalism; jails; prisons
Cardno, 167–169, 265n34
Catte, Elizabeth, 19, 25, 66, 72, 144, 173, 257n8
Caudill, Harry, 67–68, 162, 203
cells, 91, 98–99, 104, 106–108, 119–120, 190; as "cellular rural development," 72
census, 142, 174, 190, 192; and gerrymandering, 191, 244n53, 269n37
Childers, Tyler, 33, 233–234
children: and health, 78; and organizing, 209–210; and poverty, 66, 68; representations of, 23; and race, 27, 133; and social reproduction, 61, 78, 133, 183–184, 186, 194, 213, 267n14, 268n19
churches, 54, 118, 133, 139, 215, 257n5
civil rights, 71
Civil War, 76, 94
class: composition and police, 139, 162; creation of the structure in Appalachia, 12; crime and punishment as forms of working class control, 16, 190, 193, 196, 245n73; multiracial struggles, 19, 196, 208, 223; prison as racialized class war, 17, 196; racialization of, 18, 21–28, 245n67, 245n68; ruling class, 265n33, 267n63; struggle and solidarity, 92–96,

115, 117, 137, 196, 228, 232–233, 259n32; the "white working class," 19, 173
Clay County, KY, 69, 174, 185, 202, 205, 243n49
Clinton, Bill, 68, 146
coal ash, 29, 44–46, 63, 81, 191; illegal dumpsites of, 29, 44, 46, 81
coal camps, 127–128, 130–132, 137, 258n22. *See also* company towns
Coal Creek War, 94–95, 102, 115, 117, 132, 140, 255n9
coal industry: and class war, 92–96, 136–140, 196; companies, 8, 72, 75, 79, 94, 117, 127–128, 132–140, 144, 159, 216–216; corporate executives, 8, 42, 49, 52, 80, 94, 137–138, 159, 162, 168, 207, 264; decline of, 5, 14–16, 121–122, 181–182, 197, 227; dominance of, 10, 15, 144, 261; emergence of, 10–12, 41, 73, 75–76, 83, 192, 259n22, 270; employment in, 5, 14–16, 20, 32, 69, 77, 181–182, 188, 190, 192; environmental and health consequences of, 44–48, 58, 77–80, 157, 191, 200; fueling war and industrialization, 18, 26–27, 53, 61, 87, 97, 127, 228; and gender, 19–20, 192, 244n55; influence on politics and legislation, 75–76, 78, 94, 96, 159–160, 162, 167, 179, 253n57; mechanization and shifts in production 5, 15–16, 30, 73, 76–77; 91, 142, 157, 159, 164–167, 197; organizing against and opposition to, 19, 73–74, 200, 203–204, 234; and police power, 5, 17, 129–130, 136–139, 157, 196, 258n18, 261n54, 261n55; and race, 19–20, 26, 128–129 133–136; regulation of, 73–76; relationship to prisons, 41–42, 179, 183; use of prisoners, 6, 31, 92–100, 105, 108, 117, 121; and profit, 75, 122, 136–138, 157, 160; propaganda and ideology of, 10, 58, 81, 134–137, 192, 244n55, 247n91, 249n32, 253n58, 270n45; and social reproduction, 5, 157–158, 197, 259n24, 263–264n9; speculators, 8, 10, 76, 138, 144; surface, 42, 74, 77, 192; violence

coal industry (*continued*)
of, 74, 99, 121–122, 188, 190, 247n91, 261n41, 261n54; and welfare capitalism, 132–140. *See also* coal severance tax; crisis; mountaintop removal
coal miners, 52, 58; as correctional officers, 17, 124, 182–196; prisoners as 92–100; union fights of, 15, 19, 93–96, 196, 259n32, 260n34; uprisings of, 93–96, 100, 120
coal severance tax, 15, 164–167, 197, 222, 252n43; and municipal and state budgets, 164–167
coal slurry, 44, 49, 53, 62–63, 79–80, 193, 232, 253n57; impoundments, 49, 79
coalitional politics, 13, 33, 62, 159, 200–201, 204–217, 223–225, 231, 265n33; influence of the Delano II campaign on, 220, 224; and success of the lawsuit, 201, 212, 217–220, 224, 282. *See also* Abolitionist Law Center; Letcher Governance Project; United States Penitentiary, Letcher
colleges. *See* postsecondary education
colonialism: and prisons, 63, 143–144; and racism, 9, 21–22; 143–144; settler history of Appalachia, 8–12, 18, 20, 22–23; theory of Appalachia and internal, 10, 28, 88, 247n95
commons: and practices of commoning, 53, 56, 62, 118, 248n29, 248n3011; and enclosures, 53, 56, 59–62, 65, 84, 243n43, 253n65; defense of, 62, 65, 80, 200; and racialization, 243n43, 246n73
commodity frontiers, 131, 259n22
company towns, 5, 12, 17, 60, 122, 127–129, 131–132, 134–138, 144, 196, 257n5; 258n15, 260n32; role of the household garden in, 38, 112, 129, 259n24; and indoor plumbing, 77, 128–129; rents in,129, 138; role of mine guards in, 5, 129–130, 136–138, 261n55; and scrip, 94, 122, 131

conjuncture, 30–31, 65, 81, 146, 149, 155, 225; conjunctural analysis, 249n1, 264n12
Consolidation Coal Company, 127–128
convict lease system, 31, 92–96, 117, 227, 255n11
Core Civic, 31, 121–123, 127, 143–144, 146–149, 151, 222; state contracts with, 123, 126, 143–144. *See also* Otter Creek Correctional Facility; Wheelwright, KY
coronavirus, 33, 228–230
corporations: absenteeism of, 78, 162, 252n47; consolidation and reincorporation of, 8, 75; fines against, 52, 75; marketing, 51, 62, 93; power and profit of, 8–9, 12, 31, 51–53, 116, 121–122, 126, 142, 160, 208, 234, 258n18;. *See also* coal industry; company towns; Core Civic
correctional officers, 1–2, 4, 46, 52, 98, 104, 107, 109, 115, 124, 205; and "dirty work," 192–196, 270n47, 271n54; education of future, 185–190, 268n18; growth of jobs as, 14, 182, 267n5; salaries of, 148; racialized and gendered dimensions of, 17, 20, 189–193, 244n57; violence of, 100, 105, 108–110, 123, 143–144; as "violence workers," 158, 264n10, 268n18
Corrections Corporation of America. *See* Core Civic
Correia, David, 231, 259n24, 261n44, 271n54
corruption, 162, 188, 209
costs: of incarceration, 43, 151, 156, 207, 214; labor, 77, 96, 260n34; of reclamation following mountaintop removal, 74; for rural hospitals, 266–267n59; savings to the Bureau of Prisons, 169, 196; of social reproduction, 129
crime: limitations of analysis of, 4–5, 10, 43, 227, 241n4, 263n4, 268n18; organized, 8, 258n18; and punishment, 86,

227; as social control, 16, 193, 246n73, 251n21, 255n5, 271n54; War on, 30, 70–73, 80, 87, 100, 251n21; tough-on-crime era, 146, 156
criminalization, 2, 88, 118, 210, 219, 222, 229, 232; and employment in corrections, 20, 190, 194, 232; as strategy for social order, 16, 34, 87, 100, 190, 193, 246n73, 269n38; of rural communities, 181–182
crisis: coal industry declines and, 15, 20, 73, 165–167, 181, 197, 227; counties and, 8, 14, 16, 73; individual and community experiences of, 20, 157–158, 179, 192, 197; 244n66; jails and prisons as solutions to, 5, 14–16, 65, 70, 81, 84, 92–96, 117, 122–123, 152, 155–159, 181–182, 197, 200, 227, 249n49, 251n21; of pandemic and police, 33–34, 228–233; and possibilities for change, 227, 250n1; prison overcrowding as, 10, 13, 156; in rural healthcare, 177, 266–267n59; tendencies of capitalism, 15, 29, 155, 157, 224, 255n15, 263n8, 264n12; water in Martin County, KY, 79–80
Critical Resistance, 205, 207, 220, 224, 236
cultural representation: of Appalachia, 9–10, 18–28, 37, 67–68, 75, 83, 88; 114–115, 173, 178, 191–193, 203–204, 245n67, 245n68, 257n8; of incarceration, 110, 112–113; photography and, 6–7, 241–242n7; of prisoners, 64, 93, 114–116, 256n26; role of in expropriation and exploitation, 7, 9–10, 20–28, 37, 134–135, 245n71, 245–246n73

Davies, Beth, 51–53, 62–63, 65, 86, 232, 234
debt, 58, 118, 120, 269n38, 271n57
democracy: 5, 30, 71, 161, 200, 208, 223, 228
development: early stages of in Appalachia, 76–77, 131, 262n68; and extraction and waste, 63; mountaintop removal and, 83; opposition to prison-based, 62, 207, 210, 212, 221; and planning, 157–180, 265n22; prison-based, 13–17, 32, 38, 43, 48, 52, 54, 72, 80, 86, 118, 121, 140, 147–152, 182, 227, 266n40; relationship between capitalist and state, 144, 262n68; and social reproduction, 186, 189; tourism and, 92; uneven, 61, 125, 257n6, 271n56. *See also:* Brushy Mountain Development; planning
dirt, 22–23, 245n71, 246n73
disability payments, 68–69
disposability: Appalachia geography and; 87–88; prisoners, correctional officers, and, 189–190, 194; representations of, 23; resistance to, 201
disposal. *See* waste
dispossession: of land, 11, 37, 61, 88; racialization and, 21–22; and racialization of white poverty, 244n66; solidarities across rural and urban geographies of, 223; of vulnerable residents, 205
documentary: film, 39, 42, 50, 88, 120, 203–204; radio, 203–207. *See also* Appalshop; Calls from Home/Hip Hop from the Hilltop
drugs, 2, 29, 51–52, 186, 234. *See also* Oxycontin; Purdue Pharma

economy. *See* capitalism; crisis; political economy
ecotourism, 31, 91, 102, 110, 112
education: coal and, 81, 122, 131, 133 137; community-based, 52, 203–204, 234; high schools, 133, 149, 185, 209; neoliberal restructuring of, 63, 145–146; shifts in priorities and curricula, 182–187, 189. *See also* postsecondary education
Elkhorn Coal Company, 122, 127–128, 132–134, 140
Eller, Ronald, 76, 136, 257n5, 264n20
empire, 11

employment: in the coal industry, 5, 14–16, 20, 32, 69, 77, 136, 157, 165, 181–182, 188, 190, 192, 197; comparative numbers between coal and prison, 14–15, 142, 148, 182; costs of prison, 43; discourse of prison, 53–54, 72–73, 101, 115, 141, 147, 170–176, 181–189, 205–207, 221, 224; prisons and, 8, 14, 17, 20, 42–43, 72–73, 81–82, 101, 115, 121, 147–152, 181–197, 205–207, 215, 228; racialized and gendered dimensions of prison, 189–198; War on Poverty and, 68–72, 203. *See also* Appalachian Committee for Full Employment; coal industry; crisis; prisons; War on Poverty

enclosures: commons and, 56, 248n29, 253n65; history of in Appalachia, 11–12, 59–60, 131, 258n22; prisons as forms of, 29, 59, 61, 80, 84, 92; prisons, private property and, 102; racialization and, 23, 191, 243n43, 246n73, 271n57; as part of settler colonialism, 11–13

environment: coal industry propaganda and, 81, 83; coal mining effects on, 30, 58, 69, 73, 78–80, 83–85; disaster, 74, 79–80, 232; environmental activism, 33, 41, 52–53, 130, 164, 179, 200, 208, 211–212, 220, 223–224, 228, 234; law and, 33, 67, 159; prisons' effects on, 56, 211–213, 218, 221, 233; racism and, 191, 270n40. *See also* mountaintop removal; Environmental Impact Statements

Environmental Impact Statements, 169, 202–203, 207; biologists' testimonies in, 58, 212, 220, 249n31; as counterhegemonic archive, 212; debates about employment in, 172; delays to, 217, 223; oppositional testimonies in, 56, 178–179, 195, 207, 211–217; sociologists' testimonies in, 172; supportive comments in, 175–178, 183–185, 187–188

Europe, 18, 139, 243n43, 246n73, 248n30, 254n71

expenditures: federal per capita in Appalachia, 67–69; and prison-based gerrymandering, 191, 244n53, 269n37

expropriation: history of, 7, 28, 58, 87, 131, 200, 234, 254n71; and racialization, 9, 21, 191, 243n43; and settler colonialism in Appalachia, 11, 21, 234; mountaintop removal and, 60; prison and, 191, 211, 234; and relationship to exploitation, 194–196, 271n57

extraction. *See* coal industry; gas; prisons

facilities: healthcare, 32, 145–146, 188–189, 209; in company towns, 129, 136–137, 140; alternative justice, 209, 214; and social order, 162, 255n11; waste disposal, 51, 53, 65, 87. *See also* prisons.

factories, 42, 149, 196

farms, 12, 130–132, 196, 215; loss of, 60, 76–77, 130–132, 207, 258n21, 258n22; and rural "greentrification," 112, 115, 118

federal prison camp, 172, 176, 200, 202, 221; as servicing USP Letcher, 194–196

Fight Toxic Prisons, 211, 218, 220, 224

First Nations: expropriation and genocide of, 9, 11, 19, 131, 248n30, 259n22; racialization of, 21–22, 244n63, 245n71; incarceration of, 143–144. *See also* colonialism

Floyd County, KY, 44, 127, 130, 133–135, 140–142, 150–151, 174; decline of mining in, 142; income and poverty data for, 142. *See also* Wheelwright, KY

forests: 78; destruction of during colonization, 11; mountaintop removal and, 39–40, 50, 61, 67, 77–78, 85; 44, 47, 50, 248n30; prison's threat to old growth, 58–59, 61, 211–213; 85, 135, 211–213. *See also:* Lilley Cornet Woods

fossil fuels. *See* coal industry, gas

Fox Jr, John, 138–139
Frank, Jill, 1–3, 6, 37, 39–40, 43–47, 55–57, 92, 98–99, 101–108, 110–111, 114, 123–125, 141, 147, 163–164
Frazier, Mae, 131–132
Friends of Coal, 10, 58, 81, 249n32, 253n58, 270n45
Friends of the Lilley Cornett Woods and North Fork River Watershed, 220–221
funding: appropriations to federal prisons, 160–162, 208, 217; of community development contingent on prison construction, 16, 158, 161–164, 175; fights over prison, 219–224; grants, 58, 72, 140, 146, 164–166, 174–175, 183, 191; of jails, 13–14, 156–158; of state prisons, 72, 151; and Promise Zones, 174–175. *See also* coal severance tax; development; revenue

garbage. *See* waste
gas: laid off workers, 177; open wells on prison site, 169–170; opposition to industry, 204, 209; ownership of rights, 78, 144; rise and power of industry, 166–166
gender: work and social reproduction, 20, 32, 159, 189–193, 197, 244n55, 263–264n9; violence, 143. *See also* masculinities, women, work
genocide: of First Nations, 21–22; allegations of against development agencies, 162
geography. *See* abolition; carceral geography
Gidwani, Vinay, 84, 248n30, 253n65, 270n48, 271n53
Gilmore, Craig, 193, 195, 207, 233
Gilmore, Ruth Wilson, 28, 181, 193, 199, 206–207, 241n4, 263–264n9, 267n63, 268n18, 268n19, 269n38, 271n56
ginseng, 54, 248n29, 258n22. *See also* commons

government: collaboration across scales, 78, 161–170, 172, 221, 227; contradictions within, 217, 219–223; federal, 42, 67–69, 87, 146, 150, 167, 170, 174, 177; leverage of federal by activists, 74, 217, 219–221; municipal, 14, 146, 197, 208; state governors, 66, 69, 96, 123, 138, 140–141, 144–146, 148, 150–151, 176, 229; state legislatures, 72–74, 87, 165; quasi-government bodies, 161–170. *See also*: Bureau of Prisons; carceral state
Great society. *See* War on Poverty
guards. *See* correctional officers; mine guards; police

Hall, Eula, 130–131
Hall, Stuart, 15, 134, 197–198, 241n7, 250n1, 264n12
Hallinan, Joseph, 50, 73
Harkins, Anthony, 22, 245n67
Harlan County, KY, 9, 49, 187, 244n49, 258n18, 261n55; *Harlan County, U.S.A.* (film), 120
Harvard University, 78, 138, 252n57
health: consequences of coal mining, 44–48, 58, 77–80; in company towns, 128; 132; prisons' threat to, 191, 211–215, 229–233. *See also* black lung disease; cancer
healthcare: Affordable Care Act, 177, 232, 266–267n59; clinics, 51, 130, 176–177, 199, 233, 264; defunding of, 146, 177, 221; hospitals, 17, 150, 177, 187, 189, 232, 266–267, 266n58, 266–267n59; patients,145–146, 189, 232–233, 267; impact of prison on, 32, 64, 177, 187–189; workers, 176–178
hegemony: contest over, 198, 212; and identity, 20–21, 190, 192; and political common sense, 81, 84, 171, 198, 264n12; and coal company dominance, 137, 152; 244, 264n12, 267n63
Herzing, Rachel, 205, 207, 224

higher education. *See* postsecondary education
Highlander Research and Education Center, 51, 203, 209–210, 224
hillbilly, 21–22, 24, 37, 88, 210, 245n67. *See also* cultural representation
holding companies, 8, 41, 70, 75, 183
homesteaders, 12, 60, 76, 259n22
Hooks, Gregory, 206
housing: company town, 122, 128, 131–132; impact of prison on, 151–152, 187; Kentucky Housing Corporation, 140, 148
Huling, Tracy, 241n2, 242n12, 243n40, 244n53, 266n40, 266n43, 269n37, 272n11

ideology, 8, 28, 30, 65, 158, 167, 175, 197; and Appalachia, 20, 24, 28, 245n67; and the carceral state, 17, 30–31, 62, 70, 81, 113, 119, 143, 147, 152, 160, 167, 172, 179, 196, 227, 230; company towns and, 134–136; coal industry and, 10, 30, 73, 81, 84, 253n58, 270n45; criminology and, 268n18; and landscape, 82–86, 116; and photography, 6–8, 241n7; of punishment, 117; race as, 254n76; struggles over, 32–33, 62, 86–87, 158, 172, 179–180, 198, 201, 265n33; visual, 84–85, 116
images. *See* cultural representation; photography
immigrants: miners, 9, 21, 129, 136; racialization of, 222, 246n73
imprisonment. *See* incarceration
incarceration: and crisis, 5, 14–16, 65, 70, 81, 84, 92–96, 117, 122–123, 152, 155–159, 181–182, 197, 200, 227, 249n49, 251n21; federal rates of, 160, 219, 273n32; Kentucky growth of, 13, 155–156; realignment around, 17, 32, 159, 179, 201, 223; reforms to, 156; rural growth rates of, 181–182; as a strategy for social order, 190, 193; in Tennessee, 97, 119;

violence of, 107–110, 143–144, 229–231; in Virginia, 72. *See also* carceral state; correctional officers; jails; mass incarceration; prisoners; prisons
incinerators, 5, 29, 44, 46–49, 63, 81, 87–88, 191, 193–194, 216. *See also* waste
Indiana bat, 212, 220
industrialization, 144, 193, 245–246; Appalachian coal and, 18, 87, 127; and race, 9, 245n71, 246n73; waste and disorder, 193–194, 245n71, 246n73; and rural development, 70, 266n40
Inez, KY, 5, 43–46, 66, 79–80
infrastructure: Development Districts and, 164, 167–169; mining, 41, 49, 61, 127; failures of, 79–80, 166, 214; role of prisons in securing upgrades and extensions, 5, 8, 14, 16, 31–32, 64, 72, 93, 101, 151–152, 158, 175, 179, 207; Appalachian Regional Commission investments in, 68–69, 87, 264n20
Inland Steel, 127–128, 132–138, 140, 147, 152, 157
insurrections: labor, 7, 31, 94–96, 200, 227, 234, 263–264n9; in the 1960s, 71, 250–251n18; in 2020, 33, 230–234
interfaces, 4–6, 49, 125, 193, 234, 241n4
international: Appalachia's role, 75; companies involved in prison siting, 167–169; markets, 118; scope of the coal industry, 8, 61, 75; solidarity, 19; working class, 16
investment. *See* development
Island Creek Coal Company, 132, 140

jails, 5, 13–17, 33, 65, 72, 119, 121, 139, 200–201, 227; and coronavirus, 33, 229; and revenue from holding state and federal prisoners, 13–14, 16, 81, 144, 156–158, 196, 222–224; and rural incarceration, 181–182; and social reproduction, 158, 179, 196–197
jobs. *See* employment

INDEX | 311

Johnson, Lyndon Baines, 27, 66–68, 70–72, 79, 100, 251n21
Jones, Brereton, 140–141, 145
journalism, 19, 23–25, 67, 80, 102, 132–138, 145–146, 162, 173, 188, 201; coverage of prison building, 42, 188, 206; targeting of, 162; and the "Trump country" genre, 25, 173, 257n8. *See also* Catte, Elizabeth; cultural representation; media
judge-executives, 42, 141, 148, 150–152, 161, 166, 187, 250n12
just transition, 175, 200, 228

Kennedy, John F., 66–67, 203, 251n21
Kentuckians for the Commonwealth, 204, 207–208, 224
Kentucky Department of Corrections, 14, 143, 150, 156
Kentucky: African-Americans in eastern, 191–192; coal industry in eastern, 14–16, 73–77, 128–132, 164–167, 181, 192, 261n55, 262n68; correctional officers in, 14–15, 182; federal prisons in eastern, 2, 37, 200, 202, 205; healthcare in eastern, 177, 266–267n59; history of activism in eastern, 69–70, 73, 175, 177, 200, 203–204, 207–208, 234, 263–264n9; incarceration rates of, 13–14, 121, 155–157; jail growth in 13–14, 156–157, 222; neoliberalism and, 145–146; planning and development in eastern, 159–170; private prisons in, 31, 121, 127, 140–145; sentencing reform, 13, 155–156, 222; state budget, 13, 149–151; state prisons, 2–5, 127, 150–151
Kentucky Highlands Investment Corporation, 174–175
Kentucky House Bill 463, the "Public Safety and Offender Accountability Act," 13, 155
Kentucky River Area Development District, 161–164, 167–169, 172, 176

Kirby, Amelia, 50–51, 86, 204–205
Knoxville, TN, 91, 95, 100, 103

labor: arrival of wage, 13, 60, 77, 83, 120, 127–132; convict, 93–96, 121; "dirty work" and, 189–196; mechanization and, 73, 76–77, 87, 181, 260n34; militancy, 17,19, 26, 31, 92, 95–96, 115, 200, 234, 261n54, 263–264n9; and police, 17, 31, 70, 129, 132, 137–139, 196, 258n18, 261n40, 261n54, 261n55; prisoner 96–100, 117; renovation of through prisons, 13, 64, 182, 189–190. *See also* Appalachian Committee for Full Employment; coal miners; correctional officers, employment; unions
land: absentee ownership of, 12, 52, 70, 76–78, 80, 162, 204, 252n47; alternative uses of, 54–62; defense of, 53–62, 74, 76, 86–87, 200–201, 204, 216–217, 224, 234; deputization of, 112–114; effect of mountaintop removal on, 29–30, 40–42, 53, 74, 77, 214; expropriation of, 11–12, 21, 30, 58–61, 76, 200, 234, 243n43, 259n22; locally unwanted land use, 17; and racism, 9, 21, 23, 243n43, 246n73; and surplus, 40, 61, 64, 88. *See also* Appalachian Landownership Study; carceral geography; commons
landfills, 5, 29, 62–63, 87–88, 191, 193–194, 248n14, 249n38, 254n86
landowners, 33, 48, 77, 159, 180, 200, 208, 216, 220
landscape, 1–2, 5, 6; ideology of, 4, 10, 81–87, 116–117, 121, 143–144, 171, 201, 254n71; morphology of, 124; and racism, 20, 191; and representation, 22–24, 37, 67, 88, 246n73; and uneven development, 124–125, 257n6. *See also* carceral geography
law. *See* Broad Form Deed; criminalization; law enforcement; lawyers; legislation; Kentucky House Bill 463; Surface Mining Control and Reclamation Act

law enforcement, 14, 52, 71–72, 146, 167, 184–187, 222, 251n21. *See also*: mine guards; police
Law Enforcement Assistance Administration, 71
lawyers, 12, 138, 221; movement, 33, 62, 80, 159, 194, 211–212, 216–218, 220–221
Lee County, VA, 49, 51–52, 135, 187, 232
legislation: and the carceral state, 13, 146, 155–156; regulatory, 30, 73–76, 87; War on Crime, 70–73; War on Poverty, 66–69.
Letcher County, KY: competition for the prison between communities in, 168, 183; history of activism in, 203–208; history of planning and development in, 161–164; population growth and decline in, 159–160; racial demographics of, 190; revenue loss, 166. *See also* Appalshop; Calls from Home; Letcher Governance Project; United States Penitentiary, Letcher
Letcher County Planning Commission, composition of, 38; history of, 161–162; local influence of, 176–178, 183, 197, 208, 212; relationships with federal government regarding prison siting, 38, 61, 166–168, 172, 195, 202
Letcher Governance Project: analysis, framing, and strategy of, 209–212, 215, 223, 232; coalitional politics of, 211–217, 223; membership of, 208, 234; origins, 203–208, 234; vision of, 208
Lexington, KY, 5, 41, 165–166, 176
Lilley Cornett Woods, 211, 213, 220
Little, Jr., Sam, 129, 137, 148–149, 151
Little Sandy Correctional Complex, 1, 4, 46, 230
local elites: antebellum, 262n68; benefitting from prison construction, 64, 213; as "Mountain Royalty," 32; as prison boosters, 12–13, 32, 53, 121, 206, 221, 265n33; as recipients of War on Poverty funds, 30, 69–70, 162

logistics, 49, 61, 88
Louisville, KY, 41, 123, 132–133, 141, 144–146, 149, 151, 230
Louisville Courier-Journal, 132, 137, 144–146

maintenance: infrastructure, 8, 72, 117, 121, 164, 166, 179; role of prisoners in providing, 195–196
Manchester, KY, 185–187
manufacturing, 37, 196, 268n19
maps: Bureau of Prisons site, 56, 217; cadastral, 12; coal, 79, 126; of prison growth, 6; of waste and prisons, 44, 248n14
markets: coal, 61, 97, 127; renewable energy, 165; "green" commodities, 118
Martin County, KY: absentee land ownership in, 78; airport, 42, 48; carceral social reproduction in, 185–187; coal slurry spill, 79–80, 253n57; federal assistance to, 68; income data, 68; poverty rate in, 68; racial composition of, 190–191; revenue declines in, 166–167; strip mining in, 73; water crisis, 79–80. *See also* War on Poverty; United States Penitentiary Big Sandy
masculinities, 20, 190, 192, 244n55
mass incarceration, 2, 87, 100, 157, 208, 216–217; and disposal, 63; limitations of a focus on, 65, 73, 126. *See also* carceral state; criminalization; incarceration; jails; prisons
Massey Energy, 48, 79–80, 253n57
McCoy, Mickey, 43–47, 51, 62–63, 65–66, 77, 81, 86, 234
McCoy, Nina, 43, 46–47, 62, 66, 81, 86, 234
McCreary County, 174, 187, 202, 205
McDaniel, Dustin, 211, 217–218
McDowell County, WV, 128, 257n8
mechanization. *See* coal industry
media. *See* Appalshop; cultural representation; journalism

Medicaid, 52, 68, 232, 266–267n59. *See also* healthcare
Medicare, 68, 150–151, 266–267n59. *See also* healthcare
Melamed, Jodi, 20, 194, 243n43
memory, 116–117, 133, 149
men, 106–107, 113, 138, 143, 148, 191. *See also* gender; masculinities; women
mental health, 14, 71, 134, 231
Mine Safety and Health Administration, 79–80, 253n57
mineral rights, 9–10, 59, 76–78, 91, 183, 216, 252n47
Mitchell, Don, 84, 116, 254n71
mobility: of capital, 257n6; of cultural products, 31, 117; of production and reproduction, 197; of populations, 181, 191; of representations, 21, 245–246n73
modernization: of police, 72, 251n21; of Appalachia, 84–85, 254n83; of Wheelwright, KY, 133, 140;
moonshine, 91, 101, 103, 110–111, 115
Morgan County, TN, 91, 96, 115, 118–119; local development in, 101
mountains: as barriers to development, 82–83; as commons, 59, 61; deputization of, 113–114; history of Appalachian, 12, 21; and "mountain whites" and "mountaineers," 23–24, 60, 83, 139, 162, 194, 244n52, 246n77; as prison walls, 102–103, 107, 114; and waste disposal, 87. *See also* mountaintop removal
Mountain Investment, 124, 140, 148
mountaintop removal: activism against, 43, 51, 73–74, 86, 164, 200, 203–204, 208, 234; activity on following, 53–62; and bond money, 74–75; and capitalism, 40, 64, 83–85; in "distressed" regions, 77; environmental and health consequences of, 39–40, 60–61, 67, 78–80; growth of, 73–75, 77; and labor, 73, 76–77, 87, 181, 260n34; and prisons, 29, 40–42, 50, 53, 72, 78, 82, 170, 200; process of, 29, 39–41; reclamation and remediation, 42, 58, 74–75, 83, 175; regulatory law and, 30, 72–80; and waste and value, 40, 64. *See also* coal industry
museums, 104–105, 109, 116, 256n34
music, 25, 53–54, 107, 113, 203–204, 233

nation: Appalachia and, 24, 26–28, 66–68, 112–115, 203, 247n94; prison and, 112–113; symbolic production of, 23–24, 28, 112–115. *See also* carceral state
National Bituminous Coal Wage Agreement, 15, 243n37, 260n34
National Environmental Policy Act, 158, 167, 172, 202–203, 207–208, 211–212, 216–220, 223–224. *See also* Environmental Impact Statements; United States Penitentiary, Letcher
National Miners Union, 19, 244n51
"national sacrifice zone," 10, 84, 114–115
nature: capitalism and, 8–9, 40, 64, 82–83, 110–112; 118–119, 253n65, 256n29, 271n53; conservation of, 56, 61, 220; deputization of, 112–115, 256n29
Neocleous, Mark, 85, 193, 259n24, 261n40, 268n18, 271n54
neoliberalism: mountaintop removal and, 40; role of the prison and, 17, 88, 157; and state restructuring, 13, 126–127, 140, 145–146, 231, 266n40, 271n57. *See also* capital; capitalism; carceral state
Night Comes to the Cumberlands. See: Caudill, Harry
Norton, Jack, 156, 242n11; 266n42
nursing homes, 145–146, 150–151
Nyden, Paul, 19, 244n51, 259–260n32

Obama, Barack, 160, 174, 177, 208
oil: crisis, 75, 192; extraction, 12, 62, 204; rights, 78; workers, 177
Oliver Springs, TN, 95–96

opioids, 51–52, 62–63. *See also* drugs; Oxycontin; Purdue Pharma

opposition. *See* abolition; Abolitionist Law Center; activism; Appalachian Committee for Full Employment; coalitions; Letcher Governance Project; organizations; social movements

oppression, 179, 245–246n73; 261–262n55

organizations: community-based, 80, 179–180, 203–225; faith-based, 48; labor, 15, 19, 70, 94–96, 130, 120; pro-coal, 81; quasi-public, 32, 101, 158, 160–161, 170; regional development, 13, 159–172, 176; social movement, 51, 69–70, 74, 81, 159, 179–180, 203–225, 231, 234, 244n53, 251, 257, 262

organized abandonment, 193, 221, 263–264n9

Otter Creek Correctional Facility, 31, 121–122; contiguity with coal mining, 125–126; opening of 123, 140–142; reopening of, 149–152, 155, 222, 227, 229; state reorganization and, 144–146; violence in, 123, 143–144, 262

#our444million: origins of, 209–210; reach of, 215, 228; power of, 221, 223–224, 228, 231–232. *See also* Letcher Governance Project

Oxycontin, 51–52

pacification, 100, 137, 259n24, 261n40, 292

pandemic. *See* coronavirus

parole, 72, 98, 150, 156, 263n1

payments: coal severance tax, 166; debt, 58, 118; disability, 68–69; Medicare and Medicaid reimbursement to hospitals, 150–151, 177, 266–267n59; per diem to county jails, 14, 16, 156; royalty, 183; utilities, 148

Payne Gap, KY, 168–169, 183

Penitentiary. *See* prisons

Pennington Gap, VA, 49, 51, 232

people of color: coal miners, 19; prison and, 9, 18, 20, 143, 191; residents of Appalachia 9, 18–21; 66–67, 191. *See also* African Americans; race

Perry, Lisa, 128, 135–136, 140

Persistent felony offender law, 155–156, 263n1

Petros, TN, 91, 94–96, 108

photography, 1–2, 6–7, 46–48; and framing, 6–7, 241–242n7, 254n68; and waste, 47–48, 248n17

plaintiffs, 201, 218, 220, 224

planning, 32, 38, 53, 61, 151–152; composition of regional bodies, 161; and federal appropriations, 160; regional organizations and, 161–180; relationships between the coal industry and county, 159–168; across scales of the state, 170, 172, 179. *See also* development; Kentucky River Area Development District; Letcher County Planning Commission

plot, 33, 199, 225

Pocahontas Coal Company, 41, 78–79

police: brutality in the coalfields, 162, 188, 258n18, 261–262n55; defunding and abolition, 33, 209–210, 224, 228, 230–234; and company towns, 17, 129, 132, 137, 152, 157, 258n18, 261n41, 261–262n55; growth of, 71–72, 146, 233, 251n21; and incarceration, 17, 34, 193, 196, 233, 261n54; powers of the state, 70, 84, 127, 132, 137–139, 157–158, 253n66, 264n10; and production of capitalist social order, 17, 193, 251n18; 256n29, 258n18, 259n24, 261n40, 261–262n55, 271n54. *See also:* mine guards, law enforcement

politics: abolitionist, 200–201, 204, 224; across scales, 7–8, 32–33, 161, 197, 222; coal industry and, 144, 160,

162, 200, 209; federal; 80, 160–161, 217–219, 222; local, 38, 161; realignment of through prisons and jails, 13, 15, 17, 32, 159, 197, 201; solidarity, 220, 223–224; *See also* development; planning; prisons;
political economy: analysis of Central Appalachia's, 10, 22, 60, 63, 65, 142; and ideology, 17, 26; 67, 70, 81, 84–86, 196–198; prison's effect on local, 161, 169, 179, 181. *See also* capitalism; crisis
pollution: light, 211; prisons and, 233; racialization of, 37, 245–246n73, 271n54; of water, 58, 77, 157, 175, 200
positionality, 7, 109, 233
Posner, Emily, 194, 211, 216–221, 273n32
postsecondary education: neoliberalization of in Kentucky and, 145; development of criminology and criminal justice curricula and degrees, 8, 17, 182–187, 268n18
Pound, VA, 50, 168, 214
poverty: data on, 52, 68–69, 77, 142, 174; federal cuts to programs, 146, 160; prison as management, 16–17, 266n40; representation and racialization of, 10, 20–21, 23–25, 27, 193, 244–245n66, 245n67, 247n94. *See also* War on Poverty
power: corporate, 122, 126, 208; law and, 73, 76, 258n18; landscape and, 116–117; local structures, 7, 60, 69–70, 144, 155, 160–162, 205, 208, 265n22, 267n23; organizing and, 210, 223–224; photography and, 6–7, 47–48, 241–242n7, 248n17; police, 4–5, 17, 31, 70, 84, 127, 132, 137–139, 157–158, 193, 196, 253n66, 256n29, 264n10; state, 7, 28, 34, 160, 170, 177, 222, 259n24, 264n10
precarity, 43, 60, 157, 182, 196, 229
Prestonsburg, KY, 44, 46, 150, 277

Price, Edward "Jack," 133–138
primitive accumulation, 131, 243n43, 258n21, 270n48
prisons: affective importance of, 16, 20, 104, 157, 161, 192; beds in, 13, 123, 156, 221, 223, 273n32; closures of, 42–43, 92, 100, 104, 107, 116–117, 119, 123–124, 142, 147–148, 151, 174; conditions in, 108–109, 121, 137, 143–144; and crisis, 5, 14–16, 64–65, 70, 81, 84, 92–96, 117, 122–123, 152, 155–159, 181–182, 197, 200, 227, 249n49, 251n21, 255n15; data on jobs in, 186–187, 205–207; employment in, 14–15; and mountaintop removal, 42, 48, 50, 78; overcrowding, 10, 13, 31, 108, 127, 149, 151, 156, 176, 229, 273n32; and political-cultural realignment, 17, 32, 65, 183, 201, 223–224; private, 31, 122, 125–126, 144–146, 148, 156; as recession-proof, 86, 174, 176; rural proliferation of, 2, 7, 16, 29–30, 37, 41, 65, 72, 87, 125–127, 185, 1193–94, 200, 202, 273n32; and social harms, 51–51, 205–207; as waste disposal, 29–30, 41–49, 62–64, 214, 249n38. *See also* carceral geography; carceral state
prisoners: as coal miners, 6, 31, 92, 94, 96–100; coronavirus cases among, 229–230; and gerrymandering, 20, 190–191, 244n53, 269n37; held for other agencies and states, 50, 72, 143–144, 150, 222; families of, 48; as plaintiffs, 201, 218–220, 224; protests of, 93–94, 99–100; representations of, 31, 64, 86, 93, 106, 114–115, 256n26; and reproductive labor, 194–196; solidarity with, 95–96; 117, 220; violence against, 99–100, 107–110, 123, 143–144
prison boosters, 13, 29, 53, 85, 173–174, 178, 212

prison construction: alternatives to, 61–62, 149, 159, 209–215, 228; and businesses, 118, 142, 166–168, 187–189, 197, 214–215, 265n34, 267n14; coal industry and, 78, 183; in distressed regions, 2, 171; data on, 2, 44, 248n14, 171–174, 266n43; effect on habitat and health, 56–58, 211–213; effect on infrastructure, 42, 101, 167–169, 174–175, 205–207; as enclosure, 56–61, 216; fights against, 29, 200–225; funding for, 72, 151, 160–161, 158, 175; jobs in, 141, 172, 175–176, 205; justifications for, 73, 194–195, 222, 273n32; and land acquisition: 38, 202, 216; mountaintop removal for, 50–51; prisoners' opposition to, 217–221, 224; scoping and siting process for, 17, 29, 32, 54, 158–160, 169–171, 182–183, 202, 207; support for, 176–178

Prison Ecology Project. *See* Fight Toxic Prisons

prison guards. *See* correctional officers

prison populations: continued growth of despite sentencing reform, 13, 16, 123, 151, 155–156, 222; coronavirus and, 229–230; declines in federal, 160, 229–230, 273n32; shifts in composition of, 181–182; state growth of, 13, 72–73

private property: 102, 130, 138, 262n68; disputes over, 58–62, 200, 216–217; donations of to build prisons, 42, 78; and the commons, 11, 54, 61–62, 84, 253n65; mountaintop removal and, 83–84; taxes, 12, 78, 166, 204, 252n47

profits: coal industry, 8, 39, 75, 78, 129, 137, 157, 200; and prisons, 30–31, 34, 64, 86, 91, 94–98, 100, 102, 116–118, 121–122, 125–126, 144–147, 170; and social reproduction, 157, 195–197, 263n8, 263–264n9, 269n29; and uneven development, 257. *See also* capitalism; coal industry

Promise Zone, 174–175

public health, 34, 44, 78, 211–212, 229, 231–233

Pulido, Laura, 20, 37, 49, 191, 270n40

punishment: 144, 149, 151; analytical limitations of, 4–5, 10, 15, 34, 43, 117, 241n4, 256n37, 268n18; corporal, 99; cultural work of, 86, 109–110, 113, 117

Purdue Pharma, 51–52

race, 9–11, 18, 190; representations of, 20–28, 37, 243n43, 244n52, 245n71, 247n88, 254n76. *See also* racialization; racial capitalism; racism

racialization: of Appalachia as white and "unwhite," 21–28, 139, 244n62; carceral state's role in, 18, 100, 115, 143, 190; and the coal industry, 19; of common sense, 71; as constitutive of capitalism, 9, 18, 20, 22, 94, 117, 190, 194; of crisis, 20; of representations of prisoners, 93; role of in dispossessions, 21–28, 243n43; of carceral social reproduction, 32, 159, 189–198, 244n57; of surplus populations 16, 64, 96, 118, 190–191, 194, 243n43, 244n62, 245–246n73; and waste, 245n67, 245n71 of whiteness, 9, 18, 244n57

racism: in Appalachia, 19–22, 234; definitions of, 18, 21–22, 196; environmental, 20, 191, 270n40; as foundational to capitalism, 9, 20–22, 243n43, 244n62; prisons and, 18–19, 191, 196; and representations of Appalachia, 21, 245n67

radio, 203–204, 206–208

railroads, 60–61, 76, 94, 117, 127–128, 139, 159

Ray, Tarence, 166, 212, 253n58

rebellion, 71, 95, 250–251n18, 261n40

Red Onion State Prison, 50, 52, 72, 168

Reece, Eric, 39, 41, 74, 77, 85, 242n10, 258n18

reforms: to the coal industry, 74–75; healthcare, 177; limitations of

sentencing, 13–14, 121, 151, 155–156, 199, 219, 222, 230, 272n1; limitations of War on Poverty, 69; land tax, 204
regulations, 7, 30, 67, 73–76, 80, 164–165
Republican party, 48, 148, 151, 223
revenue: convict lease system and generation of, 94, 96; declines from coal production, 14–16, 32, 69, 81, 157, 165–167, 192, 197, 222, 252n43; incarceration and, 5, 10, 14, 32, 64, 86, 91, 97, 100, 148, 156, 179, 182, 206, 224
rights. *See* mineral rights
Robinson, Cedric, 139, 243n43
Rogers, Harold "Hal", 38, 160, 170, 172, 174, 202, 210–211, 219, 223
Rosenstein, Rod, 160, 219, 221, 223
Roxana, KY: 5, 178, 183, 194, 202; mining in, 8, 75; mountaintop removal in, 37–39, 82–83; history of site, 59–60, 62; uses of the land in, 53–58; utilities and infrastructure for, 166–171, 175. *See also* United States Penitentiary Letcher
rural areas: and deindustrialization, 122, 143, 157, 194; and development, 58, 62, 69, 72, 118, 143, 156, 160, 172, 224, 264n20, 266n40; and dialectical relationship with urban areas, 28, 44, 53, 65, 87–88, 100, 193–194, 232–233; and gentrification, 118–119; hospital closures in, 177, 232, 266n58, 266–267n59; increased incarceration rates in, 181–182, 199–200; prison growth in, 2, 9–10, 14, 29, 72, 126, 172–174, 190, 193–194, 205–207, 215, 244n53; representations of, 21, 23, 69. *See also* Appalachia.
Ryerson, Sylvia, 6, 33, 61, 121–122, 159, 161, 185–186, 199–225, 267n14

Sanders, Elizabeth, 6, 207, 222, 228
Sapphire Coal Company, 8, 75
schools. *See* education; postsecondary education

Scott, Rebecca, 24, 40, 83–86, 248n30
sentencing, 13, 72–73, 92, 121, 151, 155–156, 222, 263n1
sheriffs, 156; cuts to offices, 166–167, 197; role of in the coalfields, 5, 130, 138, 196, 258n18, 261–262n55. *See also:* mine guards, police
sight, 6, 81–82, 85–86, 254n68, 254n77. *See also* photography; visuality
sinks, 37–49. *See also* United States Penitentiary Big Sandy; waste
social movements: abolitionist, 33–34, 64, 201, 208–210, 223–224, 230–234; Appalachian, 17, 26, 33–34, 51, 69–70; 80, 164, 203–204, 208–210, 224, 231–234, 258n19; southern, 51, 203, 209–210, 224. *See also* abolition; activism; organizations
social reproduction. *See* capitalism; carceral social reproduction; coal industry; development; gender
songs, 25, 33, 120, 233, 261–262n55
Southeastern Correctional Complex. *See:* Otter Creek Correctional Facility
state. *See* carceral state
stereotypes. *See* cultural representation
Stoll, Steven, 12, 21, 137, 259n24, 261n41, 271n68, 273n6
Story, Brett, 39, 42, 256n34, 256n37
Surface Mining Control and Reclamation Act, 74–76, 87
surpluses: lands, 34, 40, 61, 73, 82; masculinities, 20, 192; populations, 16, 34, 40, 60–61, 64, 88, 100, 182, 189–196, 249n38, 270n48; value, 34, 249n38, 270n48. *See also* waste

taxes: credits, 174–175; evasion of by the coal industry, 12, 48, 78, 160, 204, 214, 222, 252, 276, 279; and revenue, 15, 86, 97, 164–167, 197, 222, 252n43
Tennessee, 2, 5–6, 8, 23, 31, 51, 77, 91–120, 203, 210, 227

Tennessee Coal Iron and Railroad Company, 94–96, 117
Thill, Brian, 62, 248n17
topography, 10, 23–24, 41–43, 54, 83, 114, 245–246n73
tourism: Appalachia and, 61, 67, 92; and authenticity, 109, 117; ghost, 85, 105–106, 255n24; prison, 31, 91–93, 101–102, 106, 109–110, 117–119. *See also* Brushy Mountain Development
trash. *See* waste; white trash
Travis, Merle, 120
Trump, Donald, 8, 25, 160, 173, 217, 219, 222–223, 229, 257n8
Tsolkas, Panagioti, 179, 211, 216–217, 220
Turner, Tanya, 209–210

unemployment: prison production of, 17, 175; prison as resolving crises of, 5, 10, 14–15, 17, 81–82, 122, 183, 196–197; uneven development and, 257n6; War on Poverty and, 66, 70
uneven development, 61, 68, 125, 257n6, 271n56
unions: and mechanization, 15, 73; militancy of, 94–96, 120; multiracial composition and leadership of, 19, 259–260n32; police powers against, 70, 129–130, 136, 258n15, 258n18, 261–262n55. *See also* labor; National Miners Union; United Mine Workers of America
United Mine Workers of America, 15, 137, 258n18, 260n34
United States Department of Justice, 160–161, 220–221, 223
United States House Appropriations Committee, 160, 219
United States Immigration and Customs Enforcement, 14, 222
United States–Mexico border, 219, 222–223

United States Penitentiary Big Sandy: African-American population of, 190–191; contiguity with the coal industry, 29, 41–42, 48–49, 78; cost of construction, 42, 80, 232; mountaintop removal and, 42–43; as "Sink Sink," 42, 49; and social reproduction, 185–187; and water crisis, 167, 232
United States Penitentiary Letcher: and adjacent federal prison camp, 37, 172, 194–196, 221; environmental review process for, 58, 167–170, 172, 175–180, 183–188, 202–203, 207–208, 211–220; federal allocations to, 160, 208–209, 217–219; federal budget fight over, 160–161, 219–223; opposition to and defeat of, 13, 32–34, 56, 62, 159, 180, 199–225, 228, 231; Record of Decision, 33, 58, 160–161, 168, 173, 202–203, 208, 212, 217–223, 232; site intended for, 37–39, 53–62, 82, 216–217; and social reproduction, 32–33, 157–159, 182–198, 213; utilities and infrastructure, 58–59, 167–170, 175
Up the Ridge, 50–51, 86, 204–205, 224
uprisings. *See* insurrections
urban areas: Appalachian Regional Commission strategy regarding, 162, 264n20; elites in, 23, 138; and incarceration rates, 181–182; organized abandonment and criminalization of, 193, 199; and rural coalitions, 28, 223, 228, 232–233; and rural dispossessions, 28, 88, 118, 122, 143, 191, 194, 205, 221, 232–233; War on Crime and, 70–72, 87, 251n21; and waste removal, 87–88, 194, 245n71, 245–246n73
utilities, 58–59, 82, 129, 140, 148, 167–169, 175, 265n34, 269n38

value: and commodities, 96, 102, 164, and land, 11, 59; racism and, 18, 37; and

waste 30, 40, 64, 82, 84, 181, 189, 214, 249n38, 253n65, 270n48; and young people, 186, 268n19
Vance, J. D., 24, 68
Vera Institute of Justice, 16, 156, 181
violence: of the carceral state, 7, 33–34, 50, 100, 143–144, 190, 193, 230, 233, 262n65; of the coal industry, 80, 137, 190, 234; criminalization and representations of, 31, 71, 93, 106–110, 114–117, 251n21; of enclosure and expropriation, 18, 84; of mountaintop removal, 39–41, 53, 60–61, 80; police, 33, 137, 230–234, 250–251n18, 258n18, 261n41; "slow violence," 230, 254n78, 261n41, 273n6; "violence workers," 158, 264n10, 268n18
Virginia, 2, 5, 29, 40, 168–169, 214; coal industry and police development of southwestern, 138–139; company towns in, 128; hospital closures in southwestern, 232; marketing of Oxycontin to southwestern, 51–52; mountaintop removal in southwestern, 50, 77; rise of state prisons in southwestern, 49–53, 72–73, 187, 204; tough-on-crime legislation in, 72–73
visuality, 4, 82–85, 116, 241n3

wages: in company towns, 12, 77, 120, 122, 129, 131–132, 257n5; in rural hospitals, 266–267n59; prisons and, 148, 195–196, 269n38; struggles over, 9, 15, 204, 261n54; and uneven development, 257n6; "of whiteness," 244–245n66
Wallens Ridge State Prison, 50, 52, 72–73, 83, 138, 204
War on Crime, 30, 70–73, 87, 100, 251n21
War on Poverty: convergences with the War on Crime, 30, 70–72, 251n21; and cultural representations of Appalachia, 27, 67, 203; uneven impacts of, 29–30, 68–72, 87, 161, 203; launch of from Martin County, KY, 43, 66, 77; 79–80
waste: Appalachia as dumping ground for, 44–46, 49, 51, 53, 62–65, 87–88, 234; and capitalist value, 30, 39–40, 64, 82, 84, 181, 189, 214, 249n38, 253n65, 256n30, 270n48; coal, 5, 44–46, 49, 63, 74, 76; elimination of, 63–64, 143, 170, 249n46, 267; images of, 47, 248n17, 254–255n86; infrastructure, 168–170; police and, 193, 271n53, 271n54; prison as management and "dirty work," 48–49, 63–64, 84, 113, 181, 189–196, 214; "waste land" and "waste people," 23, 63, 87–88, 245n67, 245–246n73
water: and the commons, 58–59; coal industry pollution of, 58, 75–80, 157, 200; crisis in Martin County, 79–80, 167; infrastructure, 68, 101, 166–170, 175, 207
Watts, 71, 250–251n18
welfare: capitalism of Inland Steel, 127, 136–137, 152; corporate, 144; neoliberal restructuring of 13, 48, 68, 146; welfare rights movement, 164, 234; War on Poverty provision, 71–72
West Virginia, 2, 21, 43, 127–130, 243–244n49, 249n32; organizing in, 19; mine wars, 26, 261–262n55; War on Poverty in, 66, 69; strip mining in, 73–74, 77–79, 83–85, 254n83; mining disasters in, 48–49, 74
Wheelwright, KY: amenities as a company town, 136–137, 264; as Camelot, 127–128, 132–134, 136, 147, 149; as a "model" company town 128, 134–137; welfare capitalism in, 127, 137, 140, 152
Whitaker, Mitch: analysis and history of land, 58–62, 65, 75–76, 87, 216–217, 234; impact of on defeat of USP Letcher, 217; joining coalition, 216–217; raptor rehabilitation, 56–58

whiteness: of communities with prisons, 18, 189–196, 244n57; inscription of into Appalachia, 9–10, 18–19, 21, 66, 244n52, 244n62; and masculinity, 20, 190, 192; racialization of, 18, 21–28, 244–245n66. *See also* cultural representation; race, racialization, "white trash."

"white trash," 21–23, 63, 245n67, 245n68, 245–246n73

Whitesburg, KY, 5, 38, 168–169, 176–177, 205

Williamson, Kevin, 24–25, 68

Wise County, VA, 50, 52, 72–73, 138, 204, 214

WMMT-FM, 203–204, 206–207, 232. *See also* Appalshop; Calls from Home

Wolfe, Patrick, 22, 244n62

women: incarcerated, 121, 143–144; incarceration rates of in Kentucky, 156; organizing, 130, 177, 258n19, 263n8, 263–264n9. *See also* gender

Woods, Clyde, 155, 265n22, 266n46, 267n63

work. *See* correctional officers; coal industry; employment; labor; prisons

young people; organizing of, 203, 209–210, 234; and social reproduction, 182–189, 213, 215, 268n19

ABOUT THE AUTHOR

Judah Schept is Professor in the School of Justice Studies at Eastern Kentucky University. He is the author of *Progressive Punishment: Job Loss, Jail Growth, and the Neoliberal Logic of Carceral Expansion.*

CPSIA information can be obtained
at www.ICGtesting.com
Printed in the USA
JSHW081155280223
38319JS00002B/143